Paying for Progress

FABIAN

S O C I E T Y

The Fabian Society is Britain's senior think tank. Concerned since its foundation with evolutionary political and economic reform and progressive social change, the Fabian Society has played a central role for more than a century in the development of political ideas and public policy on the left of centre. The Society is affiliated to the Labour Party but is editorially and organisationally independent. Through its publications, seminars and conferences, the Society provides an arena for open-minded public debate.

Today the Fabian Society seeks to help shape the agenda for the Labour government in the UK and for the wider international renewal of progressive politics. Particular areas of work include taxation and public services, social inclusion, globalisation and economic policy, information technology, environmental policy and constitutional reform. Analysing the key challenges facing the UK and the rest of the industrialised world in a changing society and global economy, the Society's programme aims to explore the political ideas and the policy reforms which will define the left of centre in the new century.

The Society is unique among think tanks in being a democratically-constituted membership organisation. Its six thousand members engage in political education and argument through the Society's publications, conferences and other events, its quarterly journal *Fabian Review* and a network of local societies and meetings.

Paying for Progress

A New Politics of Tax for Public Spending

Copyright © Fabian Society 2000

Fabian Society
11 Dartmouth Street
London SW1H 9BN
www.fabian-society.org.uk

First published November 2000
ISBN 0 7163 6003 9

British Library Cataloguing in Publication data.
A catalogue record for this book is available from the British Library.

Design by Emphasis Publishing Limited
Printed by Bell & Bain, Glasgow

Part One: Changing the Argument

Part Two: Connecting Citizens and Their Taxes

Part Three: The Reform of Key Taxes

Part Four: Conclusion

The Commission on Taxation and Citizenship

Chair: Raymond Plant (Lord Plant of Highfield)
Professor of European Political Thought at the University of Southampton

Fran Bennett
Independent social policy researcher/analyst and policy adviser on UK poverty for Oxfam

Jonathan Charkham
Company director and former adviser to the Governor of the Bank of England

Ruth Evans
Former Director of the National Consumer Council

Roger Jowell
Director of the National Centre for Social Research

Julian Le Grand
Richard Titmuss Professor of Social Policy at the London School of Economics

Peter Lehmann
Chairman of the Energy Saving Trust and former Commercial Director and member of the Board of Centrica

Elizabeth Meehan
Jean Monnet Professor of European Social Policy and Professor of Politics at the Queen's University of Belfast

Jim McAuslan
Deputy General Secretary of the Public and Commercial Services Union

Sir Nick Monck
Former Permanent Secretary of the Department of Employment and Second Permanent Secretary of the Treasury

Steve Nickell
Professor of Economics at the Centre for Economic Performance, London School of Economics

Brian Pomeroy
Consultant on public policy and former Senior Partner of Deloitte Consulting

Holly Sutherland
Director of the Microsimulation Unit in the Department of Applied Economics, University of Cambridge

Secretary to the Commission: Michael Jacobs
General Secretary of the Fabian Society

Original members of the Commission whose appointment to new positions required them to resign during the Commission's period of enquiry and are not therefore signatories to its final report:

Paul Johnson (member of the Commission to September 2000)
Former Head of Economics of the Financial Services Authority and previously Deputy Director of the Institute for Fiscal Studies

Wendy Thomson (member of the Commission to June 1999)
Former Chief Executive of the London Borough of Newham

Financial support for the Commission

The Commission on Taxation and Citizenship has received generous support from:

 **Public and Commercial Services Union**

Deloitte & Touche

Webb Memorial Trust

UNISON

KPMG

The research into public attitudes undertaken for the Commission was supported by:

Public and Commercial Services Union

Campaign for Fair Taxation

List of Boxes, Figures and Tables

Tables

Foreword

Taxation is once again the central issue in British politics. The Prime Minister has spoken of the relationship between tax, public spending and the wellbeing of citizens. The Chancellor of the Exchequer has called for a national debate. With its usual capacity to foresee the direction of major political arguments, the Fabian Society established the Commission on Taxation and Citizenship in September 1998 to look afresh at this subject. *Paying for Progress: A New Politics of Tax for Public Spending* is the Commission's final report.

The Commission on Taxation and Citizenship met under the auspices of the Fabian Society, and held many of its meetings at the Society's offices. The Commission would like to thank the Fabian Society for the logistical and administrative support it provided for the Commission's work.

The Commission's work was financed by grants from several sources. We are extremely grateful to the Public and Commercial Services Union and Deloitte and Touche for their generous support for the Commission at the outset and throughout its period of enquiry. The Webb Memorial Trust generously funded the Commission's research on public accountability and hypothecation, and UNISON also provided a valuable research grant. The research on public attitudes was funded by a further grant from the Public and Commercial Services Union and by the Campaign for Fair Taxation. An initial grant was kindly given by KPMG. The Commission was also generously supported by an anonymous donor.

The Commission's work was coordinated by Michael Jacobs, Secretary to the Commission and General Secretary of the Fabian Society. Michael has borne a considerable burden and deserves the Commission's gratitude. The Commission's research was primarily undertaken by two Research Fellows, Selina Chen and David Nissan, and a Research Assistant, Rocio Martinez-Sampere. The Commission would like to acknowledge the immense contribution each has made to this report. Additional research assistance was provided by Kathy Pick and Guy Lodge, and also by Daniel de Torres, David Noble and Siân Richards. Henry Russell contributed to the copy editing. The Commission is particularly grateful for the administrative support given by Margaret McGillen, Cyril O'Keeffe, Judith Begg and other staff of the Fabian Society, and to Lois Sparling, Samantha Carberry and James Sparling of Emphasis Publishing for their work on the design and typesetting of the book.

This report has been written by Michael Jacobs with contributions by David Nissan, Selina Chen, Raymond Plant, Nick Monck and Fran Bennett. Chapter 2 draws on the work of Alan Hedges, independent researcher, and Catherine Bromley, of the National Centre for Social Research, who conducted the Commission's research on public attitudes.

The Commission is very grateful to all the organisations and individuals who made written submissions, and particularly to those who gave up their time to give oral evidence and to discuss our findings. These are listed in Appendix 3.

The members of the Commission on Taxation and Citizenship are pleased to present this report. Not every commissioner necessarily agrees with every individual recommendation, but all subscribe to the general arguments and to the thrust of the recommendations as a whole. We hope that it can contribute to a rich public debate on this most important of subjects.

Professor Raymond Plant
Chair of the Commission on Taxation and Citizenship
November 2000

Executive summary and recommendations

The Commission on Taxation and Citizenship

The Commission on Taxation and Citizenship was established as an independent commission of enquiry by the Fabian Society in September 1998. Comprising fifteen people with varied experience and expertise under the chairmanship of Professor Raymond Plant (Lord Plant of Highfield), the Commission was asked to explore the principles and practice of the tax system, with the aim of contributing to a new public debate on the subject. *Paying for Progress: A New Politics of Tax for Public Spending* is its final report.

1 | Changing the argument

The need for a new debate (Chapter 1)

The Commission believes that the terms of debate about tax in the UK need to be changed. Over the last 20 years taxation has become a subject of extreme political sensitivity. A climate has been created in which rational and balanced discussion of the options for tax and public spending has become very difficult. At times the unwillingness in public life to address the question of taxation squarely—given simultaneous and widespread demands for better public services—might almost be described as denial.

Of course, taxes will never be popular. But the terms of debate have increasingly made them seem fundamentally *illegitimate*. This is not a healthy way for public debate to be conducted. Taxes are an essential part of a modern society: they pay for public services and for government. Proper debate about the nature and level of taxation is therefore crucial to the wellbeing of democracy itself.

Such a debate is particularly important today in the context of new economic and social circumstances. As service standards in the private sector have improved and consumer expectations have risen, it has been difficult for many public services to catch up. A significant widening in the income distribution has left larger numbers of people on both very high and very low incomes, with important implications for both taxation and public spending. New demands have been made of the tax system from the growing concern about environmental damage. Yet at the same time globalisation and the growth of e-commerce have led some commentators to suggest that taxes are on an inevitable downward trend. In general, modern societies face difficult choices about the level and form of public services which government should provide. But these challenges can only be addressed if taxation is seen as a legitimate part of public discourse.

It is to help stimulate a more mature and informed debate that the Commission presents this report.

Public attitudes towards taxation (Chapter 2)

Opinion surveys throughout the last twenty years have shown substantial public support for higher taxes to pay for higher public spending, particularly in the fields of health and education. The two major political parties, on the other hand, have acted as if proposals to raise taxes cannot win votes. To understand this issue more deeply, the Commission on Taxation and Citizenship commissioned independent original research into public attitudes towards taxation and public spending. This comprised both discussion (focus) groups and quantitative opinion polling.

This research revealed a rich array of perceptions of the tax system and of government and public services. But the dominant sense to emerge was of a deep sense of 'disconnection' from the taxes people pay and the public services which these finance. Partly this was a result of ignorance: many of the respondents did not understand the tax system, or how (for example) the level of tax in the UK compared with other countries. But it mainly arose because most people did not feel they knew where their taxes were going, and were not convinced that government used the money well. There was a widespread perception that public services had been getting worse for many years, and that public money was often wasted.

Yet this sense of 'disconnection' did not mean that the respondents were simply unwilling to pay more in tax. Most people strongly valued public services, particularly education and the NHS. Although they disliked the taxes they paid, they were even more concerned about the perceived decline in public services. The dominant argument to emerge was that, if people could be sure that the money were genuinely going to improve the priority public services, they would be willing to countenance higher taxation.

The Commission's conclusion from this research is that the major priority for government now in this field must be to make people feel better 'connected' to the taxes they pay and the public services they finance. 'Disconnection' undermines public support for the whole purpose of government, and fuels a certain kind of 'tax resistance'. A major part of the report examines how such disconnection might be overcome.

Some facts about taxation and public spending (Chapter 3)

Surveying the UK tax system, the report notes that the share of taxation in national income has risen slightly over the last few years. But at 37% it is slightly lower than it was on average in the 1980s and is 6% lower than the European Union average. The Government's public spending plans for the period 2001-04 will leave public spending as a proportion of GDP lower (at 40.5% in 2003-04) than when the Conservatives left office in 1996-97. Taken as a whole the system of taxation and public spending in the UK is highly redistributive from high income to low income groups. But contrary to popular perception the tax system on its own is *not* progressive: in fact the richest fifth of the population pay slightly less of their income in tax than the poorest fifth. Over the twenty years to 1998, at the same time as incomes became markedly more unequal, the tax system became less progressive. However the first four Labour budgets (1997-2000) have been redistributive in impact, both to low income households and to families with children.

Citizenship: the philosophy of taxation (Chapter 4)

Taxation is essentially a component of the relationship between the citizen and the state. Arguments about taxation tend therefore to be underpinned by different ideas about citizenship. The Commission's examination of the tax system has been based on its own philosophical and practical analysis of what citizenship means in a modern society. Arguing against the philosophy of a minimal state, the report sets out a 'strong' idea of citizenship. This sees the individual as part of a civic community. It recognises the importance of public goods to the quality of life. It argues that inequalities need to be reduced in order to maintain a socially just and inclusive society—one in which poverty is strenuously tackled and in which everyone feels they have a stake. The strong conception of citizenship insists on the openness and accountability of government to its citizens.

Objectives and principles (Chapter 5)

The Commission's principal objectives in its proposals for reform of the tax system flow from this strong conception of citizenship.

First, we are concerned that the tax system, and the political debate about it, should generate sufficient revenues to support a level of public services consonant with a strong conception of citizenship. The overall system of public spending and taxation should help to reduce inequalities of opportunity and to provide public goods which encourage a sense of community and social solidarity.

Second, we believe that the operation of the tax and public spending system should seek to 'connect' the public better to the taxes they pay and to the public services which these finance. Citizens should feel that they know what taxes they pay, what the money is spent on, and what difference it makes; and should feel greater confidence in government performance and accountability.

Third, we believe that the system of public spending and taxation should become more progressive. Given the widening dispersion of incomes over the last twenty years—and with the public apparently increasingly concerned about this—the distribution of the tax burden should be rebalanced, so that those on higher incomes pay a fairer share and more resources are directed to those on low incomes.

Fourth, we argue that the system of taxation should provide incentives to reduce socially damaging behaviour, particularly environmental degradation. This is a legitimate and important purpose of the tax system, and taxes can play an important role in supporting environmental policy.

The report sets out ten 'principles of a good tax system' which embody these objectives and other important aims. The rest of the report attempts to show how these objectives and principles can be met through various reforms to the tax system.

How much tax should we pay? (Chapter 6)

It is often argued today that globalisation will force taxes down, as mobile companies and workers relocate to where taxes are lowest. However this is not inevitable: tax is not the only factor in investment decisions and international cooperation can prevent 'beggar my neighbour' tax competition. More generally the evidence of the impact of taxes on economic performance is uncertain; at the UK's present levels of taxation the benefits of public spending would appear to outweigh any economic costs. Other European countries perform well economically with much higher levels of taxation and public spending.

It is perfectly legitimate to argue for significantly lower taxation. But this must be done honestly. It would require correspondingly large cuts in public spending. Most members of the public would not gain: they would have to replace lost public services with private spending (on education, health, insurance, transport and so on).

In fact there are good grounds for believing that the pressures on public spending will rise over the next decade. Many public services are 'superior goods', demand for which grows faster than income. There are particular pressures in health and education, in the former case from demographic and technological factors, in the latter from the growing emphasis on education and skills in the 'knowledge-based economy'. The reduction of poverty will almost certainly require higher spending. Pressures for higher public spending do not automatically imply higher taxation. But the idea that taxes should rise as a proportion of national income should be regarded as an entirely serious and legitimate proposal. A share of taxation of up to 40% of GDP—still below the European Union average—would enable considerable improvements in public services and infrastructure and further reductions in poverty. (A tax share of 39%, for example, would yield an extra £20 billion pa.) A higher tax share up to this limit should be properly debated as an option for the UK.

However, the Commission is not recommending that the overall share of taxation in national income should be raised at the present time. The Government needs to prove that the significant programme of public spending increases and associated reforms planned for the period 2001-04 can generate genuine improvements to public services. Our public attitudes research has shown that many people remain to be convinced that governments spend money well. If the public are to be better 'connected' to their taxes the Government's plans need to be given time to work before additional funding is sought. Our own proposals have therefore been drawn up on a revenue neutral basis.

2 | Connecting citizens to their taxes

Information, auditing and democracy: making government accountable (Chapter 7)

The evidence of 'disconnection' the Commission documented in our research leads us to believe that the legitimacy of taxation—and any sustained support for higher public spending—will only be achieved when the public understand better how their taxes are spent and feel more confident that they are being spent well. We describe this as a renewal of the 'civic contract' between citizens and the state.

This is partly about rejuvenating the democratic process. The most important task is to improve the quality of public services. But it is also to do with information. Public services must be effective and efficient; but they must also be *seen* to be so. Three broad approaches can help citizens understand better what is being done with the taxes they pay.

First, information about the objectives of government and its performance must be made more transparent. Despite acknowledgement of the difficulties they raise, the Commission supports the use of well designed and published targets setting out what the Government seeks to achieve.

But, second, it is then essential that government performance is independently audited. In our own research we found tremendous public scepticism about the honesty of government statements and statistics. We therefore recommend:

- *The establishment of an independent Office for Public Accountability (OPA)* combining (and expanding) the roles of the present National Audit Office and Audit Commission. The OPA would be responsible for auditing the government's achievements against its stated objectives and targets. It, rather than the government, would issue an Annual Report on government performance, along with more detailed value for money audits of public services. The credibility of the OPA would depend on its independence from the government. The OPA should be accountable to Parliament—either to a select committee of the House of Commons not appointed by party whips, or to a reformed Second Chamber.

- *Publication by the OPA and the Statistics Commission of standardised formats in which statistics about taxation and public spending should be published.*

Third, the public should be better informed about taxes and public spending. We recommend:

- *Publication (by the Office for Public Accountability) of an annual 'Citizen's Leaflet' sent to every citizen.* This would explain in simple terms how the tax system works, provide illustrations of how much tax different individuals pay in different circumstances, and set out how public spending is allocated. It would also include a summary of the OPA's annual audit of government performance.

- *Information from the OPA about public spending and government performance should be made as widely available as possible,* through the media, internet, public libraries, post offices and so on.

- *The development and use of innovative methods to involve citizens in consultations on, and evaluation of, decisions on public spending and services.*

Better information will, we believe, help people feel more 'connected'. But ultimately it is the quality of public debate about taxation and spending choices which most matters. The role of the media in holding governments to account is very important. But the bias and cynicism with which much of the media report government performance are not conducive to healthy debate. To improve the quality of public debate, we recommend:

- *Establishment of a standing Royal Commission on Taxation.* This would investigate the social, economic, environmental and other effects of proposed new taxes; investigate how government objectives are being and could be better met by the tax system; and recommend technical reforms to improve the administration of the tax system. The purpose of such a Royal Commission would be to enable ideas for new or reformed taxes to be assessed impartially before being subjected to party political conflict.

Earmarking taxes: the 'hypothecation' debate (Chapter 8)

There has been increasing interest in recent years in the idea of 'earmarking' some taxes for specific public spending purposes. In principle this would appear to be a way of 'connecting' citizens more closely to their taxes and to public spending. It was in principle also favoured by many of the respondents in our discussion groups.

There are, however, strong arguments against earmarking. It reduces the flexibility with which government can use its revenues. It is therefore likely to lead to inefficiencies, with too much or too little being spent on the designated area. If earmarking is more flexible it runs the risk of dishonesty, particularly if it is sold to the public as a way of increasing the revenues going to a specific spending area. Governments may simply divert existing funds spent in that area elsewhere.

The Commission is mindful of these risks, but argues that earmarking can nevertheless be a useful mechanism for 'connecting' citizens in certain circumstances. The report sets out four conditions which need to be met, and describes four different kinds of earmarked tax. The key condition is that a 'baseline' is set out for spending in the designated area, say for five years ahead, so that it can be clearly established that earmarked taxes are additional to existing allocations. The effects of the taxes should be publicly and independently audited. The Commission recommends:

- *The use of earmarking (where required) for time-limited taxes for special capital expenditures,* such as investment in public transport infrastructure projects. Such taxes should be abolished when the required funds have been raised.

- *The earmarking of environmental taxes.* For new environmental taxes earmarking can be flexible: expenditure can be higher than the tax revenues. But the whole of the tax revenues must be used for the designated spending area. Such flexibility is only appropriate for incentive-based taxes where the tax has an independent purpose and its rate is set according to its environmental and economic impact.

- *The use of 'tax and public service pledges' when governments seek to raise the rates of principal taxes such as income tax.* In general governments should set out what the additional revenues are designed to achieve and, where possible, the auditable improvements that will made with the funds. We believe that this will attract much more public support than tax increases for unspecified purposes.

The latter view was borne out by the Commission's quantitative opinion polling. Around 40% of people supported an increase of 1p on the basic rate of income tax for unspecified public spending. But when the spending area was specified these numbers rose substantially: to 68% for education, and 80% for health.

The Commission also examined the proposal for a fully hypothecated tax for the National Health Service. This would split income tax more or less in half, creating an NHS tax and a General Income Tax. The NHS tax, perhaps along with the revenues from tobacco and alcohol taxes, would be allocated to an NHS Fund strictly hypothecated to spending on the National Health Service. The tax would be set at a level sufficient to fund planned NHS expenditure over the economic cycle. In an economic downturn the Fund could use accumulated surpluses or borrow in order to keep tax rates stable, subject to full repayment out of future reserves.

The report sets out in some detail the arguments for and against a hypothecated NHS tax of this kind. The Commission members were themselves divided on its merits. Some commissioners argued that such a tax would in practice be as likely to obscure as to clarify the relationship between the tax and NHS spending, and by using the most buoyant tax for the most popular area of spending would effectively reduce the resources available for other areas of expenditure. A majority of commissioners, however, felt that such a tax would help to 'connect' citizens better to the tax system and to public spending, and in doing so would help to overcome the public's resistance to paying higher taxes. It would enable more funds to be allocated to the NHS and possibly to others areas as well. However the majority acknowledged that there were both practical and constitutional questions (concerning the devolution of health spending to Scotland, Wales and Northern Ireland) which needed resolving before such a tax could be introduced. On the basis of this majority, and with the minority noting their disagreement,[1] the Commission therefore recommends:

- *The introduction of a fully hypothecated NHS tax.* We acknowledge that such a tax would need considerable public debate before it could be introduced. In particular, the recommendation is conditional on both the practical and constitutional questions being satisfactorily resolved. The Commission hopes that this recommendation will contribute to such a debate.

National Insurance (Annex)

Though National Insurance contributions are not strictly speaking part of the tax system, the Commission examined the National Insurance (NI) system as an example of earmarking. The NI system was designed to give people a clear understanding of the social insurance benefits they were paying for. But the blurring of the contributory principle over recent years and the fall in the value of NI benefits (including the basic state pension) relative to average earnings threatens to undermine this sense of 'connection'. The sense that the NI system is drifting slowly but inevitably into decline is neither healthy for citizenship nor sustainable in the long term. Though the structure of social security benefits was beyond the remit of the Commission the report presents three broad options. It calls for an honest and open public debate about the principles and future of the National Insurance system.

The devolution of taxation (Chapter 9)

If citizens are to feel better 'connected' to their taxes it is important that decisions over the level of public spending are related to the democratic process. The devolved governments in Scotland, Wales and Northern Ireland, and local authorities throughout the UK, are between them responsible for most public services. In principle decentralisation should lead to higher levels of 'connectedness'. Yet turnouts in elections for local government and for the new elected Assemblies in Wales and London have been low. This would appear to be due at least in part to these bodies' lack of perceived power, particularly their lack of accountability for their own budgets.

While the Scottish Parliament has the power to vary the standard rate of income tax by plus or minus 3p, the National Assemblies of Wales and Northern Ireland—despite their substantial spending budgets—have no tax-raising power. They therefore cannot decide for themselves their own level of spending: this is determined by central government. The Greater London Mayor and Assembly have the power to raise congestion and workplace parking charges, but only to fund transport spending. Local authorities can vary council tax, but the small proportion of local expenditure funded by the tax (around 25%) means that for any given percentage rise in spending it must be raised by at least four times the amount. Changes in council tax reflect changes in central government grant as much as local spending decisions, so the connection between local taxes and political choices is obscured. Local authority budgets can still be capped by central government. In the Commission's view these arrangements create a serious democratic imbalance between the political and 'fiscal' constitutions.

The Commission believes it to be a principle of citizenship and democratic accountability that elected governments should have the ability to determine their own expenditure levels, taking into account the preference of their electorates. The report examines various options for devolved taxation, including the return of business rates to local control, local sales taxes and local income tax. The Commission rejects the view often put that local authorities or devolved institutions need to raise from their own taxation at least 50% of their spending in order to have fiscal autonomy: it is the ability to *vary* a government's total budget that is most important. We commend the model of the Scottish Variable Rate, which (contrary to the view sometimes asserted) allows the Scottish Parliament to vary its budget by a significant amount—though we believe the basic and higher rates should move together. We also regard the role of central government grants in equalising local authority finance between richer and poorer areas as extremely important.

While acknowledging that these conclusions have wider constitutional implications which will need further debate, the Commission therefore recommends:

- *The granting of a power to vary the basic and higher rates of income tax by a maximum of 3p in the pound to the National Assembly of Wales and the National Assembly of Northern Ireland,* on the general model of the Scottish Variable Rate.

- *The further devolution of this tax-varying power, if they so wish it, from these Assemblies and the Scottish Parliament to local authorities in Scotland, Wales and Northern Ireland.* However divided between them, the combined power to vary the rates of income tax held by the devolved institutions and local authorities should be limited to 3p in the pound.

- *The granting of a power to vary the basic and higher rates of income tax by a maximum of 2p in the pound to local authorities in England.* Arrangements in London—between the London Boroughs and the Greater London Mayor and Assembly—would need to be subject to further consultation. We would recommend that local authorities seeking to use this power should seek a popular mandate through a local referendum.

- *The granting to all local authorities the power to levy a supplementary business rate,* in consultation with local businesses and tied to parallel changes in council tax.

At the same time the Commission believes that council tax needs to be reformed. Council tax is regressive: taxpayers in the lowest property band pay approximately four times the proportion of their property value as taxpayers in the highest band. We therefore recommend:

- *Introduction of a new set of property value bands for council tax, splitting the top two bands (G and H) and the bottom band (A) and increasing the ratio of top to bottom from 3:1 to 7:1.* This would achieve a fairer, more progressive, structure.

- *More frequent valuations of council tax (every five years) to ensure that the tax more accurately reflects real property values.*

The Commission also considered the pressures for the relocation of tax-raising power upwards to the European level, whether through the establishment of a specific tax-raising power for the European Union, or through the harmonisation of national tax regimes and rates. We see no role at present for a tax-raising power at the level of the European Union, since there is no elected European government. As far as tax harmonisation is concerned, different principles apply to different forms of taxation.

On indirect taxation of traded goods and services, harmonisation is increasingly important, as EU rules already recognise. Differential tax rates distort trade between European countries. On corporate taxation, harmonisation is impossible while the bases and structures of corporate taxation vary so much between countries. Overall shares of taxation determine overall public spending levels, and (so long as the European Union remains an inter-governmental body) these must be a matter for national sovereignty.

3 | The reform of key taxes

Making income tax fairer (Chapter 10)

Of all the major taxes, income tax is the fairest, in the sense of being related directly to ability to pay. But the proportion of revenue from income tax has declined over the last twenty years, while that of VAT (which is regressive in effect) has doubled. During this period changes to the structure of income tax have made it less progressive, at the same time as higher incomes have grown rapidly. The Commission believes that the top income earners in British society are not now contributing a fair share towards the public purse. Our public attitudes research revealed general agreement with this view.

The Commission believes that the income tax system should become more progressive. This can be done both by reducing the level of taxation faced by the lowest income groups, and by increasing it on the highest. In practice many of those in lower income groups will be assisted as much or more by public spending as by changes in the tax system: around 14 million adults do not pay income tax.

The Commission considered five principal areas for potential reform. First, we looked at the personal tax allowance. This is regressive in its effects: it gives a larger relief to those on higher rate tax than to those on lower rates. The Commission therefore recommends:

- *Introduction of a Flat-rate Personal Allowance to replace the present personal allowance.* The flat rate allowance would give every income taxpayer (with enough income to use it in full) the same amount of money, rather like a rebate off their tax bill. We recommend an annual allowance of £1000. This would be worth around the same as the present personal allowance to a basic rate taxpayer, but less than the current allowance is worth to a higher rate taxpayer. It would not however be the Commission's intention to use this change to affect current tax bills; rather, the aim is to ensure that any future changes are worth a uniform cash amount (and therefore give a larger proportionate benefit to lower and basic rate taxpayers). In introducing it we therefore recommend that the threshold for the 40% rate of tax is raised (to £32,600) to ensure that no-one is immediately affected adversely.

Second, the Commission considered the top rate of income tax. At 40% this is considerably lower than most of our European neighbours. But it also comes in at a relatively low level of income (around £33,000-£37,000 of gross annual income, depending on pension contributions). The number of people paying the higher rate on part of their income is now 2.3 million, or 9% of all income taxpayers, compared to under 3% in 1979. The Commission believes that those on the highest incomes should pay a fairer share of tax. We also accept that there is a case for raising the threshold of the existing 40% rate to reduce the number of higher rate taxpayers. We therefore recommend:

- *Introduction of a new top rate of income tax of 50% on taxable incomes of more than £100,000 a year.* (This equates to gross incomes of generally closer to £120,000.) This would raise £2.9 billion and affect 200,000 high earners.

- *Use of the revenues from this to rebalance the distribution of the income tax burden in one of two ways: either simply taking low earners out of tax by raising the personal allowance; or taking low earners out of tax by a smaller amount and raising the 40% band threshold at the same time.* The £2.9 billion would finance an increase in the personal allowance (under the present system) by £250 and an increase in the threshold for the 40% rate to £30,000 taxable income (from the present £28,400). These changes would take 480,000 people out of tax altogether and 420,000 out of the 40% band.

The public attitudes research conducted for the Commission suggested that such a top rate of tax of 50% on incomes over £100,000 a year would be widely approved.

Third, the Commission considered the possibility of introducing an extra 'middle' band of income tax (say 30%) in order to make the overall progression smoother. As a structural change on its own at present this was not favoured: the extra administrative complexity it would create would not be worth the gains in progressivity. However we do recommend:

- *Consideration of a middle rate band where it has been decided that income tax needs to be raised to generate additional long-term revenues for public spending.* Introduction of a middle rate band (with a threshold of say £16,500 per year of taxable income, or around £21,000) would enable all those earning less than this to be protected from a rise in rates. Distributionally this would be very favourable.

Fourth, the Commission looked at the effect on overall marginal tax rates of the National Insurance Upper Earnings Limit. We recommend:

- *The gradual convergence of the Upper Earnings Limit for National Insurance contributions with the thresholds for the 40% rate, accompanied by a corresponding reduction in National Insurance rates.*

Fifth, the Commission examined the taxation of savings. We welcome the broad equivalence in the tax treatment of different types of saving (ISAs, pensions, owner occupation). However, since pension contributions are tax-exempt, the tax-free pension lump sum remains an anomaly. We suggest that this be included in a review of the rules for the use of private pensions on maturity.

Taxes on spending (Chapter 11)

Over the last twenty years indirect taxes—VAT and various excise duties—have been regarded by governments as less visible than direct taxes and therefore more easily raised. However our public attitudes research suggests that their very invisibility now makes indirect taxes particularly unpopular. Indirect taxes are also regressive in their effects, making them in principle less fair.

The Commission considered the option of reducing the share of indirect taxation and increasing income tax rates to compensate. A cut in the main rate of VAT to 15%, which is as far as EU rules allow, would require an increase in the basic rate of income tax from 22% to 23.5%. This would in principle be a progressive change. But in practice the reduction in consumer prices would probably be insufficiently visible, and we therefore do not favour this.

The Commission also examined the proposal for a uniform rate of VAT, replacing the current list of exempt, zero rated and reduced rate products with a single rate applying to all. It is often suggested that the same rate of VAT on all goods and services would bring improvements in terms of both economic efficiency and equity. It would allow the rate to be much lower, reducing evasion and creating more flexibility in the tax system.

Though European Union regulations make it illegal to reduce the standard rate of VAT below 15%, the Commission wished to investigate the option. We modelled a uniform rate of 11%, using the revenues raised to compensate those on lower incomes. The compensation, however, was not very effective. Due to the wide variations in spending patterns between households, there were still considerable numbers of 'losers' from such a change. This would bring considerable numbers of households into means-tested benefits, and by affecting real incomes at the bottom of the distribution could have potentially significant knock-on effect on labour markets. For these reasons the Commission does not believe that, in current UK conditions, a uniform rate of VAT is an acceptable reform.

The Commission accepts the justification of so-called 'sin' taxes on tobacco, alcohol and gambling, on the grounds of the social harm they cause and their addictive effects. We examined the argument that high rates of duty leads to cross-border trade and to smuggling. We accept that there are adverse effects of these kinds, particularly for tobacco, but do not believe that they would be significantly reduced by cuts in duty. Stronger enforcement measures are likely to be a more effective remedy.

The Commission examined the claim that the growth of electronic commerce would make sales taxes such as VAT very difficult to collect. Our conclusion is that the threat can be exaggerated: effective enforcement and international cooperation to establish tax jurisdictions can minimise the risk to revenues.

Taxing wealth: the reform of inheritance tax (Chapter 12)

Wealth is more unequally distributed than income and confers considerable advantages on its holders. This is particularly true of inheritance, which helps to consolidate inequality of opportunity across generations. The Commission believes that those enjoying substantial levels of wealth in society should make a fairer contribution to taxation revenues. We considered for this purpose the proposal for an annual assets or wealth tax. However we concluded that such a tax would have high administrative and compliance costs, and would be liable to evasion.

The Commission therefore examined the possibility of reforming inheritance tax. Present inheritance tax has a high threshold (£234,000) and is paid by only around 2% of estates. It therefore captures very little of the taxable capacity of wealth. Being levied on the deceased rather than on the legatees, it bears no relation to the ability to pay of those who inherit. It also allows widespread evasion, both through the use of lifetime gifts and through various reliefs. Many other countries have donee-based taxes which incorporate gifts as well as legacies.

The Commission therefore considered a proposal for a Capital Receipts Tax modelled on the Capital Acquisitions Tax used successfully in Ireland. Such a tax would be levied on the cumulative total of both gifts and legacies received by donees. It would provide desirable incentives for donors to spread their wealth, since the effective tax rate would be lower the larger the number of donees. It would also reduce avoidance by closing the lifetime gifts loophole. The Commission therefore recommends:

- *Introduction of a Capital Receipts Tax levied on the cumulative total of both gifts and legacies received by donees.* Such a tax would have a lower threshold than the present inheritance tax (say, £80,000), with gifts under £2,000 altogether exempt. The tax would have a progressive rate structure: say, 10% on the first £80,000 of receipts, rising in 10% bands to a maximum of 40%.

The Commission recognises, from our own public attitudes research, that any extension of inheritance tax would be unpopular. But we believe that the principle that wealth as well as income should contribute a fair share to the common good is important. The administration of the tax and its impact would need careful consideration. The receipts from the proposed inheritance tax are difficult to forecast. However once known, and consistent with our approach of revenue neutrality, they would allow other taxes to be reduced.

From goods to bads: environmental taxes (Chapter 13)

The Commission's principle that the tax system should be used to discourage social harm applies most strongly in relation to environmental damage. Most European countries, including the UK, now have a variety of environmental taxes. Such taxes are in general an efficient mechanism of environmental policy, and they provide incentives to continuous innovation and improvement in environmental performance. But there is a second kind of argument for environmental taxation as well. Unlike most taxes, which reduce work effort, investment, output and so on, environmental taxes *correct* existing market distortions (in the form of environmental damage). There is therefore a strong case for environmental taxation to replace other forms of taxation as a way of raising revenue: that is, for switching the burden of taxation from 'goods' to 'bads'. The Commission supports this principle, though distributional factors, including economic impacts on particular sectors, groups and regions, should temper the pace of the transition.

One of the key questions in designing environmental taxes is the use of the revenues. To achieve the maximum environmental impact it will often be useful to earmark the revenues for spending in the same field. Spending can often help to increase the elasticity of response to the tax measure and help to win public support. (An example is funding public transport from congestion charges.) But the aim of shifting the tax burden requires the revenues to be recycled into reductions in other taxes. For smaller environmental taxes the Commission supports full earmarking; for larger business taxes (as in the climate change levy on business energy consumption, the landfill tax and proposed aggregates tax) most of the revenues should be recycled to reductions in other business taxes. (If the cuts continue to be made in employers' National Insurance contributions, the implications for the NI system need to be considered.)

The Commission notes the anomaly that, with the introduction of the climate change levy, domestic energy is more or less exempt from taxation (VAT is levied at 5%). The reason for this is that a tax on domestic energy would exacerbate fuel poverty, estimated to affect 4.3 million households. Yet at the same time falling domestic energy prices (down by 35-40% since 1990) have discouraged energy efficiency measures such as insulation. The Commission therefore sought a mechanism which would encourage better-off households to install such measures while protecting those on low incomes. The Commission recommends:

- *Additional spending on domestic energy efficiency investment in low income households until at least 2005, with the aim of eliminating fuel poverty, followed by the introduction of a domestic energy tax.* Such spending could be financed in part by borrowing against the future revenues from the tax. Better off households should be encouraged to use the period until the introduction of the tax to install energy efficiency measures which would reduce their overall energy bills. An additional tax of 5% on domestic energy would raise £780m per annum.

The Commission supports the use of taxation to reduce congestion and cut pollution and carbon emissions from the transport sector. Contrary to popular perception, high petrol prices do act to reduce fuel consumption, though this effect is outweighed by the effect of higher incomes. Reductions in fuel prices would almost certainly increase demand. The Commission notes in particular that high fuel prices are one of the principal drivers of technological improvement to increase fuel efficiency. Car taxation is progressive over the population as a whole, though regressive for car owners. To mitigate the distributional effects of high fuel duty and to increase its environmental benefit, we recommend:

- *The reduction of vehicle excise duty and an increase in the differential between smaller and larger cars. The rate for the most efficient cars could be reduced to nominal levels.* This would particularly benefit lower income motorists.

- *The earmarking of increases in revenues from taxes on fuel (from a specified baseline) to spending on public transport, improved car technologies and associated measures.*

On other environmental taxes, the Commission recommends:

- *The inclusion of incineration within the landfill levy.*

- *A general environmental product tax which could be levied at different rates on particular products with adverse impacts on the environment for which substitutes are available, with the revenues earmarked for environmental spending.*

- *An international or European-wide tax on aviation fuel* or an alternative carbon emissions trading scheme.

Taxing land (Chapter 14)

Land taxation has in the past generally been considered to be a tax on wealth. The burden of a tax on land falls entirely on the landowner, reducing the value of his holding. But today land taxation is more sensibly viewed as form of environmental taxation. Development patterns in the UK are very uneven. There is enormous demand for housing in some regions, particularly on so-called 'greenfield' sites in the countryside, while in other towns and cities a spiral of dereliction has set in. It is generally agreed that there needs to be less housebuilding in greenfield areas and more on brownfield sites. The Commission examined how far taxation could help to achieve this. We recommend:

- *Granting local authorities in designated Urban Priority Areas and Town Improvement Areas the power to vary business rates* (by more than is proposed in other local authority areas).

- *Introduction of a 'greenfield levy', in the form of VAT (at the full rate of 17.5%) on the sale of new homes in designated greenfield areas.* Such a levy would raise around £1 billion, which should be earmarked to support brownfield development in urban areas.

The Commission examined the history of the attempt to capture 'development value', the increase in value of land arising from development and planning permission. We looked at a proposal to introduce land value taxation by splitting business rates into an owner's and occupier's component. Such a system has been introduced successfully elsewhere, but we are not persuaded that this would be compatible with the planning system in the UK. To examine this further, however, we recommend:

- *Establishment of pilot schemes in different local authority areas of two-tier business rates, to investigate their feasibility and effectiveness in the UK context.*

4 | Conclusion

Paying for progress (Chapter 15)

Taxation has returned to the top of the political agenda. The idea of 'taxing and spending' has even undergone a mild rehabilitation. This is welcome, but it must not mean a return to the language of the past. The public's confidence in government and their willingness to pay taxes cannot be taken for granted. The priority must be to raise the quality of public services—to 'tax, spend and improve'. We believe that the measures we have outlined to 'connect' the public better to their taxes and to public spending will help win support for this. Together with the measures we have proposed to make the tax system fairer and to discourage environmental damage, we hope that these will become part of a wider debate about how the 'civic contract' between citizens and their governments can be renewed.

Note

1   Those disagreeing with the majority recommendation for a hypothecated NHS tax included Fran Bennett, Nick Monck and Holly Sutherland.

Introduction

Taxation is central to politics. Taxes pay for government and for public services. They affect how much money people have to spend. Arguments over the level and structure of taxation are therefore a crucial part of the democratic process in modern societies. Passions are inevitably aroused, disagreements fierce.

Yet over the last twenty years public understanding of taxation and public spending in the UK has not been well served by the manner or content of political debate. So charged has the subject of tax become in modern politics, so febrile the atmosphere in which the issue is discussed, that considered argument has often seemed almost impossible. Taxation represents one of the most important relationships between the individual citizen and the state: on an everyday level, indeed, a rather more significant one to the average citizen than voting. But the connection between the taxes people pay and the public services they receive in return has often been obscured. Indeed at times the very idea of 'taxing and spending'—which is precisely what all governments do—has been treated as somehow disreputable. Since different approaches to taxation and spending represent important, often profound, choices about the sort of society we wish to be, it is difficult to argue that this has been good for the health of our democracy.

It was therefore to help stimulate a more reflective public debate about taxation that the Fabian Society established, in September 1998, the independent Commission on Taxation and Citizenship. Comprising 15 people with varied experience and expertise under the chairmanship of Professor Raymond Plant, the Commission was asked to explore both the purpose and structure of the tax system in the United Kingdom, and to make recommendations for reform. The Commission's work was conducted under the auspices of the Fabian Society but wholly independent of it. Commissioners worked part-time and unpaid. (The full list of members of the Commission is given in Appendix 1, and its Terms of Reference in Appendix 2.)

Paying for Progress: A New Politics of Tax for Public Spending is the Commission's final report.

The Commission's work

Beginning work in October 1998, the Commission on Taxation and Citizenship held a total of eighteen full meetings over a period of two years. Detailed work on different aspects of the tax system was done in five working groups of the Commission: on personal taxes, indirect taxes, hypothecation and accountability, local taxation and public attitudes. Research and discussion papers were commissioned from one full-time and three part-time research staff, and submissions were also invited and received from a range of organisations and individuals. A number of individual experts were invited to give oral presentations to meetings of the Commissioners. (Submissions by both organisations and individuals are listed in Appendix 3.)

A core concern of the Commission was the nature of public attitudes towards taxation. To explore this further original research was commissioned using both focus (discussion) groups and quantitative opinion polling. The results of this research are summarised in Chapter 2 of this report, and inform many of the arguments and recommendations. A full report of the research has been published separately.[1] The research methodology is outlined in Appendix 4.

The nature of this report

Taxation is a huge area of public policy, with an economic literature and a body of professional practitioners all of its own. The Commission's purpose was not to produce a detailed technical treatise on the design of the tax system, nor to discuss the detail of its operation. It was to explore the philosophy which should underpin the tax system, the principles deriving from this, and the broad direction of reform which might be proposed as a consequence. This report therefore does not pretend to be comprehensive, either in the subject matter it covers or in its treatment of individual issues.

In particular, there are important areas of the tax system which it does not deal with at all. Most notably, the Commission decided early on in its deliberations that it would not look at the taxation of business. Given its concern primarily with taxation in relation to the concept of citizenship, the Commission decided to concentrate on the field of personal taxation. Even here, however, there are certain issues on which the Commission has not reported—the taxation of capital gains, for example, or stamp duties. The Commission's work came to develop along particular lines of enquiry which led to a focus on certain areas of the tax system and not others.

The report makes a number of recommendations for reform. These are listed in the Executive Summary. But it does not purport to present a blueprint for wholesale change, still less does it offer a Budget. Many of the recommendations proposed are structural changes, the timing of which, should they be implemented, would need careful consideration beyond the remit of this study. No attempt has been made, quite deliberately, to present all the recommendations as a single 'package'. They are not intended to be considered as such; each stands on its own as a suggestion for how a particular area of the tax system might be improved. In nearly every case the Commission is conscious that many of the technical details will need further examination. The purpose of the report is to stimulate thought and debate on these issues, not to draft a finance bill.

In some cases the Commission has modelled its proposals and other options for reform under consideration. To do this it has used the POLIMOD tax-benefit model constructed and maintained by the Microsimulation Unit in the Department of Applied Economics at the University of Cambridge using household data from the Family Expenditure Survey. The model illustrates the ways in which policies might impact on different groups in the population; it should not be interpreted as giving forecasts. More information is given on the model in Appendix 5.

The structure of the report

The report is divided into three principal parts. *Part One*, 'Changing the Argument', introduces the subject of taxation and the key ideas and themes which have informed the Commission's work. The first chapter explains why we believe that a new kind of debate about taxation is now needed. It looks at the recent history of the tax debate in the UK and examines some of the key trends in modern society—including globalisation and the growth of inequality—which need to inform any serious discussion now.

Chapter 2 then reports on the independent research into public attitudes which was conducted for the Commission. It explores the results of both the discussion groups and the quantitative surveys. One of the main findings is the sense of what the Commission calls 'disconnection': the feeling reported by many of the members of the groups that they do not know what their taxes pay for and are highly uncertain of whether they are spent well. This theme became one of the most important in the Commission's deliberations and is taken up particularly in Part Two.

Chapter 3 presents, in as straightforward a way as possible, key facts and information about the system of tax and public spending in the UK. It looks at how the tax system has changed over time and how the UK compares with other countries. It presents some little-known information about the progressivity of the tax system—how fairly (or not) the tax burden is shared between people on different incomes. This question in turn became a second principal theme of the report as a whole, and is taken up especially in Part Three.

Chapter 4 presents the Commission's view of the philosophy of taxation. It shows how political arguments about taxation often rest on profound philosophical disagreements between different conceptions of *citizenship*. It seeks to articulate a 'strong' conception of citizenship which it is argued should underpin taxation policy today. This view of citizenship then stands as a foundation on which the rest of the report is built. It informs both the principles and the policy recommendations subsequently proposed.

Chapter 5 gathers together the key conclusions of the previous four chapters. Drawing on the strong conception of citizenship, and informed by the findings of Chapters 2 and 3, it sets out the key overall objectives of the Commission's recommendations, and outlines in simple terms ten 'principles of a good tax system' to guide them.

Chapter 6 then addresses one of the most contentious areas of the tax debate, the question of the appropriate level of taxation overall. Examining the major arguments offered in this field—including the way in which 'globalisation' may impact on the tax system—it sets out the Commission's views and recommendations on this subject.

Part Two of the report, 'Connecting People and Their Taxes', focuses on the key theme of public 'disconnection' and how it can be addressed. Three different approaches are presented. The first is an increase in the accountability of government. This is the subject of Chapter 7. It examines how information can be better presented to the public and the auditing of government performance, and makes some suggestions as to how public debate might be improved.

Chapter 8 then examines the idea that the public would be better connected to the tax system if some taxes were 'earmarked' for particular spending purposes—a proposal sometimes known as 'hypothecation'. It discusses the advantages and disadvantages of this idea, and shows how the principle might be applied to different kinds of taxes. It examines in particular the idea of a special earmarked tax for the National Health Service.

The theme of earmarking is taken up also in the Annex to the report, which discusses the National Insurance system. National Insurance is not properly part of the tax system, but many of the same issues arise. The Annex discusses these and offers some conclusions.

Arguing that taxation should be closely related to democratic decision making, Chapter 9 looks at taxes at the sub-UK-national level—in the devolved Scottish Parliament, the Wales, Northern Ireland and London Assemblies and in local government. It recommends both new taxation powers and a reform of council tax. The chapter also examines whether the case for taxation to be undertaken or 'harmonised' at the European Union level.

Part Three, 'The Reform of Key Taxes', examines particular taxes in more detail and makes recommendations for change. Chapter 10 looks at the income tax system, with the aim in particular of making it fairer. Chapter 11 looks at taxes on spending—VAT and so-called 'sin' taxes on tobacco and alcohol—and examines the balance between direct and indirect taxes. Focusing on the taxation of wealth, Chapter 12 is concerned mainly with a detailed proposal for the reform of inheritance tax.

Chapters 13 and 14 pick up the remaining theme to emerge from the Commission's view of citizenship, the use of the tax system to discourage social harm. Chapter 13 looks at environmental taxation, including the taxation of energy and of transport. Chapter 14 examines the taxation of land in various forms.

The concluding Chapter 15 brings together the principal political arguments and recommendations of the report as a whole.

Part One:
Changing the argument

1 | Wanted: a new debate about tax

The subject of taxation has long been a source of political controversy. We owe such legendary historical characters as William Tell and Lady Godiva to the periodic revolts against feudal taxes which punctuated the Middle Ages. It was the demand for 'no taxation without representation' which set off the American War of Independence. Not long after, the French revolution began with the sacking of customs posts and the burning of tax registers: the bourgeois deputies to the Third Estate marked their defiance by declaring that all existing taxes were cancelled.

Recent British politics has not seen quite this level of conflict, but tax has remained a central field of battle. During the 1980s the Conservative governments of Margaret Thatcher succeeded in establishing taxation in the popular mind as one of the key dividing lines of politics, associating themselves with 'low taxation' and Labour with a profligate image of 'tax and spend'. This has been widely regarded as one of the reasons for the Conservatives' electoral dominance throughout that decade. Yet—in common with governments in several developed countries during the 1970s and 80s—the Tories were themselves the victims of a tax revolt. It was the failure of the poll tax which many have seen as the beginning of the end of Mrs Thatcher's premiership. Arguments over taxation subsequently featured large in both the general elections of the 1990s, symbolised in now famous billboard advertising campaigns: the

Conservatives' 'Labour's tax bombshell' in 1992, Labour's '22 tax rises' in 1997.

That taxation should cause such fierce political argument is inevitable. Taxation is a method by which the state takes money from individuals and firms through compulsion: it is hardly surprising that arguments over its form and level, on what it should be levied and how much should be taken, should generate the most intense political heat. Unfortunately, however, the debate about tax in the UK in recent years has been characterised by very little accompanying light.

To start with, even basic facts about taxation have been distorted by the ideological struggle raging around them. The Conservatives did not in fact cut taxes in the 1980s: though they reduced *income* tax rates, the total share of taxes in national income rose while they were in office. Labour has also raised taxes—yet has spent part of its time in office trying hard not to acknowledge this. Certain newspapers regularly claim that the UK is a 'highly taxed' country, when this is at best relative: the proportion of national income taken in taxes in the UK is in fact less than any of our European Union partners except Ireland and Spain.[1] In these circumstances it is little wonder that many members of the public, as we found in the research conducted for this book, feel confused and ill-informed.[2]

Perhaps even more damaging is the way in which tax has been turned into an issue of hyper-sensitivity in the media. It is no surprise that Labour does not wish to be seen as having raised taxes. Almost any mention of taxation is guaranteed sensational headlines; any suggestion that taxes might be increased is seen by most of the popular press as unconscionable. As a result, it is in general only politicians who seek to reduce taxes who now dare broach the subject in public at all. Proposals for reform of the tax system as a whole, however sensible, are rare. Indeed, it is not too much to say that the fevered climate in which tax issues are reported has made rational political debate on the subject almost impossible.

This is not a healthy state of affairs. Taxation is central to democracy. Since it is taxes which pay for government, the nature and level of taxation are crucial elements in the democratic process. Modern societies face difficult and important decisions about the level and form of public services which government should provide, and about the extent to which they should seek to affect the market distribution of income. But these are inextricably bound up with the taxes their citizens pay. Without an open and honest debate about taxation, wider democratic choices cannot therefore be properly addressed.

Such a debate is particularly important today because the world is changing. The distribution of incomes has been growing more unequal, as economic patterns and labour markets change. The so-called 'globalisation' of the economy and the development of electronic commerce have led some people to suggest that the very basis of taxation is threatened, with mobile capital and people moving to wherever taxes are lowest and economic activity disappearing into a 'cyberspace' beyond the reach of tax authorities. At the same time new ways of thinking about taxation have emerged, such as on the role which taxes can play in reducing environmental damage, and their incentives effects on work and enterprise. As social and economic conditions change, new questions about both the purpose and structure of the tax system are inevitably raised.

For the sake of good government, therefore, we believe it is time for a new debate about taxation. Both the basic health of our democracy, and society's ability to address the new challenges it faces, demand that taxation is seen as a legitimate part of political discourse. We do not seek to take the passion out of political arguments about tax: on the contrary, one of the claims of this report is that such arguments are symbolic of fundamental philosophical disagreements which ought to be more clearly aired. But we do think that the hysteria can and should be removed. A more mature and informative debate is needed.

It was to help stimulate such a debate that the Commission on Taxation and Citizenship was established, and presents this report.

£

Debating tax: politics and public opinion

This chapter seeks to set out the background and context for this debate in a little more detail. What role has tax played in political argument in recent years? And what are the factors to which tax policy must now relate?

The debate about tax: a short history

Our starting place is some recent history: specifically, the way in which tax has been discussed in British politics over the last two decades. Broadly speaking there have been two phases, overlapping in the middle of the 1990s. The focus for debate in each phase has been different, but in combination a distinctive pattern has emerged.

The obsession with income tax: 1979 to 1997

The first phase, initiated under the Conservative governments of Margaret Thatcher and lasting right up to the general election of 1997, saw debate about taxation focused almost entirely on the rates of income tax. This was in one sense not surprising: between 1979 and 1997 Conservative governments cut these rates dramatically. The basic rate of income tax was reduced from 33% in 1979 to 23%, with a new 'starter' rate of 20% introduced on the first band of income; the top rate on earned income was reduced from 83% to 40%. What perhaps needs more explanation is how these policies secured for the Conservatives a reputation in the media and in the public mind as tax cutters. For in reality neither the Thatcher nor the Major governments succeeded in cutting tax. Overall, as a proportion of national income, taxation under the Conservatives never fell below the 33% they inherited in 1979. It rose to a peak of 39% in 1983 before falling back to 33% in 1994; by 1997 it was back at 35%.[3]

How did this happen? At the same time as they were cutting the rates of income tax, the Conservatives increased, equally dramatically, taxes on spending. Most notable was VAT, which rose from rates of 8% and 12.5% to a single rate of 17.5%. Certain excise duties, notably on petrol and tobacco, were subject to particularly steep rises, while new ones, such as on insurance and airport departures, were introduced. At the same time the reductions in the *rates* of income tax were partly offset by reductions in reliefs and allowances such as the married couple's allowance and mortgage interest relief, and by higher national insurance contributions. Yet for most of the Conservatives' period in office up to the mid-1990s—helped by a largely supportive popular press—these changes received very little public attention. The simple issue of income tax *rates*—particularly the basic rate—seemed to occupy almost the whole of the terrain on which taxation was debated. The political benefit to the Conservatives was obvious.

And the effect on the Labour Party was equally significant. It is now more or less received wisdom that tax was a major reason for Labour's defeat in the 1992 general election. The party had proposed increases in income tax and National Insurance contributions for those on above-average earnings, in order to pay for higher child benefit and pensions. These were then considerably exaggerated by the Conservatives' election campaign. For the subsequent architects of 'new Labour' the lesson was clear.[4] Labour had to rid itself of the 'tax and spend' image it had in voters' minds—both of wanting higher taxes and of being likely to run the economy so badly that they would be needed. But such was the focus of political debate on *income* tax, this did not require a promise to keep down tax rates in general. It was sufficient merely to say that income tax rates would not be raised.

This commitment therefore became one of the 'five pledges' the party made in the 1997 election. Indeed, with Labour promising a new 10p starting rate of income tax and the Tories having just delivered (in the budget of March 1997) another cut in the basic rate (to 23%), in tax terms that election was fought almost as an income tax-cutting competition between the two main parties. Only the Liberal Democrats demurred, promising a 1p increase in the basic rate to pay for an increase in education spending.

The discovery of 'hidden' taxes: the mid-1990s to the present

Yet in fact by 1997 the terms of debate had already begun to shift. Following the debacle of the poll tax in 1990-92, the turning point probably came in 1993 when John Major's government decided to impose VAT on domestic fuel. In both these cases the regressive effects of the tax on low income households sparked first protests, and then the abandonment of the policy. (The poll tax was replaced altogether, VAT on fuel limited to 8%.) Suddenly indirect taxes were in the headlines. With fiscal crisis forcing indirect tax rates up across the board Labour was able by the 1997 election to accuse the Tories of raising 22 separate taxes—none of them income tax.

And so the second phase of the debate gathered speed. For Labour's commitment was not just to hold income tax rates, but to reduce the large budget deficit inherited from the Conservatives. The new Government argued that high borrowing levels increased interest rates and forced too much of the Government's budget to go on repayments of debt. Even with public spending held down for the first two years, this inevitably meant that taxes overall would have to rise.

And so they did: through the windfall tax on privatised utilities, the abolition of advance corporation tax and dividend tax credits for pension funds, increases in excise duties and stamp duties and the final abolition of the married couple's and additional personal allowances and mortgage interest relief. By 1999 the share of tax in national income had risen from 35% in 1997 to 37%.[5]

The Government's strategy was in practice rather similar to that of the Tories. With higher income tax rates ruled out, other forms of taxation were required. But now public debate was focused sharply on these changes. (So sharply that Labour's own cut in the basic rate of income tax, to 22% in March 2000, seemed barely to be noticed.) Labour was accused of 'taxation by stealth', the claim being that these higher taxes were somehow hidden. On the Conservatives' part, given their own record, this was somewhat disingenuous. (After a while, there was also something slightly odd about it, since the very complaint had ensured that the taxes were highly visible.) But the accusation of 'stealth' actually carried a more powerful connotation. It implied that indirect and other less visible taxes (such as corporate taxes and changes to tax allowances) were in some way improper. 'Stealth taxation' came to suggest an underhand or illegitimate approach, as if the only acceptable way to raise tax (in direct opposition to the argument of the previous eighteen years) was actually through income tax rates.

The complaint against so-called 'hidden' taxes reached a peak in the summer and autumn of 2000 with the protests against fuel duty. An initial media campaign was followed by a blockade of fuel depots by hauliers and farmers which almost brought the country to a standstill—with the support, it appeared, of most of the public and press. Though the immediate cause of steeply higher petrol prices was a rise in the underlying price of oil rather than of tax—the Government had actually just removed the escalator originally introduced by the Tories—it was on the high level of duty that public anger focused.

The fuel protests put taxation once again at the top of the political agenda. But what was striking about much of the debate was the extent to which the demand for lower tax could be detached from its own consequences. Given the high petrol price, cutting petrol duty was not in itself an unreasonable demand. But it would inevitably have both environmental and public revenue effects. A 15p cut in petrol duty, for example, would cost around £6 billion, equivalent to six times the Government's additional spending on education in 2000-01.[6] Yet too often even national newspapers seemed barely to acknowledge that a permanent cut in duty would require public spending to be reduced or some other taxes to be raised. It was enough, it appeared, to say that the duty must come down, irrespective of the consequences.

The terms of debate: illegitimacy and taboo

So in a sense the debate had come full circle. First attention was focused on income tax, with tremendous pressure on the political parties to reduce it, or at least not raise it. Then when the prospect of increased income tax had been more or less eliminated, debate shifted to indirect taxes—again, with all the pressure being downwards. It is almost as if a pincer movement has been applied, with both the major forms of personal taxation now squeezed onto the narrow terrain of a single argument: that taxes should be reduced.

The ultimate effect has been to make debate about tax a very lop-sided affair. Governments and opposition parties are under constant pressure to promise to cut taxes, while any talk of raising them has become virtually taboo. This was powerfully illustrated by the difficulty the Labour Government had in acknowledging its own tax increases. By 1999-2000, the whole subject had become so sensitive that, despite the published statistics in the Treasury's own budget 'Red Book', Ministers tried very hard not to say that taxes had risen.[7] Eventually, the 'admission' was slipped out, not by a minister, but by the Prime Minister's spokesperson, Alastair Campbell, in a press briefing.[8] The very notion—almost universally reported in these terms in the media—that this was an 'admission', not merely a statement of fact, revealed the partial way in which the debate had become framed.[9]

At the same time the Conservative Party had developed a taxation policy perfectly attuned to the new terms of debate. William Hague's 'tax guarantee', announced in October 1999, promised that in office a Tory government would cut the share of taxes in national income whatever the prevailing economic circumstances. As almost every commentator immediately pointed out, this was almost certainly impossible to fulfil. In a recession higher unemployment pushes up social security payments, so the guarantee implied a parallel commitment to cut public spending just when the pressure for it would inevitably rise. A few months later the guarantee was dropped. But in a way it was an appropriate culmination of twenty years of debate: a commitment to reduce taxes whatever the consequences—indeed with the consequences detached altogether.

Observing this debate overall, what seems to have happened is in fact rather more profound than simply a cumulative pressure to cut taxes. Taxation has gradually become stigmatised in public life. The dominant view which governs the terms of debate is not simply that taxes should be reduced because public services do not need more money, or that it would be better spent privately by individuals. It is that taxes are somehow not legitimate at all. Taxation has become almost a dirty word.

Of course, taxes are never popular. But the process has gone deeper than this. Virtually everyone recognises that taxes are necessary to pay for public services. But this should surely then mean that taxation is regarded as a means to an end. Of course one can argue that taxes should be reduced, because public spending should be reduced. Logically, one should also be able to argue the opposite. But in fact taxation has come increasingly to be seen as intrinsically bad, so that the argument about taxation and public services is not in fact symmetrical in this way. The very language reinforces this view: the share of tax in national income is known as the 'tax burden', as if by definition—irrespective of what it is paying for—it is an unwanted load which would be better lightened. Taxation is cast as a 'necessary evil'; but it is on the evil, not the necessity, that the weight is placed.

It would be difficult to argue that this is a healthy way for public debate about taxation to be conducted. It unbalances important arguments about the appropriate level of public services and the taxes required to pay for them. Indeed, at a time when there is considerable public demand for such services to be improved, the current terms of debate sometimes seem to induce a sort of schizophrenia: a widespread desire for more spending but an aversion to the taxes that fund it.[10] In psychological terms the unwillingness in public life even to address the question of taxation squarely might almost be described as denial.

This is a particularly unhelpful state of affairs now, when the two major political parties are offering significantly different priorities to the British people over tax and public spending. In its Comprehensive Spending Review of July 2000 the Labour Government announced substantially higher funding for public services in the period 2001-4. In contrast the Conservatives have promised to cut taxes, holding the overall increase in public spending to below the rate of growth of the economy, and thereby reducing the share of taxes in national income. The flourishing state of the public accounts is such that the Government's spending increases are not projected to require higher taxes. Nevertheless they do involve asking citizens to continue paying their present taxes, when the Conservative alternative on offer is for these to be cut, paid for by substantial reductions in the Government's spending plans.[11] This is an important choice for a modern society, and it needs to be considered well. Yet it can hardly be said that the present terms of debate help in this task.

Tax, public opinion and voting

We shall return to this political choice in Chapter 6. But there is another very important dimension to the political debate which also needs to be examined. After all, the political parties and media have not been talking about this to themselves. It is ultimately voters who matter in politics. And public opinion has played a particularly important part in the politics of tax.

One of the explanations for the dominant terms of debate, it could be said, is that they simply reflect public attitudes. In particular, they reflect voting preferences: people don't like taxes and will not vote for parties which raise or promise to raise them.

Within political circles, this view is very widely held. Yet, strangely, it does not appear to be supported by the evidence of public opinion. The annual British Social Attitudes reports have been tracking opinion on this question since 1983. Asked if they would like to see 'increased taxes and more spending on health, education and social benefits', a majority of the British public has consistently said—not just recently, but since the mid-1980s—that they support higher taxes for higher spending. In 1983, 32% favoured higher spending, 54% wanted spending kept the same as it was, and 9% wanted taxes and spending cut. In 1987 the number wanting higher taxes and spending had reached 50%. In 1998 it was 63%, with 32% favouring the status quo and 3% wanting cuts. When it is pointed out to respondents that this would mean an increase in *their own taxes*, not simply those of other people, the numbers favouring higher taxes decline, but they remain majorities.[12]

But of course public opinion as expressed in surveys is not the same as voting intention. Critics point out that what is said to a researcher can be belied by what is done in the privacy of the polling booth. Surely the results of the last four general elections show precisely that the British public will only vote for low tax parties?

In fact they don't. In the elections of 1983, 1987 and 1992 a majority of the public voted for parties (Labour and the SDP/Liberal Democrats) promising to raise taxes or keep them as they were: the Tories never received more than

44% of the popular vote. It was the electoral system which generated the apparently contrary result in terms of seats won and governments formed. Moreover, detailed analyses of voters' *reasons* for voting for the different parties in these elections and in 1997 (when the two main parties did not differ on tax) do not reveal that tax policies played anything like the central role which political mythology suggests. Examination of monthly opinion polls shows that neither John Smith's Shadow Budget in 1992 nor new Labour's tax policy announced in 1997 had discernible effects on stated voting intentions. Indeed, the public perception of Labour's position on tax barely changed between 1992 and 1997. For the majority of voters, it would seem, these elections were won and lost elsewhere.[13]

What accounts then for the received wisdom that the public are highly resistant to tax increases? One possible explanation is that though taxation policy *per se* is not a determinant of voting intention, it acts as a proxy for economic competence, which is. Parties associated with high taxes—particularly the pre-1997 Labour Party—are also associated with economic incompetence, and economic credibility is the single most important ingredient of electoral success. There is indeed evidence of this—Labour and the Conservatives swapped places as being the 'best party on taxation' at exactly the same time (late 1992) as they reversed positions on having 'the best policies on managing the economy'.[14] It may well be that, though tax in itself was not the determining issue, it was partly the abandonment of Labour's 'high tax' stance that contributed to its rising economic credibility, and therefore electoral appeal, during the second half of the 1990s.

A second explanation is that overall majorities of public opinion are more or less irrelevant when it comes to winning elections. Under Britain's first past the post electoral system, it is the views only of 'swing' voters (those who might vote for either of the two main parties) in marginal seats which really matter. And the evidence is that *these* voters have indeed been resistant to tax increases. Survey evidence following the 1992 election showed that 'high taxes' were among the first things which C1 and C2 voters in the Midlands and South East of England identified with—and disliked about—Labour.[15] The party's own private focus groups over the 1992-97 period powerfully confirmed the leadership's view that to these 'aspirational' target voters tax policy was indeed a central factor in voting intention.[16]

But if these explanations are valid, they both tend to reinforce the view that public opinion is not as fixed on the question of tax as it is widely thought to be. The strong reputation which Labour in government has built for managing the economy might now allow it to adopt a quite different stance on taxes from the one it needed in the pre-1997 period. And the views of swing voters are by definition volatile: it cannot simply be assumed that the opinions which animated the key target groups before 1997 remain the same in the very different political and economic conditions which prevail now.

So we can certainly say that public opinion is very important in the debate about tax; but exactly what that opinion is is by no means obvious. On the contrary, it seemed to the Commission that it was probably an altogether more complex thing than the orthodox view allowed. If we were going to contribute to this debate we felt we needed to understand it better. To this end we commissioned independent research into public attitudes on taxation, using both discussion (often known as focus) groups and quantitative opinion polling. Discussion groups allow people to express their views in more depth and with much more time for thought than is possible in opinion polls. The latter, however, allow some estimation of the overall proportions of views of different kinds in the population as a whole. The results of this research are summarised in the next chapter, and a full report has been published separately.[17]

£

The wider context

The Commission believes that a new debate about tax is needed, then, partly because of the inadequacy, in our view, of the prevailing one. But it is also because taxation policy needs to come to terms with wider economic and social changes that have been occurring over recent years. The political context, of course, has changed since the election of a new government in 1997. But the politics of taxation needs to meet other profound challenges too.

Consumers and citizens

Perhaps the most critical is the public's experience and perception of government. For taxation is at root a relationship between the individual and the state. If there is doubt about the public's willingness to pay tax it arises in large part because the benefits of doing so are not always clear. This in turn is crucially related to people's relationship to government. Two different, though connected, social trends appear to be particularly important here.

As British society has become richer over the last twenty to thirty years, one of the consequences is that private consumption has come to play a much larger role in most people's lives. People have more money to spend, and consumer choices have become more important in shaping people's identities and lifestyles. Considerable efforts have been made by the private sector to respond to these trends (as well as to shape them). Much more emphasis is given to customer service, with the recent development of telephone- and internet-based services in particular placing a particular premium on consumer convenience. Product standards have almost universally risen. Unsurprisingly, consumer expectations have followed suit.

But this has left the public sector struggling to catch up. It is not in fact true that public sector services are worse than they used to be: in many areas, including the NHS and schools, there is considerable evidence of improvement.[18] In many cases greater demands on services mean that improvements are required even to stand still: this is true (for example) in policing, given higher crime levels, and in the care of the elderly, given an ageing population. For most of the last two decades public spending has risen more slowly than average private earnings. But public attitudes rarely take such factors into account. People's perceptions are based not on actual performance, but on the gap between their expectations and reality. And the comparison with the private sector has now raised expectations high. So what people notice— as was widely observed in our discussion groups—is that public sector services are in general not as flexible, perhaps not as efficient, and certainly not as consumer-focused, as the private services people pay for directly.

At the same time, public confidence in the political system as a whole has also been in decline. This is important, because—as the members of our groups pointed out—taxes are not paid direct to public services. They go first to the government, and the government is controlled by politicians. Trust in politicians and parties has fallen considerably since the 1970s.[19] Perhaps more significantly, turnouts in recent general, local and European elections (1997-2000) have all been at record lows.[20] In the regular British Social Attitudes opinion surveys the number of people saying that 'the system of governing Britain works extremely well' or 'could be improved in small ways but mainly works well' has fallen from just under a half in 1973 to around a third in 1996.[21]

The reasons for these trends are no doubt complex, but they also seem to reflect wider social changes. As people have become more active consumers, and perhaps as their outlook on the world in general has become more individualistic, they appear to have become more sceptical and less deferential about politics. Higher standards for their own consumption seem to have been accompanied by an increasing unwillingness to take governments on trust. For some—particularly the young—this has reduced levels of political participation. But the evidence is that those with least confidence in the political system are overall no less likely to vote than others; and indeed, for many, loss of confidence in government seems to have been translated into political support for constitutional changes to it.[22] Overall, the UK seems to have developed a more *critical* citizenry—in both senses of the word.

This is, of course, a double-edged development. On the one hand, it is surely good for government that the public wish to hold it to account, and that their criticisms are driving pressure for its performance to improve. But on the other, if the public do not feel that government is responding, the risk is that scepticism will turn into more widespread alienation and disillusion, in which people do not feel represented by government at all. The health of our democracy, already perhaps ailing, may be further weakened.

All this is highly relevant to the debate about tax. For as we have already noted, arguments about taxation are critical to wider democratic choices. Indeed, many of them are arguments about the very purpose of government. Two, complementary, conclusions would appear to follow. If public scepticism is to be turned to democratic advantage, it must involve a healthier, more open debate about taxation. At the same time, a renewed debate about tax must acknowledge the changed circumstances in which we find ourselves. Citizens and voters can no longer be taken for granted. These are conclusions to which we shall return often in this report.

Inequality and social inclusion

British society has not only become wealthier over the last twenty years. It has also become more unequal. It is a trend which has had a profound effect on the character of British society. And it is extremely important to tax policy.

Over the last two decades the gap between the living standards of those at the top of the income distribution and those at the bottom has widened. In 1978 the share of total income of the richest fifth of households in the population was three and a half times that of the poorest fifth. But by 1998-99 this had risen to seven and a half times as much. Income inequality grew fastest in the 1980s, when high unemployment was combined with significant increases in earnings for those in work. Levels of inequality were more stable in the early 1990s but over the last few years they have been rising again. Over the whole period there has been a particularly steep increase in the incomes of those at the very top of the scale.[23] Inequality in the UK has risen faster, and is now higher, than in most other OECD countries.[24]

One of the effects of rising inequality is the growth of poverty. The percentage of the population living in households below half average income (one generally-accepted measure of poverty) has risen from 10% in 1979-80 to 24% in 1998-99. One in three children live in households below this income level, compared to one in ten in 1979. Over this period average incomes have risen by 40%; but what has happened is that the extra wealth has been distributed very unequally. This is in comparison with the previous two decades, when the proportion of people in poverty remained broadly constant.[25] Poverty causes far-reaching damage to people's lives, not least stark effects on their health. People living in poverty die younger and suffer higher rates of illness than those on higher incomes.[26]

A second effect of rising inequality which is widely felt is the loss of 'social cohesion': the sense that everyone belongs to the same society and shares in a certain kind of common experience. Loss of social cohesion is less tangible than poverty, but has equally profound effects on the character of society. As people's experience diverges and their sense of connection with one another declines, it seems likely that the idea of shared responsibility for one another will also weaken.

All this has obvious implications for the tax system. For taxes are not simply a way of paying for public services. They are also a means of redistributing incomes in society.

Contrary to the view often expressed in public debate, the statement that taxation is a mechanism for 'redistribution' is one of fact, not of ideology. As would be expected in any civilised society, the tax system takes more money from the better off than the poor, while public spending, particularly on social security benefits and pensions but also in other ways, transfers more resources to the poor than to the rich. In this fundamental sense the tax and public spending system redistributes income. (It did so throughout the Conservative governments of the 1980s and 1990s, as it continues to do so today.) The question that concerns tax policy is not whether it should redistribute income; it is by how much. It is a question that cannot be avoided, since the design of the tax system must inevitably involve some choice as to how much different groups in society should pay, whatever the total level of taxation levied.

This question becomes particularly critical when market incomes in society are growing more unequal.[27] Certainly the public appear to be concerned about the growing gap between those on high and those on low incomes. According to the British Social Attitudes surveys, 81% of the British public believe the gap is too large. This majority has grown steadily since the measurements started in 1983 (when the figure was 72%). Even among people identifying themselves as Conservatives over 70% hold this view.[28] Taxation plays two different roles here. On the one hand it finances public spending in areas which help to reduce inequality—not just on social security benefits, but in employment, education and training, housing and economic regeneration, health and so on. On the other the structure of the tax system—notably its degree of progressivity—helps to determine the distribution of disposable income itself. By increasing the progressivity of the tax system (that is, by increasing the share of income contributed by the better off in comparison with those on lower incomes) the growing inequality of market income can be slowed down. In fact, as we shall show in Chapter 3, this has not been happening. Over the last twenty years changes to the tax system have made it less progressive rather than more, while the development of the social security system has left most recipients of benefits further adrift from the level of average earnings. As a result the inequality of post-tax incomes has actually risen slightly faster than the inequality of original market incomes.[29]

Some of these trends are being strongly addressed by the present

Government, notably the increases in child and pensioner poverty; a particular focus has been the drive to reduce unemployment.[30] The causes of rising
inequality are complex, relating to changes in the structure of the economy
and of labour markets as well as of government policy over a long period.
Different views on the appropriate response to inequality are possible: the
Commission will discuss its own later in this report. What cannot be doubted
is the importance of these trends to the issue of taxation policy today.

Globalisation, electronic commerce and tax

One of the contributors to rising inequality, it is widely argued, is the so-
called 'globalisation' of industrial economies.[31] But the changes gathered
under this label have other implications for tax policy too.

Indeed there is now a frequently expressed view that the whole subject
of taxation will be transformed by the new globalised economy in which we
now live.[32] As international borders become less and less relevant to
economic activity, it is argued, nation states will find themselves increasingly competing with one another in the field of tax. Multinational
companies which can choose to locate almost anywhere will start to
demand that the price of bestowing their investment on any particular
country must be a lower tax bill. Countries with high rates of tax for individuals will find themselves losing their internationally mobile top
executives and professionals, who will themselves (or the companies that
need to employ them) choose to relocate to low-tax countries. Meanwhile
taxes on goods and services will also have to fall, as increasingly competitive international trade makes it unsustainable to have a higher tax in one
place than another.

The effect of this, it is claimed, will be profound. If globalisation leads to
a constant bidding down of national tax rates under the pressure of international competition, it might prove impossible to maintain public spending at
its current levels. Nation states simply won't be able to maintain the revenue
stream to pay for it. Indeed, not only will the total yield from taxes decline,
but the distribution is likely to become much less fair. While companies, their
shareholders and high income earners pay less tax, the burden will
inevitably fall more heavily on those left behind. Those who aren't internationally mobile, people without enough money to employ a tax accountant
or to place their savings in offshore accounts, those who cannot shop around
for the best international deal—the ordinary folk, in other words, will end up
with the bill. Some commentators go so far as to predict a fundamental crisis
for the welfare state ahead.[33]

The development of electronic commerce has led to similarly gloomy forecasts.[33] As more and more goods and services are purchased electronically, it

is argued, it will be much harder for the tax authorities to trace the transactions and to levy the appropriate sales taxes on them. Indeed it may not even be clear in exactly which tax jurisdiction an electronic transaction is located. Many firms, it is pointed out, are already relocating internet-based operations to so-called 'tax havens' where taxes are lower.

When the structure of economic activity changes in important ways there are often claims that the implications are so profound as to overturn all existing assumptions. But it is not always true. In fact the Commission does not believe that the prognosis for taxation is nearly as bleak as these arguments suggest. This is partly because the character of the new global economy and the role of tax policy in it are more complex than the simple picture presented suggests; partly because we believe there are ways of countering the threats to the tax base which arise, including various forms of international cooperation. Nevertheless we certainly do acknowledge that the trends of globalisation and the development of e-commerce are important, and that the implications for tax policy must be treated seriously. The projected effects on the tax system and on public spending *could* occur; but we do not believe that they have to, and the task of policy is to ensure that they do not.

This is therefore an important subject for tax policy to address. We shall discuss the challenges of both globalisation and e-commerce further in this report and make various proposals for how they can be met.

£

Conclusion

A new debate about tax in the UK is needed, therefore, partly because the one we have had over the past twenty years has contributed so little to public understanding and considered political choice; and partly because there are important new challenges for taxation policy to face. Such a debate must escape from the stifling terms which have dominated discussion in recent years; and must be informed by an understanding of social and economic change. Taxes play an essential role in a modern society. They need to be seen to have a legitimate place in public debate. The following chapters are intended to help in this task.

2 | Public attitudes towards taxation

As part of its work the Commission on Taxation and Citizenship commissioned independent research into public attitudes towards taxation. This chapter summarises the principal findings and conclusions; the full results have been published in a separate report.[1]

Two complementary techniques were used in this research: discussion (often known as focus) groups, and a large-scale quantitative survey of the public. One question was also placed on a separate opinion poll.

Discussion groups allow people to express their views and experience in some depth and in response to the views of others. The researchers gathered eight groups of people together in different parts of the country, each group consisting of men and women of similar ages and income. The groups took place in June 2000. An experienced and impartial 'moderator' led the discussions, loosely ranging around a set of questions concerning taxation and public services. (More detail on the research methodology is given in Appendix 4.)

The survey consisted of a module of questions which were placed on the Office for National Statistics' monthly Omnibus in late June and early July 2000. A sample of 1,717 adults aged 16 years and over took part, drawn randomly from across Great Britain.

An ICM opinion poll in August 2000 was used to carry one question seeking opinions on the Conservative and Labour parties' tax and spending plans.

The analysis contained within this chapter is drawn from all three parts of the research (the discussion groups, the survey and the opinion poll); it is important to note the distinction between them.

£

General perceptions of taxation

> *Moderator:*   *What comes into your mind, when someone says 'tax' to you?*
> *M:*   *Nicking my money*
> *F:*   *Sadness at the end of each month*
>
> *[High income, London, 18-39]*

Although attitudes towards taxation differed within and between each of the discussion groups, some strong common themes emerged in all of them. The most pervasive was what might be described as a sense of *alienation* from the whole subject of taxation. Taxes were not merely unpopular: they were perceived as an unpleasant subject to discuss altogether, invoking negative feelings even amongst those who accepted their legitimacy in principle. Almost everyone acknowledged that taxes were necessary to pay for public services; but a commonly used phrase was 'necessary evil', and the stress was generally on the evil. Taxation, it was widely remarked, has an almost punitive feeling, with the Inland Revenue in particular regarded as a coercive and even threatening body.

Few people experienced taxation as a payment for services rendered. Whereas everyone could say what they would do with the money if they had it to spend themselves, few felt they knew what the government does with it. On the contrary, for many people taxes seem to disappear into a 'bottomless pit' (others used the phrase 'black hole'), with almost no visible connection at all to the things it pays for.

Knowledge and understanding

Most people taking part in the discussions had a rough understanding of the main areas of tax that affected them. However there was considerable confusion about the details, including such things as the way in which income tax rates, allowances and thresholds operate, and exactly how savings are taxed. Few people had more than a very basic knowledge of taxation issues, and most were willing to admit this. Perhaps most importantly, few people knew how much tax they paid themselves. Though income tax is visible on payslips, people noted that its impact diminishes over time and therefore tends to be discounted. It is more or less impossible to calculate how much indirect tax one pays—or even how this is changing over time. So people's perception of their overall tax bill is largely made up of images and impressions, in which particular taxes (such as petrol duty) loom disproportionately large and media reporting plays a crucial role.

Most people felt that taxes were rising, and had been doing so for ten or twenty years; certainly since Labour took office three years ago. Perhaps surprisingly, given the symbolic nature of the basic rate of income tax over recent years, by no means everyone was aware that Labour had reduced it; and many people were at least as if not more conscious of the abolition of various reliefs and allowances.

The size of the tax burden

Respondents to the quantitative survey were asked if the rates of various taxes were 'too high, too low or about right'. Perhaps unsurprisingly, when the question was put in this way (with no reference to what the taxes were paying for), a majority replied that taxes are too high. Just over half (58%) thought that income tax is too high, with 35% saying it is about right, and 7% too low. Fully three-quarters thought that both VAT and taxes on cigarettes, alcohol and petrol are too high. Although people were more negative about these indirect taxes, the most interesting variations in attitudes were found in relation to income tax. Those in their mid-forties and upwards—who can probably best remember the high income tax levels of the late 1970s and early 1980s—were less likely to think that current rates are too high compared to the younger generations who would only have started paying income tax at the earliest in the late 1980s. In contrast, views about indirect taxes were fairly consistent across the age groups.

Social class was also an important determinant of feelings about income tax. As Table 2.1 demonstrates, just under half (47%) of the survey respondents in social classes I and II thought that income tax was too high compared to over two-thirds (69%) of those in classes IV and V. The pattern of opposition to both forms of indirect taxation was identical—clear majorities thought they were too high, with those in social classes I and II being slightly less inclined to think this than the other groups. Respondents in social classes I and II are likely, of course, to have higher incomes, and therefore to be paying more in tax than those in classes IV and V.

Table 2.1: Are taxes too high?				
% saying 'much too high' or 'too high'	Class I & II	Class IIIM & IIIN	Class IV & V	All
income tax	47	61	69	58
VAT	71	81	78	76
petrol, alcohol & cigarette duty	70	80	79	75
Base	578	668	375	1716

[Source: ONS Omnibus survey, June-July 2000]

These results were echoed in the discussion groups, where many partici-pants appeared to dislike indirect taxes even above income tax. The relative invisibility of these taxes and the difficulty of identifying how much one was paying led many to feel they were a 'ploy' used by governments to raise taxes without being noticed.

Meanwhile, one of the most interesting findings among the discussion group participants was the widespread belief that the UK is a heavily taxed country in comparison with most of its European neighbours. When a chart showing comparative international tax levels was shown to the groups, they were surprised to learn that this was not so.

£

Public spending, accountability and earmarking

The state of public services

There was a very powerful perception among the discussion group partici-pants that most public services in Britain are in an unsatisfactory state—that they have been declining in quality for some time and are still doing so. This was a matter of serious and widespread concern, and a trend which people wanted to see reversed. Health, education, transport and policing were the most likely public services to be mentioned, corresponding to their relative visibility to the ordinary citizen. Some participants recalled that it was a desire to stem the decline in public services that persuaded them to vote for a change of government at the last election—but they had not generally seen much sign that improvements had yet been made.

> I felt this was happening when the Tories were in power about eight years ago and so I thought that we need to make a change. It hasn't kicked into reverse yet for me. I don't know whether it will.
> [Female, high-medium income, London, Labour supporter]

Coupled with the perception that taxes had been rising, this created a strong feeling that taxes don't provide 'value for money'. Most people felt that this was largely down to inefficiencies, waste and bureaucratic management of various kinds in the public sector rather than any intrinsic difficulty or rising expense in providing good services. A number of people felt that money was spent on the wrong things anyway: government, it was felt, had its own purposes and priorities which didn't always match theirs. Some familiar examples of 'wasted public money' (such as the Millennium Dome) were frequently mentioned.

The link between taxation and public spending

Perhaps the most powerful impressions to emerge from the discussion groups were that people did not know where their taxes were going, and were not convinced that they were being used well. A number of people pointed out that if you buy a consumer good, or pay for a service, you can judge what you pay against competitors' prices and what you get in return. But with taxation you are only sometimes aware of what you are paying, and can almost never see directly what it is being spent on. At best, people said, they had a general feeling of contributing to the cost of public services; but while the link was fairly vivid in some people's minds it was much weaker and hazier for others.

Many felt this was the fault of the government, which made almost no effort to account for the money it received. Several pointed out that their local council provided a leaflet every year setting out how council tax was spent. This didn't necessarily convince them that it was being spent wisely (and it wasn't always very comprehensible); but at least it made a connection between the tax paid and the services provided. Central government didn't even do this. When in the discussion groups some information was provided on how government revenues are in fact spent, there was considerable interest, and many people were surprised at some of the figures. Many felt that this information should be provided to them—preferably at the point of tax collection, when the 'pain' of paying is at its greatest.

Trust and accountability

But even if they knew what their taxes were being spent on, most of those who took part in the discussion groups would not, it seems, have been content. The key element missing, for many, was confidence. Simply being told what has been collected and spent in tax revenues needs to be supplemented by clear and tangible demonstrations of improvements to services.

A powerful mistrust of governments and politicians was evident throughout the discussion groups. This seemed to be non-partisan—it was widely applied to both the present Labour government and the previous Conservative one. The discussion group participants generally thought that politicians mislead people, at least by 'spinning' the facts, and often by telling downright lies. At the same time they fail to keep their promises—either because their original statements were misleading, or because they are just not competent enough to carry out their intentions.

This made the *accountability* of tax-raising authorities a crucial issue for the discussion group participants. They generally wanted to know much more about what happens to their money, and how public services do or don't get improved as a result:

> M: *But where's it going? Where's the money going?*
> M: *Nobody knows, do they?*
> F: *At the end of the day the government are there because the people as*
> *a majority have put them in. We pay the money and they are*
> *accountable to us, to tell us what they're doing with our money.*
>
> *[Medium income, Sheffield, 40+]*

This requirement for more accountability emerged quite spontaneously in most of the discussion groups—and whenever someone suggested that governments should be required to explain to the public more clearly what they have done with tax revenues the idea was usually strongly endorsed by other group members.

Tax cuts vs public spending

The view that seemed to be emerging, then, was of a public which believed taxes were already too high and did not trust government to spend public money well. One might have thought that this would then lead to a desire to see taxes cut. But this turned out not be to be the case at all.

In the separate question we asked ICM to include in their regular opinion polling respondents were asked:

> *Over the next few years the Government is likely to have enough money EITHER to spend more*
> *on public services such as hospitals, schools and transport, OR to cut taxes. Which would you*
> *prefer the Government to do?*

This question was designed to capture the basic policy positions of the two major political parties following the Comprehensive Spending Review announcement in July 2000, positions which it appeared they were each planning to sustain in the run-up to the general election. The responses clearly suggest that when faced with the choice between spending on public services or cutting taxes the public prefers the former. Fully eighty per cent opted for continued spending and just a 16% cut in taxes. As the following table demonstrates, although Conservative supporters were more likely than Labour supporters to favour tax cuts, they favoured the (Labour) policy of maintaining taxes at their present level by a margin of three to one (73% to 24%).

Table 2.2: Should the government spend more or cut taxes? by voting intention			
% in favour of	Conservative	Labour	All
Spend more on services	73	85	80
Cut taxes	24	13	16
Base	202	326	1006

[Source: ICM poll, 25-27 August 2000]

Earmarking

But what of tax *increases*? The main quantitative survey looked in detail at levels of support for increased taxes to pay for more government spending. But it did not simply ask whether people favoured higher taxes for higher spending in general. Respondents were asked first whether they would support a tax increase for unspecified public spending, then whether they would support this if the revenues were specifically earmarked for spending on health or on education. In each case half the sample were asked about a 1p in the pound increase on the basic rate of income tax, and the other half were asked about a 2p increase. The implications of the tax rise were spelled out: an average £125 annual or £2.50 weekly increase for the 1p option, and a £250 annual or £5 weekly increase for the 2p option.

The results were very interesting. Unsurprisingly, support for increased taxes varies according to the size of the increase people are asked to pay. But specifying what the additional spending would go on is a far more significant factor in determining support or opposition to tax increases.

As the table below shows, increased taxes for unspecified public spending did not gain majority support in either scenario: four in ten supported a 1p increase, while a third supported a 2p increase. By contrast when an earmarked form of spending was specified there were clear majorities in favour of both the 1p and 2p increases. Support for an earmarked tax to increase health funding was the most overwhelming, with four in five of the 1p group supporting an increase and just over 70 per cent of the 2p group doing so.

Table 2.3: The effect of earmarking on attitudes towards increases in the standard rate of income tax			
% in favour of	Public spending (unspecified)	NHS	Education
1p increase	40	80	68
2p increase	34	71	61
Base 850			

[Source: ONS Omnibus survey, June-July 2000]

This striking result suggests that earmarking taxes, at least for popular areas of spending, significantly increases public support for them. It was a finding borne out, if in rather more cautionary tones, in the discussion groups. Despite the dislike of taxes in general there was a willingness among a number of participants to accept tax increases for the sake of improving services. But this was explicitly linked to the extent to which group participants had confidence that the increased spending would genuinely be channelled towards the services in need. Just as unspecified public spending was clearly too vague for most survey respondents, so it was only the identification of a spending programme that triggered a positive response among the discussion group members. And, as the following exchange highlights, the success of earmarked taxes will ultimately lie in the ability of governments to convince the public that the earmarking is genuine.

> F: Do you ever believe anything they say?
> F: I think the older I get the less I—I get quite a jaundiced view.
> Moderator: But in principle if you really believed it was going into the Health
>   Service you wouldn't mind paying an extra penny on tax?
> M: No, nobody would.
> F: No I wouldn't, I wouldn't mind at all.
> F: No not at all, no.
> F: If I knew where it was going, not at all.
>
> [Low income, Birmingham, 40+]

It was noticeable that by far the most important factor in determining support for both the 1p and the 2p increase was whether respondents had children under 16. The gap between those with children and those without was greatest for the 2p increase—three-quarters of those with children supported the increase compared to just under six in ten of those without.

Support for the earmarked tax increase for health was so great amongst the survey respondents that variations across the population are difficult to detect. Differences in the *strength* of opinion, that is, whether people were *strongly* in favour (rather than just in favour) of the 1p and 2p increases were, however, detectable. Strong support for the 2p increase for health spending existed equally amongst those with the lowest and highest incomes, while those on middle incomes were slightly more lukewarm.

£

Fairness

One of the strongest themes to emerge from the discussion groups was the
sense that the British tax system is unfair: both through the amounts of taxation it levies and the extent of its reach. There was a very common feeling
that the state takes too many different bites at an individual's means. There
was often resistance to the idea of being taxed again when spending or
saving money which has already been subject to income tax. This was
frequently described as 'double taxation'.

Taxing higher incomes

The survey asked respondents what they thought about the income taxes
currently paid by people with annual incomes of:

- £15,000 and under,
- between £15,000 and £30,000,
- between £30,000 and £70,000,
- over £70,000.

As might be expected, and as the following table shows, those earning more
than £70,000 a year were the most likely to be thought of as paying too little
income tax, but perhaps surprisingly, this was a position held by less than a
third of respondents. Almost three-quarters thought that the levels of income
tax paid by those earning less than £15,000 was too high, and just over half
thought this of the tax faced by people with incomes in the £15-30,000
bracket. So, while there is majority support for the view that lower earners
are bearing too much of the tax burden, this is not matched by a concomitant
desire for higher earners to carry more of the responsibility.

Table 2.4: Attitudes towards the tax levels of different income groups				
	Too high	About right	Too low	Don't know
Below £15,000	72	22	1	5
£15,000-£30,000	53	38	2	7
£30,000-£70,000	32	46	11	10
£70,000+	20	40	29	11
Base 1716				

[Source: ONS Omnibus survey, June-July 2000]

It is, of course, worth bearing in mind that people are generally reluctant to
think that they themselves ought to pay higher taxes. And indeed, what

emerged quite strongly from the discussion groups was that while people were fairly ready to suggest that those earning very high incomes are under-taxed, this was coupled with a tendency to think that *very* high incomes were those considerably in excess of their own. The higher up the income scale people were, the higher the perceived threshold of the 'really rich' became. Interestingly, the feeling that those on lower incomes pay too much tax (as suggested by the survey findings) was not so apparent in the group discussions.

There was, nevertheless, a view reasonably widely held that those on very high incomes should face a higher marginal rate of tax. Many of the group participants settled on £100,000 per year as the point at which such a higher rate of tax should be introduced. Three reasons for introducing such a threshold were voiced. Some discussion group members suggested that high earners have done very well from rapidly escalating top salaries (what a number called the 'fat cat' syndrome), coupled with the abolition of the high tax rates of the 1980s (which some remembered, though many had forgot-ten). Top incomes were often seen as excessive and unjustified—and even sometimes undeserved. But there was also simply a feeling that those on the highest incomes are not now paying a fair share of the overall tax burden in comparison with those earning much less:

> There needs to be a higher tax for the real serious incomes, 'cos my sister's other half is a stock-broker and he gets quarter of a million bonuses a year, and he's paying the same tax level as me—I'm going 'Jesus Christ'.
>
> [Male, High-Medium income, Banbury, Conservative]

A second reason cited in the discussion groups was that 'they can afford it'. It was widely thought that people on higher incomes can afford to pay higher taxes without having to compromise their lifestyle. High earners were perceived to have more 'spare' money, and therefore not to be in 'need' of such a large income. At the same time taxing higher incomes more heavily was also seen as a way of raising more money for public services without hurting people on low to medium incomes.

'Double taxation'

> That's probably one of the most unfair things there is—you paid your tax when you get paid and then you go and save money, you make a little bit of interest on it and you pay tax on that again.
>
> [Male, High-Medium income, Banbury, Conservative]

Across the discussion groups there was a widespread feeling that people should not be taxed twice on the same thing. This principle is well estab-lished in tax law, but the perception of what counts as 'double taxation' seemed much broader. There was a surprising degree of consensus on this point.

These feelings may in part reflect misunderstandings about how the tax system actually works. For example, many group members overlooked the fact that pension contributions are tax deductible (and hence paid out of pre-tax income), and that only new income arising from savings is taxed. But quite apart from possible misunderstandings these views also seem to suggest that a gulf exists between the beliefs and values expressed in the discussion groups and some of the assumptions on which the tax system is based. This mismatch seemed to increase negative imagery and resentment in relation to tax.

One of the key areas where the concept of double taxation was raised was inheritance tax—because, it was pointed out, an estate is merely an accumulation of assets which have been subject to taxation during a person's lifetime. Some people even felt it is morbid for the state to ask for a cut as soon as someone dies:

> M: Why is there inheritance tax?
> M: I think that's diabolical is that—you die, you're gonna have to pay a tax on it.
> F: Well you pay tax all through your life anyway.
> M: So the money you've accrued, and saved and scrimped, that you want to pass onto your children and grandchildren, you get nailed for it.
>   [Medium income, Birmingham, 18-39]

> F: It's a bit like robbing a grave isn't it?
>   [Low income, Birmingham, 40+]

Respondents to the survey were also deeply resistant to the idea of taxing inheritances. Half thought that *no* inheritances should be taxed, while only around one in ten were prepared to support taxation even in the case of estates of over £1 million. The same proportion took this view in relation to estates over £500,000. Only one in six supported the current status quo of inheritances over about £250,000 being taxed, while just two per cent took the view that *all* inheritances should be subject to taxation.

Those arguably most likely to benefit from future inheritances—that is those in the younger age groups—were the most resistant to the idea of inheritance taxes. Those most likely to be bequeathing (those aged over 65) were less likely to say that no inheritances should be taxed. More interestingly, perhaps, people in social classes IV and V were more opposed to inheritance taxes than those in social classes I and II. This reinforces the point highlighted earlier that those in social classes IV and V are the most resistant to—while arguably least burdened by—the tax system.

Table 2.5: Opposition to inheritance taxes, by age	16-29	30-44	45-64	65+	All
% saying 'no inheritances should be taxed'	61	55	48	43	51
Base	258	488	528	442	1716

[Source: ONS Omnibus survey, June-July 2000]

£

Conclusion: 'disconnection'

Attitudes towards taxation and public spending are complex, and this has been of necessity a brief survey of a rich field. But some strong conclusions do seem to have emerged from it. What has struck us most is what we have come to call the phenomenon of *disconnection*. People feel disconnected from the taxes they pay and from the public services which these finance. Both these elements are important: the link has collapsed in people's minds both between themselves and the taxes they pay, *and* between those taxes and the public services they are being spent on. Disconnection is partly a function of lack of knowledge, both of what is paid and where it goes; and partly a sense that it's not being spent well. Within the discussion groups it was clear that feelings of disconnection were widely and strongly experienced.

Disconnection of this kind would certainly seem to provide some explanation for why the dominant terms of debate about tax we noted in the previous chapter should have gained a purchase. (Which came first, of course, we do not know: they have no doubt been mutually reinforcing.) But in fact this would be too simplistic an analysis. For despite the strongly felt dislike of taxes evident from the discussion groups, there was *also* a surprising willingness to contemplate paying more. This was not universally expressed: some in our groups were implacably opposed, arguing that taxes were high enough and they saw little reason to support public spending (such as social security payments) which went on others. But the overall consensus which emerged from the discussion groups and the survey was that *if* people could be sure that the money was genuinely going to improve the priority public services, then they would be willing to pay more in tax.

This was, however, a very big if. At present discussion group members thought it very unlikely that any extra taxes *would* improve public services, because of the ways (as they saw it) in which money was 'wasted' or diverted to non-priority causes. Moreover, they were highly sceptical that they could believe any politician who promised improvement: trust in politicians' honesty and competence was even lower than confidence in public service management. Indeed, even if public money was being spent well, our discussion group participants had so little faith in the truth of the information and statistics they were given by government that they were not sure they would believe it. Certainly, most would need a good deal of persuading that paying more tax was genuinely going to deliver the benefits they sought.

At best, therefore, this was only a qualified endorsement. But in the context of the present argument, it is an important one. For, at least among the members of our discussion groups, it shows that the 'disconnection' is not terminal. *In principle*, most people can still see the relationship between tax and public services. Moreover—as our survey shows—a majority are still willing to contemplate paying more in tax for better services. Disconnection, it would appear, could yet be reversed.

This is no doubt a difficult task, but the significant point is that it is not one which seems to require changing most people's basic attitudes towards public services and their purpose. As we have found, and as many other surveys also confirm, there is widespread support for better public services, and a willingness in principle to pay more for them.[2] In order to capitalise on such sentiments what needs to change—what has to be (re)constructed—is the sense of 'connectedness': the relationship between citizens and the taxes they pay, and between these taxes and the public services on which they are spent. The discussion groups show clearly the areas in which the building work needs to be done. People need to be given more information on the taxes they pay, and what these are spent on; and they need to be given evidence—of a kind in which they can have confidence—that the spending is efficient and on priorities they share.

These are conclusions to which we shall return.

3 | Some facts about tax and public spending

This chapter provides some background information on the system of taxation and public spending in the UK, particularly where relevant to the policy issues discussed later in this report. (Readers who already know this subject well may wish to skip part or all of it.) It covers changes in taxation and spending as a proportion of national income over the last twenty years or so; the 'fiscal rules' introduced by the Labour Government after 1997 and its spending plans announced in July 2000; some international comparisons; the structure of the UK tax system and changes made to it over the last twenty years; the distributional effects of tax and spending; and finally a brief survey of the measures taken by the Labour Government in its four budgets up to March 2000, and their cumulative distributional effects. Box 3.4 at the end of the chapter provides a glossary of principal tax terms used here and throughout the report.

£

Taxation and public spending

The purpose of taxation

The main purpose of taxation is to raise revenue to finance government spending. This includes spending on public services, such as health, education and defence, and on cash transfers, such as state pensions and other social security benefits and interest on the government's borrowing. The design of the tax system affects the proportion of total revenue borne by different groups or activities, and it affects economic activity, as individuals and firms react to the taxes they face. Because of this taxes can also have other purposes: to influence the distribution of income and to influence economic and social behaviour in various ways. We discuss these more fully in Chapter 5 below.

Broadly speaking the amount of tax revenue the Government aims to collect reflects the level of total public spending—though governments can spend more than they receive in taxes to the extent that public borrowing (and its cost in terms of interest payments) is regarded as acceptable. The public spending total itself reflects the Government's views on a range of issues including the requirements of a decent society, the impact of taxation on incentives to work, save and invest, the likely growth of national output, and its own values and political direction.

For the purposes of this chapter National Insurance contributions (NICs), paid by employees, employers and the self-employed, are included as part of the tax system. Strictly speaking NICs are not taxes: they are social insurance contributions which provide entitlements to certain kinds of social security benefit (so-called 'contributory' benefits, including the basic state pension). NICs are paid into a National Insurance Fund from which these benefits are drawn, with current contributions financing current benefits. However as an important part of the welfare state they must be included in the analysis of the system of tax and public spending as a whole. (The National Insurance system is discussed in more detail in the Annex to this report.)

The overall level of taxation and public spending

Taxation and National Insurance contributions took around 37% of the UK's national income (Gross Domestic Product or GDP) in the year 1999-2000. Figure 3.1 shows how this share has changed over time since 1978-79. It also shows movements in the share of total spending over the same period. Figure 3.2 shows the trends in public borrowing and net public investment (capital spending).

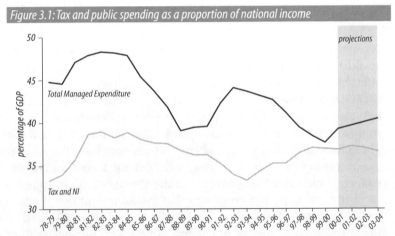

Figure 3.1: Tax and public spending as a proportion of national income

Note: If tax credits are counted as public expenditure rather than as a subtraction from income tax, the share of both taxation and expenditure would be 0.2% higher (due to MIRAS) up to 1998-99, 0.3% higher in 1999-00, 0.5% higher in 2000-01 and 0.8% higher in 2001-4.

[Source: HM Treasury, Financial Statement and Budget Report 2000, Tables C7 and C22;
HM Treasury, Spending Review 2000, Table A9]

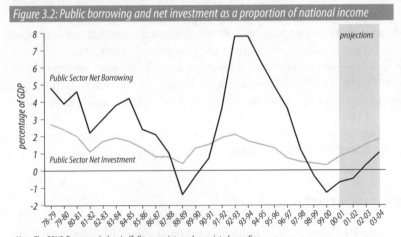

Figure 3.2: Public borrowing and net investment as a proportion of national income

Note: The PSNB figures exclude windfall tax receipts and associated spending.

[Source: HM Treasury, Financial Statement and Budget Report 2000, Tables C22 and 2.6;
HM Treasury, Spending Review 2000, Table A9]

The fluctuations in tax and public spending over time reflect not only policy changes but also the cyclical movements of the economy. In general tax revenues fall during a recession, when economic activity declines and unemployment rises. At the same time public spending normally rises, as higher demands are made on unemployment and other social security benefits. Borrowing therefore normally rises as well. This occurred in both the recessions of the early 1980s and 1990s.

The broad picture from Figures 3.1 and 3.2 is:

- After a peak in 1975 under the Labour Government, when public spending reached 50% of national income, UK governments generally attempted to reduce the share of spending, allowing for the economic cycle. They eventually succeeded in this: the share of spending in GDP fell from 44.8% in 1978-79 to 37.7% in 1999-00, which was a cyclically similar year.[1] Over the next four years however it is projected to rise.
- There have been less sustained efforts to reduce the share of borrowing by raising taxes: in 1979 and 1992 after the Conservative election victories; and from 1997 onwards under the Labour Government.
- Over the whole period borrowing has been brought down and there are a few years of budget surplus in 1988-90 and 1998-2001. In the later 1970s and early 1980s net public investment was just over half of net borrowing. But in the period from 1990 to 1997 borrowing resulted mainly from the recession as well as inadequate taxes (ie an underlying deficit after cyclical adjustment). Borrowing is projected to rise again from 2002 onwards as public investment rises.

The efforts to reduce the share of spending and borrowing in GDP over the 1970s and 1980s were part of policies designed to reduce inflation and to produce a more stable rate of unemployment and, if possible, a higher trend rate of economic growth. Lower average unemployment and small fluctuations increase the flow of revenue over the cycle. Growth in national output increases real tax revenues for a given tax system; and creates room for choice by the government between higher public spending and tax reductions. This is one reason why it is generally agreed that steadier and if possible faster growth is desirable.

Labour's fiscal rules

The current Labour Government has taken the pursuit of macro-economic stability further by introducing explicit fiscal rules.

The first is the so-called *Golden Rule* that public borrowing over the economic cycle should not exceed net investment (gross investment minus capital consumption or depreciation). This is a much tougher overall fiscal constraint than has on average been achieved in the UK since the mid-1970s. But the formulation fits in well with the Government's decision to reverse the fall over the last two decades in the share of GDP taken by public investment. The rule allows the average public sector borrowing requirement (PSBR) over the cycle to equal net public investment as a percentage of GDP.

Box 3.1: Cyclical adjustment

To help ensure that the Golden Rule is observed, the government now publishes figures for borrowing in 'cyclically adjusted' terms. Such adjustments remove the effects on borrowing caused by an economic growth rate which is temporarily above or below trend because of the stage of the economic cycle. Since faster growth adds to revenue and reduces expenditure, and slower growth does the opposite, borrowing tends to rise or fall according to the stage of the cycle. It is important to make these adjustments to avoid mistakes about the underlying state of the public finances. An apparently reassuring PSBR may actually be caused simply by a favourable stage of the cycle. But the adjustment process is highly uncertain, because the exact position in the cycle is not known at any one time and the trend rate of growth may change. When it assesses and projects the state of the public finances, the government therefore builds in a number of cautious conventions, including an illustration of the effect of a lower trend growth rate of the economy.

The Government's second fiscal rule, the *Sustainable Investment Rule*, is that, as a proportion of GDP, the cumulative total of public sector net debt should be held over the cycle at a 'stable and prudent level'.

If both rules are observed, as they have been up to 1999-00, the Government will normally be on track to meet its European commitments, under the Maastricht Treaty and the Stability and Growth Pact respectively, that General Government Borrowing should be below 3% and that gross debt should be below 60% of GDP.

Between 1996-97 and 1999-00 the public finances showed a 'fiscal tightening'—a reduction in cyclically adjusted net borrowing—of over 4% of GDP. The public finances moved into surplus on current account and the Golden Rule started to be met. This happened partly because spending was rising less rapidly than national income. But the share of taxation has also risen by about 2%, as a result partly of policy decisions and partly of unexpectedly high revenue yields. The reasons for high yields are not well understood and they may or may not be sustained.

Over the same period there was a fall in the ratio of public sector net debt to GDP from nearly 45% to 37%, leading to a sizeable reduction in interest payments. This has created room for higher current expenditure on public services and other areas within the planned total.

The shares of tax and public spending in other countries

The UK's share of tax in GDP was 6% below the average for European Union countries in 1997 (see Figure 3.3). The majority of European countries take over 40% of their national income in taxation, with Sweden and Denmark around 50%. This corresponds to higher shares of public spending. The

United States, Australia and Japan all have much lower tax shares, at around 30%, partly due to differences in the mix of public and private financing of their welfare states. Most European countries have been reducing borrowing and are expected to move into surplus by 2001. But government expenditure as a percentage of GDP is forecast to be about 6% higher in the European Union on average in 2000 than in the UK.[2]

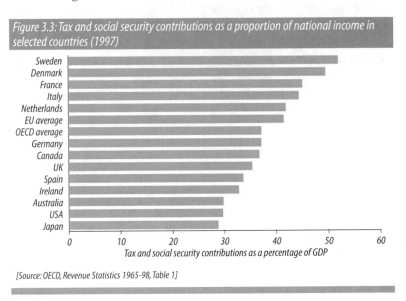

Figure 3.3: Tax and social security contributions as a proportion of national income in selected countries (1997)

Tax and social security contributions as a percentage of GDP

[Source: OECD, Revenue Statistics 1965-98, Table 1]

The growth and allocation of public spending

As the Golden Rule now allows borrowing over the cycle only for net investment, the planned level of current spending determines the minimum level of tax revenue required. In the summer of 1998 the Government announced its decision in the Comprehensive Spending Review that current spending in real terms should rise on average by 2.25% a year in the 3 years to 2001-02.[3] Including a rapid rise in net public investment the annual growth in total spending would be an average of 2.75% pa. In real terms public spending was more or less flat between 1996-97 and 1999-00 but is rising by about 6.7% in 2000-01.

The allocation of total planned public expenditure for 2000-01 is shown in Figure 3.4. Total spending is £371 billion. Social security is the largest programme, taking nearly 30% of the total. Just under half of this is made up of contributory benefits (including the basic state pension) financed out of National Insurance contributions; the rest comprises income-related and other non-contributory benefits financed by general taxation.[4] In total around 40% of social security spending goes on the elderly. The social security programme is as large as health and education put together.

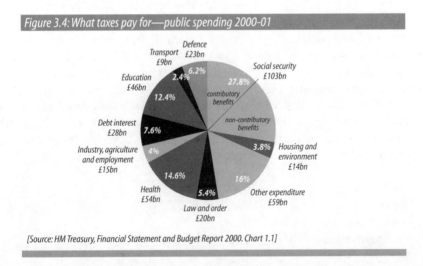

Figure 3.4: What taxes pay for—public spending 2000-01

[Source: HM Treasury, Financial Statement and Budget Report 2000. Chart 1.1]

These three main welfare state programmes account for about 55% of total spending. Their combined share rose strongly in the second half of the last century. Other large programmes are: law and order (made up of prisons, police, courts and legal aid) which has also risen very fast; defence; and debt interest. In recent decades the combined share of industry, agriculture, housing, employment and defence has been falling. The three welfare state spending programmes are the main ones which have a redistributive effect in favour of lower income households—see below.

In the Budget of March 2000 the planned annual growth of real current expenditure was raised to 2.5% in the three years to 2003-04.[5] This keeps the growth of current spending at the same rate as the 'neutral' projection for economic growth. At the same time a rapid increase in net investment is planned, from about 0.6% to 1.8% of GDP by 2003-04. This means that total expenditure will rise by 3.75% a year in real terms. So the share of total spending in GDP is planned to rise from 39.3% in 2000-01 to 40.5% in 2003-04. This compares with 37.7% in 1999-00 (which was the lowest figure since the 1960s), and with 41.2% in 1996-97, the last year of the Tory Government (see Figure 3.1).

Given the fiscal tightening of 1997-2000, it should be possible to finance these spending plans within the Labour Government's fiscal rules in the period to 2003-04 without raising the overall share of taxation, if national income rises broadly as projected.

The plans announced in July 2000, in the Government's Spending Review for the years 2001-02 to 2003-04, are for very different rates of growth in different components of the total.[6] Departmental spending is planned to rise on average by 5.25% a year in real terms. By contrast Annually Managed Expenditure (AME), which includes variable items which cannot reasonably be subject to firm multi-year limits (such as unemployment-related social security spending and debt interest) is expected to grow in real terms by an average of only 0.75% a year. The Government attributes the slowdown in AME to the successful reduction of unemployment and borrowing and vigorous action against benefit fraud. Since AME is likely to be about 47% of TME in 2000-01, this leaves room for faster growth of spending on the main public services. Average annual growth rates in real terms for particular areas of spending over the three years to 2003-04 include:

NHS	5.6%
Education	5.4%
Criminal Justice (England & Wales)	4.2%
Transport (England)	20 %

Public Service Agreements have been agreed for all departments and for certain cross-departmental programmes setting out objectives and targets to be achieved with the funds allocated.

Finding room for these departmental spending plans within a total growth in real current expenditure of 2.5% a year depends on limiting the real growth of social security. The growth rate of GDP will be crucial for this, because of its effect on unemployment and on tax revenue.

£

The structure of taxation

The present structure of the UK tax system

The contribution of different taxes to total revenue in 2000-01 is shown in Figure 3.5 and, in more detail, in Table 3.1. In declining order of size the main sources are: income tax (25%), national insurance contributions (16%), VAT (16%), other indirect taxes (13%), corporation taxes and non-domestic rates (13%).

Figure 3.5: The sources of government revenue 2000-01

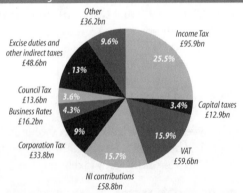

Other
£36.2bn

Income Tax
£95.9bn

Excise duties and
other indirect taxes
£48.6bn

9.6%

25.5%

.13%

Council Tax
£13.6bn
3.6%

Business Rates
£16.2bn
4.3%

3.4%

Capital taxes
£12.9bn

9%

15.9%

Corporation Tax
£33.8bn
15.7%

VAT
£59.6bn

NI contributions
£58.8bn

[Source: HM Treasury, Financial Statement and Budget Report 2000, Table C9]

Table 3.1: Sources of government revenue, 2000-01

Sources of revenue	2000-01 (£bn)	% of total
Income tax (net of income tax credits)[1]	95.9	25.5
National Insurance contributions	58.8	15.7
Capital taxes		
Capital gains tax	3.4	0.9
Inheritance tax	2.3	0.6
Stamp duties	7.2	1.9
Value added tax	59.6	15.9
Other indirect taxes		
Petrol duties	23.3	6.2
Tobacco duties	7.4	2.0
Alcohol duties	6.6	1.8
Betting and gaming duties	1.4	0.4
Vehicle excise duty	4.9	1.3
Air passenger duty	1.0	0.3
Insurance premium tax	1.6	0.4
Landfill tax	0.4	0.1
Customs duties and levies	2.0	0.5
Corporation taxes		
Corporation tax[2]	33.8	9.0
Petroleum revenue tax	1.2	0.3
National non-domestic rates	16.2	4.3
Oil royalties	0.5	0.1
Council tax	13.6	3.6
Other taxes and royalties	8.2	2.2
Interest and dividends	4.4	1.2
Gross operating surplus and rent	19.6	5.2
Other receipts and accounting adjustments	2.3	0.6
Current receipts	**375.6**	**100.0**

1 Gross income tax minus income tax credits.
2 Includes residual advance corporation tax (ACT) repayment of £0.2 billion.

[Source: HM Treasury, Financial Statement and Budget Report, 2000, Table C9]

More details on the structure of individual taxes is given in the different chapters below, notably Chapter 9 (local taxation), 10 (income tax), 11 (VAT and indirect taxes), 12 (inheritance tax), 13 (environmental taxes) and 14 (taxes on land).

Changes in the UK tax system 1979-2000

Over the two decades between 1979 and 2000 the tax system in the UK has been changed in a number of different ways. Box 3.2 summarises them and Figure 3.6 shows the effect on the shares of different taxes.

Box 3.2: Summary of main tax reforms 1979-2000
(including reforms announced but not yet introduced)

Personal Income Taxes
Basic rate 33% down to 22%
Top rate 98% (unearned income), 83% (earnings) down to 40%
Lower rate 25% down to 10%
Independent taxation introduced
Married couple's allowance abolished, children's tax credit introduced
Mortgage interest tax relief abolished
Life assurance premium relief abolished
PEP, TESSA and ISA introduced

National Insurance
Rate for employees increased from 6.5% to 10%
Rate for employers reduced from 13.5% to 12.2%
Ceiling (upper earnings limit) abolished for employers
Cuts for low earners ('entry fee' abolished)
Alignment of floor with income tax allowance
Imposition of NI contributions on benefits in kind
Structure of self-employed contributions reformed

VAT
Standard rate increased from 8% to 17.5%
Higher rate of 12.5% abolished
Reduced rate of 5% introduced on domestic fuel, energy saving materials and women's sanitary products

Excise duties and other indirect taxes
Large real rise in duties on road fuels
Smaller increase in tobacco duties
Slight real decrease in duties on beer, larger decline for spirits
Small increase in real duties on wine
Insurance premium tax and air passenger duty introduced
Landfill tax introduced

Corporate taxes

Rate cut from 52% to 30%, 20% for small companies
100% first-year capital allowance replaced by 25% writing-down allowance
Advance corporation tax and refundable dividend tax credit abolished
Windfall tax on privatised utilities introduced (1997 only)
Climate change levy introduced on business energy consumption (2001)
Aggregates tax introduced (2002)

Capital taxes

Capital gains tax at income tax rates and taper introduced
Capital transfer tax replaced by inheritance tax
Stamp duties raised and graduated

Local taxation

Domestic rates replaced by council tax (via poll tax)
Locally varying non-domestic rates abolished, replaced by national non-domestic rates

[Source: Andrew Dilnot et al, A Survey of the UK Tax System, Briefing Note No 9, Institute for Fiscal Studies, 2000; Lucy Chennells et al, The IFS Green Budget, Institute for Fiscal Studies, 2000.]

Figure 3.6: The structure of taxation 1978-79 to 2000-01

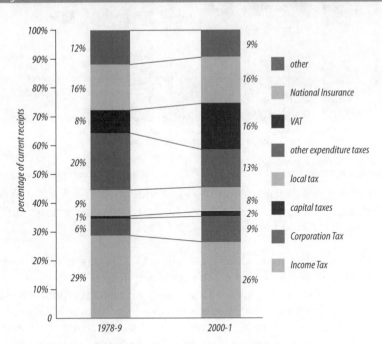

Note: Local tax is comprised of local authority rates, both domestic and business, for 1978-79 and council tax plus (national) business rates for 2000-01.

[Source: Andrew Dilnot et al, A Survey of the UK Tax System, Briefing Note No 9, Institute for Fiscal Studies, 2000.]

The effects of these changes included a widening in the tax base for income and corporation tax and a sharp reduction in the headline rates for both these taxes; and an increase in the opportunities for tax free savings income. The share of VAT within the total for indirect taxes has doubled, but the balance between total direct and total indirect taxes has changed little, as Figure 3.6 shows. The share of income tax in total revenue has fallen from 29% to 26%, offset by a rise in corporation tax revenue. The share of capital taxes and 'other taxes' has risen. The share of local tax has fallen.

Tax systems in other OECD countries

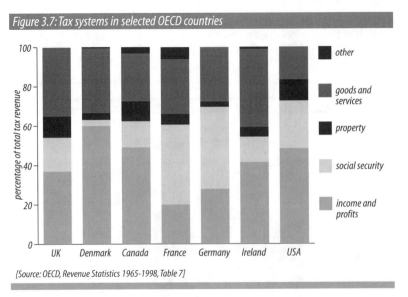

Figure 3.7: Tax systems in selected OECD countries

[Source: OECD, Revenue Statistics 1965-1998, Table 7]

The tax systems of different countries vary widely. As Figure 3.7 shows, tax can be collected in very different ways. Comparisons are therefore difficult, but the following broad observations can be made:[7]

- The UK relies more than most other OECD countries on taxes on goods and services, particularly on excise duties
- The UK relies less on taxes on income—income tax, corporation tax and national insurance contributions (NICs). In particular NICs produce a smaller share than many other countries' social security contributions.
- The UK raises a larger share of total revenue from property taxes than most European countries
- Central government in the UK raises and determines a larger share of total taxation than in most other countries.

How much tax do you pay?

The amount of income tax and National Insurance contributions paid by individuals depends not only on their income but on a variety of other factors. These include the source of that income, the level of any private pension contributions they make, and on certain other aspects of their status, such as age and number of dependent children. There are different personal allowances for elderly people; those with children get (from 2001) a special tax credit; the tax on savings income depends on whether or not the capital is in a tax exempt account; National Insurance is not charged on savings income or pension income. Hence individuals with the same gross income will not necessarily pay the same total level of tax.

The amount of indirect tax paid, meanwhile, depends what the income is spent on. Although many basic goods, such as food, water, transport and children's clothes, are zero-rated or exempt from VAT, around 56% of consumers' spending is subject to VAT at the full rate of 17.5% and another 3% bears a reduced rate of 5%. It is difficult for consumers to avoid this tax. But other indirect taxes can be avoided or minimised by those who don't smoke and drink, don't have a car or don't travel by air.

Taxes paid by businesses eventually fall on individuals, passed on through higher prices, lower wages, reduced dividend payments and so on. It is almost impossible, however, to identify the precise incidence of business taxes, so these are normally ignored in calculations of the taxes individuals pay.

Since every person will pay a different amount in tax, depending on their income, status and consumption patterns, averages or 'typical examples' have to be used to illustrate how much tax an individual or a household pays. One way of doing this is to use the average figures for the different fifths (or 'quintiles') of household income. National Statistics calculate these every year: their calculations for 1998-99, the latest available, are given in Table 3.2.

To see how this works, let us look at the middle fifth (by household income) of households in 1998-99 in Table 3.2. For this group of households the average original or market income (the income received before any state benefits were received or tax paid) was £16,570. The household received £3,440 in cash benefits. Adding these together gave a gross income of £20,010. Out of this income the household paid an average of £3,680 in direct taxation—income tax, employee NICs, and local taxes. This left a disposable income (the amount left to spend) of £16,330. Of this indirect taxes took £3,820.8 Total direct and indirect taxation for the average household in this group therefore took a total of £7,500 or about 37% of gross income.

Table 3.2: Summary of the effects of taxes and benefits by quintile groups[1] 1998-99						
(£ per year)						
Income, taxes and benefits per household	bottom	second	third	fourth	top	all households
Original income	2,940	7,260	16,570	26,700	51,220	20,940
Plus cash benefits	4,810	5,170	3,440	2,030	1,120	3,310
Gross income	7,740	12,430	20,010	28,720	52,340	24,250
Less direct taxes and employees' NIC	920	1,710	3,680	6,130	12,660	5,020
Disposable income	6,830	10,730	16,330	22,590	39,680	19,230
Less indirect taxes	2,190	2,650	3,820	4,840	6,340	3,970
Post-tax income	4,630	8,070	12,500	17,750	33,340	15,260
Plus benefits in kind	4,190	3,400	3,340	2,630	2,100	3,130
Final income	**8,820**	**11,470**	**15,840**	**20,380**	**35,440**	**18,390**

1 Households are ranked by equivalised disposable income.

[Source: Tim Harris, 'The effects of taxes and benefits on household incomes 1998-99', Economic Trends, April 2000]

The table also shows an estimate for the *benefits in kind* the household received in terms of free and subsidised direct public services—mainly health and education. These totalled £3,340. Added to the cash benefits this gave the household a total of £6,780 in direct benefits from public spending, leaving a so-called *final income* of £15,840.

The table also shows the same calculation for the other fifths of households (ranked by income) and the average for all households.

£

The distribution of taxes and public spending

How progressive is taxation and public spending?

The analysis presented in Table 3.2 allows us to see how taxes and public spending differ between different household income groups in the population. (It is important to note that the year for which the analysis is done, 1998-99, was before many of the reforms introduced by the Labour Government, such as the Working Families Tax Credit, came into operation. We discuss these reforms below.)

Table 3.3 shows the effect of taxes and public spending together on household income. It gives final income (ie after taxes and benefits) as a percentage of original income. This shows that the overall effect in 1998-99 of tax and expenditure in combination was markedly progressive. On average, households in the bottom 40% of the income distribution received more in benefits than they paid in taxes. (As Table 3.2 shows, the average gross income of those on the lowest incomes is largely made up of cash benefits.) Those in the middle fifth gained around the same in benefits as they paid in taxes. Those in the highest two fifths of households paid considerably more in taxes than they received in benefits. Another way of putting this is that the combined system of taxation and public spending is highly *redistributive*, with net taxes taken from those on higher incomes going in net benefits (both cash and in kind) to those on lower incomes.

Table 3.3: The distributional effect of tax and public spending 1998-99

Quintile groups of all households	bottom	second	third	fourth	top
Final income (% of original income)	300%	158%	96%	76%	69%

[Source: Tim Harris, 'The effects of taxes and benefits on household incomes 1998-99', Economic Trends, April 2000]

This progressive structure, however, is almost entirely the result of the effects of public spending, rather than the effects of taxation. Table 3.4 gives the percentage of gross income (that is, original income plus cash benefits) paid in taxes. This shows that total taxes paid were broadly proportional to gross income: each fifth of the population paid on average around the same percentage of their gross income in tax. In fact, between the bottom and top quintiles the tax system is slightly regressive, with the bottom quintile paying around 40% of their gross income in tax and the top around 36%.

Table 3.4: The distributional effect of taxation 1998-99[1]

Percentage of gross income taken in direct and indirect tax by quintile group

	bottom	second	third	fourth	top	all households
Total direct taxes	**12**	**14**	**18**	**21**	**24**	**21**
Income tax[2]	4	6	10	13	18	14
Employees' NIC[3]	2	3	4	5	4	4
Local taxes[4]	6	5	4	3	2	3
Total indirect taxes	**28**	**21**	**19**	**17**	**12**	**16**
VAT	11	8	8	7	5	7
Duty on petrol/oil	3	2	2	2	1	2
Duty on tobacco	3	2	2	1	..	1
Duty on alcohol	1	1	1	1	1	1
Other indirect taxes[5]	10	8	7	6	4	6
Total taxes	**40**	**35**	**37**	**38**	**36**	**37**

1 Households are ranked by equivalised disposable income.
2 Income tax is net of tax relief on mortgage interest and life assurance premiums.
3 National Insurance Contributions.
4 Council tax, domestic rates and water charges after deducting discounts, council tax benefits and rates rebates.
5 Includes intermediate taxes, vehicle excise duty and lottery and betting taxes.

[Source: National Statistics]

The separate rows of Table 3.4 show the reason for this. Income tax is markedly progressive: as a proportion of gross income the top 20% of households pay on average four and a half times as much income tax as the bottom 20%. Employees' NICs are progressive but not so much so, the top fifth paying only twice as large a proportion as the bottom. (This is because NICs are not paid on income above the Upper Earnings Limit of around £28,000 pa gross income or on savings income.) Local taxes, however, are substantially regressive, those on the lowest incomes paying on average three times as much of their income proportionally in council tax and water charges as those at the top. (The regressive nature of council tax is analysed further in Chapter 9.)

Indirect taxes contribute most to this regressive effect. The bottom fifth of the household income distribution pay around 28% of their gross income in indirect taxes, compared to only 12% of the top fifth. Even though many basic goods are exempt from VAT, it is still very regressive in its effect, as are most excise duties. Only the duty on alcohol is neutral. Overall the bottom 60% of the income distribution pay on average more in indirect tax than they do in direct tax.

One way of expressing the effects of different stages of government intervention is to look at the ratio of the income received by the top fifth of households to the income received by the lowest fifth, on each of the 'stages of income' given in Table 3.2. These ratios are set out in Table 3.5. At the level of original incomes the top fifth receives over 17 times that of the lowest fifth. The addition of cash benefits reduces the ratio sharply to 6.8. Direct taxes are progressive, reducing the ratio to 5.8, but the regressive nature of indirect taxes increases it again to 7.2. The addition of estimated benefits in kind reduces the ratio to 4.0.

Table 3.5: Ratio of incomes received by top and bottom fifth of households 1998-99	
Definition of income	Ratio (top:bottom)
a Original income (before government intervention)	17.4
b Gross income (a plus social security cash benefits)	6.8
c Disposable income (b minus income tax, employee NICs and local taxes)	5.8
d Post-tax income (c minus indirect taxes)	7.2
e Final income (d plus education and health benefits in kind)	4.0

[Source: National Statistics]

The proportional, rather than progressive, nature of the tax system has been known for at least a decade, but it is rarely mentioned in public debate. Of course, it can be argued that what matters is the overall distributional effect of tax and spending together, rather than that of the tax system alone; as we have seen, the former is very progressive. (Around half of the gross income of the bottom 40% of the income distribution anyway comes from the state.) So long as there are any indirect taxes at all, the tax system will inevitably be partly regressive. Nevertheless, it can equally be argued—and this report indeed makes this case in Chapter 5—that the tax system overall could be more progressive than it is.

Changes in the distribution of income 1978 to 1998-99

How has the distribution of income changed over time? Table 3.6 shows the shares of the total income of all households enjoyed by each fifth of the income distribution in 1978 and in 1998-99.

Table 3.6: Percentage shares of total original, gross, disposable and post-tax income by quintile groups of households		
Quintile of equivalised original income	1978	1998-99
Bottom	3	3
Second	10	7
Third	18	15
Fourth	26	25
Top	43	52
Quintile of equivalised gross income	1978	1998-99
Bottom	9	7
Second	13	11
Third	18	16
Fourth	23	23
Top	37	44
Quintile of equivalised disposable income	1978	1998-99
Bottom	10	7
Second	14	12
Third	18	16
Fourth	23	23
Top	35	42
Quintile of equivalised post-tax income	1978	1998-99
Bottom	10	6
Second	14	11
Third	18	16
Fourth	23	22
Top	36	45

[Source: Tim Harris, 'The effects of taxes and benefits on household income, 1998-99', Economic Trends, No 557, April 2000]

On all four definitions of income, inequality—and in particular the ratio between the top and bottom quintiles—increased over this period. The upper panel of the table shows the sharp increase in the top quintile's share of original income—up from 43% to 52%. The share of the bottom quintile remained at 3%. The second panel shows that in 1998-99 cash benefits raised the share of gross income going to the lowest quintile of income to 7%, but that this was lower than in 1978 when the share was 9%. At the same time the share of the top quintile in gross income rose from 37% to 44%. The third panel shows that changes in the shares of income after direct taxes were in the same direction. In 1978 the share of disposable income going to the top fifth was three and a half time that of the bottom fifth (35% to 10%); but in 1998-99 it was six times higher (42% to 7%). The bottom panel shows that when indirect taxes were taken into account, the difference had grown even larger. In 1978 the top fifth had three and a half times the share of the bottom fifth (36% to 10%). But in 1998-99 they enjoyed a share seven and a half times larger (45% to 6%). Their share of post-tax income was actually slightly larger than their share of gross income in that year (45% compared with 44%).

These figures show that overall the combined benefits and taxes were still clearly redistributive in 1998-99. But the sharp increase in the top quintile's share of original income over the period was reflected in its increased share of post-tax income; both rose over the period by 9 percentage points. During the period social security benefits were generally uprated in line with prices which meant that their incomes rose more slowly than that of the earning population. For the Commission the key point is that, as a result of changes over the period in the rates and structures of direct and indirect taxes, the tax system as a whole has become slightly regressive instead of slightly progressive. It has added to the growth of inequality rather than moderating it.

These figures do not mean that better off people are not paying more in tax. They are, particularly in income tax. The highest paid people now pay a larger proportion of total income tax receipts than they did twenty years ago. (The top 1% of income taxpayers now pay 20% of all income tax receipts, compared with 11% twenty years ago; the top 10% pay 48%, compared with 25% in 1978.[9]) But this is a reflection of the very large increases in market income these groups have experienced. The difference between the incomes of the highest earning 1% and 10% of the population and those of households nearer the average is much greater now than it was at the end of the 1970s. At the same time social security benefits have been uprated during this period only in line with prices, not earnings. So the income of those dependent on benefits has grown further behind average incomes of the earning population.

Figure 3.8 shows the changes in the proportion of gross income paid in tax by each fifth of the household income distribution over this period. The highest-earning fifth of households are now paying a lower proportion in tax (direct and indirect combined) that they were twenty years ago (35% to 37%). By contrast the bottom fifth are paying considerably more (38% in comparison with 31% in 1979).

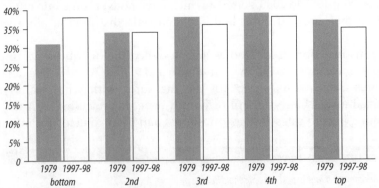

Figure 3.8: The tax burden on individuals 1979 to 1997-98

Direct and indirect taxes as a percentage of gross income by quintile of disposable household income

[Source: Robert Twigger, 'The Burden of Taxation', Research Paper 99/67, House of Commons Library, June 1999]

The distributional effects of Labour's budgets 1997-2000

Box 3.3: Principal tax and benefit measures affecting household income distribution 1997-2000

- *Reduction in the basic rate of income tax to 22%*
- *Replacement of the initial 20% rate of income tax by a 10% starting rate*
- *Reduction in National Insurance contributions (NICs) for the low paid (completed in April 2001)*
- *Real increase in the Upper Earnings Limit for National Insurance contributions for employees*
- *Abolition of mortgage interest relief*
- *Abolition of the Married Couples Allowance. Introduction (from April 2001) of the Child Tax Credit*
- *Replacement of Family Credit (a means-tested social security benefit) by the Working Families Tax Credit. This is more generous than its predecessor, is withdrawn more slowly as earnings rise, and is intended to be administered differently, through the tax system and the pay packet rather than as a cash benefit.*
- *Higher rates of universal child benefit*
- *Higher elements for children in means-tested benefit rates*
- *Higher winter fuel allowance for pensioners (£150 per year)*
- *Higher rates of Income Support for pensioners (the so-called 'Minimum Income Guarantee')*
- *Abolition of special benefits for lone parents*
- *Reduction in Incapacity Benefit for those with pension incomes*
- *Higher duties on tobacco and petrol*
- *Lower VAT on domestic fuel*

The distributional impacts discussed so far do not take into account the impact of the measures introduced in the Labour Government's first four budgets from 1997 to 2000, some of which have not yet come into effect. The principal measures affecting household income distribution are given in Box 3.3.

The Institute for Fiscal Studies has modelled the distributional impacts of these measures, as shown in Figures 3.9 and 3.10.10 The analysis compares the eventual effects of the measures with what would have happened under the system of taxes and benefits prevailing in April 1997 (assuming benefit rates and tax thresholds had been adjusted for inflation).

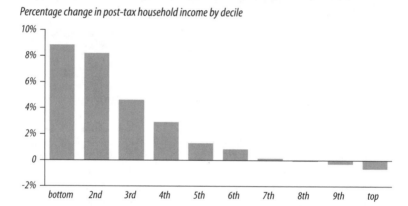

Figure 3.9: The distributional impact of Labour's budgets 1997-2000, by household income

Percentage change in post-tax household income by decile

[Source: Michail Myck, Fiscal Reforms since May 1997, Briefing Note No 14, Institute for Fiscal Studies, 2000]

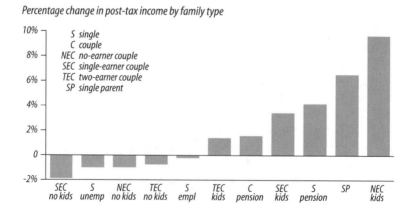

Figure 3.10: The distributional impact of Labour's budgets 1997-2000, by household type

Percentage change in post-tax income by family type

[Source: Michail Myck, 'Fiscal Reforms Since May 1997', Briefing Note No 14, Institute for Fiscal Studies, 2000]

The principal results are as follows:

- The measures are 'vertically' highly progressive: they give consider-ably more benefit to those on lower incomes than to those on higher incomes. The post-tax income of households in the lowest tenth (decile) of the income distribution is projected on average to rise in real terms by almost 9%. This will occur mainly because of increased income support for pensioners and the Working Families Tax Credit. The next six deciles in the income distribution also gain on average but by smaller percentage amounts. Those in the top 30% will experience on average small losses, around 0.5% for the richest tenth. This will arise mainly because of increased NICs and the abolition of the married couple's allowance and mortgage interest relief.
- The measures are highly progressive 'horizontally', towards house-holds with children. All types of family with children will gain on average, whether in or out of work. This is mainly as a result of the Working Families Tax Credit, the Children's Tax Credit and increases in Child Benefit and Income Support rates for children. Two earner couples with children gain less than other families with children as higher incomes make them less likely to benefit from the WFTC and CTC or from higher Income Support rates. Couples with children but no earner gain most, an average of £18.70 a week. It is independently estimated that the number of children living in poverty—that is, in households receiving less than half mean income—will be reduced by these measures by 1.25 to 1.5 million, or around a third; though this depends on unemployment remaining low.[11]
- The measures also benefit pensioners in general. Both single and married pensioners will on average be net gainers (and particularly poorer pensioners). This will occur as a result of increased age-related personal tax allowances, preservation of the Married Couple's Allowance (MCA) for people born before April 1935; increased Income Support rates; and the winter fuel allowance. Poorer pensioners will benefit from the Minimum Income Guarantee which is uprated in line with earnings.
- By contrast all non-pensioner households without children lose from the changes. For them the reforms to NICs and direct tax rates are outweighed by loss of the MCA and by higher excise duties.
- The number of lower earners facing a 'marginal deduction rate' (MDR) of 70% a more has been reduced by about 500,000. (MDR is the proportion of any increase in income lost through reduced benefits or increased taxation.) However an extra 200,000 face an MDR of 60% or more. This is mainly because of the longer, shallower taper of the Working Families Tax Credit in comparison with its predecessor Family Credit.

It should be noted that these are the results *on average* for different groups. Within groups there can be both losers and gainers.

These effects, which will eventually show up in future National Statistics analyses of income distribution, result from changes in social security spending as much as from changes in taxation. Increases in planned spending on health and education, the main redistributive benefits in kind, will in due course add to the overall progressivity of recent reforms.

Box 3.4: A glossary of tax terms

- **Direct taxes** are levied on individual and corporate income. They can take various forms, including income tax, employees' National Insurance contributions, corporation and capital gains taxes. **Indirect taxes** are taxes levied on expenditure. These include VAT, excise duties on vehicle fuel, tobacco, alcohol, and other taxes on expenditure such as air passenger duty. **Intermediate taxes** are levied on businesses, such as employers' NICs and business rates may be included in indirect taxes.

- The **tax base** is the range of income or expenditure on which a tax is charged. Thus the base for income tax is all income minus personal allowances, pension contributions up to a certain limit, income from savings held in tax exempt accounts, pension income, and so on. By contrast the base for employees' National Insurance contributions is the range of earned income between the upper and lower earnings limits only. The base for VAT excludes the 41% of total consumption made up of goods which are exempt or zero-rated.

- The **tax burden** or **share** is the percentage of national income (Gross Domestic Product or GDP) taken in taxation and social security contributions (in the UK, National Insurance contributions or NICs). It can also be the percentage of the income of an individual, household or group taken in tax.

- A tax is **progressive** if the proportion it takes out of income is lower for people with lower incomes than for people with higher incomes. A tax is **regressive** when the reverse applies. If the share is the same for all income groups it is **proportional** or **neutral**.

- **Vertical redistribution** occurs when a tax and spending system takes money in net terms from higher income groups and gives money in net terms to lower income groups (ie when it is progressive). **Horizontal redistribution** occurs when a tax and spending system gives money or services in net terms to a particular group in the population (irrespective of income)—such as households with children or the elderly.

- The **incidence** of a tax describes where its cost ultimately falls—that is, who pays it. A tax may be levied on one economic agent (a business, say), but its effective incidence may lie elsewhere. For example, the business may decide for competitive reasons not to 'pass on' the full amount of a sales tax but to absorb part of it. The net effect on the customer will be smaller than the full tax. So the incidence will be shared between the consumer and the business.

- Response to a tax is **price-elastic** if demand for the taxed product changes by more proportionally than the change in tax. It is **price-inelastic** if behaviour changes by less than the change in tax. The concept of elasticity can also be applied to income (changes in behaviour in relation to income) and to the price of substitute products.

- A tax is **buoyant** if revenue from it rises, without any policy change, at least as fast as national income. For example income tax will normally be buoyant as earnings rise over time broadly in line with GDP. Under existing legislation income tax personal allowances are automatically raised each year in line with retail prices, unless this is specifically over-ridden by the government. As earnings usually rise faster than prices, the effect is that tax thresholds fall as a percentage of incomes. The share of national income taken by income tax will therefore rise. This effect is known as **fiscal drag**.

- The **average tax rate** is the percentage of total income (or expenditure) taken in tax. The **marginal tax rate** is the percentage of the last (or next) pound of income taken in tax. The average tax rate determines the amount actually paid; the marginal rate generally affects incentives (such as the incentive to work or save) more strongly. If a tax has a progressive rate structure (such as with income tax) the average rate will be lower than the marginal rate.

- The **marginal deduction rate** is the proportion of any increase in income lost through the combined effect of reduced benefits or increased taxation. For people on lower incomes, high marginal deduction rates often occur when benefits are withdrawn as income rises. They can cause a **poverty trap** when higher earnings do not result in high-er income, and/or an **unemployment trap** when there is little financial benefit in working.

- A tax **allowance** is an amount of income (or expenditure) exempted from tax; that is, allowed before tax is charged. A tax **threshold** is the level of income (or expenditure) at which a certain tax rate starts. A tax **relief** is an expenditure (such as contributions to a private pension) allowed to be deducted from gross income before tax is charged. **Taxable income** is the range of income on which tax is charged, ie income after reliefs and allowances.

- A **tax credit** is a deduction from an individual's or household's tax liability. Tax credits can be of two kinds. One is an allowance whose maximum cash value is set by restricting the income tax rate applied to it. This is known as a **'non-refundable' tax credit**. Before its abolition the Married Couple's Allowance was an unrefundable tax credit, restricted first to the basic rate and then to 10%. The Child Tax Credit to be introduced in April 2001 is also of this kind. It can only be claimed up to the limit of tax liability. By contrast a **'refundable' tax credit** can be claimed in full even where it exceeds tax liability. An example is the Working Families Tax Credit (WFTC). In such cases the credit will often leave the taxpayer with more than his or her pre-tax earnings. The extra cash given to the beneficiaries will require addi-tional money to be collected from taxpayers if it is not to add to borrowing.

- Non-refundable tax credits are treated in the public accounts as **tax expenditures**, like allowances. They reduce the share of taxation rather than increasing public spending. Although refundable tax credits such as WFTC are replacements for cash benefits (which are counted as public spending) they are also treated by the Government as tax expendi-tures. This definition affects the measurement of the shares of taxation and of spending as a proportion of GDP, reducing both. It does not affect the share of borrowing. Treating the WFTC not as public spending but as 'negative tax' in 2000-01, its first full year of opera-tion, reduces the estimated share of tax and public expenditure in GDP by about 0.5%, and *by 0.8% in 2001-2. National Statistics and international statistics treat refundable tax credits as public expenditure: the key argument for this is the extra revenue needed to finance them for a given budget balance.*

- *Several different **concepts of income** are used to show how taxes and spending affect households. **Original** or **market income** is income received, largely from employment and investment, before government intervention of any kind. **Gross income** is original income plus cash (social security) benefits. **Disposable income** is gross income minus direct taxes paid. **Post-tax income** is disposable income minus indirect taxes paid. **Final income** is post-tax income plus benefits in kind from public spending on health, education and other subsidised direct services.*

- *A **household** is defined as people who live at the same address and share catering for at least one meal a day. A **benefit unit** consists of people whose circumstances or income are assessed together to determine how much they should receive in cash benefits or Working Families Tax Credit. (For example in a household including a married couple, a child and one retired person, there would be two benefit units—the retired person and the nuclear family.) Income tax is generally assessed on individuals.*

- ***Equivalised incomes** provide a standardised basis for ranking households by income, taking into account their size and composition. The intention is that different households with the same equivalised income can be regarded as equally well off. In the 'equivalence scales' used by National Statistics in their analysis of the effects of tax and benefits on household income, married or cohabiting households are given a value of 1.0. A single person has a value of 0.6. The value for a child rises with age up to 0.36 for a child of 16-18 years. Actual income is then divided by the total equivalence number for the household to produce equivalised income. The effect is that equivalised income is lower than actual income for households larger than a couple and higher than actual income for smaller households.*

4 | Citizenship:
the philosophy of taxation

In Chapter 1 we argued that a new public debate about taxation was needed. Taxation will always be a subject of intense political controversy and passion. But a more reasoned kind of national argument about it is necessary if British society is to meet the challenges it now faces.

In our view such a debate needs not merely to examine alternative options for tax *policy*. It needs to go deeper, to the philosophical principles which underlie different policy prescriptions. Only if these are properly understood are the moral and social choices represented by different kinds of tax and public spending options likely to become clear.

In fact disagreements about taxation policy are almost always based on prior and more deep-rooted arguments about the nature of *citizenship*. This is because, at root, taxation is a relationship between the citizen and the state. Taxation secures from citizens the financial resources through which governments then attempt to serve their needs and interests. But exactly what these needs and interests are, and how they should be determined, depends upon one's view of what citizenship *is*. That is, it depends on the conception one holds of the rights and responsibilities which define the relationship between individuals and government, and the force, if any, of the bonds connecting individuals to one another in the civic community.

Since taxation uses the power of the state, it is vital that it is underpinned by a distinctive moral framework: only this can ultimately give it legitimacy.

But there is no neutral idea of citizenship—no uncontroversial set of moral or political values—from which ideas about the role of the state or principles of distribution can simply be 'read off'. Notions of citizenship are profoundly contested, and it is in these disagreements that arguments about taxation ultimately lie.

In this chapter we shall seek to explore some of these philosophical questions. It is particularly important to do so because of the role they have played in the politics of taxation over the last twenty years. As we noted in Chapter 1, the dominant view that taxes are essentially illegitimate came from clearly-defined philosophical origins. The philosophy of 'neo-liberalism' was strongly promoted in public debate during the 1980s, and it has been explicitly revived in recent speeches by the Leader of the Opposition.[1] Since our own view of the legitimacy of taxation differs quite markedly from this, it is incumbent upon us to show why we do not accept the neo-liberal case. Even more importantly, the different view of taxation policy we wish to put forward needs to rest on an alternative philosophical position. It is this that we seek to articulate here.

This chapter therefore starts by explaining the neo-liberal conception of citizenship and pointing out what we believe to be its weaknesses. We then go on to define a different conception underpinned by a rather different set of moral values. This view—what we come to call the 'strong' conception of citizenship—will then inform the arguments and recommendations in the rest of this report.

£

Weak conceptions of citizenship

As we observed in the last chapter, taxation has three main purposes and impacts. It raises funds to pay for expenditure by government. It affects the distribution of income, both in its collection and through the spending it finances. And by changing the relative prices of different activities it influences economic and social behaviour. Different theories of citizenship correspondingly seek to answer three questions. What kinds of public expenditures are legitimate? Under what principles should the costs and benefits of taxation and spending be distributed? How far is it legitimate deliberately to influence behaviour? And a fourth question follows. Through what kind of relationship between the individual and the state do decisions about taxation and spending get made?

It is useful to regard the idea of citizenship as covering a spectrum of possibilities. At one end of the spectrum is a minimalist notion of citizenship.[2] This 'libertarian' view sees individuals as essentially separate, pursuing their own private interests. The state should therefore be confined to the provision of a narrow class of public goods which the market cannot provide. It has no right to engage in redistribution based on notions of social justice: the market should be left to determine the distribution of rewards in society. Taxation, which is essentially coercive, should therefore be kept to a minimum.

Towards the other end of the spectrum lies a more expansive conception of citizenship. This sees the individual as belonging to a civic community essential to the realisation of his or her potential. Many of the goods needed for wellbeing are public or social goods which require collective provision of some kind. Market outcomes are not simply accepted: social justice requires that resources, benefits and burdens are redistributed more fairly. This larger role for the state in turn legitimises a more substantial power of taxation.

The libertarian position has been very influential at a philosophical level, but the impracticality of its notion of a minimal state in a modern society has reduced its relevance in public debate. Politically, the much more important conception of citizenship has therefore been the 'neo-liberal' one. This lies, as one might put it, a little way in along the spectrum. It shares many features of libertarianism but accepts a rather larger—if still small—role for the state. As expounded, notably, by the philosopher FA Hayek and the economist Milton Friedman, it represents a modernisation of the classical liberal theory of *laissez faire* and has had a profound influence on modern political thought on the right.[3] It is therefore this position which we shall examine here.

Individuals, rights and freedoms

The neo-liberal conception of citizenship starts with its view of the individual. This view was perhaps most famously articulated by Margaret Thatcher, in her assertion that 'there is no such thing as society, only individuals and their families'. For the neo-liberal the individual is autonomous, independent of others; the relationship between individuals is instrumental, based largely on free exchange. In turn, every individual has the right to keep whatever he or she can earn in the market and to consume whatever will fulfil his or her own desires. No-one else can know what will achieve this.

For the libertarian and neo-liberal, the essential illegitimacy of taxation follows. Taxation is effectively confiscation. Thus the philosopher Robert Nozick argues that taxation is 'morally equivalent to forced labour': it expropriates private earnings for purposes determined not by the individual but by government. This view has subsequently given rise to the notion—first promulgated in the USA and now imported into the UK—of 'Tax Freedom Day', the supposed day in the calendar when the individual stops earning money simply to pay it over to the overweening state and starts working for him/herself.[4]

Politically, the autonomy of the individual is expressed in the idea of basic 'negative rights': the rights not to be interfered with or coerced, of freedom of expression (ie not to be silenced) and so on. The state is then seen simply as a contractual relationship between individuals to protect these negative rights. Neo-liberals accept that there are public goods which the market cannot provide, because their consumption is essentially collective and free-riders cannot be excluded: national defence, policing and the judicial system, clean air. But the state's role should not go much further than the provision of these goods. Hence taxation, alongside government, should be kept to a minimum.

Obligation and ability

The insistence that citizens have only 'negative' rights, to freedom from coercion, assault and so on has crucial implications for taxation. Neo-liberals explicitly reject the idea of so-called 'positive' rights, to resources such as health, education and social security, which might imply a larger role for the state and hence for taxation.

Their reasons for doing so have to do with the nature of the corresponding obligation. My right not to be coerced, etc, puts an obligation on you not to engage in acts of coercion. This duty is categorical. It can always be performed: since you cannot run out of not doing things, it does not run up against any constraint of scarcity. Moreover one knows precisely what one has to do to discharge the duty and when one has done it. In contrast, the neo-liberal argues, rights to resources such as health care or education cannot be genuine rights because the corresponding duty involves action (rather than inaction) and thus may run up against constraints of scarcity. Since the corresponding obligation is a duty to provide resources, it cannot be categorical: one can never know when one has done enough. Because of the scarcity constraint, positive rights will always be subject to rationing. But the neo-liberal argues that nothing can be a right if it is subject to such rationing. So only negative rights are defensible.

The neo-liberal makes a second argument against positive rights, and the taxation that they might entail. This is that freedom and ability are categorically different. Being free to do something is not the same thing as being able to do it or having the resources to do it. Freedom is strictly negative. I am free to do those things only that I am not intentionally prevented from doing; whether I am able to do them is quite a different matter. In a free society it is possible for the state to secure to its citizens equal negative liberty by imposing a set of laws which prevent assault and coercion of various kinds. This is part of the legitimate public good for which taxation can be used. But it is not legitimate in a free society for the state to seek to provide the resources to give individuals the ability to do these things. (As the Conservative minister Sir Keith Joseph put it, 'poverty is not unfreedom'.[5]) The idea that lack of this ability is a constraint on freedom would open up a bottomless pit of public expenditure—and the taxation to pay for it.

These arguments for a purely negative view of the citizen's rights and freedom, however, begin to break down as soon as they are examined more closely. Let us start with the neo-liberal view of obligation. The problem here is that if this is valid it undermines the idea of negative as much as of positive rights. The basic question here is: do we have a right to the *protection* of our rights, whether these are negative or positive? If the answer is no, then it is not at all clear that we have rights in any meaningful sense. We have all sorts of desires, needs and interests, but what turns some of these into rights is that they are *enforceable*. But if this is the case, rights of all sorts immediately run into resource considerations. The mechanisms for enforcing negative rights include the police, the courts, prisons etc. These are funded by taxation (indeed, they are very expensive, and have become increasingly so over recent years).[6]

But then there is always a question, which can only be answered by democratic deliberation and choice, about the level of resources we wish to commit to enforcing such rights. This is exactly the same as for social and economic rights.

The neo-liberal critic will argue that the costs are different in the two cases. In the health service, for example, doctors and managers have discretion about how to use scarce resources. So a right to health care cannot be absolute. But the same is true of the protection of negative rights. The amount of money allocated to the police and courts (ie to the protection of the right not to be coerced) is as essentially discretionary as the amount committed to health care. Police commanders make decisions about which kinds of crimes they will prioritise just as hospital managers make decisions on medical treatments. It is simply wrong to believe that negative rights imply easily defined 'categorical' obligations whereas positive rights involve political or bureaucratic discretion. Decisions about the allocation of resources—and therefore of the role of taxation—lie at the heart of the enforcement of negative rights too.

A similar weakness is evident in the neo-liberal attempt to separate freedom and ability. For why should I want to be free from coercion, to have negative freedom? The answer surely has to be expressed in terms of what I am able to do if I am free from coercion—namely, that I am able to live a life shaped by my own priorities and my own interests. Or put another way, if I am free in negative terms I shall be able to do things that I was not previously able to do. Thus the *worth* of negative liberty—the justification of its value— has a great deal to do with ability.

To see this further, consider how we compare freedom between countries.[7] If freedom were simply about negative liberty we should have to describe North Korea as freer than the UK. Many more things are illegal in the UK than in North Korea: there are myriad laws and regulations covering employment, the production and retailing of goods and services, land use planning and so on. These aren't necessary in North Korea because poverty and underdevelopment allows far fewer things to be done in the first place. It is not the number of constraints under the law which determines freedom, but the *ability* to do those things which we hold valuable. It is this that makes the UK a freer country than North Korea.

This is an important point, and it is one to which we shall return. It suggests that in assessing questions of freedom it is essential to have some conception of the abilities or 'capabilities' which we regard as central to human flourishing.[8] In fact these capabilities play an important role in the stronger conception of citizenship which we describe below. They justify a concern both for positive rights and for the just distribution of resources in society. They thus have a crucial bearing on the role of taxation.

The critique of social justice

The neo-liberal view of citizenship not only rejects a role for the state in providing the resources to realise social and economic rights. It also rejects the idea that taxation can be used to achieve any kind of social or distributive justice. Unlike the true libertarian, the neo-liberal accepts the idea of a minimal welfare state. Hayek, for example, argues for a level of social security expenditure which will prevent destitution. But the provision of a welfare safety net is sharply distinguished from an attempt to secure 'social justice'. To the neo-liberal, the latter concept has neither meaning nor ethical coherence.

In the first place, it is argued, those who lack resources are not, in a market economy, suffering from an injustice. For Hayek injustice can occur only as the result of intentional action. The so-called 'distribution of income' that arises at any point out of the operation of a free market is not actually a 'distribution' at all. It is rather an unintended and unforeseen consequence of millions of acts of economic exchange between individuals. Since those who end up at the bottom of the pile are not there as the result of anyone's intentional act, their situation is one of misfortune not injustice. Their rights have not been infringed, and the rest of the population bear no collective moral responsibility for them. For the neo-liberal there is therefore no moral case for the state to impose taxes to secure a more equitable distribution of resources.

Second, the neo-liberal argues that, even if we thought there was a general moral case for redistribution, there will be no agreement on the principles under which it should happen. Resources and goods could be distributed by a whole range of mutually incompatible and incommensurable criteria: need, merit, equality, marginal contribution and so on. In a morally diverse society it will not be agreed which principle should be paramount, or how different principles should be weighted. This means that distributive politics takes place in an ethical vacuum: the moral principles underpinning it are just not available. Hence the effects of any taxation and spending regime will be essentially arbitrary.

Foreseeability and distributive principles

But again these arguments prove weak under closer scrutiny. First, consider the point about intention. Outside the economic field, we do not normally argue that justice and injustice can only result from intentional action. In law, for example, the fact that a consequence of one's action or inaction was not intended does not automatically absolve one from responsibility for it. The key question is whether or not it could have been foreseen. (This is the basis, for example, of the crime of manslaughter.) Similarly, if economic outcomes are foreseeable there can be responsibility for them. It will not do for neo-liberals to argue that economic consequences are unforeseeable, since they are so keen to argue for the extension and deregulation of markets precisely for what they believe to be their foreseeable consequences—higher production, lower prices, and so on. If these things are foreseeable then we can also be responsible for the other foreseeable consequences of market activities, including poverty and inequality.

Let us take a real example. In the emerging 'knowledge-based economy' it is fairly predictable that those who lack education and information technology skills will end up near the bottom of the income distribution. But if this can be foreseen, and we can do something about it (for example, investing in training and access to resources) then we become responsible for the consequences if we fail to do so. So it cannot be the case that the question of justice or injustice is settled by intention; foreseeability also counts. Indeed, it can be argued that this is crucial to the very notion of civilisation itself. One of the main forces of progress has surely been the transition from a view of events as being the result of impersonal forces—acts of God and nature and the like—to the view that they are the result of human organisation and action (and inaction). Far more falls within the domain of human responsibility and thus of justice than the neo-liberal allows.

It is difficult, in fact, to see how the neo-liberal can avoid acknowledging the concept of social justice. As we have seen, Hayek himself argues in favour of a minimalist welfare state to prevent destitution, and even libertarians accept that the state needs to provide a minimum level of public goods (national defence, clean air, and so on.) But as soon as the need for either of these forms of public expenditure is conceded, the question arises of who will pay for them. Any form of taxation and spending is distributive: it involves some allocation of benefits and burdens between citizens. Whatever decision is made on this, it is a distributive decision.[9] This really cannot be escaped: the idea that we have moved into an era in which the question of distribution no longer matters is simply an illusion. The question is under what principles and values the redistribution takes place.

Hayek argues that because we live in a pluralistic society, we cannot agree on principles of social justice. It is certainly true that there is no universal or foundational theory of social justice. But this is to misunderstand the nature of political argument. In a democracy, competing interpretations of philosophical ideas (freedom, justice, democracy itself) are part of public debate. There is no philosopher's stone which will solve the question of distribution. Such issues can only be settled by democratic argument: this is what politics is for. The crucial need is not to try to eliminate politics, but to make public debate more open and decisions on the distribution of resources more transparent. We shall return to this below.

Taxation and charity

The rejection by neo-liberals of the claim of social justice does not mean that the idea of a moral obligation to the poor is eschewed altogether. The remedy for poverty lies not in the public duties of citizenship—in taxation and expenditure by the state—so much as in private acts of altruism. Beyond the provision of a basic safety net to prevent destitution, the issue is not one of justice but of charity.

The importance of charity and its relationship to taxation has been specifically taken up by the present Leader of the Opposition, William Hague.[10] Mr Hague has argued that taxation 'crowds out' voluntary charitable giving, and so reduces moral virtue in society. He points to the difference between the USA and the UK, arguing that the lower tax share in the former is directly related to the higher average level of charitable donation.

The empirical argument here is not cut and dried: both incomes and tax incentives for charitable giving are greater in the United States. But the moral case, and the view of citizenship it embodies, can certainly be contested. If more social needs were to be met by voluntary giving, the consequences would be wholly arbitrary. The point about charitable giving is that it is discretionary—this is part of its value. I choose to whom or to what cause I shall give. This inevitably means that some groups of people or causes will not be chosen, or will receive considerably less than others. But justice at its most minimal means treating like cases in like manner. Charity will never do this, nor could it seek to. This is why it has been accepted by British governments for nearly a century that the funding of basic social goods should *not* be based upon charitable giving but upon a predictable and inclusive form of state support.

There is something odd, too, about the claim that a low tax society with a higher rate of charitable giving is a more moral one. This argument locates morality in the virtue of the person donating to charity. But many people will prefer an idea of morality that gives greater priority to the individual's impact on the world. As a comparison of the United States with most of continental Europe shows, charitable giving (much higher in the US) leaves huge amounts of poverty. By contrast taxation (higher in Europe) tends to prevent and alleviate it. In these circumstances it is not clear that the USA should be regarded as the more moral society. Indeed, there seems every reason why an individual should claim as much personal virtue from willingly paying taxes, and voting for them, as her neighbour claims from giving money to charity (especially as very few people, even in the United States, give anything like the level of money to charity as they pay in taxes).

The state

Underpinned by the principle of negative freedom, and rejecting social justice, the neo-liberal view of citizenship sees the state as essentially coercive. But this is not the only reason why for the neo-liberal the activities of the state—and the taxation that pays for them—should be reduced as far as possible. There is something rotten in the very idea of the modern state itself.

Hayek makes this point most strongly.[11] In the absence of a core set of publicly agreed distributive principles, Hayek warns, governments inevitably fall victim to coalitions of powerful interest groups bent on extracting resources from the state, each demanding their 'just' share of the benefits to be distributed. At the same time, in providing public services, the bureaucracies of the state inevitably find themselves with a great deal of discretionary power. Given that public officials, in the neo-liberal view, tend to maximise their own status, the state will almost inevitably become unaccountable and self-serving.

Few people would deny a certain truth in this picture. But as an argument for a minimal state it is surely overblown. Since distributive politics are endemic to any kind of state, even a minimal one, interest groups are an inevitable corollary. There is no reason to see them as damaging: on the contrary, they embody the negative right of free association. One might indeed regard interest groups as a healthy feature of a strong civil society. That is not to deny that their demands are often incompatible. But reconciling and managing them is precisely what politics is for. Citizenship does not seek to diminish politics but to make it more accountable.

In this respect, perhaps curiously, many of the mechanisms espoused by neo-liberals for controlling the state can also be used by those who see the state's role as more expansive. Performance indicators, charters, league tables, even earmarked taxes: as we shall see below and in Part Two of this report, these can all be used as part of a much richer account of citizenship and the relationship between the individual and the state.

From weak to strong

The connection between the neo-liberal conception of citizenship and its view of taxation should therefore be clear. The individual with minimal obligations to other people gives rise to the state with minimal responsibilities for social goods. To tax is essentially to infringe the citizen's freedom; the state has neither the need for, nor the right to, tax revenues. But we have also seen how the arguments justifying these positions are unstable. Negative rights turn out not to be so different from positive rights. No tax and spending regime can avoid the question of distribution. Charity is no substitute, either practically or morally, for collective provision of basic goods. The state must be made accountable rather than simply reduced.

These arguments challenge the view that taxation is essentially illegitimate; but they do not yet construct a positive case for an alternative. It is to this task, therefore, that we now turn.

£

A strong conception of citizenship

Our starting point, again, is the notion of the individual. A strong conception of citizenship does not see individuals as atoms, entirely responsible for the satisfaction of their own needs. We do not spring up like mushrooms, fully formed. Rather, the individual is located in a community of mutual dependence. We are daily reliant on the civility and cooperation of the strangers with whom we share the same geographic space, and on their participation in the provision of shared goods. The money we earn does not come simply from our own efforts, but from the education and culture we have acquired in society, and from the social institutions in which we are inescapably embedded.

Public goods and the quality of life

A crucial element in this mutual dependence is the role played by public goods. The strong conception of citizenship sees no need to limit the provision of public goods simply to those falling under the economist's strict definition. Public or social goods include any collectively financed public services: education, health care, roads and public transport, culture, environmental spending and so on. Their justification lies not in the impossibility of private provision—many public services could be privately paid for—but in the contribution they make to individual and social welfare.

To put it in simple terms: taxation can make you better off. Public spending contributes to everybody's living standards. Indeed at the margin, where taxes are varied, it can contribute more than the private spending which it replaces. The issue of transport illustrates this well. Extra private income, spent on more private car use, will make the problem of road congestion worse. Extra public income, spent on public transport and infrastructure, will make it better.

The crucial recognition here is that public spending, financed through taxation, can achieve some of an individual's objectives better than his or her own private spending. The neo-liberal argument assumes that this can never be the case: individuals are always best placed to satisfy their own needs, the state can never know better. But this is not always true. My desire for safe streets and a low crime rate cannot be satisfied through my own private spending: I need the community to pay for policing and for social expenditures which reduce the problem at source. I cannot buy clean air (and only a minority can buy their way into the diminishing number of neighbourhoods which have more of it); this must be secured collectively, through reductions in road transport emissions. I can pay out of private income for my health care; but this is very unlikely to cover all my health needs, and for the system as a whole private funding is much less efficient than a publicly financed health service. (Americans pay nearly twice as much for their health insurance as Britons pay for the NHS in tax.[12]) For most people, paying for private education would be similarly more expensive than tax contributions.

This does not mean that any level of taxation and public spending can be justified. A test of public benefit must be passed. But it does acknowledge that, in an interdependent society, collective or social goods make an important contribution to wellbeing. It would be helpful, in fact, if we had a better language with which to express this. Living standards are not only about private consumption; they are about public spending too. Yet it is notable how difficult it can be to get this across in discussions of taxation. Take, for example, the way in which Budget statements are reported by the media. The question is always whether tax changes have made the typical person 'better off' or 'worse off'. But tax changes alone can never measure this. It depends on what is done with the money, on the spending side of the equation as well as the revenue raising. A new way of articulating and measuring 'overall living standards' or quality of life, encompassing public and social goods as well as private ones, would surely help here.

The justification of taxation is not simply about the collective nature of public services. For many could be financed at least partly through the greater use of charges and fees. Taxation rests on the principle of equity: that public services should be available to all, and therefore should be paid for according to ability to pay rather than use. In fact this principle is not absolute: partial charging for public services is commonplace, whether for swimming pools, prescriptions or (less formally) through school fundraising events. There are legitimate arguments to be had about where lines should be drawn—as witnessed, for example, over national museum charges. But the general principle remains an important feature of a tax-funded system of public services.

Self-reliance

The principle of equity is not universally accepted, however. One of the arguments sometimes used by neo-liberals against the provision of social goods is that it undermines the promotion of 'self-reliance'. Taxation, it is said, 'diminishes the ability of the individual to take responsibility for his or her own life'.[13] It is morally better for individuals to make private provision for their health, education and welfare insurance than to pay taxes and allow these services to be provided by the state. But this argument is surely dubious. If I buy an education for my children at a private school, why should I be regarded as any less dependent on this than I am on the state if my children go the local comprehensive? If I am required to buy private welfare insurance, why does this make me more self-reliant than if I pay contributions into and get benefits out of the National Insurance system? These are alternative ways of paying for comparable goods; for anyone on average income or above it isn't clear why one should be regarded as promoting more 'self-reliance' (or why this should be seen as more virtuous) than the other.

But of course that is the rub. The claim about 'self-reliance' is not really about those on average earnings purchasing goods in different ways. It is about people in poverty. For public services are redistributively financed. For those on low incomes, self-reliance—the private purchase of social benefits—means paying more than under a system of taxation. (Effectively, it means becoming poorer.) So the argument turns out not really to be about self-reliance at all, but about the morality of redistribution. Should the better off subsidise the social goods enjoyed by those less well off?

This question lies at the heart of the strong conception of citizenship.

Social justice and equality of capability

We have already seen how any system of taxation and spending must be redistributive in one sense. It must involve some allocation of the costs and benefits between different individuals and groups in society. For public goods and services which benefit more or less everyone, this is a question of how far the system of funding should redistribute between those on different incomes. But much public spending is not universal in this way. The claim that 'taxes make you better off' applies directly, after all, only to those public services used by all, or nearly all, citizens—health, education, law and order, public transport. (Even those who do not use public transport almost always need others to do so.) But a considerable proportion of public spending, both on social security and on programmes to tackle social exclusion such as in urban regeneration, support services for lone parents, and so on, appears to the majority of taxpayers essentially as transfers to other people. The tax and spending system therefore has two different kinds of redistribution going on. How are these justified?

For the strong conception of citizenship the answer requires us to return to the idea of negative freedom. It will be recalled that the freedom to do something cannot be separated from the ability to do it. For a society seeking to promote freedom the question is therefore not just how constraints on action can be removed, but what kinds of abilities will contribute to human wellbeing. We need some conception, that is, of the capabilities people need to live a flourishing life. What makes freedom worthwhile?

The answer has powerful implications for the idea of equality. The neo-liberal accepts a basic principle of equality of opportunity. Negative freedom is a universal right: hence no-one should be prevented by discriminatory laws from pursuing their interests (so long as these do not infringe the liberties of others). But if freedom requires some notion of capability, equality of opportunity implies a much stronger ideal. To be properly free, every individual needs access to a basic set of goods and resources to enable him or her to realise the opportunities available.

What are these goods and resources? People have a wide range of goals and purposes. It cannot be the role of the state to ensure that opportunities are extended to all individuals to pursue their goals whatever they are. What we have to do therefore is to identify a set of goods which are fundamental to realising human potential in general. That is to say, we need to identify the core goods which are necessary to enable the pursuit of any other goods at all.

Such goods will include the neo-liberal freedoms of non-coercion, non-interference and non-discrimination: one can only live a life shaped by one's own purposes if one is free in these ways. Equally important, however, are the positive generic goods needed to achieve any sort of chosen goal. Exactly how these are specified can be debated at length, but few people would surely dissent from the view that they include health, education, shelter and security of income. A richer view of human flourishing would add others, such as access to arts and culture and environmental integrity. In turn these generic goods[14] must then be specified in the particular context of a modern society. So for example the good of education entails training and lifelong learning; security of income requires access to employment opportunities; shelter requires a decent home and local environment. As general living standards rise, the level of goods and income which ensures reasonable equality of capability will inevitably rise too.

It is in this way, from the foundational value of freedom and autonomy, that the strong conception of citizenship comes to a powerful view of the need for equality. All people are born of equal worth, and all have the right to realise their potential. But in practice this right will only be exercised if everyone has access to resources to develop their capabilities. This does not mean equality of income or result. Every individual will use his or her capabilities differently. But it does mean that the inequalities generated in the market—inequalities which in our present society are growing larger—must be tempered.

Reciprocity and ability to pay

This is what taxation does. In the strong conception of citizenship, taxation is justified to secure the resources which ensure that everyone has access to similar capabilities, measured in terms of the basic goods necessary for human flourishing and autonomy. This will inevitably be redistributive: the resources will primarily come from those who have more and mainly go to those who have less. But it is important to recognise that this is based, not on the altruism of the better off or (simply) the needs of those in poverty, but on the principle of *reciprocity*.

We all share the need for basic social goods: these are the requirements of autonomous and flourishing citizens. Although we may not share our ultimate goals or purposes in life, everyone can recognise that in order to meet our divergent goals we need access to these goods. But if each citizen has a right to these goods, so each has a corresponding obligation to provide for them when they are able. There can be no free riders; equally, those who have benefited more from the distribution of income and wealth in the market have a duty to contribute more in return. Thus the strong conception of citizenship not only justifies public spending to equalise capabilities; it creates the civic duty of taxpaying according to ability to pay.[15]

It is interesting to note that when people are asked what they understand by citizenship, the duty to pay one's taxes is one of the first that comes to mind.[16] Similarly, research has shown that attitudes towards government and perceptions of the fairness of the tax system are significant factors in explaining rates of tax evasion.[17] Taxpaying is a civic duty, legally enforced; but considerations of citizenship do appear to underpin voluntary attitudes towards compliance.

Public services and social inclusion

The principle that the cost of taxation should be distributed according to ability to pay justifies a progressive tax system, one in which the proportion of income taken in tax rises as income rises. But the idea of reciprocity goes more deeply even than this. It reflects a fundamental view of the relationships people have to one another in society, the recognition of mutual dependence and belonging.

For one way of interpreting the obligation on the part of the better off to pay for equality of capability would be to see it simply as a way of transferring incomes from rich to poor. But this is not our view of the strong conception of citizenship. It is vital, we believe, that public services in general remain designed for and accessible to everyone, and as far as possible universally used.

This is partly for prudential reasons. Only if better-off taxpayers feel that they are getting good value out of public spending themselves are they likely to continue supporting and paying for it. A system of taxation and spending that was *purely* redistributive would surely be subjected to constant downward pressure. But it is also because of the nature of such services themselves.

The value of tax-funded public services lies not simply in their efficiency but also in their contribution to social inclusion or cohesion. Public services, commonly experienced, act as a sort of social glue. We all have an interest in them; and it is in using them (schools, hospitals, public transport) that we meet our fellow citizens. The deep public support for the NHS, despite all its faults, is surely an expression of this sense of commonality: it is one of those institutions that binds the nation together. Yet at the same time one of the results of rising inequality is precisely the sense that some citizens are opting out of this common experience, using private education, health care, welfare insurance and transport; and even in some cases—as in the US—barricading themselves behind gated residential communities. Retaining high-quality, tax-funded public services is therefore an essential bulwark against the 'social exclusion of the rich' as well as that of the poor.

We acknowledge that this is easier said than done. To retain universal use when many people can afford to exclude themselves many public services need to improve.[18] But the basic principle remains intact, and it justifies a level of taxation which can secure it. Citizenship in this view can then be seen as an expression of belonging to the civic community. But a sense of belonging in modern society cannot be taken for granted. It has to be constructed: and the stake that every citizen has in the public services for which they pay seems likely to be one of the essential building blocks.

Of course, there *is* an element of pure income redistribution in the tax and spending regime. Contrary to media perception, much of the social security system actually redistributes across individuals' lifetimes, building up savings and insurance against future contingencies; but it also does transfer from richer to poorer groups. But here too a view of citizenship as the holding of a stake in society helps to cast this in a different light. The problem with huge and growing inequalities of income and wealth is not simply that they deny to some people, through relative poverty, the resources which make possible the full realisation of individual potential. It is that they sever the bonds which tie people together in a civic community. Social inclusion, the sense we have of living in a single society, is a difficult concept to define in the modern world; but it is something of whose loss many people have become acutely aware. Its rebuilding is one of the demands a strong conception of citizenship inevitably makes.

The economic basis of taxation

The strong conception of citizenship therefore argues for a view of the citizen as an individual bound into wider social relationships, both contributing to and receiving benefits from the civic community. Such a view supports the role of a progressive tax system in financing a wide range of public goods and promoting social justice. But it must also acknowledge that taxes do not arise from nowhere. They come from productive economic activity which generates incomes and permits consumption. Taxes in themselves can impact negatively on this activity, reducing the rewards to work and investment. They cannot therefore be levied without acknowledgement of their economic impacts. A balance must inevitably be struck between the benefits of the social goods for which taxation pays and the productivity of the economic base from which they are generated.

Fortunately, the tension implicit in this balance is not as severe as it might be. In an economy in which 'human capital' is becoming the crucial resource, much social spending is economically productive, ranging from education and health care to employability and skills training programmes. Infrastructure investment, such as in transport, has evident economic benefits. There is even evidence of the value which 'social capital' in the wider sense has on economic performance.[19] This is not to say that the tension does not remain: it does. But in some respects economic efficiency and distributive justice can reinforce one another. (In this sense the old idea that production and distribution were entirely separate spheres can now be abandoned.)

Neutrality and social harm

Taxation not only has economic impacts; it can influence behaviour in many different ways. Indeed, as we observed earlier, one of the questions raised by the concept of citizenship in relation to taxation is how far such influence can be justified. Is it right to use the tax system to encourage particular patterns of social behaviour and to discourage others?

There are certainly strong arguments that the tax system, like the state, should be neutral between the different conceptions of the good which people hold (so long as these conceptions do not harm others). The reason for this follows from the basic autonomy of the individual. People have different goals and purposes. So long as the pursuit of one's own view of the good does not interfere with others' pursuit of theirs, then the state has no business either encouraging or discouraging it through the tax system. This suggests, for example, that the tax system should not be used to favour one particular form of relationship (such as marriage) over another—unless a convincing case can be made that the absence of marriage is actually a harm to others.

Where harm is done to others, however, the principle of neutrality does not apply. Where the actions of an individual or firm damages the basic interests of others, there is a strong case for the tax system to discourage such behaviour. (Of course, it may be that the legal system should otherwise control it too.) In general it would seem that social harms are much more readily identifiable and agreed upon than social goods.

This applies particularly strongly in the case of environmental damage. In a modern industrial economy such damage is more or less endemic. Taxation policy has increasingly come to be seen as an effective and efficient instrument through which disincentives can be applied to damaging behaviour and incentives given for environmentally more benign alternatives.[20] Indeed, taxing the 'bad' of environmental damage is in principle more economically efficient than the equivalent taxation of 'goods' such as income or consumption. Given the importance of the environment to human health and wider flourishing, the use of the tax system is in our view entirely justified for these purposes. We explore this much more fully in Chapter 13.

A more difficult case concerns not harms to others, but harms to self. It is the discouragement of such harms that lies at least in part behind so-called 'sin' taxes on alcohol, tobacco and gambling. Of course, excessive consumption of these things, certainly of alcohol and tobacco, causes social harm as well. Both tobacco and alcohol create significant costs for the health service, while alcoholism is also a major contributor to social disorder and violence. But there is another, citizenship-based, justification for these taxes too. Each of these activities is addictive; and addiction is an impairment of the autonomy of the individual. So here we would accept that discouragement of these particular self-harms through the tax system is justified. We shall discuss these taxes further in Chapter 11.

The citizen and the state

We come then to the final element in the strong conception of citizenship. This is the relationship between the citizen and the state. So far we have characterised this relationship simply in terms of the taxes paid by the citizen, and the public goods and services provided by the state. But this cannot be sufficient. The state does not simply do whatever the citizen wants. There must be a mediating process through which citizens express their desires and values and government decides how to turn these into public goods and services of various kinds. We could call this process the negotiation of the 'civic contract' between the citizen and the state.

At one time this contract might have been seen as relatively straight-forward. Citizens voted every four or five years, and the governments they elected provided public services. But today such complacency cannot be sustained, and rightly so. Political citizenship means more than periodic voting. The very processes of democracy come under scrutiny: the ways in which public debate is conducted; the mechanisms by which governments listen to, consult and seek the participation of the governed; the legitimacy won by politicians and political institutions for the decisions they make.

This is particularly important in relation to taxation. Taxes are payments to the state. A strong conception of citizenship recognises the essential need for accountability which follows. Governments must explain what they have done with the money they have received, and report on the performance of the services they have provided. Accountability demands that there is a constant drive to improve public services, to become more responsive to the citizen and consumer—in short, to use taxes well. This is a much more active, dynamic relationship between the citizen and the state than was once thought necessary.

And it does not simply operate on one level. The state is multi-layered: there are governments or quasi-governments right up from local scale through the national to the international (in the European Union). The notion of citizenship must apply wherever there is government, and wherever taxes are paid. We are 'concentric citizens', members of a civic and political community at each level.

Conclusion

Thus the strong conception of citizenship we have outlined contrasts strongly with that of the weak or neo-liberal interpretation. It starts from a different view of the individual, as a member of a civic community of mutual dependence. It acknowledges the central role played by public goods in human wellbeing. It argues for a radical notion of equality of capability, ensuring that each citizen has the core goods necessary to realise his or her potential. It seeks a universal system of public services and to reduce major disparities of income in order to promote social inclusion. In all these ways it justifies a progressive tax system, based on ability to pay, to finance public spending. At the same time it argues that taxation can legitimately be used to discourage social harms, particularly environmental damage. And it demands an active relationship of democracy and accountability between the individual citizen and the state.

Much of this, we are happy to acknowledge, would have been included in the standard account of the social democratic view of citizenship which underpinned the establishment of the postwar welfare state. But this does not make its restatement redundant. Challenged by the philosophy of neo-liberalism, social democracy has needed updating and articulating afresh for new times. The kinds of arguments and values expressed here need, we believe, to become once again the common currency, and the philosophical underpinnings, of the national debate about taxation and public spending. The rest of this book seeks to do just this.

5 | Principles and objectives

In Chapters 1 to 4 we have set out the grounding on which the Commission's deliberations about the tax system have been based.

- We believe that British politics needs a new *kind* of debate about tax, in which the essential legitimacy of taxation is accepted, and through which therefore a more open discussion about political choices can be held.
- We have argued that taxation is essentially a matter of citizenship; and have set out a 'strong' philosophical idea of citizenship which we believe should underpin the tax system and debate about it.
- Our research into public attitudes has led us to be particularly concerned about the 'disconnection' which many people appear to feel from the tax system and the public spending which it finances. This seems to be both a response and a contributor to the loss of legitimacy, and needs therefore urgently to be addressed.
- We have expressed particular concern about the growth of inequality in British society over the last two decades, a trend fundamentally incompatible with our conception of citizenship. We have noted that the tax system is not, overall, progressive, and has become less so in the recent past: it has therefore in general contributed to, rather than countered, this trend.
- We are conscious of the relationship of taxation to powerful new economic developments and forces. A tax system for the 21st century

must respond to (among other things) globalisation, the growth of e-commerce and environmental degradation.

In the rest of this report we shall discuss in more detail the issues that arise from these starting points. We shall make various recommendations for changes to the tax system—and in some cases discuss possible reforms suggested by others with which we do not agree. But to do this we need more than just the general conception of citizenship set out in the previous chapter. We need some more concrete principles to guide our proposals.

In this chapter therefore we set out ten 'principles of a good tax system'. These arise both directly from our conception of citizenship and more generally from an analysis of what makes a tax system function effectively.

These principles are not always mutually compatible. As in all fields of human endeavour, values and principles conflict. In the design of any tax system, therefore, it is inevitable that principles must be reconciled and to some extent traded off against one another. The following principles are intended to guide reform; they cannot in themselves determine it.

£

Principles of a good tax system

1 Legitimacy

Both the purpose and the operation of the tax system should be seen to be legitimate by taxpayers.

Public support for the taxation system depends on its purposes being broadly understood and accepted and its operation being seen as fair.

Legitimacy operates at two levels: what might be called the political and the personal. At a 'political' level it is likely to be increased when reliable information, not just about the tax system but about public spending, is provided to individuals and in public debate. The public need to understand how taxes are used, and to feel that government is accountable to them. We discuss mechanisms which might help to achieve this better in Chapters 7 and 8. But the design of the tax system itself, and its impact at a personal level on individuals, are also important. The crucial element here, we believe, is *clarity*. Both the purpose and the operation of the tax system need to be clear to those asked to pay. As our own research into public attitudes has demonstrated, this is not always the case today.

Clarity is not the same as simplicity. Over recent years many commentators and tax practitioners have argued that the tax system has become too complex, and needs to be made simpler.[1] We would agree with this. But simplicity should not be regarded as an end in itself. The simplest tax system would consist of only a small number of taxes, and all at flat rates. But this would not be desirable: it would conflict with more or less every other principle listed here. A really simple tax system would almost certainly not be progressive; it would be unlikely to be very flexible; it would make no allowances to encourage entrepreneurship; it would certainly be unable to encourage the reduction of socially damaging behaviour; and so on.

The tax system is complex for two reasons. The first is because it has several different objectives. As we argue here, this is entirely appropriate: one should be careful of arguments for simplicity which are really disguised ways of opposing important aims such as progressivity and environmental incentives. Second, complexity in the tax system reflects the complexity of the world with which it is dealing. Many small provisions in the tax laws are designed to be fair to those in unusual circumstances. It would certainly be possible to eliminate many such provisions. But this could only be done by riding roughshod over the particular circumstances of many individuals. The result would be a powerful sense of unfairness, which would not be conducive to legitimacy at all.

Our view is that clarity is a more helpful principle than simplicity alone. In many instances clarity will be served by greater simplicity, but the primary aim should be to ensure that the tax system is comprehensible to taxpayers and that compliance is straightforward. The impact of taxes should be clear to those on whom they are levied—a principle by no means always applied at present. Tax returns, particularly for individuals and small businesses, should in normal circumstances be easy to complete. Where complexities are introduced, there should be a careful assessment that their benefits outweigh the disadvantages of additional complexity. Just as importantly, the purpose of such provisions should be made clear to those affected.

Complaints about the complexity of the tax system came to the fore in the spring of 2000 when the post-Budget Finance Bill turned out to be 558 pages long. It has not been our remit to review the detailed list of anomalies compiled by others.[2] We note, however, that the Chartered Institute of Taxation has called for a Royal Commission on Taxation to investigate the growing complexity of the tax system.[3] This seems to us a sensible proposal—it would make a suitable subject for the (rather wider) Royal Commission we ourselves recommend in Chapter 7.

As we argue in Chapter 7, one of the keys to 'political' legitimacy is accountability: the sense that government must account for the taxes it receives. But this also operates at a personal level. The individual taxpayer must feel that the Inland Revenue (or Customs and Excise) is accountable for its actions, and that redress will be swiftly provided if mistakes are made. The Inland Revenue Ombudsman plays an important role in this respect.

2 Progressivity
The tax system should take a higher proportion of income from those with higher incomes and wealth than on those with lower incomes and wealth.

Our view of citizenship leads us strongly to support the principle of progressivity. This is based on the simple idea of 'ability to pay'. Those on higher incomes are more able to contribute to the common good than those on lower incomes. Each pound is worth less to them; a progressive scale therefore represents an 'equality of sacrifice' from everyone.

The principle of progressivity need not apply to every tax. But it should apply to the system as a whole. As we saw in Chapter 3, in fact the British tax system is not progressive, but more or less proportional. That is, every income group pays around the same proportion of its income in tax. As we saw in Chapter 3, when public expenditure is included—ie when the impact of tax and spending together is analysed—the system becomes progressive.

In many ways it is easier to affect the overall progressivity of the system through public expenditure than through taxation. Since many of the poorest groups in society do not pay tax, the tax system on its own cannot affect their incomes. Benefits, in-work tax credits and spending on public services can therefore have the largest impacts at the bottom of the income distribution. In the middle range both taxation and spending are significant, while taxation has a particularly important impact on those at the top of the scale. On its own the tax system probably cannot be made *very* progressive, since as long as there are indirect taxes (which are almost always regressive) those on lower incomes will pay a significant level of tax. Many indirect taxes (such as those on tobacco, alcohol and petrol) have important social and environmental purposes. Nevertheless we do believe that the tax system on its own can be made a little more progressive. We make various proposals for this in relation to council tax (Chapter 9), income tax (Chapter 10) and the taxation of wealth (Chapter 12). It also affects our view of VAT (Chapter 11).

3 Economic efficiency
The tax system should encourage work, enterprise, saving and economic efficiency.

There is an inherent conflict embodied within almost all tax systems. Taxation is necessary to fund public services. But most taxes reduce economic activity, by reducing the reward for work and investment. This means in effect that taxation risks undercutting its own base. It is important therefore that the tax system in general is designed to support economic effort—work and entrepreneurial activity—rather than hurting it.

In practice many taxes have contradictory effects: at the same time as reducing effort, they can also stimulate it in order to raise income to a desired level.[4] But in general it is recognised that marginal tax rates—the tax rate which applies to the next slice of income—can have an impact on work effort. It is therefore important that marginal tax rates should not rise too high. How high this is should be based on empirical evidence of their effects.

The argument that marginal rates of income tax should be kept down is often applied in relation to the higher reaches of the income scale: it was the (public) motivation behind the cuts in higher rates of tax introduced by the Conservative Governments of the 1980s. There is some evidence to show that in some circumstances lower rates can actually yield larger revenues, because they stimulate greater economic activity.[5]

But this depends very much on the level of marginal rates over which the change is made: the lower marginal rates are, the less this is likely. Lower rates of income tax at the top of the income scale conflict with the aim of progressivity, so the desire to encourage economic activity must be balanced with the former principle.

In fact marginal deduction rates tend to be much higher at the bottom of the income scale than at the top. This arises from the interaction of the taxation and benefit systems. As earnings rise, benefits get withdrawn, leaving an effective marginal rate of 'tax' (ie net deduction from income) which in some instances can rise to more than 90%.[6] High marginal rates of this kind reduce much of the incentive for people on benefit to work—particularly (as often happens) if the work is of uncertain duration—and to earn more. These are the so-called 'unemployment and poverty traps'. It is therefore highly desirable for such marginal tax rates to be reduced. (The present Government has made a number of reforms through both benefit structures and in-work tax credits to reduce the highest of these rates, although the number of people on slightly lower rates (60-70%) has increased.[7])

The tax system should also encourage saving. Saving is an important form of security for individuals and households. We discuss the tax regime for saving in Chapter 10 on income tax.

This report is not primarily concerned with business taxation. But we recognise that levels of business taxation can be an important element in determining the overall level of investment. There is particular justification for the tax system to reward entrepreneurship: the initial process of setting up a company and establishing new business ventures. This might include, for example, taxing non-established income (such as share options) in a new business differently from established income. But such exemption has limits: ultimately business income and wealth are forms of income and wealth like any other and should be taxed as such.

4 Discouragement of social harm

The tax system should provide incentives to reduce socially damaging behaviour.

The tax system can be a powerful mechanism for influencing behaviour. By raising the price of an activity or product, taxation (normally) reduces demand for it. The application of different rates of tax to activities or products which act as substitutes for one another can strongly affect the operation of the market between them.

As a general rule (see below) we do not believe that the tax system should seek to affect the private choices individuals make about their own consumption. But where individuals' or firms' choices damage others, this principle can legitimately be breached. Then private choices are no longer private: they affect the interests of others. As we argued in Chapter 4, it is the interaction of individuals with one another in this way—generating social goods or social harms—that helps to ground the strong principle of citizenship.

Environmental damage constitutes probably the most important single category of social harm. The tax system can play a major role in providing incentives to reduce environmentally damaging behaviour (such as the consumption of fossil fuels and the production of waste and pollution) and to increase environmentally benign alternatives. This is in fact an application of the principle of economic efficiency. Unlike most taxes, taxes on environmental damage are economically productive: they help to direct resources away from where they will generate harm towards more productive uses. This is often described as the taxation of 'bads' rather than 'goods'. Shifting the burden of taxation in this way onto environmentally damaging activities is in general a desirable goal and we explore it further in Chapters 13 and 14.

The discouragement of social harm is also the principle which underpins so-called 'sin taxes': duties on alcohol, tobacco and gambling. We discuss these in Chapter 11.

We make an important distinction between social harms and social goods. Some politicians and commentators believe that the tax system should provide positive incentives to socially beneficial behaviour: marriage is the example usually given.[8] The problem here, however, is that what constitutes a social good is highly contested in a way that social harm is not. Few people would disagree that pollution is a bad, and less pollution a good. But many people do not accept that marriage is in itself socially beneficial, and 'less marriage' harmful. For many, marriage is a private choice which may benefit the individuals involved, but which in itself has no particular impact on society in comparison with other forms of partnership. Potentially the tax system could discriminate in favour of all kinds of activities regarded by some people as socially beneficial. But this would quickly become a mine-field of competing claims. The tax system is much more likely to retain its general legitimacy if it focuses only on generally agreed social harms.

5 Horizontal equity
The tax system should treat people in similar circumstances similarly.

We noted above that the tax system can legitimately discourage socially damaging behaviour. But in most circumstances the tax system should not discriminate between the ordinary choices made by individuals on how to live their lives. This is sometimes known as the principle of 'horizontal equity'.[9] It means that, for example, individuals should not be taxed differently just because they prefer to spend their money on different things. We discuss this further in Chapter 11 on consumption taxes.

How this principle is applied, however, will depends on what counts as 'like'. One of the important principles of the welfare state has been (and remains) the provision of support to parents for their children. Child benefit and other benefits aimed at children are based on the principle of horizontal equity, since they recognise that having children raises household costs. On the premise that the welfare of children is a concern for society as a whole, child benefits attempt to compensate parents for these costs. They seek equity by helping to equalise the net income of parents and non-parents. The same principle underpins many benefits made to disabled people, who bear higher costs to achieve a comparable standard of living to the able-bodied. Horizontal equity can be promoted through both the tax and the benefits systems.

6 Individual independence
The tax system should tax individuals separately.

The principle of independent taxation allows individuals to have financial autonomy. This is not to deny the value of inter-dependence within families, just to permit individual adults to make decisions about their incomes on an independent basis. It therefore derives from an important principle of citizenship, and has particular value in recognising gender equality. It ensures that the tax system treats women in the same way as men. It also places on an equal footing the value of inter-dependence between adults who are not married to each other.

Independent taxation has several components. The most often cited are the right to privacy in tax affairs and the ability for couples to file separate tax returns. These are important, but we believe that there is an additional more fundamental principle that applies. This is that each individual's liability for tax should be determined by their own income alone, and should not be affected by the income of anyone else. In practice this means that the income of one married person can never be treated as part of their spouse's income and that each individual is allocated their own tax allowances, reliefs and credits and that these are not transferable and are not split on the basis of income.

Taxation systems that allow the income of the husband to affect the tax paid by the wife (or vice versa) result in the second earner facing higher marginal tax rates than those faced by the first earner on entry into work or on increasing the amount they earn. In practice this results in adverse affects on women's work incentives. The principle of independence ensures that the tax system does not exacerbate gender inequalities and underpins the notion of financial autonomy.

7 Broad basis
The tax system should have a broad base.

The 'base' of the tax system is the range of activities and income on which taxes are levied. The tax base is broadened if a wider range of activities and income is charged to tax, and if reliefs and exemptions of various kinds are reduced.

The advantage of a broad base is that it enables lower rates of tax to be charged for the same revenue. In general lower rates are likely to be perceived as more acceptable, thereby increasing the legitimacy of the tax system. They are also likely to affect economic behaviour less. Just as importantly, lower rates tend to reduce the extent of avoidance and evasion, since the losses are smaller. (To take an example, one of the penalties of the high rate of VAT is that many small service providers seek to evade it through cash transactions. This encourages law breaking by both the businesses and their customers.)

Exemptions and reliefs to taxes also tend to encourage avoidance and evasion. Many exemptions and reliefs are designed to provide incentives to particular kinds of behaviour, such as business investment. But they frequently end up providing a means of tax avoidance. The notorious Business Expansion Scheme in the 1980s provides a case in point. Reliefs on inheritance tax have a similar effect. (We discuss these further in Chapter 12.) In general such reliefs and exemptions should be avoided.

8 Administrative efficiency
The tax system should be cost-effective in collection and compliance and effectively enforced.

All taxes cost money to collect. It is important that the ratio of administrative cost to revenue is as low as possible. A tax which raises little more revenue than it costs to collect is clearly inefficient. But it is also important that the costs to taxpayers of *complying* with tax laws is also held down. Over recent years the tax accountancy profession has grown larger and richer as incomes have risen and the tax system has become more complex. It is estimated that around 25,000 people now work in the private sector tax industry.[10] In terms of the total welfare of society (and with all due respect to tax accountants and lawyers) money spent on tax advisers is not productive: it would yield more welfare if spent elsewhere. Reducing compliance costs is therefore an important goal. Making the tax system simpler will be an important element in this.

It is also very important that taxes are effectively enforced. Tax evasion undermines the legitimacy of the whole system, and effective enforcement acts as a deterrent as well as a means of catching evaders.

9 International cooperation

Countries should cooperate with one another in order to maintain their tax bases.

Taxation can no longer be considered a national matter. This is partly because in an international economy companies, and to some extent individuals, operate in different countries and tax regimes need to take account of this. Bilateral agreements between countries to ensure fair and efficient tax treatment have been common for many years. But taxation must also be considered on an international scale because of the effect of differences between national tax regimes.

There are two separate issues here. One concerns the extent to which tax 'harmonisation' is required in a single market such as the European Union. The answer depends on the kind of taxation concerned; we shall discuss this in more detail in Chapter 9. The other issue concerns the use of so-called 'tax havens'. A number of countries around the world offer very low tax rates for savings and profits and require little or no disclosure of a company's or individual's tax affairs. These regimes effectively provide companies and individuals with a means of avoiding, and in many cases illegally evading, taxes due in their own countries. At the same time many multinational companies are able to arrange their internal accounting (through the use of 'transfer pricing', so-called 'mixer companies' and other techniques) so as to minimise their tax bill and to pay it in countries with the lowest rates.[11] These practices tend to undermine national tax revenues, with the effect that tax rates are forced up for others unable to take advantage in the same way. But in order to tackle this issue countries need to cooperate with one another. As the effects of economic globalisation gather pace, this will become more important.

10 Sufficiency

The tax system should raise sufficient revenue to fund the desired level of public expenditure.

That the tax system should raise enough money may seem rather obvious, but it has important implications. In particular, it focuses attention on the medium-term sustainability of revenues. We have already mentioned in Chapter 1 the apparent threat to tax revenues represented by the growth of electronic commerce and the increasing mobility of certain kinds of capital and labour. We discuss some specific responses to these developments in Chapters 6 and 11, but the broader conclusion is that the tax system must always be kept under review to guard against risks to its sustainability.

One important implication of this principle is the value to the tax system of 'buoyant' taxes—those (such as income tax) which automatically yield additional revenues as the economy grows. Another implication is that the tax system should be flexible. Yields from taxes are uncertain: if a tax does not yield as much as it is projected to do, it should be possible either to raise its rate or to raise another tax (and vice versa if yields exceed forecasts).

The sufficiency of tax revenues does not, of course, mean that tax rates must rise whenever revenues fall short of the level of public expenditure which has been decided on. Within sustainable limits governments can raise borrowing levels during economic downturns. By the same token, however, it also means that the tax system must raise enough revenue not to exceed the desired or acceptable level of borrowing.[12]

£

The Commission's objectives

As we emphasised above, these principles cannot all be applied in every aspect of the tax system. They sometimes conflict with one another. In making proposals for reforms to the tax system we are therefore very conscious of having had to reconcile opposing principles in particular cases, and of balancing the different principles in our recommendations as a whole.

As we explained in the Introduction, the Commission has not sought to examine or make recommendations for every area of the tax system. We have concentrated on those areas which flow from the grounding explained at the beginning of this chapter—from our initial analysis of the need for a new debate, and our strong conception of citizenship. Before we embark on our detailed analysis and recommendations, therefore, it may be helpful if we set out the principal objectives which these are intended to meet.

First, we are concerned that the tax system, and the public debate about it, should generate sufficient revenues to support a level of public services consonant with a strong conception of citizenship. The overall system of public spending and taxation should help to reduce inequalities of opportunity and to provide public goods which encourage a sense of community and social solidarity.

Second, we believe that the operation of the tax and public spending system should seek to 'connect' the public better to the taxes they pay and to the public services which these finance. Citizens should feel that they know what taxes they pay, what the money is spent on and what difference it makes; and should feel greater confidence in government performance and accountability.

Third, we believe that the system of public spending and taxation should become more progressive. Given the widening dispersion of incomes over the last twenty years the distribution of the tax burden should be rebalanced, so that those on higher incomes pay a fairer share and more resources are directed to those on low incomes.

Fourth, we argue that the system of taxation should provide incentives to reduce socially damaging behaviour, particularly environmental degradation.

The rest of this report

The rest of this report seeks to examine the implications of these objectives in more detail. In the next chapter we ask how much tax needs to be raised to realise our ideas of citizenship. Should taxes be higher or lower? The aim of 'connecting' the public better to their taxes then forms the subject of the whole of Part Two. We look at various ways in which such 'connection' might be achieved: improving government accountability (Chapter 7), the possibility of 'earmarking' taxes (Chapter 8), and the relocation of taxation powers, both to sub-UK-national and to European Union levels (Chapter 9).

The objective of making the tax system more progressive inevitably runs through every chapter, since every tax has an impact on it. But it forms the main focus of Chapters 10 and 12, on income tax and on the taxation of wealth. It is also an important issue in the discussion of indirect taxes in Chapter 11. This chapter also addresses (in relation to so-called 'sin taxes') our concern to reform the tax system so that it discourages socially damaging behaviour. But the main focus in this respect is on the ways in which the tax system can help to reduce environmentally damaging behaviour. This is addressed in Chapters 13 and 14 on the taxation of the environment and land.

It is to the overall level of taxation, therefore, that we now turn.

6 | How much tax should we pay?

In Chapter 4 we argued that the general public legitimacy of taxation is central to a modern society founded on a strong notion of citizenship. The kind of philosophical arguments presented there provide an essential grounding, we believe, for a public debate about tax. But they don't answer the question that really matters in the hard world of politics. Should we pay less tax, or more? Or is the level of taxation more or less correct as it is?

Of course this isn't actually the right question at all. It falls into the trap which we noted in Chapter 1 had been far too common in political debate over the last twenty years: it focuses on only one side of the equation. Taxation pays for public services, so the question of whether we pay too much or too little tax can only properly be answered by rephrasing it. Are governments taxing and spending too much, too little, or about the right amount?

This is not an issue about individual tax rates. Whether income tax rates are too high or too low, or similarly the rates of corporation tax, or VAT, or any other specific tax: these are a different sort of question. They concern the proportion of total tax revenues which come from different *sources*; and the *distribution* of taxation across different groups in the population. These are also important issues, and we shall deal with many of them later in this report. But the subject that concerns us here is the total level of taxation in the economy, measured as the proportion of national income which is taken in taxes and social security (National Insurance) contributions.

This is generally known as the 'burden' of taxation. But this term is not always a helpful one. Since a 'burden' is almost always negative, it has a pejorative connotation, and can therefore tend unwittingly to bias the debate. Taxation is certainly often felt as a burden; but as we observed in Chapter 1, in an almost unnoticed way the term can contribute to the idea that taxation is essentially illegitimate. We therefore prefer the neutral term the 'share' of taxation to mean the proportion of tax in national income.

As we saw in Chapter 3, in the UK the share of taxation is currently around 37% of Gross Domestic Product (GDP). The share of public spending is a little higher than this at 38%: the difference is largely made up by government borrowing and the proceeds of privatisations and other asset sales (see Figure 3.1). Over the last twenty years the shares of both tax and public spending have fluctuated. From 33% in 1979, the tax share rose to 39% in 1985, and then fell again to 33% in 1994. Since 1997 there has been a small increase; government projections are for this to peak at 38% in 2002 before returning to 37% by 2004. Broadly speaking the share of spending has followed a similar trend, though borrowing and privatisation proceeds have also fluctuated significantly. From 45% in 1979 public spending peaked at 48% in 1983; at 38.5% in 1999, it is projected to grow to 40.5% by 2004.[1]

In certain newspapers it is often said, and appears from our public attitudes research to be commonly believed, that the UK is a 'highly taxed' country. But in fact the tax and spending shares in the UK are below average for OECD countries (see Figure 3.3). In the European Union, for example, the average share of tax in national income is 41.5%. In Germany, France and Italy the shares are 37%, 45% and 44% respectively, while in Denmark the share is 49.5% and in Sweden 52%. Alone of West European countries Ireland and Spain have lower shares than in the UK. The United States, Australia (both at 30%) and Japan (at 29%) have much lower shares of tax in GDP, reflecting their very different structures of public and private spending.[2]

This chapter examines some of the arguments used, both to suggest that the tax share should be reduced, and that it should be raised.

£

Taxation in a global economy

As we noted in Chapter 1, one of the claims most commonly heard today is that taxation is on an inevitable downward trend because of the impact of a more globalised economy. Countries which wish to compete successfully will have to reduce their taxes; only in this way will they be able to compete for mobile capital and labour. More generally, it is sometimes argued that taxation is itself damaging to economic performance, reducing both the level of national income and its rate of growth. Do these arguments mean that taxation in the UK should be reduced?

Globalisation and tax

The argument that countries will be forced to reduce their tax rates because footloose capital and highly paid professionals and executives will only locate where taxes are low is most commonly applied to corporate taxes and income tax. But since indirect taxes are also effectively taxes on labour (reducing the purchasing power of earnings) the globalisation argument in practice is more far-reaching. It suggests, and its proponents claim, that economic success in the new economy requires a reduction in the overall share of tax in national income.[3]

One response to this, of course, is that the issue must depend on the current tax share in any particular country. Since the argument turns on comparative tax rates, the argument must apply very differently to Sweden, which takes over half of its national income in tax, compared with, say, Ireland, which takes only a third. And since the UK is at the low end of the range of industrialised countries in terms of tax share, the argument would seem, even if true, to have considerably less force here than elsewhere. The UK, one would imagine, would have considerably more room for manoeuvre than some other countries.

But is it in fact true? Does globalisation make it inevitable that taxes must come down? It is important to distinguish between different kinds of claims being made. First, we should be careful not to assume that international competition automatically means that tax rates are bid down. It is certainly the case, particularly in the case of goods and services, that different tax rates in different countries will affect the pattern of trade. Ferryloads of both legitimate shoppers and law-breaking smugglers crossing the Channel to buy alcohol and tobacco on the continent provide ample evidence of this. But eliminating tax differentials does not imply that they must be reduced. It is having taxes at a common level that counts: this could equally be at a higher level as at a lower one. So globalisation may well have the effect of making the rates of certain taxes in different countries *converge*; but this does not mean that it must inevitably cause the overall yield from tax to decline. This will depend on how countries cooperate with one another, particularly in the European Union.

We must also be careful about assuming that multinational corporations automatically locate in countries where tax is lowest. This is an easy threat to make: when in the mid-1990s the Chairman of Daimler-Benz warned members of the German Parliament that the company's tax bill would need to be reduced to zero if its factories were to stay in Germany, alarm bells started ringing.[4] But the evidence suggests that international investment decisions are much more complex than this. Comparative tax rates can play some role, particularly in comparisons between developed and developing countries, but they are by no means the only determining factor. Skills, wage levels, communications, language, currency, state aid and other factors can all be at least as, and often more, important.[5] In general, so far, any pressure to reduce corporate taxation levels in developed countries has been successfully resisted. It is true that corporate tax *rates* have come down, but this has been accompanied by a broadening of their base. In the European Union the yield from corporate taxation has actually increased over the last twenty years, both as a proportion of GDP and as a share of total tax revenue.[6]

On the other hand, it is certainly true that differential tax regimes in different countries leads to widespread avoidance by multinational companies and financial institutions. The practice of 'transfer pricing' allows companies to sell goods and services between their own subsidiaries in such a way as to minimise the profits, and therefore the taxes, they pay overall. The use of so-called 'mixer companies' (mixing the profits from several sister firms) ensures that profits are registered in the lowest tax jurisdiction. Meanwhile the use of offshore 'tax havens' (countries such as Bermuda and the Cayman Islands which set out to attract mobile capital through very low tax rates) has increased substantially.[7] Already significant parts of the financial services industry, such as hedge funds, are located offshore. Much less tax is consequently being paid by these sectors now than would have been the case (if all other things had been equal) a few years ago; but since we do not know how they would have performed under a different tax regime, it is difficult to say by precisely how much such behaviour has actually reduced the tax yield.

Meanwhile the number of internationally mobile high income earners has certainly increased, but the evidence does not suggest that migration has yet reached such a level—or indeed, will do in the foreseeable future—that tax rates will inevitably be bid down. As with investment, choices of where to live and work are determined by many factors, of which tax is only one. Indeed, the quality of public services—which is likely to correlate with tax rates—is another. So far, certainly, most national tax regimes have not yet felt required to respond. Germany has announced that it will reduce its top rate of income tax (from 52% to 42%) in 2002. But Sweden, with a top rate of 56% and a business community complaining loudly that it cannot attract the best workers, has so far resisted. Public spending has been regarded as more important than cutting tax, even if some mobile workers are lost abroad. The range of top income tax rates in European countries remains wide, from 40% in the UK and Portugal to 60% in the Netherlands.[8]

Policy responses

These trends must certainly be watched, and the Commission has no doubt that the globalisation of economic activity must be taken seriously by tax policy. But the evidence does not suggest that the share of tax in national income has inevitably to be reduced, particularly in a country such as the UK in which it is already on the low side. Two kinds of approach are available to tackle these issues.

The first is greater cooperation between nation states in the tax field. International competition (and increasing electronic commerce) will only force down tax revenues if countries fail to work together to counter them. This is, in fact, what is already happening. Both the OECD (the association of developed countries) and the European Union have set in motion initiatives to address the issue of 'tax competition'.[9] Some of the measures being proposed are controversial, and some of them may well be difficult to execute. Securing cooperation from countries outside the OECD and EU, in particular, may be difficult. But the principle that international cooperation is required is the important first step, and as we pointed out in the last chapter it is one we strongly endorse. We shall explore the particular issue of cooperation at a European level a little further in Chapter 9, and examine possible responses to electronic commerce in Chapter 11.

The second way in which the tax system can respond to globalisation is to shift the burden of taxation between different factors rather than to reduce the total. If it is indeed likely that international competition (and electronic commerce) will cause tax yields to fall from mobile factors of production, it will be sensible to look at ways in which factors which cannot be so easily moved can bear tax instead. Land, energy and other environmental factors are likely candidates here. There will still be a need for international cooperation, since differential tax rates can always be avoided by relocation. In the end, all taxes are paid by people, so tax-induced migration is always possible. But if the incidence of tax between mobile and less-mobile people and enterprises can be changed, this may make it easier to withstand any pressures for lower taxes overall. This is one of the reasons why land and environmental taxes have indeed become more popular over recent years. We shall explore these further too in Chapters 13 and 14.

Does taxation weaken economic performance?

A more general kind of economic argument is also sometimes used to argue that taxes should be reduced. This is that taxation is intrinsically damaging to economic performance. By reducing the rewards to entrepreneurship, savings and work, it is argued, taxes reduce the levels of investment and productivity. Private investment is 'crowded out' by less productive public investment. Both the level and the rate of growth of national income are then reduced.[10]

Unfortunately there is little conclusive evidence on the relationship between taxation and economic performance, and indeed attempting to calculate it is fraught with difficulty. Separating out the impacts of tax policy changes from other economic factors, and the effect of the structure of taxes from that of the total tax share, is very difficult.[11]

Individual taxes clearly do create disincentive effects. In the absence of any individual tax economic production would be higher. But the overall effect on the economy must take into account the economic benefits of some aspects of the public spending which taxes pay for. Many aspects of public investment make a crucial contribution to economic health and vitality. Spending on education and training, on transport systems and communications infrastructure, on research and development and in similar fields are all essential in modern economies. Indeed, over the last two decades the UK's consistently low level of public investment and associated spending (such as in education), relative to its OECD competitors, is widely argued to be one of the reasons for its continuing failure to match the rates of productivity growth achieved elsewhere. Other forms of public spending, such as so-called 'active labour market' policies like the New Deal, in-work tax credits and other 'welfare to work' measures (along with education policy), are designed to reduce structural unemployment, and thereby reduce wage inflation. These are generally considered supportive of good economic performance rather than the reverse.[12]

The OECD's review of the evidence in this field suggests that a higher tax share has a small effect on the level of savings, a somewhat larger effect on the level of foreign investment and an uncertain effect on labour supply, depending on the flexibility of labour markets and the progressivity of the tax system. Overall, tentative estimates suggest that the 10% average increase in the tax share experienced by OECD countries over the past 35 years may have reduced annual growth rates by about 0.5%.[13] But at the same time these higher taxes have paid for public spending which most people appear to regard as worthwhile in creating higher living standards and a more cohesive society. Whether in the health service, education, crime prevention, urban regeneration or in pensions and social security, any costs to the overall rate of growth must be set against the benefits to society more generally that higher taxes and spending have brought.

There is clearly a trade-off here. A level of taxation which seriously reduced economic performance would not generate the resources to pay for valued public services. But the Commission does not believe that we are at this point today. Indeed, it has to be observed that considerably higher levels of taxation and spending in most of our European partners have not given them worse economic performance—or lower living standards—over the last decade than the UK. In many cases the contrary is true. Given the UK's current and projected share of taxes in national income it is not therefore our view that lowering taxes is necessary or desirable for economic reasons.

£

The benefits of public spending

For many people who argue that the share of taxation in the UK should be reduced, technical arguments about economic performance are not in fact paramount. Their claim is that, whatever the level of national income, we would simply be better off if more of it were spent privately and less by the public sector. Since individuals always have a better idea of what will improve their lives than the state, giving them more money to spend privately would inevitably create a richer and happier society. Some go so far as to propose that the share of taxation and public spending in national income should be cut drastically—to as low as around 30%.[14]

Public vs private spending

These arguments must be taken seriously. But one must ensure that the kinds of reasoning employed here are valid. First, consider the case of public services which provide benefits to the individual, which could in theory be bought privately instead. Seen from the perspective of an individual, it is almost always true that having more money to spend privately will make one feel better off. All other things being equal, we would all be pleased to find ourselves with a higher income. But taxation cannot be viewed in this way, as if a cut in tax were simply a windfall to the individual. If taxes are reduced, so (usually) must public spending.

But then all other things are no longer equal. The individual may have more money to spend, but he or she has more things to spend it on. If there is less spending on the national health service, more people will feel required to take out private health insurance. If state education is under-funded, more people will send their children to private schools. If public transport is worse, more people will end up buying more petrol. If pensions and social security benefits decline, more people will take out private schemes. If spending on law and order fails to match crime rates, insurance premiums will rise. Even if something as simple as public spending on swimming pools declines, the admission price to public pools will almost certainly have to rise, so private spending will go up.

In all these cases, and many others, reductions in tax will give many households more income, but at the same time require them to spend that income privately to replace the services which are no longer publicly funded. Over the last twenty years, as public funding has declined or not kept up with demand in many areas, this phenomenon has already been widely observed, from spending on private health, education and social insurance through higher prices for publicly funded services such as swimming pools and museums to higher insurance premiums.

So the net effect for the individual is not necessarily an increase in spending or wellbeing: this is a misleading way of presenting the argument. On the contrary, the evidence suggests that for many people private spending in many of these areas is likely to be *more* expensive than the equivalent payment made through taxation. This would appear to be true in the field of health, for example, where American experience of private health insurance gives a direct comparison with a publicly funded service. Americans pay twice the proportion of their national income on healthcare (14%) than is the case in the UK, and its coverage is still far from complete. A publicly funded health service appears to be more efficient than one based on private insurance.[15]

In general, whether or not an individual or household would be better off with a private system of welfare spending or a public one obviously depends on their position in the income distribution, since one of the functions of the tax system is to redistribute resources from higher earners to those on lower incomes. In practice, on average, households in the bottom 50% of the income distribution gain more in social benefits (both for social insurance itself, and when health, education, housing and transport are added in) than they pay in taxes; those in the top 50% less.[16] So for around half of the population, at least, the welfare state represents a rather good deal on simply a private basis—quite apart from its beneficial effects on social equity and cohesion. In the case of some public services, such as crime prevention and policing, the benefits of public and private spending may simply not be comparable. Most people, given an equivalent choice, would surely rather pay higher tax and have less crime than face more crime and pay higher insurance premiums. Few people would claim that they like paying taxes; but as Maurice Chevalier pointed out when asked what it was like being old, the alternative is worse.

Reasoning about public goods

So the first point it is important to remember when considering the appeal of lower taxation is that lower taxes do not necessarily mean more money for the individual to spend on things which he or she cannot afford today. Of course, the individual could choose not to buy the things which the state provides. There are no doubt many items of public expenditure which many people would not choose to purchase privately. But this then leads to a second flaw in these kinds of argument. Most areas of public spending which do not provide basic goods to individuals (in the way that education and health services can at least partly be seen) provide public goods which individuals could not buy privately anyway. In practice it simply isn't possible for individuals to buy a judicial system, or environmental protection, or national defence, or the eradication of poverty. So here arguments for the advantages of lower taxes need to compare, not an individual's private spending with his or her tax contributions, but a society with these public goods and one without them—or with worse public goods, consequent upon reduced funding.

It is easy, when asked to imagine a society with lower spending on public goods, to pick this or that item of expenditure of which one disapproves, or whose benefits seem unclear. Whether it is spending on social security fraud, or asylum seekers, or the Millennium Dome, or the Royal Opera House, or whatever, most people can provide an example of public spending they think should be cut. (All these, and many others, were mentioned in our discussion groups testing public attitudes.) But arguments of this kind need careful reasoning.

First, one cannot argue for tax cuts on the basis of small cuts in public spending if the numbers simply don't add up. Other things being equal, a 1p cut in the basic rate of income tax requires spending cuts of £2.65 billion. It is disingenuous (at best) for some politicians and commentators to claim that reducing spending, say, on asylum seekers—even were this desirable— would enable taxes to be cut. In 1999-2000, spending on asylum seekers amounted to £590 million.[17] Taxes can only be meaningfully cut if significant reductions are made in spending. Moreover many such reductions are much easier to talk about than to achieve. Every government would like to cut social security fraud. A succession of government initiatives to tackle it have been introduced over the last twenty years. These efforts should continue. But if the available savings were as easy as it is sometimes claimed, it is hard not to believe that they would have been found by now.

Second, public spending on public goods is not a matter of personal preference. We all have to recognise that other people will have other preferences which won't necessarily match our own. For every item of spending we would like preserved, or even increased, someone else will want it cut. Both minority preferences and deeper principles, such as justice and human rights, must be taken into account. We elect political representatives precisely because decisions on public goods need considered and informed deliberation, not simply the aggregation of immediate preferences. In a democracy, one must expect a compromise with one's own personal desires.

Third, some cuts may sound desirable in general, but look less attractive when it comes to the specifics. One of the items for reduced spending most commonly cited by those proposing lower taxes is social security. But it's easy to say this in general, much harder to say exactly where the cuts should fall. In eighteen years of government, throughout which there was an objective to reduce social security spending, it is notable that the Conservative administrations never managed to achieve it. This was partly because these governments' other economic and social policies increased the numbers of people in unemployment and poverty, so forcing spending to rise. But it was partly because in a decent society there proved to be clear limits of tolerability to the reductions which could be made to spending on the least advantaged in society.

The Conservatives' dilemma is mirrored in public opinion. Spending on 'social security' or welfare is often considered unpopular. But when the issues are explored in detail, there are few items most people would actually like to see cut. The 1999 British Social Attitudes survey asked people about the level of social security spending on different groups of people: those caring for the sick and disabled, disabled people unable to work, the retired, working parents on very low income, single parents and unemployed people.[18] For none of these groups did a majority of respondents want spending cuts. Even for the 'least popular' groups, unemployed people and single parents, around two-thirds or more of respondents wanted spending maintained or increased. (It is notable that when the Government tried cutting lone parent benefits, in 1997-98, there was a public outcry, and the effect was subsequently reversed for most of those affected.) For all the other groups, two or more out of every three people wanted spending increased, and under 3% wanted it reduced. Despite all the pejorative connotations commonly attached to 'social security' or 'welfare', it seems that most people recognise that spending in this area is necessary and valuable. It makes for a better society, not a worse one.

None of these arguments means that reductions in the overall share of taxation are ruled out. In a democratic society it must be possible to argue for lower levels of public spending and for lower taxation. But we do not believe that the share of taxation as it stands at present can be cut to a significant degree, let alone very easily, in the way that some politicians and commentators suggest. In a modern society cuts in public spending sufficient to achieve a significant reduction in the share of taxation will be hard and painful, involving losses of valued private benefits and public goods.

£

Should taxes be higher?

So far we have addressed some arguments which suggest that the share of taxation in GDP in the UK is currently too high. But what of the counter-argument, that taxes are in fact too low?

Pressures on public spending

There are certainly reasons to think that pressures on public spending will grow over the next decade. The gradual rise in the share of taxation and public spending which has occurred throughout the industrialised world over the last forty years has after all not been without cause.

First, many public services, particularly health and education, are what economists call 'superior goods'. That is, as income rises, demand for them increases more than proportionately. Most people find that as their income rises they spend more of it on so-called 'higher needs' and pleasures and less on the basic requirements of subsistence. So, as nations grow richer, demand for education and health (and for other similar goods such as environmental improvement, tourism and cultural activities) grow larger. Where such goods are provided within the public sector, the share of public spending in national income tends to rise.

Second, the cost of such services will also be subjected to powerful upward trends. Most public services are labour-intensive, and many find it difficult by their very nature to increase productivity as quickly as is possible in more capital-intensive manufacturing and commercial sectors. Yet public sector wages and salaries tend (understandably) to follow the general patterns set by the private sector. So the cost of public services per unit of output rises over time. In turn spending on them rises as a proportion of national income.

There is no reason to think that these trends will come to an end over the next decade. But there are other grounds too for believing that demand for public services will rise in the future. Both demographic and technological forces are creating pressures for higher spending in the health service. Since it is in the last years of life that most people require most healthcare, an ageing population has considerable implications for health spending. Higher life expectancy does not in itself imply higher spending, but if longer lives mean longer periods of illness towards the end of life (which is not certain), total demand will rise. An increase in the number of elderly people will certainly have this effect: the large post-war 'baby boomer' generation will reach retirement in 2010 and beyond.

Both larger numbers of elderly people and longer lives will of course require increases in spending on pensions. On the other hand, an ageing society also means fewer children, which reduces spending on education, child benefits and so on.

New technologies and other advances in medicine do not automatically imply that health costs will rise. Some technologies, such as new surgical procedures, are cheaper than those they replace; and expensive proprietary drugs become much cheaper once patents run out. But at the same time there can be little doubt that many new medical developments are more expensive. As new drugs and other forms of treatment are developed they create demands for health provision where none existed before. At the same time, the public's expectations of standards of care are also constantly rising: as standards have risen elsewhere in society, what would have been acceptable twenty years ago—in terms of the convenience of appointments, speed of treatment, accommodation, catering and so on—is inadequate today.[19]

Similar kinds of pressures exist in the field of education. The natural tendency of rich societies to spend more on education as a superior good has been accentuated by the premium now placed on education and skills in the so-called 'knowledge economy'. These are now widely believed to be the key to success, both for the individual and for the economy as a whole.[20] It has been acknowledged for some time that educational standards in schools need to be raised; some experts believe that this will not be possible without significantly higher funding.[21] Already over the last decade the number of entrants to higher education has almost doubled, with around a third of all 18- to 21-year-olds now going to university, along with much expanded numbers of mature students. There is much higher demand for lifelong learning and skills training of all kinds. Higher education funding is under considerable pressure, with expenditure per student in real terms a little more than half what it was a decade ago.[22]

Comparable demands for higher spending to improve public services also exist in many other fields: public transport and road maintenance, policing, social services, housing, the arts. It is not our place to judge all of these. We certainly acknowledge that higher spending is not the only way of improving public services: new and more efficient ways of carrying them out can no doubt be found. But it seems likely nevertheless to play some role. We note the sense experienced by many people, for example, that public services are often better in continental Europe. (This was one of the comments made at several of our research discussion groups.) But a comparison of spending levels suggests that this is perhaps not surprising. The UK spends 5.3% of its GDP on public health care, against an EU average of 6.1%. Germany spends 8.1%, France 7.7%. The UK spends 4.6% of its GDP on education (down, incidentally, from 5.3% in 1979). The EU average is 5.1%. Germany spends 4.5%, France 5.8%.[23]

Perhaps most of all, we are conscious that the eradication of poverty will almost certainly require higher spending. We have already set out in the previous chapter how a strong view of citizenship seeks a reduction in social inequalities. As we noted in Chapter 1, in the UK today one in four people lives in poverty as generally defined—having an income less than half the average. For children the figure is one in three.[24] There are major differences in health between those on different incomes: poorer people live shorter lives and suffer worse rates of many major illnesses. Social exclusion is experienced in high unemployment, low educational achievement, poor housing conditions, high rates of drug use and so on. As we have already said, we believe that the UK cannot properly call itself a civilised country while these levels of inequality and exclusion persist.

The Government has committed itself to ending child poverty in twenty years, and halving it in ten. It has also declared that it seeks to end pensioner poverty. Achieving these goals is not simply about spending more money. A major task is to continue to reduce unemployment, which requires a whole series of policies: to increase demand, to improve education and skills, to improve incentives and support for people to enter work and so on. Increasing saving rates so that fewer people are dependent on benefits alone will help in the longer term. Changing the way particular services are delivered—in education, health, housing and so on—may make a significant difference to the experience of exclusion. Much will depend on the private sector—through wage levels, prices and investment decisions. The voluntary sector has an important contribution to make. But however much can be achieved in these ways, it seems very unlikely that poverty can be eradicated without additional spending from the public purse.

Partly this is for the simple, if unfashionable, reason that the levels of state benefit remain an important contributor to poverty.[25] Many people on low incomes—the elderly, disabled people, carers, lone parents with young children—are unable to work, or insufficiently to earn a decent income. They are therefore dependent on social support. In the short to medium term raising certain benefit levels is therefore likely to be part of a strategy of raising the incomes of these groups. By raising child benefit and income support rates for children, and through the introduction of the Working Families Tax Credit and the forthcoming Integrated Child Credit, the government has already raised substantially some benefit levels.[26]

But this is not simply about social security. Many of the 'welfare to work' measures precisely designed to take people off benefit—the New Deal and other training and lifelong learning programmes—cost money. Regenerating disadvantaged estates, renovating social housing, programmes such as Sure Start to support disadvantaged parents, measures to tackle educational under-achievement: none of these is cheap, as experience in other countries has shown.[27] We do not know what the gradual eradication of poverty will cost: it will depend on many factors, not least wider economic conditions. Some of these, such as a further reduction in unemployment, will reduce rather than add to spending. But it is difficult to conceive that this goal, which we believe to be an important part of the strong conception of citizenship, will not add to the pressures for higher public spending overall.

The Government's plans

The Government has of course responded to many of these pressures. In its Comprehensive Spending Review in July 2000, considerably higher spending plans were announced for the period April 2001 to March 2004. Overall public spending is to grow by 3.1% per annum over the three-year period, including current spending by 2.5%. There are particularly large rises planned for education (5.4%) and health (an average of 6.1% pa over the four years from April 2000) but almost all departments have larger real allocations than in the previous period.[28]

These are significant sums, particularly for health and education, but their effect should not be exaggerated. Over the first two years of the present government's period in office, public spending actually fell, at a time of strong economic growth. Over the whole period from 1997 to 2004 the average rate of spending increase planned is only 2.3% per annum. Hence spending as a proportion of GDP, 41.2% in 1997, is only planned to reach 40.5% by 2004. This remains well below the EU average. The NHS budget will grow by 35% in the four years to 2004. But health spending will remain less than the current EU average, as will education.[29] (Of course, if other European Union countries maintain their own rates of growth, the gaps will be even larger.) We doubt, therefore, that the present spending plans will exhaust the demand for higher public spending. Though certainly eased, we suspect that the pressures we have outlined will continue to apply after 2004.

Spending and taxes

None of these arguments implies that public spending will inevitably rise. In the first place, it has not been our role as a Commission to examine and assess the merits of every item of public expenditure. We are therefore not in a position to say whether, *overall*, public spending should be higher. What we have been arguing is that there are very likely to be *pressures* for higher expenditure in certain important areas. We can ourselves see strong citizenship arguments for spending more in some of them. But such demands must always take account of their costs. Whether they should be met—and which ones—must be a matter for democratic debate and political choice.

Perhaps most importantly, it must be recognised that higher spending does not necessarily mean a higher tax share. Overall spending depends on the sum total of individual areas of expenditure. It is always possible that some acceptable cuts in spending can be made. Significant cuts do not appear obvious at the present time, but they cannot be ruled out in principle.

It is also possible that new forms of finance may be found. In spring 2000 the Government sold by auction the third generation of telecommunication licences. The yield of £22bn was seven times the anticipated revenue. By using the revenues to reduce the national debt, the Government has cut its interest payments by approximately one billion pounds a year. In turn this has allowed higher expenditure without higher taxation. (An alternative would of course have been for part of the money to be spent directly.) Other sales of public assets or public-private finance arrangements may also be available.

At the same time it may be possible to increase the efficiency with which public services are delivered. Over recent years most of the public sector has been forced to raise its productivity (sometimes, it is claimed, at the expense of overall quality of service). The extent to which continuing significant gains are still possible will vary from service to service; but the search for further improvement is clearly important. To the extent that efficiency gains are made, higher *effective* spending can be achieved—in terms of real input—without additional calls on resources.

Perhaps most importantly, the relationship between spending and taxation depends on the state of the economy. In simple terms, public spending can be increased at the same rate as the growth of the economy without the share of taxes needing to rise. This is essentially what is planned by the Government over the period 2001-2004, though in addition to a rise in current spending of 2.5% pa (equal to the projected rate of economic growth), the Government is planning a (short-term) increase in capital spending as well. The Government's economic and fiscal projections suggest that these increases in spending can be achieved while the overall share of taxation in national income actually falls slightly.

Are these projections realistic? At the time of writing the Government's revenues actually appear to be very buoyant.[30] But there are reasons to be cautious. An economic downturn might reduce the projected rates of economic growth. Anticipated cuts in social security spending resulting from such growth may not materialise. Forecasts of government revenues do not always prove accurate: actual receipts fluctuate in a manner not always understood even by the Treasury. Much of the current surpluses may prove to be cyclical rather than structural—as similar surpluses have proved in the past. At the time of writing, therefore, we would see no reason to revise the Government's cautious projections.

Higher taxation and disposable income

A final point is worth making. A higher share of taxation in national income does not necessarily mean that individuals have less money to spend privately. When the economy is growing, and particularly when average earnings are rising, both taxation and disposable income can rise. Imagine that average earnings are rising in real terms, by, say, 3% a year. If the share of taxation rises by 1% in a year, and assuming it is evenly distributed, this still leaves net disposable income higher than the previous year. Effectively what is happening is that, though more is taken in tax, this remains less than the additional money earned, leaving a net growth in disposable income.[31]

Of course in practice not everyone will experience the increase in the average national share of taxation: this will depend on which taxes are increased and on an individual's earnings. Some people (mainly above average earnings) will generally pay more than the average, others—particularly on lower incomes—less. In any case, as we suggested in the last chapter, prosperity or quality of life cannot simply be measured by disposable income. To get a real measure of the effects on individual wellbeing of a higher tax share, the benefits of the public goods and services bought with the extra taxes—the schools, hospitals, police officers and so on—need to be added back in.

£

Conclusion

We draw five conclusions from these arguments. First, it is entirely legitimate to argue for spending and taxation to be reduced as a proportion of national income. But any such argument should be accompanied by an honest account of the price that would be paid, in terms both of compensating private expenditure and reductions in public services and goods. We believe that for any significant cuts in the overall share of taxation this price would be considerable.

Second, and equally, raising the share of taxation in national income should not be regarded as impossible or unconscionable. We see no overwhelming economic reason why the share of spending and taxation should not rise to something closer to the European Union average. If the share of taxation were increased to, say, 39% of GDP, this would mean additional revenues over 1999-2000 levels of about £20 billion. If the demand for public spending continued to grow—for any of the reasons we have outlined—and a government could win a democratic mandate for such a policy, we believe that a gradual increase to this kind of level should be regarded as entirely legitimate. Certainly, there is no reason why higher taxation and spending should not be debated as serious options for the UK.

Third, we are not recommending that the share of taxation in national income in the UK needs to be raised at the present time. We are publishing this report at a time when the Government has just embarked on a significant programme of annual spending increases which have yet to prove their effectiveness. Our public attitudes research has shown that many members of the public are not convinced that the government spends its revenues well. They wish to be convinced that higher spending will genuinely improve public services. In these circumstances we believe that the Government's current spending plans, and its various associated programmes of public service reform, should be give time to work before the public is asked for additional funding.

The Government has taken the unique opportunity presented to it by current fiscal conditions to increase the funding of key services by substantial amounts without seeking tax rises. There is a great deal to be done to ensure that this money leads to serious and perceptible improvements in public services and a reduction in poverty. Over the next three years efforts should be concentrated on these reform and modernisation programmes. We do not believe that raising further revenue, through a higher share of taxation in GDP, is necessary. Rather, the priority is to ensure that the British public feel more 'connected' to the taxes they pay and to the services which these finance. We shall explore this further in Part Two.

Equally, however, and fourth, we do not believe that a lower tax share is an appropriate goal in current circumstances. The needs for public spending in many areas are very great, and the likelihood of long-run fiscal surpluses highly uncertain. The priority at the present time must be to improve public services with the revenues now available. We see no grounds for general tax cuts.

Our final conclusion is to reiterate the central argument we made in Chapter 1. In an advanced industrialised society, facing the multiple challenges of a changing world, the levels of taxation and public spending represent fundamental political choices. In some ways they help to define the kind of country we seek to live in. The issues raised both by proposals to cut taxes and others to increase spending are profound. They should be debated with equal legitimacy, and with a clarity and honesty that have not always been seen in recent years. The British public, who have not been very well informed about taxation in the past—and who need to be now—surely deserve no less.

**Part Two:
Connecting citizens
and their taxes**

7 | Information, auditing and democracy: making government accountable

In the last two chapters we have argued that taxation should be regarded as fundamentally legitimate: not merely a 'necessary evil' which in an ideal world there would be less of, but a defining component of modern government. Taxation is central to citizenship. We have observed that this view has come under considerable attack over the last two decades and needs to be positively articulated. Politicians and others who agree with it need to say so publicly, so that it becomes once again an accepted part of public discourse and understanding.

But we have also noted the huge barrier standing in the way of this ideal. Taxation is not popular because citizens do not in general know how their taxes are used, and many suspect that they are spent wastefully or on things of which they disapprove. In the language used in Chapter 2, citizens feel 'disconnected' from the taxes they pay and from the public spending which this finances. Some of this disconnection arises from ignorance, a simple lack of information about the levels of tax and the uses to which it is put. But much of it arises from a deeper and more fundamental suspicion of government. Taxes have become illegitimate in many people's minds because government itself has come under question.

As we pointed out in Chapter 1, this questioning comes in different forms. The public's trust in politicians has declined dramatically. But perhaps more important has been the weakening of belief in the basic institutions of democracy. Turnouts in elections have reached record lows, and commitment to political institutions among young people is noticeably lower than among older generations. Meanwhile attitudes towards public services are mixed. The troubles of the National Health Service tend to be blamed on a historic lack of funding as much as poor management, but many other services are regarded as simply unsatisfactory. As we found in the research commissioned for this report, there is a widespread if rather inchoate feeling that public services are almost by definition inefficient—that there is something intrinsic to the public sector which means that the money it receives from taxes is not used well. As consumers have become much more critical and demanding in the last two decades, and many of the market-based services supplied by the private sector have improved, public services have not in general compared favourably.

£

'Connectedness'

How then can the legitimacy of taxation be restored? We believe that the central objective must be to 'connect' citizens more strongly to the taxes they pay and to the public spending which these finance. The public need to know how their taxes are being spent, and to feel confident that they are being spent well. This is not just a reflection of the need for active citizens. The strong conception of citizenship we outlined in Chapter 4 depends upon it. So long as people feel alienated from their taxes, their commitment to public spending, both for public goods and for social justice, will always be undermined. Certainly, any explicit goal of raising taxation to pay for higher public spending in the future looks politically difficult so long as present levels of 'disconnection' persist. The evidence of alienation discovered in our own research has convinced us that increasing people's sense of 'connectedness' is the principal political task for taxation policy today.

In this chapter and the next two, therefore, we shall propose various mechanisms which we believe will help to do this. This chapter focuses on mechanisms to make government more accountable and to provide better information to its citizens. The next looks at ways in which taxes can be linked to the spending at which they are directed. Chapter 9 examines the role of taxation in bringing government closer to the people, at local and sub-UK-national levels.

Before we start on this, however, it is worth making a linguistic point. The task of countering public alienation from political institutions is sometimes described as that of restoring the public's 'trust' in government.[1] But this term needs to be used with care. Trust in government is not necessarily a good thing, if by this is meant a blind faith that government will always perform efficiently and honestly. Several decades ago it was probably true that people did trust governments more. They believed that public services were basically more efficient and politicians more honest than most people do today. In general, public attitudes were more deferential to authority. But we should not regard this as the ideal to which we must again aspire. It is good that people have become more questioning, less trusting, when we know that public services can be inefficient and that politicians are not always wholly truthful. Critical consumers—and demanding citizens— should be encouraged as much in the public sector as in the private.

Making people feel more 'connected' is therefore not really about increasing their levels of trust. It is about increasing their *confidence* that government is performing effectively and efficiently on their behalf. Public confidence is in a sense the reverse of trust. It is generated through knowledge, not faith. People will feel confident that their taxes are being wisely used when government is not only performing well, but also being seen to do so. It is therefore a product of, on the one hand, transparent mechanisms through which government performance can be clearly judged—both what government *intends* to do and what it *is* doing; and on the other, of a well-informed public keeping a good watch. If trust implies a passive, acquiescent citizenry, confidence requires an active one, ever vigilant that government is held accountable for its actions. As we argued in Chapter 4, this is an important part of what citizenship means.

We shall often talk in this chapter about making people feel more 'connected' to the taxes they pay. This idea is sometimes expressed in terms of 'reconnection'.[2] But this is another formulation which needs to be used with care. It might be taken to imply that there was once a golden age when people loved their taxes and paid them willingly to a government they regarded as entirely beneficent. We doubt very much that such an age existed. It probably is true that people have become more resistant to paying taxes than they used to be. But we do not suppose that people were ever much more knowledgeable about where their taxes went, or how efficiently government used them, than they are today. Increasing the sense of 'connectedness' is therefore not about restoring something that may or may not have existed before. It is about seeking a new relationship between citizens and the state in the particular circumstances in which modern societies find themselves today.

The civic contract

Increasing the legitimacy of taxation, we believe, therefore depends on making people feel more 'connected' to their taxes and to public spending. This in turn is part of a wider project of increasing public confidence in government. One way of putting this is that it is about renewing the implicit 'civic contract' which exists between citizens and the state. But there are three distinct elements to this, and while increasing public confidence requires all three, we are primarily concerned in this book with only one of them.

The first and most basic element in the civic contract is the democratic one. Governments and parliaments are democratically accountable, through elections, to the citizens entitled to vote for them. There can be little doubt that this element in the civic contract has become tarnished over recent years, as evidenced in declining turnouts and public cynicism about elected politicians. This is true at both national and local levels.[3]

Constitutional reform is part of the response to this, but it is unlikely to be sufficient on its own. Devolution to Scotland, Wales and Northern Ireland, the reform of local government structures such as the creation of elected mayors, reform of the House of Lords, the introduction of proportional representation for a variety of elections, including possibly to the House of Commons—all these measures are intended to increase the sense of representation which the public feel towards government. They may do so. But the *culture* and *processes* of politics may also have to change. The ways in which political debate occurs, both inside Parliament and other elected chambers and in the media; the sense of involvement people have in decisions that affect them; the opportunities available to engage with decision-makers directly; these too affect the public's sense of 'ownership' of and commitment to democracy. A number of proposals have been made for participatory and deliberative methods to be used to increase public involvement and government accountability between elections. This is not the place to explore such ideas.[4] But we acknowledge that they are important in any properly rounded discussion of how public confidence in government as a whole can be renewed.

The second element of the civic contract is what might be called that of 'service delivery'. Public services need to be efficient and effective. Taxes pay for them; the public have the right to see the money being used well. Improving public sector performance has been a concern of governments of both colours for several years now. Changes to organisational and management structures, to financial incentives, to public information, in some cases to ownership itself: a whole raft of policies and techniques has been applied to try to improve performance levels. Many of these are, we recognise, controversial; but it is not our place to discuss them here. We simply acknowledge that the task must continue. Few can deny that in many areas public services can still improve considerably. The comparison with private sector services will often be invidious: in relation to the resources made available to it, the demands on a service free at the point of use will always be different from those on a service operating in a market. But it must nevertheless be true that without continuous improvement in the quality of public services it is unlikely that public confidence in government can be increased. When, as for the next few years (at least in comparison with the last few),

substantially increased sums of money are being spent on them, the impera-
tive becomes all the stronger. If public services are not perceived to have
improved under these circumstances, the loss of public confidence in
government's ability may well be terminal.

When we speak of renewing the civic contract, the service delivery
element is therefore almost certainly the most important. But our concern in
relation to taxation is with the third element. This is that of *information*. For it
is not enough that public services should be effective and efficient. They
must also be seen to be so.

This is not as straightforward as it sounds. Public services are only
partially visible to the average citizen. If you have children in school, evidence
of government policy and spending is usually fairly obvious: it can be seen in
initiatives such as literacy and numeracy hours and aptitude tests, curriculum
changes, the existence (or lack) of books and equipment, class sizes, the repair
of buildings and so on. But for those without children in school, these things
are not directly visible at all. One hears about them only from others. The reliability and frequency of bus services will be experienced by some people, but
others may hardly be aware of them at all. Many people will have direct experience of their local GP surgery, and some people of the accident and
emergency unit at their local hospital. But many parts of the NHS—those
providing treatments for cancer or heart disease, conducting hip operations,
providing mental health services, and so on—are only directly visible to relatively small numbers of patients and their families. *Improvements* in such
services may hardly be witnessed at all, since most patients will not experience the service on different occasions to enable them to judge any change.
(Few people will actually *experience* a reduction in the average time spent on
a waiting list, for example—let alone in the numbers of people on it.)

This means, inevitably, that the public's knowledge of most public services is second-hand at best. Much no doubt comes from other people who
have direct experience themselves: friends, family, work colleagues and
neighbours. But these perceptions will also be very partial, concerning
particular conditions in certain places. For a wider, more general understanding of how public services are performing, most people must inevitably
depend on the media. Yet *this* is hardly a sufficient answer. In the first place,
many activities of government go barely reported at all. Examples abound:
community regeneration on housing estates, youth work, most crime
prevention activities, social services and social work, overseas aid, most
foreign policy, many environmental policies and so on. Perhaps even more
importantly, where these 'unglamorous' activities of government *are*
reported in the media, it is almost always when something has gone wrong.
Failure makes a story; boring, ongoing success does not. This must inevitably
distort the public's perception of public services, making them appear less
successful and efficient than they actually are. It is hardly surprising if many

people feel money is not spent well.

This reflects the major difference in the 'customer' relationship between private and public services. When private goods and services bought in the market are not up to standard, this is generally immediately obvious to the customer. Redress can then be sought: whether simply through the market by taking future custom elsewhere, or through complaints procedures of various kinds, including those established by consumer protection regulation. Where public services are provided directly to individuals or households, comparable procedures for complaint and redress are very important. They are in many cases still not adequate. But for many areas of public service, taxpayers simply do not have enough *information* about the services they are effectively 'purchasing' to know how well they are being provided. Purchasing here does not mean simply for private use: as citizens and taxpayers we purchase public services of all kinds, whether of direct benefit to ourselves or for the wider public good. As citizens, purchasing collectively, we should have the same right as customers buying privately to know that the money is being used well. But this is a much harder right to implement. How can it be done?

£

Auditing government

We believe that three broad approaches need to be followed. First, information about the objectives of government and its performance must be made more transparent. Second, government performance should be independently audited. Third, information about taxation, public spending and government performance should be publicised more clearly and more directly to citizens. These improvements should then allow a fourth, critical, development: that political debate about taxation and public spending be conducted in a more considered and informed manner.

Transparency and targets

Considerable effort has already gone into the first of these approaches over recent years. Starting with 'customer charters' and similar mechanisms introduced under the Conservatives, there has been a strong move throughout the public sector to identify service objectives and standards and to set these out clearly and transparently for the public. This has been rationalised and strengthened by the Labour administration's 'modernising government' agenda, set out in its White Paper of that title.[5] The centrepiece of the

Government's approach has been the establishment of Public Service Agreements between the spending departments of government and the Treasury.[6] Under the government's Comprehensive Spending Reviews, first in 1998 and again in 2000, every department has been required to set out precisely how it will use the monies allocated to it by the Exchequer. Each department has published a set of 'performance targets': the performance standards, goals and outcomes which the department aims to achieve in each area of policy over the three-year period covered by the funding allocation. In the first Comprehensive Spending Review there were over 600 performance targets throughout central government. After criticism that this was too many, this has now been reduced to around 160. These represent each department's strategic priorities, and there are additional targets for a number of cross-departmental objectives, such as on welfare to work and action on illegal drugs. Each department is required to report annually on its progress against these targets.[7]

The Labour Government has instituted another, rather similar process, in addition. Each year since 1998 it has published an 'Annual Report'.[8] This sets out what the Government believes it has achieved, based on the commitments it made in its manifesto. The first report actually listed the manifesto commitments and reported directly against them; the second and third merely provided a general account of the Government's record, from its own point of view.

These processes represent an important development in the administration of government. But they have been subject to two different criticisms.

The first concerns the use of measurable targets as a way of evaluating government performance. A number of commentators and practitioners have argued that such targets are not conducive to good government.[9] It is widely noted, for example, that targets can distort service delivery. The Labour Government's election pledge to reduce hospital waiting lists by 100,000 has been widely criticised for its effect on health spending priorities. Hospitals, it is argued, have been effectively forced to treat minor cases before more critical ones in order to get a larger number of patients off the waiting list. Others have pointed out that measurable indicators may lead to non-measurable aspects of public services (such as the time spent by carers with elderly people in social services, or creative and community-oriented activities in schools) being ignored or downgraded. Other indicators (like school league tables which ignore social conditions) may give misleading information on real performance.

Another objection is that over-specified targets imposed on services from above may stifle innovation, creativity and local choice, and undermine the autonomy of professionals working in the service. (These kinds of remarks are sometimes made about the Government's targets for school standards, for example.) There has also been concern about the way in which targets are attached to financial incentives. One use of performance measurement has been to reward achievement, providing additional resources to public services which have met or exceeded their targets. This may provide incentives for some. But it also risks distorting the allocation of resources towards the already successful, rather than towards those less successful parts of the public sector (whether schools, health services or anti-poverty programmes) which may actually need them more. More generally, 'government by target' has been criticised as overly 'managerial' in style. Critics have argued that it turns the essentially political and deliberative processes of governance into the mechanistic requirements of a corporate business plan.

These are important arguments. They force serious consideration of the kinds of indicators and targets which genuinely enhance performance and those which do not, and of the levels of different targets which can adequately balance competing objectives. They mean that other, non-quantitative evaluation methods are required as well, and that the use of targets is kept under constant review. But we do not believe that they argue against the use of targets altogether.

In a context where the public is deeply sceptical about government, its purposes and its efficiency, it is essential that what government is trying to do is clearly set out. This should be, first, in descriptive prose: quantitative measures can only ever illustrate public purpose, they cannot explain it. But in a sceptical age general description will not suffice. The public want to know not just that the government intends to improve the health service, but what this will actually mean in terms of patients treated or illnesses suffered. For the government to commit itself to making the UK a fairer society (say) is not sufficient: people need to know how this will be judged, and what will count as success. This is not just because the general aims themselves can too easily sound like mere rhetoric. It is because the public want to know whether, when it comes to judging the government in an election, its goals and pledges have been fulfiled. It is inevitable, we believe, that—whatever else is used as well—quantitative measures will be sought to establish this sharply and clearly.

This is not to deny that direct personal experience counts for more than statistics when most people judge government performance. But as we have already acknowledged, in many areas personal experience is not available, or will not necessarily tell a general story. Nor is it to reduce governance to mere management. It is simply to recognise that measurable change constitutes an important *part* of political debate. Quantitative indicators and targets do not—and should not—substitute for political and ideological purpose; they make it tangible.

In fact, in its latest Public Service Agreements (2001-4), the Government has made considerable progress towards a system of targets of an appropriate kind.[10] The 600 targets in the original Public Service Agreements involved a fundamental confusion, failing to distinguish between *management* targets designed to assist internal administrative planning and *communicative* targets aimed at informing the public about key objectives. The new, slimmed down targets constitute a much more manageable set for the purposes of public information. There are up to twenty for each department, defining its principal objectives, along with several more for cross-departmental areas. In its Comprehensive Spending Review document, the Government has also regrouped most of these targets under the more 'political' headings of its four 'key objectives' ('increasing opportunities for all', 'building responsible and secure communities', etc). In this way the targets are attached to the Government's overall political and philosophical narratives.

As Box 7.1 shows, there may still be something of a problem in the combination of different *kinds* of targets. Some set out the ultimate 'state of the world' it is hoped to secure (such as levels of crime, or smoking rates), but which are not under the direct control of government action itself. Others define the kinds of 'performance outcomes' the services aim to achieve themselves (such as user satisfaction ratings in the criminal justice system, or the percentage of international development assistance going to the poorest countries). Some, such as for the building of an 'enterprise society' remain extremely vague and largely unmeasurable. These different kinds of indicator measure different types of 'performance', and it is important that evaluation recognises this. But so long as this is done most can be of value.

Box 7.1: Selected Public Service Agreement targets 2001-4

- *Increase the percentage of pupils obtaining 5 or more GCSEs at grades A* to C (or equivalent) by 4% between 2002 and 2004 (Department for Education and Employment).*
- *Guaranteed access to a primary care professional within 24 hours, and to a primary care doctor within 48 hours by 2004 (Department of Health).*
- *Increase bus use in England (measured by the number of passenger journeys) from levels in 2000 by 10% by 2010, while at the same time securing improvements in punctuality and reliability (Department of the Environment, Transport and the Regions)*
- *Reduce domestic burglary by 25%, with no local authority area having a rate more than three times the national average, by 2005 (Home Office).*
- *Help build an enterprise society in which small firms of all kinds thrive and achieve their potential, with an increase in the number of people considering going into business, an improvement in the overall productivity of small firms, and more enterprise in disadvantaged communities. (Department for Trade and Industry)*
- *An increase in the percentage of DIFD's bilateral programmes going to poor countries Department for International Development).*
- *Achieve by 2004, in the 500 Sure Start areas, a 10% reduction in mothers who smoke in pregnancy (Sure Start cross-departmental PSA).*
- *Improve by 5% the satisfaction level of victims and witnesses with their treatment in the Criminal Justice Service by 2002 (Criminal Justice System cross-departmental PSA).*

[Source: HM Treasury, Spending Review 2000: Public Service Agreements 2001-2004, Cm 4808, Stationery Office, 2000]

With this caveat we regard the 2000 Public Service Agreements as a useful model for establishing the Government's principal objectives. More importantly, it provides a benchmark against which the government's performance can be judged in the future. It enables the public to know what the Government has said it is trying to do, and therefore whether it has succeeded in doing it. Of course, the public may not agree with the Government's priorities. There is an important issue of how these are chosen, to which we shall return. But the public cannot now say that the Government's ideals are just rhetoric. They are very concrete indeed, and their achievement can be very strictly measured. For all the reservations which can be expressed about this approach, this is we believe a good thing. It will help to connect the public better to what their government is doing with their taxes.

The problem of evaluation

But this then brings us to the second criticism which has been levelled at the Government's approach. It is all very well providing information to the public on the Government's objectives. But how is the public to judge whether government is performing well? After all, many of the targets are for the end of the three-year spending period—or even later. How is performance judged in the interim? Only part of public spending will be going on the main performance targets. How do we know how well the rest of the money is being spent, particularly on less high-profile activities?

Most importantly, how do the public know whether they can believe what the government says? All governments seek to present facts in as favourable a light as possible. In recent years the perceived pervasiveness of so-called 'spin' has been in itself an important contributor to public disaffection from politicians and political institutions. As we found in the research conducted for this book, many people are thoroughly suspicious of almost all 'official' information, fearing it is likely to conceal as much as it enlightens.[11]

The Government's annual reports have attracted particular opprobrium on these grounds. Many commentators have likened them to a schoolchild's end of term report written by the pupil herself. The tone is largely self-congratulatory, with all problems well on their way to solution and some areas of poor performance or other difficulties excluded altogether. But even if this were not the case, the very fact that these reports are evaluations *of* the Government *by* the Government undermine their credibility. They could be paragons of self-criticism and they would still be regarded as suspect by the media and the public.

This is the problem. For whatever reason—and the reasons are not difficult to understand—we live in an age when the government is essentially not believed. This is partly why the public feels such 'disconnection'. To counter this it is not enough that the government should give the public information on its objectives and performance. The evaluation of government must be independent of government itself—and be seen to be so.

There are of course already mechanisms for independent auditing of government performance. At a central government level this is principally the task of the National Audit Office (NAO). Through its head, the Comptroller and Auditor General, the NAO reports to Parliament on the spending of public money. Most of its work is concerned with the financial auditing of departments' and agencies' accounts, but it also conducts around 50 'value for money' reports every year on government performance. These investigate the 'economy, efficiency and effectiveness' of public spending, what the NAO calls 'spending less, spending well and spending wisely'.[12] The NAO's reports are then examined by the Public Accounts Committee of the House of Commons. At the same time a parallel body, the Audit Commission, conducts similar value for money investigations of local government services and the National Health Service in England and Wales (as well as being responsible for their financial auditing.) Audit Scotland, the Auditor General for Wales and the Northern Ireland Audit Office perform similar roles in relation to the devolved institutions.[13]

The 'value for money' audits conducted by these bodies perform a very useful role. They assess how different areas of government and public service are performing, identifying good and bad practice and making recommendations for improvement. This has been particularly productive in local government and the health service, where the Audit Commission compares performance levels across the country, providing benchmarks of success and identifying the gap between the best and not so good.

Nevertheless, there is still in our view an important element missing. Only a relatively small number of value for money audits are conducted by these bodies each year, covering particular parts of services only. For the NAO value for money audits are clearly secondary to its principal purpose of financial auditing, and (reflecting this) the choice of subjects tends to focus on services where there have been concerns about the mis-spending of public money. (Recent examples include reports on the Passports Agency, Millennium Dome and defence procurement.[14]). The Audit Commission seeks and often gets publicity in the media for its reports, and in this way disseminates its findings to the wider public. But most of the National Audit Office's work is conducted out of the public eye, directed at the departments and agencies themselves. The language of its reports tends to be very dry and cautious; they are generally agreed line by line with the department under investigation, which has left it open to the criticism that its conclusions are sometimes compromised.[15] It does not help that the parliamentary select committee which receives them is often ignored by the media.

An Office for Public Accountability

In our view a wider function is needed. This is the regular, independent assessment of the performance of government services as a whole, and the reporting of this to the public. It is excellent that every department of government's annual report must now evaluate progress against the 'key targets' each has set. But this will not be publicly credible so long as such evaluation is carried out by the department itself. Departmental reports provide valuable information, but as accounts of success and failure they are inevitably partial, reflecting the internal view of the departments themselves (along with the political needs of the government). What is needed is independent assessment, and it is this role of overall, 'big picture' evaluation of departmental and service performance which the current audit bodies do not undertake. The same is true of the government's overall annual report. The idea of an annual report of government is an excellent one; it takes seriously the idea of explanation and accountability to the public. But it needs to be presented and audited by an independent body if it is to carry credibility with the public.

And it is to the public that independent assessment should be aimed. Departmental reports are written for specialists and parliamentary committees, and barely reported in the media. If the public is to be 'connected' better to the governments it elects it needs to be presented much more accessibly with information on how they are performing.

In the Commission's view a properly independent and authoritative body is needed which will systematically examine the performance of public services and government administration and report to the public on them. The credibility of this body is absolutely essential to its role. In our own public attitude research we found considerable support for the general idea of such a body—several people in our discussion groups indeed suggested it spontaneously. But equally many felt that they could not trust anything which appeared to be part of, or linked, to the government, or which could be 'influenced' to report favourably towards it.

Our proposal is that the expertise in the National Audit Office and Audit Commission should be brought together in a single new body combining both their functions in one, with a remit right across the public sector. It should be accountable to Parliament. Related bodies should operate in Scotland, Wales and Northern Ireland with accountability to the devolved institutions. The combined UK-wide body might be called the Office for Public Accountability or OPA.

The Office for Public Accountability as we envisage it would maintain the roles of the NAO and Audit Commission in conducting and supervising financial audits of public sector bodies. It would conduct, as the NAO does now, specific investigations into areas of public administration where concerns have been raised, such as overspending of budgets or allegations of impropriety. It would also maintain both the NAO's and Audit Commission's work in providing detailed 'value for money' assessments of particular service areas, relating to both national and local government (and indeed, the relations between them). But in addition it would have two new, or strengthened, functions relating to government accountability as a whole.

First, it would be responsible for auditing central government's performance against its declared targets, notably the 'key targets' embodied in the Public Service Agreements. These assessments should be published on a departmental or service area basis on a regular annual cycle. The OPA, rather than the government, should then publish the Annual Report on the government's overall progress.

Second, the OPA should have a specific remit to make its audits as widely available to the general public as possible. Its purpose and ethos should be of a body reporting to the public rather than simply to government or Parliament. It should seek and be given a high public profile, with its reports debated in Parliament and publicised and commented upon in the media. We shall discuss this specifically in the next section.

It is important to understand the boundaries of the audit function we are proposing. The OPA's remit must be limited to assessing performance against the Government's own stated objectives and targets. Independent auditing should be as far as possible an impartial evaluation of whether stated objectives and targets have been met or not, not a subjective—and inevitably political—assessment of whether they were the right ones in the first place. This is vital, for the OPA cannot have the democratic mandate to question the elected government's priorities. That task must lie elsewhere, in the formal political arena. The purpose of independent auditing is to discover whether the Government is spending public money effectively and efficiently in carrying out those priorities—and to tell the public the results.

This should not be simply a statistical or top-down exercise, however. One of the key elements in evaluating performance should be the attempt to discover the experiences and perspectives of those who use public services, and of the citizens who pay for them more widely. It is the public, after all, whose evaluations really count; and imaginative ways of involving them should be an essential element of the audit process. This can play an important role, we believe, in giving evaluations public credibility.

There will be grey areas here, of course. Where a government has devised poor kinds of targets that don't measure properly the achievement of its broader stated objectives, or where a survey of the public has revealed altogether different priorities, the OPA should of course be able to point this out. It should be able to suggest alternative indicators to measure performance.

But the anchor for its evaluation must always be the government's stated objectives; the founding principle is that of the democratic mandate of the government.

Even with this carefully defined role a high profile body reporting on government performance will inevitably be seen as 'political', and its reports highly charged. That is why it is vital that the OPA itself be accountable to Parliament. But we do not believe that it would be appropriate for the OPA to be accountable to a select committee whose membership had been selected by party whips. This would badly undermine its independence in the public eye.[16] If accountability is to the House of Commons, we would seek the establishment of an independent backbench committee. We would argue that the reports of the OPA should be debated on the floor of the whole House.

An alternative would be for the OPA to be accountable to a reformed Second Chamber of Parliament. It is unclear at present how the present House of Lords is to be reformed, and what its functions will be. But the case for one of its major roles being the oversight of the Executive is a powerful one; and in those circumstances having responsibility for the independent audit of public services and government administration would naturally follow. An independent Office for Public Accountability instructed by and reporting to a powerful and independent-minded Second Chamber (and it would have to be clearly seen to have these qualities) might provide both the public credibility and authority needed.

In the current context we see the OPA's role as an auditor of national government as the most important priority. The parallel bodies in Scotland, Wales and Northern Ireland would perform the same task in those areas. But in expanding the work of the Audit Commission there is every reason for a similar function to be carried out for individual local authorities and other non-national public bodies such as English Regional Development Agencies. There would be tremendous public interest at local and regional levels, we believe, in evaluations of public service performance of this kind. Given the number of local authorities and regional bodies, these might be undertaken on a two or three yearly cycle.

£

Public information

The independent auditing of government performance, however, is not sufficient on its own to increase public confidence and make people feel better 'connected'. People have to know what the audit has concluded. Indeed, the need starts even earlier than this. Much more straightforwardly, the public have to know how much tax they pay and what it is being spent on.

In our public attitudes research we found considerable ignorance and confusion about the way the tax system works, how much individuals pay and what taxes are spent on. Moreover, the respondents in our discussion groups were generally aware that they did not know; indeed, they felt that lack of information was part of the reason for their general sense of 'disconnection'. Many pointed out that their local council sent them a leaflet each year with their council tax bill, setting out how the council spent its money. But there was no equivalent for central government. True, most of our respondents admitted that the council's leaflet went straight in the bin. But many had looked at it in one year or another; and at least, they remarked, the local authority was trying to tell taxpayers what their taxes were spent on. Central government, it was widely observed, didn't even bother doing this.

The 'Citizen's Leaflet'

We believe that, like local authorities, central government should tell every citizen, every year, what it is doing with public money. A leaflet should be sent to every individual or household—produced and distributed by the Office for Public Accountability, not by the Government itself, to ensure its credibility. This should:

- Explain in simple terms how the tax system works and how individuals pay tax.
- Set out illustrations of how much tax different individuals pay in different circumstances, and how an individual in slightly different circumstances can calculate (roughly) their own tax bill.
- Explain how public money is spent: not just using the standard pie chart of departmental spending, using the total sums expressed in billions of pounds, but related to the individual's own tax bill. That is, of the, say, £5,000 which an individual pays in tax each year, the leaflet should say how many hundreds (roughly) go on education, how much on health, how much on National Insurance and social security, law and order, environment, defence, etc.
- Include a summary of the OPA's annual audit of government performance, saying how far progress is or is not being made towards the government's objectives.

Following its Budget in March 2000, the Government did produce a public information leaflet, though its distribution was relatively limited.[17] But this was not of the kind we seek. First, it was focused on the measures in the Budget rather than on taxes and public spending as a whole. But more importantly, its tone was rather too propagandist. Although factually accurate, it contained only positive news, and its language marked it out as a 'New Labour' product. (Its very subtitle—*Prudent for a Purpose: Working for a Stronger and Fairer Britain*—made clear its origin.) However genuinely inform- ative, we fear it will have been dismissed by many of its readers for this reason. The Citizen's Leaflet we seek would be written in an accessible form for as wide a readership as possible, but the tone would be politically neutral. It would say what the Government had said it was trying to do, and what the OPA concluded that it had done.

One way of distributing such a leaflet would be to enclose it with tax self- assessment forms. But only a minority of the population receive such forms. Another way would be to ask employers to distribute it with the end-of-tax- year P60 slips which tell people how much income tax they have paid. But, apart from requiring the cooperation of employers, this would only reach those who pay through PAYE. It is crucial to recognise that all citizens pay tax, through indirect taxes even if not income tax. So we believe that such a leaflet should be distributed to every household door-to-door.[18] This would be quite expensive; but as a service to democracy and public confidence in government we believe it would be money well spent. (A comparable leaflet could be produced for businesses, again giving information on the taxes they pay and how this is used.)

Wider public information

The Citizen's Leaflet would be the basic source of direct information provided to all citizens. But this would only be the start. More detailed information should also be made widely available. The internet is an obvious medium, and the Government has already put considerable amounts of information on its websites. A general Government 'portal' (www.ukonline.gov.uk) is being developed to enable such information to be accessed from a single site. The Inland Revenue's website already allows an individual to calculate his or her own income tax—though since the IR does not collect indirect taxes this does not allow a broad calculation of taxes paid. It should.

With an independent Office for Public Accountability, information put out by the government should be augmented by the OPA's reports. This must go much further than use of the internet, where information will only be seen by certain groups in the population, and only if specifically sought. What is needed is nothing less than a new public culture of information about what government is doing. Citizens should have an expectation that they will be well and independently informed. And they should be helped in every way to become so. This should be the OPA's mission. Each report it produced should be summarised in leaflet form and placed in libraries, post offices and other places where public information is found. Ministers should be encouraged to discuss government performance in the light of its reports in public meetings, 'webcasts' and in the media. Perhaps most of all, the media would be expected to cover the OPA's reports fairly. This requirement is crucial and we shall return to it below.

Government information

Another function of the Office for Public Accountability would be to produce guidelines for how government information should be published, and to audit government statements on this basis. The Government has already established an independent statistics commission to ensure that all official statistics are seen to be objective. It has also got the National Audit Office to audit its economic forecasts presented in the Budget and pre-Budget report. The OPA (or, under present arrangements, the NAO) should play a similar role for wider government information, particularly on spending and taxation.

The present Government has already run into trouble in this field. Its Comprehensive Spending Review in 1998 was widely criticised—though not till many months afterwards—for the way in which public spending totals were presented. The famous '£40 billion' extra (£19 billion for education and £21 billion for health) which the Government announced was calculated by a form of treble-counting. These sums represented, not the additional amounts which would be spent over previous plans in the third year of the spending review, but the sum of the extra money spent in all three years.[19] So the announced total made it sound as if spending would be more than double what was actually planned. It is unfortunate testament to the poor quality of media coverage that the £40 billion figure was faithfully reproduced more or less everywhere without explanation.

The Government has learned its lesson, however, from the criticism it attracted. As recommended by the Treasury Select Committee, the Comprehensive Spending Review in 2000 presented its spending plans in more conventional form. This is to be welcomed.

There are still further improvements which can be made in this area, however. It remains absurd that when a Chancellor announces a Budget there can still be confusion for several days as to what the measures in fact mean, with media analysts and tax accountants having to work it out for themselves. The Government knows what its measures imply: it should publish this in the 'Red Book' in a standard format. For example, after the 1999 Budget there was some confusion as to whether the share of taxation in national income had risen or not. Careful study of the published figures did in fact reveal the answer, namely that that particular budget had reduced the tax share but by less than previous budgets had raised it, so overall the share was still going to rise. But this was not highlighted in the Budget presentation or even stated as such in the Red Book. This gave rise to several months of highly misleading public debate. As the Treasury Select Committee has recommended, Budget information of this sort should be presented in a clear and standardised form in the Red Book.[20]

In doing so the government—and the opposition parties too—should follow agreed guidelines on how they present spending and taxation statistics and plans. This is an area offering unlimited scope for confusion of the public. There are always different ways of calculating fiscal statistics. They can be made in cash terms or in real terms (allowing for inflation). Percentage increases and information on trends over time can start from different base years, giving different figures or graphs. Governments and oppositions can either compare their spending plans with actual current figures, or with future planned ones. Changes to taxes and spending can be given in simple actual terms, or 'cyclically-adjusted', where the fluctuations caused by the business cycle are removed to reveal the underlying trends.

There is always a temptation for governments, and for opposition parties, to present statistics in as favourable a light as possible. But their propensity to do this is one of the causes of public cynicism about politicians and of people's disconnection from politics more generally. As our own research showed, people know that statistics can be 'damned lies', and have become minded not to believe anything official they hear. Manipulating numbers for partisan advantage may seem to bring short term advantage but in the long term it simply brings the whole business of politics into disrepute. We do not suppose that politicians are likely to renounce this practice altogether; but it should certainly be possible to draw up standardised formats in which government information on taxation and spending will be presented.

We would propose that the Office for Public Accountability (or at present, the National Audit Office) should work with the Statistics Commission in drawing up such guidelines. Governments could of course present information in other ways, but they should be required to use the standardised formats as well. If all the major political parties could publicly agree on these formats, this would be a valuable advance. It would particularly help the analysis and discussion of these issues in the media, and therefore the public's understanding of them.

Self assessment

One way it is sometimes proposed the public could become better informed about taxation is the more widespread use of self-assessment. Currently, under arrangements begun in 1996-97, around nine million taxpayers (around a third of all those liable for income tax) calculate their own direct tax liability through self-assessment forms. This gives them, it can be argued, a much clearer idea of the tax they pay than is provided to those whose tax is assessed and collected simply through the Pay As You Earn (PAYE) system. PAYE, administered by employers, has the great advantage of administrative efficiency, but it is not a very transparent mechanism for the individual taxpayer. It means that around 17 million taxpayers barely have to think about paying their taxes at all.

Advocates of more widespread self-assessment argue that PAYE creates an essentially paternalistic relationship between the Inland Revenue (IR) and taxpayers, who must rely on their tax office to calculate their tax liability and get it right.[21] Near-universal self-assessment would not abolish PAYE as a method of paying tax; it would simply require citizens to calculate it—and in doing so force everybody to think more responsibly about the taxes they pay. It is pointed out that once every taxpayer was required to fill in a form, this could also be used to promote greater public consultation about tax and spending matters. In the US virtually every state now includes 'check-offs' on its tax return, through which individual taxpayers can choose to contribute to charities and other programmes of various kinds—educational, environmental, medical research and so on. (The federal tax form includes a check-off for the Presidential Election Campaign Fund.)[22] Tax forms could even, it is argued, be used to conduct informal public 'referendums', asking taxpayers to indicate their public spending priorities and whether or not they wanted taxes to rise or fall in consequence.

We are not, however, convinced by these arguments. The cost of introducing near-universal self-assessment would be very high, and we are not persuaded that it would have the educative function which its advocates assume. On the contrary, we suspect that forcing people to fill in a form which was not actually necessary for the collection of revenue would cause considerable annoyance. The present system of self-assessment, applying to only a third of income tax payers, has already caused considerable problems, substantially increasing the revenues of the accountancy profession. Internet-based filing of tax returns will no doubt reduce some of the costs, but not most of them. As for the use of tax returns for informal referendums, this has some attractions. But since even under near-universal self-assessment there would still be many people not completing such returns we would be dubious about their democratic validity. It is not only income tax payers who have votes.

The use of self-assessment is increasing, as more and more people have more complicated working lives, with more than one source of income and rising rates of self-employment. Moreover the extension of means-tested in-work tax credits, such as the Working Families Tax Credit, increasingly require incomes to be assessed for tax purposes. If this means that more people are understanding the tax system better we welcome it. But it is still a very long way from being universal and we do not believe that it would be desirable to make it so simply on transparency grounds.

We do have one proposal to make here, however. In the public attitude research we conducted several members of the discussion groups complained that no-one ever thanked them for paying their taxes. Taxes were subjected to 'demands' to pay them; the Inland Revenue was seen as grasping and punitive. We think this can be easily remedied. Taxpayers *should* be thanked for paying their taxes. Tax self-assessment forms and P60s should say explicitly that taxes are necessary to pay for the public services that everyone needs, and then thank the taxpayer for making his or her contribution. Rather than the curt and demanding tone of the Inland Revenue's current tax notices and forms, containing only the minimum information required to say how much tax is owed, the taxpayer should be treated as a responsible citizen fulfiling a civic duty which the state—representing the wider community—appreciates. It is surely not too much to ask.

£

Democracy and debate

We have suggested various mechanisms by which more and better information can be provided to the citizen about taxation and public spending. We believe that these will help to make people feel more 'connected'. But these are still only information mechanisms. They do not in themselves generate properly active public debate about taxation and spending choices. Information is important: it is a prerequisite for good debate, and its publication helps to spark such debate off. (For all their flaws, it is notable that the three Annual Reports which the Government has published have each stimulated considerable media discussion about the Government's performance.) The better the information the better the debate should be. But ultimately it is the debate which matters.

For at the heart of the strong conception of citizenship we seek to promote is the idea that decisions about taxation and spending are really issues of democratic choice. They are about the kind of society which we want as citizens and as a community, and how the resources available to us are spent to achieve this. As we argued in Chapter 1, what is needed is a more constructive and mature public debate about this. Better information on how government is performing currently is part of this; but the prior and more important argument is about whether it has the right priorities and objectives in the first place. In a vibrant civil society this argument should be constantly renewed.

The role of the mass media in conducting such a debate is vital. It is through the newspapers, television and radio that the vast majority of citizens receive information and ideas about politics and government. A crucial role for the media is to hold government to account, checking what it is doing, ensuring that what it says is accurate, discovering failures the government might prefer to cover up. But it should also be to report successes where these occur. At present the media cannot be said to report government performance fairly. (This is not about the present Government, but all governments.) Bias and cynicism too frequently infect news reporting as well. This can only contribute to public disaffection.

A diverse network of media is critical to civic debate; and political partiality is an essential part of this. But in a flourishing civil society citizens deserve reasonably fair and unbiased reporting of what their government is doing. We hope that, if information on government performance is published by an independent body, such as the Office for Public Accountability we propose, it may be more fairly reported than is often the case at present.

We have one specific proposal for encouraging a better debate about taxation and spending choices as a whole.

A Royal Commission on Taxation

As we remarked in Chapter 1, one of the obstacles to good debate about taxation is the hyper-sensitivity with which all tax proposals are treated in the popular media. It is very difficult for a government or opposition party to propose almost any significant reform of the tax system without political controversy. Any proposal which the government (or an opposition party) wished to investigate and consult on would automatically be regarded as a firm policy and criticised by the other side as such. Such a climate must inevitably inhibit sensible debate about tax reform.

One way of overcoming this problem would be to establish a standing Royal Commission on Taxation to examine proposals for tax reform. The purpose of such a Commission would *not* be to make independent recommendations on taxes. Both the structure and rates of the tax system are intensely and intrinsically political matters which should not be taken out of the hands of elected governments and politicians. The role of a Royal Commission, rather, would be to provide impartial evidence on how possible new or reformed taxes would work, and how the tax system could be improved to meet the government's existing stated objectives.

Specifically, such a Commission would:

- Recommend technical reforms to improve the tax system, such as in administrative arrangements, clarity and so on. We note that the Chartered Institute of Taxation has also called for a Royal Commission for this purpose.[23]

- Investigate the economic, social, environmental and other effects of proposed new taxes.
- Investigate how objectives set out by government (such as environmental incentives, progressivity or work incentives) are being and could better be met by the tax system.

We would envisage a Royal Commission being asked to study particular subjects either by the Government, or by Select Committees of the House of Commons or a reformed Second Chamber. It could also choose subjects for itself. We would envisage a structure somewhere between those of two similar standing commissions, the Royal Commission on Environmental Pollution (RCEP) and the Law Commission. Like the RCEP a Royal Commission on Taxation would acquire its credibility from an eminent and independent membership: perhaps ten to fifteen people from a variety of relevant backgrounds. Like the Law Commission it would need to be serviced by a permanent and well-resourced research staff who could work on several projects at a time. It should make use of existing independent research organisations such as the Institute for Fiscal Studies. One of its functions would be to consult widely on the proposals under investigation. It should report to Parliament and its conclusions should be debated there.

Having a standing Royal Commission on these lines would, it is hoped, take some of the heat out of political discussion of tax reform. It was noticeable, for example, how the Task Force headed by Sir Colin Marshall in 1998 helped to win agreement for the climate change levy through an impartial study of the evidence prior to the Government making its decision.[24] We hope that a Royal Commission would be able to perform a similar role. While many reform proposals will inevitably (and rightly) generate controversy, at least their effects can be subject to independent assessment. This might help to allow the arguments (both for and against any proposal) to be debated in a more deliberative and less hysterical way. Several of our own recommendations in this report would make useful subjects for such a Commission's programme.

Involving the public

So far we have spoken about public debate on taxation and spending decisions as if this is entirely conducted in the media. But this need not be so. In recent years governments at both national and local level have experimented with various mechanisms to consult and involve the public directly in public decision-making and in the holding of government to account. Techniques have ranged from traditional consultation methods using leaflets and public meetings through opinion polling, 'People's Panels' and focus groups to more in-depth processes such as citizens' juries and internet-based consultation. We see every reason for these techniques to be applied to taxation and public spending issues. This is not to take decisions on these matters out of the hands of elected governments. It is simply to give citizens a greater opportunity to make their views known directly to decision-makers and to ensure that governments are informed about them. Appropriately used and reported, such techniques can both increase the public's sense of participation and encourage them to feel that the government is 'listening'. They can also help to educate the public in the complex issues involved. Both can only help enhance citizens' sense of connectedness.

In certain circumstances an even more powerful participatory tool might also be tried. This is the referendum. Referendums should be used sparingly, and there are few taxation and spending decisions which are simple enough to be amenable to the simplicity of a referendum vote. But we do not rule out its use for the very specific choice of whether or not a particular headline tax should be raised or reduced. This would not be normal. But in exceptional circumstances, we can envisage a government asking the public whether or not they wanted, say, income tax to be raised by a specified amount to protect or improve a particular public service. As we argued in Chapter 6, such a rise should be regarded as legitimate if there is a clearly identifiable need for the revenues. But faced with this option a government might wish to secure the legitimacy of a popular mandate.

We believe referendums have a particular role at local and sub-national levels, where taxation and spending choices are more immediate and generally clearer than on a national scale. Some councils, such as as Milton Keynes, have already conducted referendums on their tax and spending plans; the Government has given general approval to the idea.[25] We shall return to this in Chapter 9.

Conclusion

The proposals in this chapter have all been designed to increase the public's understanding of, and confidence in, the government's taxation and spending decisions. They seek to make government more accountable for its actions and for the revenues it uses. We hope by these means to increase the public's sense of 'connectedness' to their taxes and to the spending which these finance. But there is another way in which this might be done as well, which relates to the nature of the taxes themselves. It is to this that we now turn.

8 | Earmarking taxes: the 'hypothecation' debate

In the last chapter we examined various measures which might help to 'connect' citizens better to the taxes they pay and to the public services which these finance. These focused on providing more and better information to the public about taxation and public expenditure. But there is another, perhaps even more tangible, way in which citizens might be 'reconnected' to taxation. This is to earmark particular taxes for specific spending purposes.

At present, with a very small number of exceptions, revenues from all the different sources of taxation—income tax, VAT, excise duties, corporation tax, capital gains tax and so on—go into a single 'pool' in the Treasury. From there funds are taken out to be used for spending on all the various programmes of government—education, health, law and order, transport etc. The tax streams channelled into the centralised pool, and the spending flows pumped out of it, are not linked in any way.

This arrangement—which is used for the bulk of taxes in almost every industrialised country—provides for maximum flexibility for the Treasury. The government can fund the desired level of expenditure without reference to any particular source of revenue. But for the public it makes for a very opaque system. All that most citizens can see is that they pay taxes of different kinds into a single large pot, and then by a more or less invisible process—in which there is almost no public consultation or participation—an allocation of spending emerges. This system almost certainly contributes to the sense of 'disconnection' from their taxes which many people feel.

In recent years, for this reason, there has been increasing interest in the idea of 'earmarking' certain taxes for specific spending purposes. The technical name for this is 'hypothecation'. We prefer the term 'earmarking': not just because it is more easily understood, but because 'hypothecation' has a strict technical meaning, namely the complete funding of an area of expenditure from a single tax source. We use 'earmarking' to mean any form of explicit connection between a tax and a spending purpose. We shall discuss four different kinds below, of which only the last takes the form of 'strict' hypothecation. The four are:

- Special time-limited levies for capital expenditures.
- Flexible earmarking of incentive-based taxes, particularly environmental ones.
- 'Tax and public service pledges': political promises to spend additional tax revenues on specific public service improvements.
- Strict hypothecation of a principal tax for a mainstream spending programme (we shall look in particular at the proposal to hypothecate part of income tax for health or education).

£

The general arguments

Current earmarked taxes

The idea of earmarked taxes is not new. On the contrary, most of the earliest taxes were earmarked ones, levied by sovereigns and governments, right up to the 18th century, to pay for specific wars. It was the growth of the centralised administrative state in the second half of the 19th century which established the mechanism of the single Treasury pool; in local government different services were funded by separate rates until the 1930s.[1]

New taxes have often been earmarked: vehicle licence fees were originally paid into a Road Fund (created in 1921) to pay for roadbuilding; in the late 1940s a special levy was charged on cinema seats to fund the British film industry. The television licence fee remains a fully hypothecated charge to fund the BBC. And of course the National Insurance system is also based on the principle of earmarking. National Insurance contributions paid by employees, self-employed people and employers go, not into the main Treasury pot, but into a separate National Insurance Fund, from which the basic state pension and other contributory social security benefits are then paid. (The

National Insurance system is discussed in more detail in the Annex.)

In the last few years, in fact, earmarked taxes have undergone something of a revival. In introducing the landfill tax on waste disposal in 1996, the Conservative Government earmarked a proportion of the revenues for environmental spending through a special fund (Entrust). The National Lottery was created as a kind of voluntary earmarked taxation, the revenues specified for a range of popular (and some not so popular) 'good causes'. The new Labour Government's first tax measure was the windfall tax on the profits of privatised utilities—earmarked for the New Deal programme to assist unemployed people into work. Since then the Government has declared that the increases in tobacco duties announced in the 2000 Budget will go towards the NHS, while any future increases in petrol duty will be earmarked for transport spending. In Scotland the proposed arrangement to replace student tuition fees is based on an earmarked graduate endowment fund. The terms of the UK climate change levy to be introduced on business energy consumption in 2001 include around 15% of revenues earmarked for energy efficiency programmes. The Government's transport programme goes even further. It gives local authorities the power to levy congestion charges on motorists in urban areas and taxes on workplace carparking spaces—but only if the entire receipts are earmarked for spending on public transport and related measures.[2]

Arguments for earmarking

Interestingly, many of the advocates of earmarked taxes have come from the right of the political spectrum.[3] For them such taxes have had two attractions. On the one hand they are seen as a way of reining in the power of the state. A fully hypothecated tax requires that all the revenues must be allocated to the given spending programme, and the whole of the spending must come from the tax. Such an arrangement limits the power of government to spend as it chooses. For neo-liberals and others who fear that the state has an in-built tendency to grow big, when it ought to be kept small, hypothecation forces governments to justify every new area of spending and to raise specific new taxes to pay for it. If a tax raises more money than is required for the desired level of the spending programme, governments cannot use the surplus to do something else: the tax rate must be cut. So earmarked taxes effectively control government expansion.

At the same time, those on the right argue, hypothecation allows citizens to choose which areas of government they wish to finance and at what level. For so-called 'public choice' theorists, government should not be seen as a collective process of decision-making in its own right, but as an aggregation of many individual ones.[4] They advocate not merely earmarking separate taxes for different spending programmes, but a system of popular referendums on each one. This allows the citizen to make an essentially 'private' decision on which areas of government he or she wishes to fund. Instead of having to vote on a 'bundle' of taxes and spending choices made by government, the citizen can choose the specific amounts of tax and forms of spending he or she desires. Thus government decisions, it is argued, become more representative of the public's preferences.

Moreover, on this model taxes can then be targeted only at those who will benefit from their associated spending. Only motorists need pay for road-building (and they should pay no more than is necessary to finance it), while those who take out private health insurance can be relieved from paying for the NHS. Under such a so-called 'benefit principle', earmarked taxation becomes essentially a kind of user charging: a form of private spending on individualised benefits.

This is one, extreme, way of understanding earmarked taxes. But it is not a necessary one. As we argued in Chapter 4, a strong conception of citizen-ship rejects the idea of government simply as a way of aggregating private preferences. Citizenship implies a connectedness between the individual and other people in society, and demands the proper provision of public goods whose benefits are shared with them. Against the 'private' benefit principle of taxation, this view argues that taxes are the individual's contribution to the common good—democratically decided—as well as to his/her own. And they should be based on ability to pay. In this context earmarking is simply a way of connecting a tax to a spending programme to make its purpose more transparent: it need have no basis in public choice theory.

Making government more responsive to public concerns, however, is not an aim confined to those who want the state to be smaller. On the contrary, as we have already argued, improving the democratic accountability of government is an important corollary of citizenship. Long experience of the ways in which the state can 'fail' has rightly fuelled the demand that public decisions should be made in as open and transparent a manner as possible. Earmarking taxes, it can be argued, may help this. There need be no assump-tion that individuals simply want to choose the public services that benefit them: even the most altruistic or socially-minded taxpayer wants to ensure that his or her taxes are being spent well.

From this perspective earmarked taxes can be seen not as a way of minimis-ing government, but of legitimising it.[5] The problem with pooled taxes is that they make the purpose of taxation obscure. The processes by which govern-ments decide how to allocate spending between different areas are locked inside a 'black box', hidden from public view. By linking taxes to expenditure, earmarking can help citizens see more clearly what they are paying for. Choices on spending are brought out into the open. If its goals are made more transparent in this way, it can be argued, earmarking may come to make taxa-tion seem more legitimate, and therefore more publicly acceptable.

This is likely to be particularly true whenever government seeks to introduce a new tax or to raise an existing one. The public are surely more likely to accept this if they know (and support) the uses to which the extra revenues will be put. Indeed, earmarking can do more than make government more accountable; one could say that in an interesting kind of way it makes the public more account-able too. If voters want more spending on a public service, an earmarked tax may make it clearer to them what they will have to pay to get it.

Arguments against earmarking

From the point of view of citizenship—of 'reconnecting' people to their taxes—there does therefore seem to be a case for earmarking. Yet the major-ity of experts, in both the tax and general public policy fields, have long been against it. Why?

The first and most basic objection to earmarking is that it impedes the flexibility and efficiency of government. The great advantage of central tax pooling is that governments can make decisions on the allocation of spend-ing according to perceived needs, without reference to choices on tax. Earmarking—at least of the strict hypothecation kind—would restrict this ability. This is of course precisely what the neo-liberal advocates of hypothe-cation seek. But for anyone who regards public spending as essentially legitimate, and wants governments to be able to respond sensibly to chang-ing social and economic circumstances, forcing all the separate streams of revenue and expenditure into equally-sized channels looks fundamentally unhelpful.

There is no reason why any particular tax should yield just that level of income which government believes is required for any particular spending programme. Why, for example, should the politically and economically desired level of the vehicle licence fee just happen to bring in precisely the same amount of revenue as the government seeks to spend on roadbuild-ing?[6] The two sums are simply unconnected. Tying them together through strict hypothecation is therefore always likely to generate either too much revenue or not enough. In the first case the government will end up spend-ing more than it wants to on the expenditure programme; in the second it will be forced to spend less. Both results are inefficient. Of course, the tax can be constantly adjusted up and down to bring its yield into line with the spending need. But then the government may find itself foregoing a good source of taxation simply because it doesn't want to spend so much money in a particular area—or dependent on a bad source of taxation because it does. Some taxes are particularly efficient, or progressive, or economically less damaging than others; if so, they should be used to bring in revenue irre-spective of the desired level of spending in some arbitrarily related area.

For most of the tax system, in most circumstances, these are good arguments, and they make a convincing case against generalised hypothecation of government revenue. It would clearly be absurd to tie all or even most areas of government expenditure to particular tax sources. But this does not mean that earmarking is therefore ruled out altogether. In the first place, it might still have a useful role to play for specific taxes and specific areas of spending. If the Treasury's need for flexibility is maintained for taxation in general, it might still be possible for specific sources of revenue to be earmarked. This is, as we have seen, already occurring, and we shall return to it shortly.

Moreover, the objection only properly applies to strict hypothecation, where the expenditure programme is completely funded by the full revenues from the tax. But what if earmarking were less strict? Two possibilities might be allowed: either that the tax revenues could be spent on areas other than the given spending programme if more money was raised than required; or that the spending programme could also be funded from other sources if the specific tax revenues were insufficient. Either option (or both) would get round the objection of inflexibility, while still maintaining a basic link between the tax and the spending.

Most forms of earmarking now proposed are of this more flexible kind, in fact. It is not suggested, for example, that local authorities' spending on transport should be limited to the revenues from congestion and workplace parking charges; they will be able to spend more than this, from other sources, if they wish (though they will not be able to spend less). But while such 'flexible earmarking' overcomes the problem of inflexibility, it does so at a considerable cost to transparency. Indeed, for many critics of earmarking, it makes the whole process potentially something of a sham.[7]

Strict hypothecation may be inflexible, but it is at least absolutely clear. The tax pays for the spending. If the public wants to see more spending, it must pay more tax. If the government wants to cut spending, it must cut the tax. But once that strict link is broken, allowing flexibility on either side, this transparency disappears. Now higher spending need not require higher tax; it can simply come out of general funds. So the public are not really being told through earmarking what they have to pay to receive a particular level of government service. If flexibility operates on the tax side, allowing surplus revenues from the tax to be spent elsewhere, earmarking does not even tell the public what their taxes are being spent on. When this happens, say the critics, earmarking could even become rather dishonest, a mere public relations stunt. It would pretend to be establishing a clear link between the tax and the spending, but would in practice make no difference whatsoever to the budgetary or decision-making practices of government.

This problem becomes particularly acute when earmarking is sold to the public as a way of increasing the revenues for particular spending programmes. For many of its advocates, this is precisely the attraction of earmarking: it helps increase the political acceptability of raised or new taxes. It is, to take an example, almost certainly how urban congestion and workplace car parking charges are being presented. As well as deterring traffic directly, such charges will help fund the extra public transport, cycle lanes, traffic calming measures and so on which will help to encourage people out of their cars.

But how do we know that this will be the case? Local authorities already spend money on these things. How can we be sure that they will spend more money as a result of these new revenues? In the first year the charges come in, and for any subsequent years in which the authority has a pre-existing transport plan it will be fairly obvious, since we can compare transport spending with the planned budget. But gradually, over time, who is to say how much the authority would have spent on transport in the absence of the charges—and therefore whether all the extra revenue is really going towards extra spending? There will surely be a temptation for councils to allocate rather less of their general funds to transport, now that they have so much extra money to spend on it. Many will regard education, or social services, as a higher priority. It is not difficult to foresee the gradual withdrawal of general funds from transport, and their redirection to these or other spending areas. (In the case of capital spending, local authorities have to bid for funding allocations from central government. So the temptation may fall on central government to reduce the amounts available.[8])

This is, after all, what many people believe has happened with the National Lottery. The government insisted at the outset that all Lottery monies would be additional to mainstream government spending programmes—but how do we know what the Government would have spent on sport, arts and voluntary organisations (and now on health and education as well) if the Lottery money had not been available? It is widely regarded as implausible to think that, given total Lottery spending of £9.7bn since 1993, there has been no displacement of general funds at all.[9]

But this possibility represents a very serious problem for earmarking. The purpose of earmarking is to make government more transparent to its citizens, to help increase the public legitimacy of taxation. But if the public find that in fact earmarking has turned out to be a con, with the extra taxes they are paying actually funding other programmes altogether, this will surely have precisely the opposite effect. It will lead the public to trust politicians even less. Taxation will be made less legitimate, not more. For those seeking a stronger citizenship basis to the political process, this would be the worst of all possible worlds: a mechanism claiming to 'reconnect' people to their taxes which actually did exactly the opposite.

Public attitudes

This was, in fact, precisely the view we found in the public attitude discussion groups conducted for the Commission.[10] Many people in the groups commented that they would feel better about paying tax if they knew more clearly what it was being spent on—particularly in the case of priority areas such as health or education of which they approved. The idea of earmarking taxes was generally considered attractive for this reason.

But this view came with a big rider attached. Many respondents were mistrustful about whether the money would *actually* be used for the promised purpose. They felt that governments often say they will do things but then don't keep to their pledges. How would the public know whether the money was in fact being used as promised or not? At the very least, they argued, there would need to be believable feedback on how earmarked taxes were being spent. Even then, this would not guarantee that extra money would lead to a better service. Earmarking sounded attractive in principle, it was concluded, but there was still much to do to convince people that it would actually work.

The challenge

So we seem to be left with a challenge. Though earmarking taxes in general is not sensible, in principle earmarking some kinds of taxation would seem to be a useful way of making government more transparent, and helping thereby to legitimise the tax system. Tentatively, the evidence does appear to show that earmarking would make people feel more connected to the taxes they pay, and therefore more accepting of them. But if earmarking is abused, with governments using the cover of flexibility simply to break the link between the tax and the spending altogether, the opposite result is likely. The challenge therefore is to design a framework for earmarking which prevents—or reduces the risk of—both inflexibility and sham. Can this be done?

£

Conditions for earmarking

We believe it can. We shall suggest four general conditions which need to be met, and then show how these would work for the four different types of earmarked tax we identified above.

Condition 1: the tax-spending relationship

The first condition is to specify clearly the relationship between the earmarked tax and the spending area to which the revenues will be put. As we shall show below, in the case of a fully hypothecated tax, the link should be strict. The spending area must be wholly financed by the revenues from the tax, and the revenues must not be used for anything else. This should be publicly announced when the tax is introduced. With special levies for capital expenditure programmes and 'tax and public service pledges', the general spending area may not be wholly funded by the tax, but the specific spending programme must be identified, and in relation to this the earmarking must be strict.

In the case of incentive-based taxes, however, we do not believe that strict hypothecation of this kind is necessary. Earmarking can be 'flexible'. But such flexibility can only be in one direction. The designated expenditure programme may be allowed to receive funds from general revenues as well as the earmarked tax; but the whole of the revenues from the tax must go towards that area of spending.

This condition allows a new or raised tax to fund an existing area of spending, and means the spending level does not have to be determined solely by the revenue from the tax. (Or to put it another way: governments have a choice, when expenditure is raised, whether or not they also raise the tax.)

But does this not fall foul of the 'sham' objection? The answer is no. In the previous section we spoke as if the two kinds of flexibility—on the spending side, and on the tax side—were essentially the same. But this is not true. The purpose of earmarking is to guarantee to the public that the tax they are paying is going on the expenditure programme of which they approve (or at least, of which they have been told), not being spent elsewhere. If the government can use 'surplus' revenues from the tax on other programmes, this promise is broken. Hence flexibility on the 'tax' side of the relationship would indeed make earmarking the sham that its critics suggest. But flexibility on the 'spending' side does not have this effect. When taxpayers are told that the taxes they are paying will go on the spending programme, this is entirely true. All the revenues will be spent in the designated area. More may be spent if need be (drawing on other revenue sources)—but less will not. It is after all the tax which is being earmarked, not the spending. It is the tax which the public wants to know is being spent in the way that is being promised; and this is the case.

It is true that one of the elements of transparency is broken by such flexibility. If the public wants more spending, it may not be required to pay more tax: the government may be able to find the additional resources from elsewhere. But we do not believe that earmarking is only worthwhile if this kind of transparency is achieved. For some taxes it may be—in which case strict, non-flexible hypothecation is required. But for most environmental and other incentive-based taxes, the purpose of earmarking is simply to guarantee to taxpayers that the monies they are paying are genuinely going on the designated spending programme, not being used merely as an additional source of revenue for the Treasury. Few firms or consumers, we think, will want the level of (say) environmental expenditure to be limited to the level of environmental taxes they pay; what they want to ensure is that it is not less. This is what one-way flexibility guarantees. As long as this relationship is made clear to the public, we believe that the credibility of the earmarking will be maintained.

Condition 2: the 'baseline'

But there is another guarantee taxpayers will want as well. As we argued above, earmarking will be exposed as fraudulent if governments use the additional revenue from a new or higher tax simply to displace existing spending. To be credible, the public must be assured that the additional revenues are genuinely going to fund extra spending in the designated area.

In the case of a fully hypothecated tax, this is not a problem, since the entire sum of expenditure must come from the tax. But where earmarking is flexible, an additional mechanism is needed. The government or local authority responsible needs to identify publicly a 'baseline' of existing expenditure, to which the new revenues will be clearly additional. Such a baseline will need to extend, we would argue, for at least five years into the future. This will guarantee to the public that the revenues from the new tax will lead to additional spending in the designated area for at least that period.

In some cases, such baselines already exist. In the case of road congestion charges, for example, local authorities are now required to have five-year transport spending plans, so the baseline for future spending can already be identified. (A new plan could be required if charges are introduced halfway through an existing five-year cycle.) Central government now has a ten-year spending plan for transport investment, so its baseline is guaranteed for even longer. Though such long-term spending plans do not yet exist for other areas of capital spending, there are good reasons (on policy planning grounds) for them to do so. For current spending the Government now has three-year spending plans. Local authorities could follow suit, particularly since councils' central government grant is now fixed for a three-year period.

So for the first three years of an earmarked tax the 'baseline' expenditure to which the tax revenues would be additional should be identifiable. For the fourth and fifth years a promise could be made to maintain at least the baseline level of spending planned for the third year. Even if there is no actual baseline for years four and five, such a promise should maintain the credibility of the earmarked tax.

An objection might be raised here, however. If the government knows that it is going to levy an earmarked tax, could it not just reduce its planned baseline expenditure, in order to bring in the extra money without actually having to spend more than it was already planning to do?

The answer, of course, is yes, the government could do this. But it would be stupid to do so. Since the baseline budgets can always be compared with previous years' spending, it will be pretty obvious if a government has cut its planned spending as soon as the new tax revenues become available. Any government which tried this would be quickly exposed by both the media and opposition parties; so quickly, in fact, that the incentive would surely operate in the opposite direction, with governments leaning over backwards to ensure that the earmarking was as transparent to the public as possible.

This is, of course, precisely as it should be. For in a sense the objection misses the point. The purpose of earmarking is to help increase the legitimacy of government spending and taxation. Our assumption is that governments wish to do this. There is nothing formally to stop a government abusing earmarking if it wants to. But if it does so the exercise will soon be exposed as a sham. The public credibility of the government, and the legitimacy of spending and taxation, will then be severely diminished. In this sense it will be the opposition parties, media and public who will be the guardians of earmarking, not the government. Governments must always be held to account: one can merely hope that if virtue alone is insufficient motivation, fear of exposure will provide a suitable back-up.

Beyond the baseline period

For current spending we believe that a five-year planning timeframe is about right. (For capital spending, an even longer period could be adopted.) It would ensure that for what in political terms is quite a long period the public could be sure that the revenues from an earmarked tax were genuinely additional. It would also ensure that the earmarking extended beyond the life of one government (whether at central or local level). This would help to discourage the earmarking becoming a matter of party political contention. While it would be perfectly reasonable for a party to go into an election promising to abolish the tax altogether, it would be much harder to campaign on ending its earmarking. In this way, the credibility of the earmarking promise would be protected, which is our prime concern.

For current spending a planning period much longer than five years is unrealistic. Indeed it is undesirable. Circumstances and priorities change, and it would be wrong (and as time went on, absurd) to tie governments indefinitely to spending a certain amount of money in a certain area. So the question arises: what happens after the baseline period?

In the case of time-limited levies for capital expenditures, as we shall explain below, the question does not arise. The tax is abolished after a specified period. But for taxes which are intended to be permanent, this is an important question. After the initial planning period a new spending plan would have to be set. But now we would argue that there should be no need to maintain the distinction between 'baseline' and 'additional' expenditure. With the tax in place, and the revenues from it established, governments should be able to determine spending levels according to need judged at the time. The only requirement, as set by our first condition above, would be that the spending could not decline below the level of revenue received from the tax. Once the plausibility of a pre-existing 'baseline' has disappeared it is impossible to say what is or is not 'additional' expenditure, since we cannot say what expenditure would have been in the absence of the tax. The earmarking promise should therefore revert to the basic requirement that at least all the revenues from the tax will be spent in the designated area.

In theory, relaxing the requirement for a pre-determined 'baseline' beyond the initial planning period could lead governments suddenly to reduce their spending, possibly to a level no more than the revenues from the earmarked tax. In practice, however, this seems unlikely; partly because in most cases we may presume that at least part of the spending will have been deemed useful, and worth continuing; and partly because this would again risk political opprobrium. But it should be possible, nevertheless. If the spending really isn't worthwhile, it should be cut; and governments should be able to justify this to their electorates without the earmarking itself being called into question (so long as the earmarked revenues themselves are still being spent in the designated area).

In effect what we are proposing is that two different earmarking promises should be made. In the short to medium term, for a time-limited period, the revenues will be additional to a pre-determined baseline of expenditure. Subsequent to that, in the long term, all the revenues will at least be spent in the designated area. In this way, we believe, flexibility and credibility can both be achieved, in the real world of both politics and government budgeting.

Condition 3: the spending programme

One objection which might be made to earmarking on this basis is that it will lead to inefficiencies. Although spending will not be wholly determined by the revenues from the tax, it will still be linked to it. What if the government feels that the given level of spending (either within or after the initial planning period) is more than required for a rational expenditure programme? Will the government not be forced to spend 'too much' money in the spending area?

This is a possibility in theory, but in practice it can be easily avoided. The key lies in the definition of the spending programme on which the revenues will be spent. This must be defined sufficiently narrowly to link the tax to the spending: an environmental tax, for example, must be earmarked to environmental improvement programmes. But it should not be defined so narrowly as to risk obsolescence as conditions and spending priorities change.

We believe that in the real world such judgements will be relatively easy to make. To take an example: earmarking road congestion charges to particular bus priority measures would not be sensible. Such measures might prove ineffective, or not require as much money as the levy could sensibly yield. But defining the designated expenditure as being for 'transport spending' would allow for enough flexibility to adapt the spending according to need while still tying the tax to a clearly related area of expenditure.

Condition 4: public auditing and information

As with all taxes, we regard it as essential that earmarked spending programmes should be independently and publicly audited for their effectiveness. Indeed we would go further. For each earmarked tax, its taxpayers should be given information each year on how much has been collected, what the revenues have been used for, and the environmental and other impacts which this spending has had. Those paying congestion charges should receive such information with their smart card or licence renewal notice. Employers paying workplace carparking charges should receive copies to give to all their affected staff. Firms paying water or waste charges should receive the information with their tax demands. Firms and households paying an energy tax should get it with their energy bills. In this way the earmarked tax and its associated spending can be linked not only in the government's accounts, but in the minds of the public as well. This will surely be the key to earmarking's political success.

£

Three kinds of earmarked tax

It is important to distinguish between different forms of earmarking, and to identify the different purposes for which they can be used. Too much of the debate about 'hypothecation' assumes that there is only one kind, and that all earmarked taxes must conform to it. It is particularly important to focus on real world examples rather than purely theoretical ones. As set out above, there are four main kinds of earmarked tax. We shall deal with the first three here.

Time-limited taxes for special capital expenditures

The most straightforward form of earmarking is one where the relationship between the tax and the spending programme is completely transparent. This condition is met where a new and time-limited tax is levied to finance new capital expenditure. An example might be a special levy on businesses and residents in a city to finance capital investment in the transport system.

From the earmarking point of view, the key feature of such a levy would be its time-limited nature (perhaps five years in the London case). Of course, capital investment in the transport system will always be required. But, as a result of under-investment over the last twenty years, there is a specific need now for a much higher rate of capital spending than would normally be needed to maintain the system. The government's 10-year transport investment plan may provide enough. But if it does not, and anyway in principle, it is plausible to think of introducing a special levy for a limited period only. This would need to be long enough (depending on the rate) to meet the accumulated backlog of investment needed, but not permanent. (Given the practicalities of major investment, the period of spending can be longer than the period of the tax.)

Crucially, a time-limited levy overcomes much of the problem of ensuring that the monies are genuinely additional to what would anyway have been spent. This can provide a 'baseline' against which to measure the additional spending. In this way taxpayers can be assured, both at the time the levy is introduced, and subsequently during the period of its operation, that the extra money they are paying is genuinely financing more investment than would otherwise have been possible. Clear and public auditing of the spending programme, to ensure that the money is being well spent, and to inform the public of this, is essential. At the end of the specified period, when the required money has been raised, the tax is abolished.

We see every reason to use earmarked taxes for special capital expenditures in this way. They improve transparency, and seem likely to increase the public acceptability of taxation. They may even make possible tax rises which would not otherwise be politically viable. Using such taxes to finance local investment programmes of the above kind—on transport or on other economic development projects—would seem to be particularly appropriate. As we argue in the next chapter, local authorities should have the power to levy them.

But it is also plausible to see a similar mechanism being used occasionally at a national level. An example might be the levying of a special tax—a temporary surcharge on income tax, perhaps—to finance additional capital spending in education. This is another field in which a huge backlog of investment need, in school buildings and equipment, has built up over many years. Again, as in transport, the government has significantly increased the sums available for capital spending. But, coming out of the general fund, this money still competes with other spending priorities, in education and elsewhere. If at the end of the current spending round more monies were seen to be required, a special time-limited 'schools levy', aimed at a well-defined programme of capital investment, might attract public support.

Environmental taxes

In Chapter 5 we argued that one of the legitimate purposes of taxation is to discourage social harm. Where an economic activity has an adverse 'external effect' on other people or on the environment, the tax system can be a useful way of influencing behaviour to reduce the harm caused. This is the main justification for taxes on environmental damage, transport and land use, and in Chapters 13 and 14 we discuss these in more detail. In all these cases there are strong arguments for earmarking the revenues raised.

Environmental taxes (grouping all the above under this general heading) are intended to discourage firms and consumers from causing pollution and wasting resources, while encouraging more environmentally efficient kinds of behaviour. But their success in doing this varies according to the issue and the tax. Some forms of behaviour (like car driving) are not very responsive to price changes. So then it makes sense to use the revenues to bolster the incentive. Better public transport, for example, should increase the responsiveness of motorists to congestion charges. Similarly, using the revenues from (say) a tax on pesticides to help farmers reduce their chemical inputs will help increase its effectiveness in tackling agrochemical pollution.

Earmarking revenues in this way is also likely to make such taxes more publicly acceptable. Most firms and consumers whose behaviour causes environmental damage are now aware that they are doing so. But they may still object to paying tax on the activity if they do not believe that it will actually make any difference to the environmental problem. Cynicism can quickly set in: the government may claim that the tax is being introduced for environmental reasons, but many of its targets may actually feel that it is really just a way of milking more revenue for the Treasury. Earmarking such taxes to spend on environmental improvement will almost certainly increase their political acceptability.

But if earmarking environmental taxes seems in principle a useful idea, strict hypothecation does not. It is not sensible to require environmental spending to be limited to whatever revenues environmental taxes happen to yield. Decisions on the appropriate level of taxation and the appropriate level of spending are independent of one another; so if earmarking is to work it will need to be flexible. We have already discussed how we believe this can be done.

We would argue that all environmental taxes should be at least partially earmarked. We include in this category taxes on energy, resources, waste disposal, pollution and transport. (Some of these are already levied or have been announced; others might be introduced.) Transport taxes include duties on road fuels, vehicle licences, urban congestion and workplace carparking charges and any possible road tolls.

For many of the smaller environmental taxes, full earmarking to environmental expenditure programmes is possible. But for those yielding larger revenues, it will not always be feasible to earmark the entire sum for spending purposes. In some cases this will be because the tax is being 'earmarked' in another way. As we shall explain in Chapter 13, one of the aims of environmental taxation is to shift the burden of taxation from taxes on labour and income to taxes on environmental damage. Most of the revenues from the present Government's new climate change levy and aggregates tax, therefore, are being used to finance a parallel reduction in employers' National Insurance contributions. This represents, not additional income, but a transfer of income from one tax source to another. Only a proportion of the revenue is therefore available for earmarking to environmental spending.

In other cases, the total revenue from an environmental tax may simply exceed desirable spending in a related field. This is the case, notably, with petrol duty. In 2000-01 the duty is projected to raise £23 billion per annum; total annual spending on transport (both current and capital) is only around £5 billion.[11] So unless the tax were simply reduced, in which case another tax would have to be raised to make up the (very considerable) shortfall in revenue, full earmarking of the tax is not possible. This does not rule out earmarking altogether, however. Two options are available. One the government has already done, earmarking all *increases* in the tax for additional transport spending. The other is to earmark a minimum proportion of the entire revenue (say, one-third) for transport expenditures. By creating a link between the tax as a whole and the spending programme, this might increase the public acceptability of the duty. It was notable in the summer of 2000 that the high rate of petrol tax was being criticised at almost exactly the same time as the government was promising a ten-year programme of higher transport spending. If the two had been formally linked, public acceptance of petrol taxation might have been greater.[12]

So long as the relationship between the tax and the spending is made publicly clear, and the government keeps to it—that is, that our first condition is fulfiled—partial earmarking of a tax in this way is entirely consistent with the principle. But this raises another objection. Where earmarking is not 100%, it might be asked, what is the justification for the rest of the tax? A similar question might arise in relation to permanent earmarked taxes extending beyond an initial baseline period. We have observed above that after the end of the initial planning period governments may wish to reduce their expenditure, eventually perhaps to no more than the level of the tax revenues. But in these circumstances shouldn't they in fact just reduce the level of the tax?

The answer is: possibly—but not necessarily. What the objection highlights is the reason we have suggested that flexible earmarking be used only for incentive-based taxes. If a tax has no justification other than to raise revenues for the spending programme (as, for example, with a special levy for capital expenditure), then the size and purpose of that programme should indeed determine the rate and duration of the tax. But incentive-based taxes do have such ulterior justification: they are designed to change behaviour or to penalise social harm. They are intended, in the environmental case, to make 'the polluter pay'.

In these circumstances, if the specific spending need changes, or the tax brings in more revenue than is required for an initial spending programme, this is not a reason of itself to say that the tax or its rate can no longer be justified. Earmarking the tax adds to its justification—the tax now has a twin effect on the problem, on both tax and spending sides—but it is not the sole reason for levying it. The design and rate of the tax are set according to an independent judgement of its incentive and other economic and social effects, not simply its projected revenue yield. Hence if the need for spending rises, it does not mean that the tax must rise. If the tax has an independent justification, it cannot be set at whatever level is needed to fund the spending: its level must depend on the effects it will have.[13] It is for this reason that the transparency achieved by strict hypothecation—forcing the tax to rise if spending rises, or to fall if spending falls—is not in fact desirable. We do not wish to link the two in this umbilical way.[14]

Tax and public service pledges

In principle, other incentive-based taxes could also be earmarked. So-called 'sin taxes' on alcohol and tobacco, for example, could be earmarked for health spending. The problem here, though, is that (unlike most environmental taxes) such taxes are already well established, and merely declaring that they were now to be earmarked would not in itself provide any extra money to the NHS. So this would be almost entirely cosmetic—*unless* it were part of a thorough-going hypothecation of health spending. We shall return to this latter possibility below.

Another, simpler option for sin taxes would be to say that any *new* revenues, from increased rates of duty, should be earmarked. This is in fact what the Government has done with tobacco duty. In his March 2000 Budget the Chancellor raised the duty and announced that the extra revenues would be earmarked for the NHS. This was a more plausible pledge, since in the same Budget health spending was substantially increased. But the rather vague nature of the announcement—the Chancellor did not say on what kinds of spending the extra revenues would go, and the additional spending commitment on the NHS was vastly more than the additional tobacco revenues—made it a rather woolly kind of promise, and it made little apparent public impact.

We believe that a different approach should be taken here, and not just with sin taxes. The process should in fact be conducted the other way round.

We argued in Chapter 6 that it should not be politically impossible for governments to raise taxes, and opposition parties to commit themselves to doing so. It is perfectly appropriate for a government or party to regard any given level of public spending as insufficient. If the desired level of expenditure cannot be achieved at the current level of tax receipts (combined with an acceptable level of borrowing), a government or party should be able to explain to the public that taxes (in some form) need to be raised. But we also recognised that this is much easier said than done. Raising taxes has never been popular, and political memories of the last decade—the 1992 election for Labour, the 1992-97 period for the Tories—have made it even harder.

In this context we believe that earmarking could have a role. Where a government or party wishes to raise taxes to pay for higher public spending it should publicly earmark the extra tax for a specific spending purpose. It should then make a clear 'pledge' to the electorate: in return for the tax increase, the government guarantees that a certain level of measurable improvement in the public service will be achieved.

Let us say, for example, that a government believes that an extra £3 billion needs to be spent on schools per annum. It cannot find the money in efficiency savings or in cuts to other budgets, and is at the limit of its borrowing constraint. The proposal is that it should then present to the public a 'tax and public service pledge'. The public would be asked to pay (say) an extra 1p in the pound on the basic rate of income tax. The government would then pledge that the money would be used to achieve stated improvements in health outcomes: smaller class sizes, more books and equipment, repairs to buildings, or whatever. The pledge would be time-limited: these improvements would have to be achieved by a specified date, say three or four years ahead. At that point (and probably at intermediate times as well) the pledge would be independently audited, and the public told whether or not it had been met. It would be important not to suggest that the targets could be achieved too quickly: there is always a time lag between additional spending and perceptible improvement, and this would have to be made clear in the timetable set.

(Sometimes, in adverse economic circumstances, a rise in the rate of tax may be necessary, not to increase current spending, but simply to maintain it. But again this can be specified in a 'pledge'. In such a situation the government could make clear the levels of public services that would continue to be achieved using the additional revenues.)

The higher tax rate itself would not be time-limited. If it were used to finance current expenditure, it would be implausible for the government to suggest that the tax would be reduced again at the end of the period. Unless some other new source of revenue replaced it, cutting the tax would require cutting the spending as well. Since the point of the tax would be to improve the level of public service, making it worse again at the end of the period would hardly be sensible. The point of the specified date would therefore be simply to ensure that the service improvement had a properly measurable target. The pledge the government would make, rather, would be of the following kind: 'Allow us to raise the tax and we will improve the service. At the end of the period, an independent audit will determine whether we have done this. If we have, we will then ask you to continue paying the higher level of tax to continue receiving the improved level of service. If we have not, judge us accordingly.' Of course, the extra tax *could* be cut again at the end of the period: if the service improvement had not been made, the government or opposition party might argue that it were not worth paying. But this would not be the earmarking pledge made at the outset.

Specifying the pledge in terms of a particular, and measurable, improvement in the public service is crucial to this kind of earmarking. It makes it more than just a typical political promise to 'raise spending'. Members of the public are not interested in spending levels per se: what they want to know is whether the public services are improving or not. This is what the pledge specifies.

Of course, spending levels are also relevant. The public will certainly want to be sure that the additional revenue is genuinely going on the area of spending the government has promised. The public service improvement is not in itself a guarantor of this, since one way of achieving it might be to cut some other area of the service without spending any extra money. The pledge will therefore need to be accompanied by a planned expenditure 'baseline', of the kind we have already discussed. The government's three-year spending plans should make plausible baselines possible. Even if the higher rate of tax is pledged for a longer period, the rate of spending, or spending growth, in the last year of the plan can be extended into the future to give a credible baseline figure. The public can then be assured that the revenues from the higher tax will constitute genuinely 'additional' spending.

Again, cynics will no doubt point out that a government could secretly adjust its spending plans downwards, allowing it to spend no more than it had already decided and effectively diverting the extra revenues to other areas of spending. But, as before, this is surely unlikely. In the first place, it is not unreasonable to assume that a government taking the risk of asking the public to pay more tax actually does want to improve the public service it says it does. But even if we cannot rely upon basic integrity, it is difficult to imagine a government getting away with this. If its baseline figures do not look plausible in the light of previous expenditure plans, this will be exposed by the media and opposition. And if this is insufficient incentive, the public service improvement pledge itself—along with effective scrutiny of the rest of the service—should act as a safeguard: if the money is diverted elsewhere, we would expect it to be very difficult for the government's targets to be achieved.

Public attitudes

Raising taxes is never easy. But would a tax and public service pledge of this kind make a tax rise more publicly acceptable than it would be without it? We sought to test this claim in the public opinion research conducted for the Commission by the Office for National Statistics.[15] We asked respondents if they would support a 1p or 2p increase in the basic rate of income tax, making clear how much this would cost the average taxpayer (£2.50 or £5 a week respectively). We asked first if they would support the increase for unspecified public spending, then if they would support it if the money was specifically set aside for education or for the NHS.

The results were very significant. Neither the 1p nor 2p increases for unspecified public spending got majority support: 40% supported a 1p increase (41% against), only a third a 2p increase (50% against). But support for the earmarked increases was substantial. Eighty per cent of respondents supported a 1p increase for health, and 71% a 2p increase.Sixty-eight per cent of respondents ten supported a 1p increase for education, 61% a 2p increase.

So it would appear that the 'tax and public service pledge' would have a very considerable impact on people's sense of connectedness to their taxes, making it considerably easier to win public support for a tax rise—should it be necessary—than an unspecified increase.

A government or party seeking public legitimacy for a tax rise of this kind might even make it the subject of a referendum. Many politicians and commentators do not believe opinion polls such as the one we conducted. So why not ask the people? Now that referendums are being used rather widely in British politics, this might just be the way to test whether the opinion surveys are indeed correct—whether the British public, as one might phrase it, are prepared to put their money where their mouths appear to be. For a government unsure of the popularity of such a measure, it would be a useful way of leaving the decision to the public itself.

Such referendums have indeed already been proposed by the Government—for local authorities rather than for itself.[16] We would support this. When local government wishes to raise council tax (or any other kind—see Chapter 9) in order to raise its spending (or sometimes, in order to spend the same amount, if the grant from central government is otherwise insufficient) it should also make a tax and public service pledge. That is, it should set out measurable improvements in local public services which the extra money will pay for, and subsequently bring in the Audit Commission (or the Office for Public Accountability we proposed in Chapter 7) to assure the public that the improvements have been made. A local referendum of precisely this kind has already been conducted in Milton Keynes. It is interesting to note that, offered lower, standstill and higher tax options, with their associated spending commitments, the citizens of Milton Keynes voted for higher council tax and higher spending to improve services.[17]

Tax and public service pledges will therefore be particularly appropriate for local government. But we should note that at central government level they should not be thought of as limited to income tax rises. In principle any rise in a tax rate not accompanied by an equivalent fall in another should be explicitly justified when introduced. As with the Chancellor's tobacco duty announcement, it would be highly appropriate if this were done by earmarking. But unlike the case of tobacco duty, this would best be done through the particular mechanism of a tax and public service pledge, where the additional revenues can be measured against specific and auditable commitments to improve the public service.[18]

The tax and public service pledge is therefore a way of linking a tax rise to a specific spending purpose. We believe it may prove particularly useful where there are strong pressures for greater public expenditure which can only be achieved if taxes are raised. But there is another, rather important, implication of this argument. This is that the need to say what tax changes are for should not just apply to new or higher ones. It should also apply when governments or political parties make promises to *cut* taxes. Here too they should specify the implications for public spending (or for other taxes). Cutting taxes always looks like a popular option; but politicians should not be allowed to get away with pretending to the public that it is a free lunch. They should be asked to specify which areas of public spending (or growth in spending) will be cut, or which other taxes will be raised. We might even describe this as a kind of 'reverse earmarking'. It would do much to improve the maturity of public debate.

£

A hypothecated health tax?

The tax and public service pledge earmarks an increase in tax to an improvement in a specific public service. But there is another, more radical alternative. This is to earmark the *whole* of a tax for the entire spending budget of that service. If the argument for earmarking is to make taxation more transparent to the public, it can be argued that this would be better achieved if the entire tax-spending relationship were brought out into the open. Why not define a specific tax (a slice of income tax, or VAT, for example) for a specific area of spending, and earmark it for the full spending amount?

While in principle any spending area could be considered for a fully earmarked tax of this kind, the obvious candidates today would be health or education, because of their political and public priority and the pressures in each to spend more. A fully earmarked health or education tax would then make it absolutely clear to the public what they were paying for the service; and even more importantly, how much extra they would have to pay if they wanted spending on it to be higher. Instead of being hidden away in the Treasury black box, the relationship between taxation and spending would be visible to all. Moreover, it would be visible not just in relation to the overall budget, but in its implications for each individual taxpayer. Taxpayers would be asked to face squarely the consequences of their own desires. If people wanted health or education spending to rise, they would have to pay for it.

Such a tax would have to be strictly hypothecated, with no flexibility allowed. If the spending could be topped up from general revenues, there would be little point to it. The transparency would be lost: spending could vary independently of the tax, and the tax rate faced by taxpayers would no longer reflect the spending need. (As we argued earlier, flexibility is only suitable for incentive-based taxes which have independent justification.)

At first sight it might appear that the arguments for a fully hypothecated tax of this sort would simply mirror those for less strict forms of earmarking—perhaps applying even more strongly. But in practice full hypothecation is rather complex, and it raises new issues altogether. Neither its transparency, nor its effect on public support for higher taxes, are self-evident. It will therefore be helpful if we set out the arguments for and against, first in general and then in respect of the specific proposal for a health tax, before reaching our conclusions.

The principle of full hypothecation

For advocates of a fully earmarked tax, the immediate and primary aim is transparency. By having a significant proportion of their tax bill tied to a (popular) public service, citizens would be able to see exactly where a significant proportion of their taxes was being spent. This, it is argued, would be likely to increase their sense of 'connection' to the tax system and their confidence in its effective use. Their basic confidence in government would rise.

But the argument for hypothecation in practice goes beyond this. Advocates claim that transparency will help to loosen 'tax resistance': that it will make it easier for governments to seek—and to receive public support for—higher taxes to pay for higher spending. The argument points to the evidence from public attitude research. A majority of people, as our own survey reported above indicates, would be willing to pay more tax for higher spending on health or education. But—as our discussion groups have shown—they do not trust governments sufficiently to spend the money where they want it to go. But if lack of trust is the primary source of 'tax resistance' in these areas, it is argued, hypothecation may be a way of overcoming it. If a more direct relationship were established between what people paid and the service government provided, the public's latent willingness to pay more tax might be released. Much more strongly than a simple political pledge, hypothecation would guarantee to the public that the higher sums they were being asked to contribute were genuinely being spent where they wanted them.

But there is another side to this argument. It is quite possible, critics agree, that the public would be willing to pay more for a tax hypothecated to health or education. But this does not mean that they would be willing to pay more tax overall. It would simply expose the rest of the government's budget to greater downward pressure. Now that they could see exactly how much of their tax was being spent on the popular services, it would also show them what was going on the less popular ones—social security, overseas aid, defence, and so on. Yes, the public might be happy to pay more for the hypothecated services, but this would then simply encourage them to demand that the government spend less on the rest. Far from leading to a higher overall willingness to pay tax, hypothecation could lead to the opposite result altogether: greater tax resistance to the rest of public spending. An unscrupulous political party could easily engage in populist politics to exploit this, promising to cut social security, say, to pay for greater expenditure on health. Such behaviour, after all, has not been unknown.

The force of this argument cannot be that it would be better if the public did not know how much was being spent in areas they did not particularly like. Such an argument is not available here: it would run counter to the whole project of 'connecting' people to their taxes. We have already argued that better information is an important part of increasing the trust or confidence of citizens in government. We believe strongly that governments must be able to explain and defend all their expenditure, even that which may appear to be unpopular. (Indeed, we suspect that better public information may actually decrease the unpopularity of certain areas of spending rather than increase it.) If hypothecation increases public understanding about expenditure as well as taxation this must be considered a good.

The argument here, rather, concerns the relationship between the spending area and the tax. As we shall explain below, the usual candidate for a hypothecated health or education tax is income tax. This is partly because it is one of the most 'buoyant' taxes: that is, its revenues naturally rise faster than economic growth. But then, critics argue, there is something very odd about earmarking the most buoyant tax for the most popular area of spending. One of the only two areas of spending for which it might have been possible to ask the public to pay higher taxes (health or education) is the one which gains the benefit of naturally rising revenues, while those areas of spending which are less immediately popular are funded out of revenues which do not naturally rise in this way. Surely it should be the other way round?

There is another argument, moreover, which can be used against mainstream earmarking of this kind. Noting how those on the political right have wished to use earmarked taxes as a way of implementing the 'benefit principle' of taxation, in which taxes are paid solely by the beneficiaries of the associated spending, critics argue that earmarking may encourage people to feel that the tax is a personal payment for the public service. In turn they may then come to believe that they should receive benefits in proportion: that high earners paying more tax should receive a better quality service than poorer people paying less (or indeed no) tax. Indeed, those who do not use the public service—who have no children, for example, or who educate them privately, or who use private health insurance—may claim the right to opt out of the tax altogether. If an earmarked tax comes to be seen in this way, as effectively a form of user charge, a fundamental principle of a tax system based on citizenship would be undermined.

An NHS tax

The area of spending most commonly seen as the principal candidate for a hypothecated tax today is health.[19] There are strong reasons for this. Health is a universal need, so the basis of the health service in the concept of citizenship is easily understood. Public support for a health service which provides free care to all at the point of need, funded out of taxation, is very substantial.[20]

Perhaps even more importantly, there are very strong pressures in the health field for increases in public spending. Health care is a 'superior good'—as incomes rise, demand appears to rise even faster. Over the next five decades an ageing population will place considerably greater demands upon the service. At the same time, rapid advances in new forms of treatment—in both drugs and technology—constantly raise expectations of what can and should be offered. New treatments may not always be more expensive than those they replace (for example, new types of surgery may reduce the length of time patients spend in hospital). But where altogether new kinds of drugs and techniques become available—the case of Viagra being one now famous kind of example, and infertility treatments another—the pressure to increase spending becomes ever more acute. Since the establishment of the NHS, real spending has risen on average by 3.4% per year. Under the Government's plans it is now rising by 6.1% a year for four years—but the 'aspiration' announced by the Prime Minister in January 2000 to match the average rate of health spending in the rest of the EU implies an annual increase in spending of around 8.5%.[21]

Many of these argument, however, also apply to other areas of spending. Education is also a basic need and a superior good, and in the new so-called 'knowledge-based' economy it is becoming ever more important in the labour market. The numbers of people seeking higher education is continuing to rise, putting tremendous pressure on university funding. Education spending in the UK is also below the OECD average.[22] Like health, universal free education has wider public support; there is no guarantee that health spending will always be seen as having the greater priority. The choice of health for hypothecation, it is argued, privileges one area of spending which is indeed very important, but which should not automatically be regarded as having a higher priority than others. If hypothecation makes it easier to raise taxes, there may be other areas of spending—even beyond education, such as measures to tackle poverty—which need more funding at least as much.

We shall return to these arguments later. But since it is important to have a real tax in mind when discussing the arguments for and against, for now we shall use the health tax as our exemplar. In fact 'health tax' may be the wrong term. Public spending contributing to improved health occurs across a range of government departments and local authority services—social services, environment, anti-poverty programmes and so on. What is meant here is really an 'NHS tax', funding only those health-related expenditures carried out by the NHS. (We shall use both terms below for simplicity.)

How would a hypothecated health tax work? In principle any tax which raised sufficient funds could be earmarked. For example, with receipts of £54 billion, VAT actually yields almost exactly the sum which the Government intends to spend annually on the NHS over the next few years. But VAT would in practice be a rather bad tax to earmark for health. It is regressive, taking a much higher proportion of income from the poor than from the rich. So as health spending grew, and if VAT rates were required to rise faster than they otherwise would, those on lower incomes would find themselves contributing proportionately more to the total tax revenue than high earners. This would be widely and rightly perceived as unfair.

The obvious tax to use, in fact, is income tax. Income tax is progressive. It is also highly buoyant, meaning that, in times of economic growth, its revenues rise faster than national income. (Income tax revenues are determined both by the level of employment and by earnings growth.) This makes it particularly suitable for an area of spending which is also rising faster than national income—it means that the *rates* of tax would actually not have to rise as fast as spending.

At present income tax raises around £100 billion per annum. Spending on the NHS is around £50 billion. So to create a UK-wide hypothecated health tax, at present income tax would be cut more or less in half. (We shall consider the implications for devolution of a UK-wide tax below.) One half would be labelled as the NHS Tax, with the other half perhaps now called General Income Tax. To ensure that the hypothecation was properly trans-parent, they would be listed separately on payslips. Assuming, at least initially, that the present structure of income tax were maintained, this would mean that each of the two new taxes would at the outset levy 5% (rather than 10% as now) on the first £1520 of taxable income, 11% (rather than 22%) up to the higher rate threshold of £28,400, and 20% (against 40%) thereafter.

Creating a health tax would not be as simple as this, however. In the first place, *actual* government receipts and expenditures never conform to their planned amounts. There are too many uncertainties in revenue projections and unforeseen issues in spending outcomes. So while the government can set the planned spending total and the level of the NHS tax to match one another, considerable leeway will in practice need to be allowed. (It would in fact be quite a coincidence if the NHS tax raised just the right amount of revenue for any given year's health spending!) Perhaps more importantly, there is the problem of the economic cycle. Income tax is buoyant in times of economic growth, but in recession receipts decline. Most governments would not want health spending to be automatically cut in a recession simply because tax receipts had fallen. So if the tax were set to match antici-pated spending its rates would have to go up and down quite considerably over an economic cycle. Not only would this be rather disruptive to the taxpayer, it would also be economically destabilising, with taxes rising in recession and falling in boom—the exact opposite of the desirable effect.

An alternative arrangement, therefore, would be for the tax rate to be set not at the level required to finance the next year's spending, but at a level which would fund the planned rate of spending throughout a forecasting period, perhaps even an economic cycle. An NHS Fund would need to be created. Tax receipts would go into the Fund and the Fund would then finance the NHS. The Fund would build up surpluses during periods of above trend economic growth, and would use these surpluses, or borrow in anticipation of them, when the economy turned down and receipts declined. In this way the Fund would smooth out the natural fluctuations in revenues from the tax, giving the NHS a predictable stream of income over a period of several years. The Fund might even be constituted at arm's length from the Treasury, with an inde-pendent NHS Fund Analyst (rather like the Government Actuary who advises on the National Insurance Fund) appointed to ensure that projected receipts were sufficient to fund planned spending.

With a hypothecated NHS tax of this kind, its advocates argue, a govern-ment could raise public spending faster than if health were simply funded out of general taxation. The greater transparency of a hypothecated tax, attached to the assumed public desire to see higher spending, would enable the NHS tax to be raised in a way which governments may well feel is impossible for general taxation (even with a tax and public service pledge).

Now of course it may be possible to fund significant increases in health spending without raising taxes. The government's Comprehensive Spending Review in 2000 indeed promises just this: a 6.1% annual rise in spending for four years without any projected increase in tax.[23] But this does not itself make hypothecation redundant. In the first place, such a rise has required other areas of spending to be held lower than they would otherwise have been. It is true that buoyant government revenues mean that several other areas (including education, law and order and transport) have in fact been allocated substantial rises of their own as well. But these rises, it is argued, are less than would have been available if health spending had been separately financed and its hypothecated tax increased. (A 6.1% annual increase in health spending, while total current spending is rising by 2.5%, inevitably means that other public services cannot rise by as much.) In this sense, though 'tax resistance' may not at present be constraining *health* spending, it cannot help but squeeze other budgets. In these circumstances, it is argued, a hypothecated health tax would allow other areas of spending to rise even if health spending were kept at the same level of growth as presently. By loosening tax resistance, utilising the public's willingness to pay more for health, more general tax revenues would become available for education, law and order, transport and other needs.

Let us in fact imagine that the 6.1% annual increase in spending now planned by the Government were to be financed through an NHS tax. Strict hypothecation means that the whole of the increase would have to come from the tax. The natural buoyancy of income tax receipts over the next few years is projected to bring in around 60% of the extra required without a change in tax rates. But even after this an average increase of around 0.75p in the pound on the standard rate of the NHS tax each year would still be needed.[24] Beyond this period, or if such a tax were introduced after it, the level of the health tax would depend on the desired level of health spending and the projected revenues from income tax. So long as health spending rose faster than income tax revenues, the health tax would be required to rise.

Hypothecation in practice

But this is then where the effects of an NHS tax become rather more complicated than they might at first appear. If a health tax were introduced in present circumstances, at a time when the Government has flourishing tax revenues, the public might ask why their taxes had to rise. The Government's projections suggest, in fact, that over the next three years it can finance the planned increase in health spending, plus additional spending in education and other areas, without raising taxes. Yet with a hypothecated health tax the rise in health spending would enforce a rise in the tax rate.

What would then happen? Three alternatives are possible. One is that the Government would tell the public that the rise in the NHS tax was required to pay for the rise in health spending, and point out that it left larger sums available for education, transport, the eradication of child poverty and other priorities. The overall share of tax in GDP would rise, with higher public spending than currently planned in non-health areas. A second possibility is that the Government would simply reduce the remaining General Income Tax to compensate for the rise in health tax, thereby leaving total income tax unchanged. This might look slightly odd, since in one sense it would rather negate the point of having the tax; but it would be perfectly possible (and politically no doubt quite attractive). In this case the health tax would not be a mechanism for loosening tax resistance. It would not change the overall share of tax in GDP or total public spending, either for health or other areas; its only effect would be greater transparency. A third option would be for something in between: a partial but not full compensation for the rise in health tax through tax cuts elsewhere.

The possibility that a hypothecated NHS tax might *not* be used to raise taxes overall suggests, perhaps unsurprisingly, that it would be more valuable in less favourable economic times, when higher spending cannot be funded simply out of buoyant revenues. In these circumstances, if the public were prepared to see a rise in the tax, it might permit higher spending in a way which would otherwise not be possible.

But an economic downturn raises the possibility of another complication. One of the consequences of a recession might be to alter projections of the tax yield, making future revenues look insufficient in relation to planned spending. In these circumstances the government would be forced either to borrow more or to raise the tax rate. Yet raising taxes in recession is economically highly undesirable. Indeed, it is quite possible that alterations of forecast income might require the health tax to rise even when the NHS Fund was in surplus. This would be consistent with the principle of a fully-hypothecated Fund; but it might prove politically rather difficult. It might not be easy for ministers to explain to the public why their taxes had to rise when the NHS Fund had more than enough for current spending needs. Even more importantly, it might undermine the very transparency which hypothecation was intended to create. Once current spending and current taxation diverged in this way, the clear relationship between them intended by earmarking would start to become clouded.

Obviously, careful management of the NHS Fund would attempt to avoid this. But opponents of earmarking fear that the transparency of hypothecation would not survive a severe economic shock. In a recession the NHS Fund could of course borrow to make up for the loss of tax revenue. (Health spending could also be cut: there is nothing in the principle of hypothecation which demands that spending is always maintained, whatever the circumstances.) But any borrowing would have to be repaid in a subsequent economic upswing. The risk, it is argued, is that this would simply not happen. It would require the health tax to rise without additional current spending, simply to pay for past spending. Even though this is implicit in the whole principle of earmarking, governments, it is warned, will not want to do it. In practice they are more likely to allow the debt to accumulate, and eventually to write it off. This is, after all, precisely what happened to the old nationalised industries, which were also meant to break even, but which, when they did not, simply built up debts which were eventually written off. If this happened to the NHS Fund, the principle of hypothecation would be broken. Effectively, health spending would no longer simply be funded by the health tax; general revenues would ultimately come to be used as well.

For proponents of hypothecation, however, this is not properly an argument against. There is, to be sure, nothing to stop a government breaking the principle of hypothecation if it wishes to do so. But this cannot then be held against the principle, only against that government. In any case, it is not in fact necessary for any debt built up by the NHS Fund to be repaid immediately in full. There is no reason why the Fund should not operate with the same rules on borrowing as the rest of the Treasury. That is, it could be allocated a proportion of the government's total borrowing requirement. It could then be required, not to pay off its entire debt, but only to service it, in proportion to the government's total debt. It is true that this would mean that the NHS tax would almost always—throughout the economic cycle—be higher than required for current health spending. But just as the rest of the government's borrowing is currently an accepted feature of the public accounts, so it could be for the NHS Fund. Opponents of the health tax fear that any divergence between current taxation and current spending would make the system less rather than more transparent than at present. But advocates claim that the basic relationship—that the tax pays for the spending—would remain valid and clear.

A further case can be made against the hypothecated tax. It is the basic objection made at the very start of the chapter, that hypothecated taxes are less flexible than general taxes. Because it must take all its revenues from just one source (in fact, half of one source), the NHS Fund cannot take advantage of the buoyancy of the whole system. As we have seen, over the next few years the projected increase in total tax revenues is in fact sufficient to fund the whole of the Government's planned increases in health spending. This is why the Government need not raise taxes in its current plans. But by limiting health spending to just the one tax, hypothecation forces the tax rate to rise. If revenues from some other tax happen to be high in one year, these can't be used to fund health spending: any increase in spending must come from the hypothecated tax. If it seems politically easier to raise some other tax, this won't do: such an increase can go to fund other areas of spending, but not health.

One way of getting round this inflexibility might be to hypothecate not just part of income tax but some other taxes to the NHS Fund. Obvious possibilities would be alcohol and tobacco duties, where the earmarking would have an incentive-based logic. This would increase the flexibility of the Fund somewhat: now three different taxes could be raised and their buoyancy used to fund health spending. In principle, part of other taxes might be earmarked as well: perhaps a part of corporation tax, since the NHS keeps employees healthy; perhaps part of petrol duty, since motor vehicles cause pollution. But there is evidently a limit to this process: too many taxes or part-taxes earmarked for health would simply get us full circle back to a general tax pooling system. In the end it has to be accepted that funding health spending from a hypothecated tax simply would be less flexible than from general taxation. But to advocates of full hypothection this is an acceptable price to pay. The important principle is transparency, since it is this which will achieve the greater sense of 'connection' between citizens and their taxes—and from this the possibility that it would be easier to get taxpayers to pay for spending increases.

One final issue needs to be considered. We have so far assumed that an NHS tax would be UK-wide, since income tax is levied on a UK-national basis. But this cannot be taken for granted, since health spending is a devolved matter, the responsibility of the Scottish Parliament and the Wales and Northern Ireland Assemblies. If the tax were UK-wide, this would effectively fix spending levels, removing the power of the devolved institutions to determine their own health spending. On the other hand if the NHS tax were separately levied in Scotland, Wales and Northern Ireland—or if the devolved institutions were given the option of either having or not having a hypothecated tax—this would represent a fundamental constitutional change, with a considerable tax power being devolved. It would not be possible for the devolved institutions to receive their own allocation from a UK NHS tax and then add to it (or subtract from it) from general funds, since this would undermine the fully hypothecated (and therefore transparent) character of the proposed tax. The Scottish Parliament could decide to use its 'Variable Rate'—the power it has been granted under the Scotland Act to vary the basic rate of income tax—to raise or lower the NHS tax. But even if this were possible it would still lose a degree of autonomy, since at present it can vary health spending without any use of the Variable Rate. This option is not available at all to the Wales and Northern Ireland Assemblies, which do not have a tax-varying power.

The Commission acknowledges that the devolution of health spending when the determination of income tax is a UK-wide matter complicates the proposal for a hypothecated NHS tax. It would seem, certainly in Wales and Northern Ireland, that either the principle of devolved health spending or that of a single UK structure of tax would have to be compromised, or a tax-varying power would need to be granted to these institutions as well as to the Scottish Parliament. (We discuss this further, in fact, in the next chapter.) It was not within the Commission's remit to investigate these options further. However we recognise that resolving them would be a precondition for the introduction of such a tax in the UK at the present time.

Conclusion

The proposal for a fully hypothecated tax—whether for health or some other spending area—is not, therefore, a straightforward one. There are at least five competing arguments to be considered. First, there is one of principle. Does full hypothecation make people feel more 'connected' as citizens to taxes and public spending? Or will it encourage a 'consumer' attitude that taxes are really user charges, from which non-users have a right to opt out? Second, there is an argument about spending priorities. Does hypothecation of a buoyant tax for a popular service unbalance the relative priorities of differ-ent areas of spending and the funds available to them? Or, by loosening tax resistance, will it release more funds for spending in all areas?

Third, there is an argument over transparency itself. Will hypothecation make it easier for people to see where their taxes are going? Or will the complexity of the mechanisms required to smooth tax revenues over an economic cycle—and the risk of governments reneging on the strict hypoth-ecation principle—actually make the relationship more opaque? Is full hypothecation necessary for transparency, or would earmarking of an increase in tax do just as well? In turn this raises an argument over the need. If one aim is to win public support for higher spending, cannot the tax and public service pledge achieve this just as well? Last, there is the argument about flexibility. Do the advantages of the closer tax-spending relationship outweigh the loss of flexibility in how spending can be funded?

The Commission considered these arguments at length. It acknowledges the strength of the case on both sides. But after due deliberation a majority of the members of the Commission believe that the benefits of a fully hypothe-cated tax outweigh its disadvantages and possible risks. Such a tax would, it is felt, make a significant contribution to making people feel more 'connected' to the tax system. Given the public attitudes we have surveyed, and the importance the Commission places on this goal, the majority view is that a fully hypothecated tax would be a valuable and feasible reform. A minority of the Commission members disagreed, believing that such a tax would not achieve the benefits claimed, and might even prove damaging, both to the public's sense of connectedness and to wider values of citizenship.*

The majority view of the Commission is therefore to recommend the introduction of a fully hypothecated tax. However we acknowledge that there will need to be considerable public debate about this before it would be politically feasible to implement the change. In particular our recommendation is conditional on the practical and constitutional issues we have raised being satisfactorily resolved. (This would be a highly suitable subject for examination by the Royal Commission on Taxation we proposed in the last chapter.) We hope that our recommendation—and our discussion of the issues—will help to stimulate this debate.

The preference of a majority of the Commission members is for a hypothecated NHS tax. This is partly because of expected demands on the health budget; and partly because the central role played by local authorities in allocating education spending would make an education tax much more complicated to administer. Since almost everyone uses the NHS, the idea that people not using the service could 'opt out' would be less likely to gain a foothold than for an education tax.

A health tax is therefore, on balance, our preference, but we accept that the spending area for a fully hypothecated tax should also be part of the debate we are calling for; and that the decision should rest ultimately on both practical feasibility and public opinion. Since it would be difficult anyway to implement full hypothecation before the second half of the current spending round, this would be an appropriate time in which to judge the relative merits and needs of the two priority spending areas.

In recommending a hypothecated NHS tax in these terms, the Commission is extremely alert to the danger that this could be misrepresented as a kind of user charge on the benefit principle of taxation. We are insistent that it should be articulated, as with all our proposals, as part of the strong conception of citizenship to which we are committed. This is how we believe the vast majority of people in the United Kingdom will understand it. A hypothecated tax would pay for public services which benefit everyone in society. The health and education services, largely free at the point of use, represent social investments in a civilised society. The tax which pays for them is too. Its aim is to connect people better to this basic principle of citizenship.

---

* These included Fran Bennett, Nick Monck and Holly Sutherland.

9 | The devolution of taxation

In the last two chapters we have proposed two different sets of reforms which might help people feel more 'connected' to their taxes and to public spending. In this chapter we examine a third kind of reform which we believe can also contribute to this objective: the devolution of taxation powers to levels of government beneath that of the nation state. At the same time we shall examine the arguments for the relocation of taxation *upwards*: from the nation state to the European Union level.

£

The fiscal constitution

As we argued in Chapter 4, one of the fundamental elements of our strong conception of citizenship is an active democracy. In the last two chapters we have argued about how reforms to the system of tax and public spending could help to make government more democratically accountable. In doing so we have referred up to now almost entirely to the national (UK) level. But democracy occurs at a variety of levels. In a wider sense, we are citizens not just of the nation state, but in each geographical area where there is an elected government.

Decentralisation and 'connectedness'

In this respect the constitution of the United Kingdom has been through a fundamental change since 1997. New elected governments have been established in Scotland, Wales, Northern Ireland and London, creating in these areas a more devolved, and more richly textured, democracy. In certain parts of England, passionate arguments are taking place about whether elected governments should also be created at the regional level. Local government, which has been democratically constituted for over a hundred years, is also undergoing a period of intense reform, with changes to both the structures and powers of local authorities.

At each of these levels governments are responsible for providing public services, and for allocating public revenues to them. The Scottish Parliament and the Wales and Northern Ireland Assemblies indeed have overall responsibility for almost all public services—in education, health, social services, economic development, agriculture, environment, planning, housing, transport, culture and so on. (The Northern Ireland Assembly has slightly fewer responsibilities than the Welsh Assembly and Scottish Parliament.) With the exception of health and agriculture, many of these services are actually provided, throughout the UK, by local government. Local councils also provide many other services such as refuse collection and street cleaning, leisure facilities and amenities, libraries and parks.

This devolution of government is very important both to democracy and to the provision of public services. Centralised government is almost inevitably more remote government. It is hard for most people actively to participate in the national democratic process; the greater the distance, the larger the number of people whose interests must be served, the less open it seems to influence by the ordinary citizen. Survey evidence suggests that most people identify quite strongly with their local community and take an interest in local affairs—around three in four adults, for example, read local newspapers.[1] Decentralised democracy allows more people to participate, both in general political debate and in the formal institutions of elected government itself. It is therefore an important arena for the development of an active citizenship.

At the same time there is good reason to think that decentralised government is in general more likely to deliver services responsive to local needs and adapted for local circumstances. Decentralisation tends to foster experimentation and innovation in service delivery. It allows the development of diverse models of good practice—which through learning and imitation can then lead to improvement elsewhere as well.

In principle, therefore, decentralised government should lead to higher levels of 'connection' between the public and government. Yet on at least one measure the evidence in the UK is in fact of very low levels of participation. Turnouts in local elections average under 30%, with some areas in recent years recording much lower rates. Even the election for the London mayor and Assembly in 2000, which was accompanied by high levels of publicity, attracted only 34% of voters to participate. Turnout in the first elections for the Welsh Assembly in 1999 was just 48%. Only the Scottish Parliament (58%) and Northern Ireland Assembly (70%) saw turnout above 50%. These figures compare poorly with comparable elections in the rest of Europe, where turnouts in local and provincial or state elections regularly exceed 70%.[2] Turnouts are not the only measure of democratic health, but they are surely an important one; and they suggest that, even more than at a UK national scale, at a sub-UK-national[3] level democratic citizenship is in rather poor condition.

There are obviously a number of reasons for these low turnouts. But many people have argued that one of them is the lack of power held by local and devolved government—with the notable (and given the turnout rates, significant) exception of the Scottish Parliament. Whereas the Scottish Parliament—and to a lesser degree, the Northern Ireland Assembly—have primary legislative power, the Welsh Assembly has control only over secondary legislation. The powers of the elected London mayor and Assembly are extremely limited, being concerned largely with strategic planning and coordination. Meanwhile local government in the UK has no formal constitutional status at all—its duties and powers are prescribed by Parliament in statute and central government keeps a very close watch on its activities. Over the last twenty years the capacity of local authorities to determine their own affairs has been considerably reduced. Some service areas have been substantially or completely removed—much council housing, virtually all higher and further education, the careers service, waste regulation, for example—while others are now subjected to much greater central government control and direction.[4]

Taxation and the devolved institutions

But the power that concerns us here is that of taxation. One of the features of the limited set of powers held by each of the levels of sub-UK-national government where turnouts have been low is an inability to determine, or severe constraint on determining, its own level of spending.

The Scottish Parliament does have a power of taxation. Although the vast bulk (indeed, at the present time, the entirety) of the Scottish budget is decided by central government in London, the Scottish Parliament may vary this if it so chooses through its own tax power. This was specifically decided by the Scottish people in a second question (won by 63.5% to 36.5%) in the referendum which decided on devolution in September 1997.

The mechanism for this is the so-called 'Scottish Variable Rate'. The terms of the 1998 Scotland Act give the Scottish Parliament the power to vary the basic rate of income tax in Scotland by plus or minus 3p in the pound. 3p is equivalent to around £690m, or 4%, of a total Scotland budget (in 2000-01) of £16.7bn. The Scottish Variable Rate is thus an important symbol of self-determination. It enables the Scottish Parliament to decide (within the limits of the allowed variation in income tax) the total level of public spending enjoyed by, and the overall level of taxation levied on, the Scottish people. This power of taxation has not yet been used (the Labour-Liberal Democrat administration elected in 1999 declared that it would not seek any change in tax in its first term of office); but it is in principle a significant instrument of Scottish governance—and potentially a major focus for democratic debate about political choices. Indeed, it already has been the focus of such debate: in the first elections to the Scottish Parliament in 1999 the Scottish National Party proposed to raise the basic rate of income tax by 1p to fund higher social spending. (Some commentators argued that this policy contributed to the party's defeat.[5])

The Scottish Parliament's legislative powers are therefore backed by the power of taxation. But this is not true of either the Wales or the Northern Ireland Assembly. These Assemblies, and their governments, cannot raise their own funds. They are wholly dependent on the amount determined by the UK Parliament and government as a whole at Westminster.[6] Though they can choose (by and large[7]) how to allocate their grant *between* different areas of public spending, if they feel the total is too much or too little they can do nothing to change it.

The same is not quite true of the Greater London Assembly and the elected London mayor. Here there is a power of taxation: the mayor (subject to the approval of the Assembly) can levy road congestion and workplace parking charges. But this is not a general tax power: the revenues raised have to be earmarked for transport spending. For all other areas of spending, there is again complete dependence on the grant from central government.

These differences in tax-raising powers reflect differences in the constitutional position of the different devolved bodies. In general, constitutional questions are beyond the purview of the Commission. Nevertheless, on principles of citizenship the lack of tax-raising powers of the devolved Assemblies does look anomalous. After all, the levels of government beneath them, local authorities and even parish councils, have such powers. The devolved bodies are elected by citizens, and provide or are responsible for public services; yet they cannot determine their overall level of expenditure. This represents, it seems to us, an imbalance between the political and what we might call the 'fiscal' constitution.

The financing of local government

The situation in local government is more complex. Local authorities do have a taxing power: they levy Council Tax, based on the value of local domestic properties. But this covers only around 25% of local authority finance. The remaining 75% comes from central government. The bulk of this is given in the form of Revenue Support Grant, calculated on the basis of an annual 'Standard Spending Assessment' or SSA. Part is returned to local authorities from the National Non-Domestic Rate (NNDR) levied on business properties. These systems are explained more fully in Box 9.1.

Box 9.1: Local government finance

Except in Northern Ireland (which retains a system of rates), around a quarter of local author-ity current revenue comes from the **Council Tax***, levied by local authorities on domestic property. Properties are banded according to an assessment of their market value (as at 1 April 1991), with councils individually determining the rate levels levied on these bands. The ratio of tax rates between the bands is fixed, expressed in terms of their relationship to band D. (The bands and ratios are set out in Table 9.1 below.) Single people get a discount of 25%, with a number of other reliefs and exemptions for other categories. A special means-tested Council Tax Benefit provides support to those on low incomes. Council tax is projected to raise around £12.8 billion in 1999-00.*

Other than council tax, the two main sources of local government finance for current spend-ing are the Revenue Support Grant and the National Non-Domestic Rate.

Around 45% of local authority revenue income comes from central government. Most of this is in the form of **Revenue Support Grant** *(RSG). This is calculated in England on the basis of a Standard Spending Assessment or SSA. The SSA is a measure of each local authority's 'need to spend', as decided by central government. The RSG takes account both of the 'needs' of the author-ity (such as the number of elderly people and school-age children resident in its area) and its 'taxable capacity'—how much it can raise from council tax. Councils with higher SSAs receive a bigger Revenue Support Grant per head of population than those with lower. By this means the Grant 'equalises' the resources available to each authority. The principle is that, if each authority spends at the level of its SSA, it can provide exactly the same level of services at the same level of council tax. The process of determining SSAs is in practice very complex and subject to much dispute in the annual negotiations between the Department of the Environment, Transport and the Regions and local authorities. Similar systems, with different names, operate in Scotland and Wales, where grants are determined by the Scottish Parliament and Welsh Assembly. A different system (the General Exchequer Grant) operates in Northern Ireland, where local authorities are smaller and have fewer responsibilities.*

Although based on an assessment of various kinds of spending needs, the Revenue Support Grant is a block grant which local authorities can allocate to different areas of spending as they choose. However in some fields, such as police, community care and under 5s education, **special 'ring-fenced' grants** *are given which can only be spent for specific purposes. These* *make up around 9% of central government grant.*

*A further 22% of local authority revenue income is raised from the **National Non-Domestic Rate** (NNDR), sometimes known as the Uniform Business Rate. The NNDR was established in 1990, replacing the former system of business rates set by local government. The NNDR is a tax levied on the rateable value of business properties. It is set by central government at a uniform level throughout the country, so every business pays at the same rate whatever its location. Collected from businesses by local authorities, the tax is pooled by central government and then redistributed to local councils on an equal per capita basis. The NNDR is increased every year in line with inflation.*

*Local authorities also levy various **fees and charges** for certain services, such as libraries, car parking and waste collection. Together with sales of assets these make up around 11% of total local authority income.*

*The Transport Act 2000 gives local authorities a further tax power, allowing them to levy **road congestion and workplace carparking charges**, with the revenues earmarked for local transport spending.*

In addition local authorities' capital spending is financed from a variety of sources: own revenue, capital receipts, government grants and borrowing.

There is good reason for part of local authority finance to come from central government. Local government is not independently constituted. Many of the services which local authorities provide and fund are deeply affected by national government policy and political debate—notably education, police and social services, but also in other areas such as town and country planning, environmental health and waste recycling. Accordingly, over recent years central government has increasingly laid down minimum service standards which local authorities must reach, and other policy regulations and guidelines which constrain and direct their work. In these circumstances it is inevitable that a significant part of local government finance should come direct from central government.

Central government grant moreover plays an important role—for the devolved institutions as well as for local authorities—in the geographical redistribution of resources. In any political jurisdiction, full financial autonomy would mean that only revenues drawn from that area could be spent in it. This would benefit richer areas, but severely disadvantage poorer ones: those with the most needs would have the least resources. One of the functions of UK-wide national government is therefore to redistribute tax revenues across the country, taking resources from richer areas and households to spend on poorer ones. Scotland, Wales and Northern Ireland all benefit very substantially from this redistribution,[8] as do poorer local authorities in inner city and other disadvantaged areas. In principle (there is certainly room for dispute about who in fact should benefit and by how much) this is entirely as it should be, and represents an important justification for retaining a system of significant central government grants.

Yet at the same time there is a tension between these roles of central government and the view of local authorities as a forum for local democratic choice. This tension is evident in public debate. On the one hand, many politicians and commentators (and sometimes the public) profess a wish to see local democracy enhanced and councils given more freedom to 'do things differently'. Local government has indeed been given (in the Local Government Act 2000) a new general power to promote the social, economic and environmental well-being of its area, so increasing its autonomy and power to innovate. Yet at the same time the same politicians and media (and public) frequently complain when service standards are different in different areas. In key fields (such as education and social services) there is an insistent demand for national direction to guarantee uniform standards—against the principle of local variation.

This tension between local autonomy and national accountability lies at the heart of a genuine constitutional debate about the role of local government. In principle it needs to be resolved before an appropriate system of taxation can be agreed.[9] Yet in practice almost any acknowledgement of the democratic role of local government—a role which on citizenship grounds we believe to be vitally important—lends itself to dissatisfaction with present arrangements.

The most obvious cause of such dissatisfaction lies in the size of the central grant relative to locally raised revenue. In fact the proportion of its own finance raised by local government has fallen by more than half over the last ten years. In 1989-90 local taxation raised around 55% of the cost of local services. The proportion is now less than in most other European countries (see Figure 9.1). This decline has occurred as a result of two reforms introduced by the Conservative administration in the 1990s. The first was the abolition of the old domestic rates and their replacement (after the short interregnum in 1990-93 of the 'community charge' or poll tax, levied on individuals) by council tax. The second—and in numerical terms more

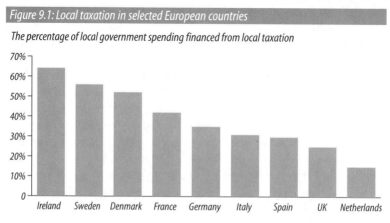

Figure 9.1: Local taxation in selected European countries

The percentage of local government spending financed from local taxation

[Source: Congress of Local and Regional Authorities of Europe]

important—was the effective 'nationalisation' of business rates in 1990. This removed around a quarter of local authority finance from local control.

At the same time a third Conservative reform, 'capping', further limited the ability of local authorities to raise their own revenue. Under capping legislation, central government in the 1980s and 1990s was able to determine the total budget set by individual local authorities where it claimed they were 'overspending'. Capping in effect limited councils' financial autonomy: elected local authorities were not able to decide their own budgets. Though it has not yet used it, the present Labour government has retained a 'reserve power' to cap local authority spending.

The problem of council tax

Capping clearly constrains local authorities' powers of taxation. But even aside from this, the small proportion of local authority spending raised by council tax has a crucial bearing on local councils' financial autonomy.

Within capping limits, a local authority can raise council tax if it wishes to increase its expenditure. But it has to do so in percentage terms by much more than the rise in spending. Since council tax finances only 25% of total expenditure, a rise in the total of, say, 5% requires a rise in council tax of 20%. This is known as the 'gearing ratio'. For poorer local authorities, whose central grant funding makes up an even larger proportion of total income, the required rise in tax is greater still. Thus a local authority such as Mole Valley in Surrey which has a large council tax base (being an area of high property prices) and a relatively low level of need (being relatively affluent) gets a small Revenue Support Grant, giving it a gearing ratio of only 1:2. By contrast a council such as Tower Hamlets in London, with a small council tax base and extensive needs, gets a large RSG and consequently has a gearing ratio of 9:1.[10] That is, for every 1% that Tower Hamlets Council might wish to raise its level of expenditure it would have to raise council tax by 9%.

As can immediately be seen, high gearing ratios distort the relationship between the council and its voters and taxpayers. They send out misleading 'price signals' about the cost of local spending choices. Even a small increase in expenditure requires a very large increase in taxation.

In fact the situation is worse than this. As the only source of income which local authorities can vary, council tax inevitably takes up all the slack when the level of central government grant is changed. Over the last decade the grant settlement for local authorities has frequently been very tight. Inevitably many councils have wished to maintain their levels of service even when their grant has been cut. They have been required to raise council tax to do so. In other cases councils have cut back their spending to match their grant: inevitably, the force of such cuts is taken by discretionary activities rather than statutory ones, so reducing local autonomy still further.

This effect is compounded by the nature of council tax itself. Council tax is not a buoyant tax: its revenue does not rise automatically with economic growth. Its rates therefore have to be adjusted every year in order simply to account for inflation. (Although house prices tend to rise with economic growth, the base for council tax is a historic valuation, not present property values. We discuss this further below.)

For all these reasons, council tax is an extremely opaque system of taxation. It is very difficult for taxpayers to see exactly what changes in council tax represent. A rise in council tax could be funding a genuine rise in expenditure—but if so the percentage increase will be much less than the percentage rise in tax. It could reflect a reduction in the grant from central government, with no change in expenditure. Or it could simply be an adjustment for inflation.

This situation is deeply unsatisfactory. It would seem almost inevitably to reduce the sense of 'connectedness' between local taxpayers and the local authority. It makes many local authorities more reluctant than they would otherwise be to change their total spending by varying local taxation—a legitimate (if always difficult) political choice which should on democratic principles be available to them. In general it makes the tax-public spending relationship far from transparent.

Some hint of the level of public misunderstanding in this area is indeed revealed in public attitude surveys. A study for the Department of the Environment, Transport and the Regions in 1999 suggested that over 80% of people thought that councils receive either equal amounts of money from council tax and central government, or more from council tax than from the government.[11] It should hardly be surprising then if people do not understand what changes in council tax mean for local services.

The democratic deficit

In the Commission's view, these arrangements, in both the devolved institutions and local government, create a serious democratic imbalance between the political constitution of the UK and what we might calls its 'fiscal constitution'. Key tiers of government do not have a tax-raising power at all. Local government does have such a power, but one which operates in a constrained and misleading way.

In the Commission's view this is not conducive to the effective realisation of citizenship. The power of taxation is an important element in accountable government. As a principle we believe it is wrong that an elected government responsible for spending money should not be at least partly responsible for raising it—and raising it in such a way that it is transparent to the voters and taxpayers what it is doing. We are by no means the first to believe this. The idea that the power to raise money and the power to spend it should be in the same hands was articulated as long ago as 1912 by the Primrose Committee examining the fiscal arrangements for Irish Home Rule. Over sixty years later it formed the basis of the conclusions of the Layfield Committee on Local Government Finance.[12] There are three main grounds for this view.

First, separating responsibility for spending and taxation almost inevitably leads to less responsible government. It allows politicians and governments at the sub-national level to blame their failings on the lack of money they have been given by central government. In turn it can lead devolved and local governments to become more like pressure groups seeking greater funds from the centre than bodies taking responsibility for their own decisions. In the devolved areas it can even tend to undermine the constitutional settlement, encouraging opposition parties, particularly nationalist ones, to claim that power is really being exercised by the centre rather than by the devolved administration.

Second, and from our point of view even more importantly, the division of fiscal responsibility violates a basic principle of democratic government. This is the right of electors to choose the overall level of resources their government will spend—and the level of taxation they will face to pay for it. The ability of government to allocate resources *between* different spending areas is obviously important: this each of the levels of sub-UK-national government can (to varying extents) do. But it is also important that the *total* level of spending can be chosen. This requires an effective power of taxation. Without it the exercise of citizenship is fundamentally constrained.

Third, and consequently, lack of effective tax-raising power would seem likely to reduce citizen participation in the democratic process. If voting and other forms of involvement in debate and policy-making can have little or no influence on the total level of expenditure, many people will surely regard participation as correspondingly less worthwhile. Coupled with the relatively restricted range of powers of the devolved institutions (with the exception of Scotland) and local government, this may well account, at least in part, for the low election turnouts we noted earlier.

The principle of expenditure determination

For all these reasons the Commission believes that the imbalance in the fiscal constitution needs to be corrected. The principle we would propose is simple. All elected governments responsible for significant public spending should have the power to vary their total level of expenditure. The ability to determine the total level of public expenditure—an ability which requires a power of taxation—is part of the democratic promise.

The principle, it should be noted, is not that elected governments should raise all, or even most, of their own finance. It is that they should be able to vary the total. For it is in the variation, not the collection, that democratic choice lies. A devolved or local government could collect 100% of its revenue from one form or another of sub-national tax, but if the level of its budget is externally constrained, it will not have proper financial autonomy. Many local and provincial or state governments in other European countries, for example, have revenues from national taxes 'assigned' to them on the basis of population. But this in itself does not give them financial autonomy: it is the ability to *vary* tax levels which does this.

This is an important point. In the local government field, in particular, many commentators (and, through their representative association, local authorities themselves[13]) have argued that local financial autonomy can only be achieved if councils are once again made responsible for at least 50% of their own revenues. At least three official enquiries into this subject over the last 25 years have recommended this.[14] But we are not persuaded that the percentage of total revenue is really the nub of the matter.

Clearly, revenue-raising is an important symbol of autonomy. When local authorities in the UK raised over 50% of their own revenue this gave them a fiscal status and responsibility which, arguably, they do not have now (though the loss of other powers has probably been a more significant contributor to their decline). If other things were equal, a larger percentage of revenue raised locally would be desirable. But what truly gives fiscal autonomy is the ability to vary the budget at the margin, not the total amount raised. The Scottish Variable Rate illustrates this well. The Scottish Parliament does not have a general responsibility to raise tax—and few people have argued that it should do so. But it still has a significant degree of financial autonomy (sufficient to be made the subject of a referendum), because of its ability to levy a supplementary income tax at the margin. This is what gives it the crucial self-determining power over the size of its budget.

The key principle, we believe, is therefore that elected governments should be able to vary the total level of their budgets. The power of variation should not be unlimited: central government has a legitimate interest in maintaining overall control over the level of public expenditure. Even in federal states (which is the UK is not) there are often limits to the extent to which sub-national levels of government can levy or vary taxation. But the power of variation within the limit should be able to be exercised without undue constraint. Of course, if the amount of variation allowed is very small, very little democratic choice will in practice be available. But it is important to note that the variation allowed does not have to be very large as a percentage of the total government budget to make the choice significant. This is because most of any government's budget is fixed, largely impervious to substantial financial change. The important political choices almost always occur at the margin.

The Scottish Variable Rate (SVR) again illustrates this. As we noted above, the ability of the Scottish Parliament to vary the basic rate of income tax levied in Scotland by plus or minus 3p in the pound represents a maximum variation of 4% of the total Scottish budget. This is often said to be rather insignificant. But in terms of democratic choice over spending it is substantial. Compare, for example, the equivalent at a UK-wide level. Four per cent of the UK government budget is around £13.7bn, which—as either an increase or a cut in spending—few people would regard as politically insignificant. (It is about a quarter of annual spending on health.) To change expenditure by this sum would require an increase or decrease in the basic rate of UK-wide income tax of around 5p—hardly an insignificant figure.

How should our principle, that all elected institutions responsible for public spending in the United Kingdom should have an effective—or more effective—power of taxation, be achieved? In the new constitutional context, we need to look not only at the devolved institutions and local government separately, but at the relationships between them.

£

Options for devolution

There are three broad options for giving sub-UK-national governments greater fiscal autonomy. The first is in practice only a serious proposal for local government, the other two could in principle be applied to the Wales and Northern Ireland Assemblies as well—and indeed potentially also to English regional government, were this to develop in the future. These are:

- Returning business rates to local control
- The introduction of new local taxes
- The creation of tax-varying powers.

We shall examine each in turn.

Returning business rates to local control

Two theoretical possibilities for giving local government greater fiscal autonomy are not generally considered serious options. These are increasing the proportion of council tax in local spending and an increase in fees and charges. Few experts believe that council tax can bear a larger load than it does at present: it is neither buoyant nor sufficiently progressive (and even if reformed would be unlikely to become so—we shall discuss this further below). Any significant increase in the rates of fees and charges for council services would also have unacceptably regressive impacts, in some cases tending to limit universal access to important services.

The main option generally discussed, therefore, is to allow local authorities once again to set business rates. This is the method favoured by the Local Government Association and by both the Parliamentary select committees which have examined this issue in the last five years.[15] The aim would be to increase the proportion of local finance raised locally to around 50%. This would reduce the gearing ratio of council tax changes to spending changes to (on average) a more manageable 2:1. (That is, for each percentage increase in total spending, an overall tax rise of twice the size would be required, rather than four or five times, as now.) The problem of lack of transparency would not be reduced altogether: as long as there is a central grant, its variation will tend to cause changes in local taxes unrelated to changes in service levels. But it would clearly help. (By providing for three year grant settlements the present Government has already achieved a welcome reduction in the instability of central funding, and has made further proposals to increase stability in its Green Paper of September 2000.[16]) A higher level of self-financing, it is argued, would increase the responsibilities and status of local government.

But it is not obvious that it would also improve local democratic accountability. Since businesses do not have votes, raising or lowering non-domestic rates has no direct impact on a council's relationship with its electorate. Local authorities argue that their consultations with local businesses are weakened by the lack of a tax relationship, but most business organisations argue the opposite: that it would be too easy for local authorities to increase business rates because there would be no direct voter comeback. This problem could be partially solved if (as the Local Government Association accepts) increases in business rates were only allowed if they were tied to similar increases in council tax. In this way any tax rise would be shared between local businesses and householders. Since both groups (in general) benefit from improvements in local services, this proposal would seem fair.

The re-localisation of business rates would nevertheless carry economic costs. The uniform business rate means that all firms face the same relative tax burden irrespective of their location, and can plan on the basis of predictable inflation-based tax rises. In 1989-90, before 'nationalisation', business rates in some areas were three times higher than in others. A return to variations on this scale could affect business competitiveness, particularly for small firms. Over time there might be a risk of firms tending to locate in low-rate areas in preference to high-rate ones.

These variations arose because of the different taxable capacities of different authorities. In some areas there are many businesses, so yields are high; in others there are few. This means that it is almost inevitable (as happened before) that the poorest areas will levy higher levels of business rates in order to achieve the same yield; but in terms of economic development this would have just the opposite effect to the one desired. In depressed areas where the rating base fell over time (or where appeals otherwise reduced it), rate rises on surviving businesses would be required simply to maintain overall yield. This disparity in taxable capacity would force the remaining Revenue Support Grant to bear an even larger load of 'equalisation' or redistribution than it does at present.

In practice, therefore, returning business rates to local control would have a very uneven effect on the gearing ratio. For local authorities with high taxable capacity locally-set business rates could yield significant additional income, allowing a considerable reduction in the gearing ratio. But for rural areas, inner city authorities and others with relatively few businesses, business rates would yield less income than they receive at present from the national pool. Revenue Support Grant would have to rise rather than fall. The gearing ratio for council tax would not therefore in practice decline very much. Indeed, if such authorities felt constrained to hold business rates down in order to sustain the local economic base, it might hardly fall at all.

We are therefore not persuaded that returning business rates to local control would have the unalloyed benefits, particularly for poorer authorities, that its supporters claim. We do not rule this out as an option, but we wish to explore alternatives as well.

New devolved taxes

Another way of increasing local authority self-financing would be to introduce new taxes at a local level. Such taxes could also be used to provide self-financed income for the devolved institutions in Scotland, Wales, Northern Ireland and Greater London, and for any future regional governments in England. In principle, such local or sub-national taxes could replace a proportion of national tax revenue. This is what happens in effect in many other countries, where local and state or regional taxation raises a higher proportion of total public revenues than in the UK and national taxes are correspondingly lower. In the UK such a change would allow central funding of local government and the devolved institutions to decline, and by giving them an additional source of income would increase their flexibility in raising revenues. Two principal kinds of local or sub-national tax are generally considered serious options: sales taxes and income taxes.[17]

A devolved sales tax

A local or sub-national sales tax could take a variety of forms. (For simplicity of expression, we shall include sub-national in the term 'local' below.) It could operate as a local surcharge on VAT, or simply an additional excise duty levied on retail sales. If levied by local authorities, it is estimated that (in either of these general forms) an average tax rate of around 4.5% would raise around the same amount as council tax, thereby doubling the proportion of local revenues under local control.[18] A third possibility would be a tax levied just on utility bills (gas, water, electricity), an administratively much simpler proposal (since it would be collected by a very small number of utility suppliers) but one whose restricted base would require a much higher rate to raise the same level of revenue as a general sales tax.

Local and sub-national sales taxes of various kinds operate in a number of other countries, most notably the USA. However, these are almost all federal countries and many such taxes operate at state or provincial rather than local level. This is for the obvious reason that sales taxes levied at different rates in different areas will tend to encourage 'cross-border shopping'. The larger the area the less likely this is to occur, since fewer people will be close enough to a 'tax border' to make such trips worthwhile. In the UK, where most local authorities do not cover large areas, local sales taxes would not be feasible in our view for this reason. They would be more acceptable at the level of the devolved institutions in Scotland, Wales and Northern Ireland or in the English regions (should regional government be introduced). But even here considerable inefficiencies (and we suspect public irritation) would be caused. If the problem of cross-border shopping led all authorities to impose the same rate of tax, much of the point of expenditure variation would be lost.

There are further objections in principle. A local sales tax would be unlikely to add very much to the sense of local 'connectedness'. It would not fall only on local voters, and wrapped into local prices it would almost certainly be invisible. It would do little therefore to increase accountability. Moreover, like all indirect taxes, a local sales tax would be regressive. Its impact would fall more heavily on poorer people than on the better off. (This would be particularly true of a utilities tax, since the proportion of household income spent on fuel and water tends to be higher in poorer households.) For all these reasons we do not believe that sales taxes are an appropriate form of local revenue-raising in the UK.

A devolved income tax

The other major possibility is a local or sub-national income tax, again envisaged as a partial replacement for UK-wide national income tax. This was proposed for local government by the Layfield Committee in 1976 and has since been the subject of periodic analysis and advocacy (and, by government, rejection).[19] Income tax has the great advantages of being progressive, buoyant and easily understood. If a local income tax were designed to raise 25% of local authority expenditure (around £17 billion in England and Wales), an average basic tax rate of 6-7% would need to be levied—with a corresponding reduction in national rates of income tax. The local income tax would be levied on residents (not employees) in each local authority area—or the equivalent for an income tax at the devolved level. Local and state or regional income taxes are levied in a number of other developed countries, including Norway, Denmark, Sweden, Finland and Japan. Indeed, in Sweden income tax is primarily local, with national income tax levied only above a certain threshold of income. In the current constitutional context, and given the existence of the Scottish Variable Rate, we do not believe that it would be appropriate for a full income tax to be levied by the devolved institutions. It remains, however, an interesting proposal for local government.

There are two principal arguments against local income tax. The first is that variations in local tax rates would be economically inefficient, creating incentives for people to move from high to low tax areas. But it is unlikely in practice that much migration of this kind would occur. In the first place many people will have reasons to stay in higher-tax areas—employment opportunities, family ties, preferences for particular locations and so on. Since the higher tax ought in principle to reflect better public services, there may even be positive incentives to do so. If migration did occur on any scale, demand for housing in low-tax areas would rise, bidding up prices and thereby reducing the gains from moving. While there might still be some tendency among higher-earning individuals to move, this could be reduced by limiting local income taxes to the basic rate, thereby 'capping' the differences in total tax paid in different areas. The larger the areas levying different rates the smaller any migration effect would be.

The second and more powerful argument against local income tax is that it would be costly and complex to administer. But this depends partly on how it is designed. If local authorities themselves became tax collectors, the costs would be higher than if the Inland Revenue remained the collecting body. Including income from investments and capital gains would add to complexity, since these are not part of the PAYE system: basing the tax simply on earned income would keep costs down. Giving local authorities the power to choose their own tax base, thresholds and number of tax rates would raise costs; requiring them to follow the structure of national income tax would reduce them.

It seems most appropriate, therefore, to consider the simplest form of local income tax. This would be levied on earned income and collected on behalf of local authorities by the Inland Revenue. Local authorities would set their tax rates and notify the Inland Revenue of these. Self-employed people would then be informed of the tax rates applying to them and charged in the normal way. At the same time the Inland Revenue would inform employers of the residence of their employees, and provide several sets of tax tables to be used according to the residence of each employee. (Every employee would be given a suffix on their tax code to indicate their tax rate.) Payslips would have a separate line for local income tax to ensure that the tax was visible and to bolster local accountability. Employers would remit their tax take to the Inland Revenue without needing to apportion it between national and local taxes. The Revenue would then redistribute the money to local authorities on the basis of their local yield.

This would be the simplest form of local income tax; but it would still introduce significant new costs into the system. The development of computerisation and self-assessment now probably makes it relatively easy (though not necessarily cheap) for the Inland Revenue to identify the residence of every employee and notify this to employers. However, the use of multiple tax tables for different employees would clearly add to the costs faced by firms, particularly small and non-computerised ones.

It would be more straightforward if the local authorities had only limited discretion over the rates of tax they could levy—say, being able to change the rates only by multiples of one half or perhaps a quarter of a penny in the pound. This would reduce the flexibility and precision with which local authorities could raise funds, but would also reduce the number of different tax tables faced by employers.[20]

We have not been able to estimate the total costs, either to the Inland Revenue or to employers and employees, of a system of local income tax of this kind. However, if these costs proved reasonable it would clearly be a progressive and easily understood mechanism for increasing the financial autonomy of local government. It could also in principle be used for the devolved national governments or (potentially) for English regional government.

An important proviso, however, needs to be added. Any system of local income tax (like, indeed, any system of greater local taxation) would require a very substantial equalisation mechanism. As with business rates, there are enormous differences between the taxable income capacities of different areas. To illustrate: the mean income in the Royal Borough of Kensington and Chelsea in London in 1999 was £33,500, whereas in Kingston upon Hull it was £15,100.[21] This means that Kensington and Chelsea could raise much more from a given tax rate than Hull. Consequently the Revenue Support Grant provided by central government would need (as with the local business rate option) to have a much larger equalisation or redistributive component. It would have to ensure that at the same rate of local income tax every authority could provide a similar level of service.[22]

Even with such a mechanism in place, however, it needs to be recognised that different taxable capacities allow richer authorities much more financial autonomy than poorer ones. However much it gets in equalisation grant, a low-income authority will raise less money per penny of local tax than a high-income one. Its gearing ratios will always therefore be greater. This is an inevitable consequence of any move towards greater financial autonomy. Richer authorities will benefit more than poorer ones. But it is a consequence of inequality of income between areas rather than the proposals for financial autonomy *per se*.

In the context of the present report, one further consideration has to be acknowledged. A local income tax which reduced the basic rate of national income tax by 6-7% would almost certainly not be compatible with a fully hypothecated NHS tax which removed an additional 10-11%. This would leave general national income tax at only around 4-6%. This would in our view be insufficiently large or flexible to finance general national public spending. If a local income tax were in principle supported, a choice would therefore need to be made between these two proposals.

Tax-varying powers

For local government, our conclusion is therefore that both the return of business rates to local control and a local income tax are viable options, but that both have costs associated with them, whether economic or administrative. A third kind of option—both for local government and for Wales and Northern Ireland—consequently presents itself.

We argued earlier that the key to fiscal autonomy was not the total amount of revenue collected locally but the ability to vary expenditure at the margin. This could be achieved simply by giving local authorities and devolved governments a power to vary national taxes, rather than by giving them responsibility for collecting the revenue as a whole. Shifting the responsiblity for the whole tax creates administrative burdens and costs whether or not there is any change in the total amount of income local authorities actually receive. Giving a power simply of local variation ensures that these costs are only incurred when changes in tax rates are made.

Our model here again is the Scottish Variable Rate. The Scottish Parliament was not given, and few people have argued that it should have, responsibility for collecting income tax in Scotland as a whole. What it has is a power to change the rate at the margin if it seeks a higher or lower budget allocation than that provided by Westminster. Can the same power to vary national taxes be given to the devolved in institutions in Wales and Northern Ireland and to local government?

We need to begin here with local government in England. Since in England there is no tier of government between local authorities and central government, proposals for local authorities can stand on their own. In Scotland, Wales and Northern Ireland the devolved institutions are responsible for local government financing, so the taxation powers at the two tiers of government need to be considered together. We shall come to this therefore below.

Local variation of the business rate

The Government has in fact already proposed a variable or supplementary local business rate in England.[23] Local authorities are to be given the power to levy a supplementary rate of up to 5% of the national rate (building up from 1% over a five-year period). By the same token, local authorities will be able to give a rebate on the national business rate to local businesses of up to the same amount. This provides in effect for a local tax-varying power on the national business rate system. Local changes in business rates will need to be matched by parallel changes in council tax, to ensure that businesses do not bear the whole burden of changes in council expenditure. Business will need to be consulted on the changes.

This system of local variation of an otherwise nationally determined tax appears a sensible way of giving local authorities greater fiscal autonomy without incurring all the costs, both to business and in administration, of widely differing rates in different areas. It would reduce the gearing on council tax without (contrary to the conventional assumption) requiring a large increase in the proportion of tax raised locally. While we would recommend that the supplementary rate should be introduced and its impact assessed before further changes are made, in principle we do not see the 5% limit as necessary. So long as changes to the business rate must be matched by changes to council tax and done following consultation, the principles of financial autonomy and responsibility for local government would suggest that no centrally determined constraints are required: the workings of local democracy should be sufficient.

Local variation of income tax

In principle (and within reason) the more sources of income available to local authorities the better: there is greater flexibility and the gearing ratio is reduced on each. By itself the supplementary business rate does not lead to greater accountability to local citizens. We therefore think it appropriate that local authorities should have a third general tax power: the ability to vary the basic rate of income tax on the lines of the Scottish Variable Rate. In areas with two councils, this should be limited to the upper tier only, to avoid confusion.

We would propose in fact one difference from the arrangements in Scotland. In our view the power to vary income tax should apply to the basic and the higher rates together. At present in Scotland only the basic rate can be changed. This makes any variation less progressive than it could be. By requiring both the basic and the higher rate to be varied, the change in the basic rate (for any given total revenue requirement) would be reduced, thereby increasing the likely political acceptability to the majority of taxpayers. The distribution of the extra burden borne would be fairer.

In effect this proposal is for a form of local income tax; but one which would only be levied where a local authority specifically desired to increase its total expenditure by more than it felt able to through council tax and the supplementary business rate. We can envisage this happening, for example, if a local authority wished to raise its education spending on local schools above the allocations suggested by central government grant. A local *reduction* in income tax would also of course be possible: this would trigger an equivalent reduction in Revenue Support Grant.

The mechanism for such a Local Variable Rate (LVR) would be as described above for a full local income tax. The Inland Revenue would notify employers of the residence of their employees and would supply alternative tax tables. The tax would then be collected through PAYE and the normal taxation of the self-employed. It would appear as a separate line on payslips to ensure its visibility. In order to keep the number of alternative tax tables manageable, it would be necessary to limit the number of variable rates which a local authority could levy: perhaps again in half-pence steps up to, say, 2p in the pound. This would leave five tax tables in normal use (the standard one plus four additional local tax rates), with a further four potentially required where local authorities decided to reduce spending and cut income tax.

The advantage of the variable rate over the full local income tax proposal is that the administrative costs should be significantly less: the tax would only be collected where a local authority made use of the tax varying provision. For this reason it is difficult to say what these costs would be. But some estimates have been made of the cost of implementing the Scottish Variable Rate.[24] The annual cost to employers is suggested to be of the order of £6-£15 million, with setting up costs (which could be phased) of around £50m. Costs would vary from firm to firm, but it is estimated that a small employer with five Scottish residents would typically face set-up costs of £50-£100, while larger firms could expect costs of around £5 per employee. In addition the Government (the Inland Revenue and Department of Social Security) would incur set-up costs of around £16m and running costs of around £9m. Given potential revenues from the SCR of £450m, these represent administrative and compliance costs of around 2%, which is comparable to the cost of national income tax. These costs would clearly be higher for a UK-wide system with a larger number of potential tax tables, but reduced insofar as they were not universally used. Though not insignificant, we believe costs of this order of magnitude would be acceptable for the benefits in local autonomy and accountability such a system would bring.

Clearly the design and implementation of a local variable rate would need much further specification: the definition of local residence, the interaction with the benefit system, the timing of budget decisions, and so on. (Many of these issues have in fact been explored in the preparations made for the Scottish Variable Rate.) But in principle a local variable rate would be, we believe, an important option to make available to local authorities.

Referendums

We would make one further recommendation, however. Changing the rate of income tax faced by local citizens is a very significant decision. To ensure full accountability to local taxpayers a local authority ought to have a specific popular mandate for it. It would be advisable, we believe, if local authorities proposing to use the variable rate held a referendum of local voters to approve this (or not).

One local authority has already conducted a local referendum on its options for taxing and spending. In February 1999 Milton Keynes Council asked its citizens how much council tax they wished to pay, relating this to the level of public service they wished to receive. Three options were presented in a detailed leaflet sent to every voter. These were for a council tax rise of 5%, necessitating some cuts in services; a rise of 9.8%, giving a standstill budget, and a 15% rise, allowing extra spending on services. The results were instructive. 24% of people voted for the 15% rise, 46% for the 9.8% rise and 30% for the 5% rise. The 9.8% rise was therefore chosen, more than twice the increase in council tax advised by central government. Perhaps even more interestingly, the turnout in the referendum was 45%, compared to the 26% who voted in the previous local elections. This indicates a relatively high level of public engagement with the question of tax and public spending levels.[25]

We are impressed by this example of the public's 'connectedness' when faced by a real choice about taxation and public spending in this way. In principle the use of referendums for major budget decisions of this kinds seems to us highly desirable.[26]

For example, it is possible that one of the main circumstances in which a local authority might wish to levy a local variable rate would be to spend more on schools. In effect the authority would be offering the option of earmarking an income tax increase to local education spending. With the referendum provision this would then become a choice made by local citizens. Given the high priority which education spending gets in public opinion surveys and the control of education at local level, this seems a good mechanism for translating public concerns, if so desired, into higher public spending.

Taxation and the devolved institutions

We also believe that the principle of fiscal autonomy or expenditure determination should be applied to the Wales and Northern Ireland Assemblies.

Obviously, this is a matter of constitutional as well as taxation policy. Giving these institutions a power of taxation to enable them to vary their total level of expenditure would change both their own powers and their relationship to the UK government. We are therefore conscious that this proposal will need wider constitutional debate. It would clearly need the assent of the institutions themselves, and of their electorates, possibly in a further referendum. But in principle, from the point of view of citizenship, our recommendation is that each of these elected institutions should have its own tax-raising power. If elected assemblies are established in the English regions with significant public spending responsibilities, they too should be able to vary, through taxation, their total level of expenditure.[27]

We believe this should be done by granting the Wales and Northern Ireland Assemblies a Variable Rate power like that of Scottish Parliament. We would recommend a similar limit for variation of 3p in the pound, in half pence steps. We would propose that the basic and higher rates should be varied together.

Of itself, this would not give local authorities in Scotland, Wales or Northern Ireland a tax-varying power comparable to that of local authorities in England. We believe that this should be a matter for the Scottish Parliament and Wales and Northern Ireland Assemblies themselves. These institutions should be able to devolve part of their tax-varying power down further to their local authorities. The devolved institutions could then decide whether to retain the entire 3p variation power for themselves, or to devolve up to 2p of it to local authorities in their jurisdiction. In this way the maximum variation of 3p would be retained, but this could be split or not according to the choice of the devolved institution. As in England, however, our recommendation would be for a maximum 2p variation power at the local level, with a minimum of 1p retained at the level of the Parliament or Assembly.[28]

These arrangements, we believe, would be in the spirit of our principle of expenditure determination, giving the devolved institutions the primary right to decide how this is to be allocated. In London we would suggest that the arrangements between the London boroughs and the Greater London Assembly and Mayor should be subject to further consultation.

Better government

An effective power of taxation is, we believe, an important feature of accountable government, and therefore a requirement for the proper exercise of citizenship. In principle we believe it is likely to 'connect' people better to the taxes they pay and to the public services which these finance. This is particularly important at the devolved and local levels, where participation rates have been low. We cannot guarantee that election turnouts would be higher if local authorities and devolved assemblies had greater autonomy to determine their own budgets. But we think this would be more likely, as the referendum in Milton Keynes seems to suggest.

But none of this will have any effect unless both the standard of public services and the standard of political debate improve. As we noted in Chapter 7, these are the first requirements for better 'connection'. Giving governments greater tax powers will only be publicly acceptable if the services which they pay for are seen to be effective and efficient. And such powers will only increase the public's political engagement if the kinds of debate conducted by politicians and in the media reflect in a mature way the genuine choices available. The Government and local authorities have embarked on a series of 'modernisation' reforms to local government structures and processes which are designed to improve accountability and performance standards.[29] Each of the devolved institutions is carefully examining its own performance with a view to improvement. This is not the place to discuss these initiatives. But their importance in making devolved and local tax powers worth having cannot be underestimated.

£

Reforming council tax

We have so far discussed ways of increasing the tax power of local government by introducing new taxes in addition to council tax. But council tax also needs reform.

The regressive character of council tax

Council tax is a property tax, levied on domestic property values. In principle this makes it an attractive form of taxation. It widens the tax base to include a large part of taxable capacity (property-based wealth) which would not otherwise be taxed. In particular, it creates a level playing field between different forms of wealth and income, ensuring that owner-occupiers pay tax on the effective 'income' they earn from not having to pay rent. It also ensures that homeowners contribute to the communal investments which help to increase the value of their property—schools, roads, amenities and so on. Since occupiers of local domestic properties are those who primarily benefit from the services which council tax finances, it creates an immediate form of democratic accountability. Since houses are visible and immobile, council tax is very easy to administer and collect and very difficult to evade.

Unfortunately, however, the particular way in which council tax is presently structured has serious flaws.[30] Most important of these is that council tax is severely regressive. The structure of the banding system and the difference between the level of council tax paid in different bands mean that the rate of tax actually falls the greater the wealth on which it is levied (see Table 9.1 and Figure 9.2). Someone living in a house worth £1 million pays only twice the amount of someone living in a house worth £70,000, and only three times the tax paid by those in the poorest accommodation.

Table 9.1: Council Tax bands

band	lower threshold	upper threshold	current multipliers (overall 3:1 ratio)	distribution of dwellings by band %
A		£40,000	6/9	26.4
B	£40,000	£52,000	7/9	19.4
C	£52,000	£68,000	8/9	21.6
D	£68,000	£88,000	1	14.7
E	£88,000	£120,000	11/9	9.1
F	£120,000	£160,000	13/9	4.8
G	£160,000	£225,000	15/9	3.5
H	£320,000	£500,000	18/9	0.5

Figure 9.2: The regressive nature of Council Tax

Council Tax as a percentage of highest value in band (assuming £500 a year for band D)

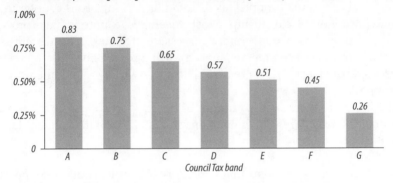

[Source: Peter Kenway and Guy Palmer, Council Tax: the Case for Reform, New Policy Institute, 1999]

Indeed in many of the poorer local authorities outside the south east of England, the banding system effectively turns council tax into a flat-rate tax. In the north east, north west, Yorkshire and Merseyside over 50% of properties are located in band A (worth less than £40,000 in 1991), and in individual authorities the numbers are even higher. In these areas therefore most people, whatever their income, pay the same amount of tax—making council tax alarmingly similar to the poll tax it replaced.

The infrequent valuations of property conducted for council tax (the last one was in 1991) create a further anomaly. As house prices in the south east of England and certain other regions have dramatically increased over the last decade, the valuations used for the tax have diverged further and further from actual property values. Again, the beneficiaries have been the richest households in society. Many have been further helped by the provision under which second and third homes attract only half the tax rate of first homes. This is one of the contributing factors which have pushed up prices in commuter and holiday villages, resulting in many young people and families being priced out of their home communities.

The regressiveness of council tax is relieved to some extent by Council Tax Benefit, a means-tested benefit which is claimed by almost half of all households in the lowest band. (Council tax is unique among taxes in having its own special benefit, a function of its regressivity.) However, this has other negative impacts, creating a 'poverty trap' for those in work or seeking to enter it. The withdrawal of benefit if earnings from work rise above a certain level contributes to very high effective marginal 'tax' rates, and consequently disincentives to work. In addition, take-up of the benefit is only around 70%, with many pensioners in particular not claiming their entitlement.[31]

Potential reforms

The regressive nature of council tax is unfair and as such runs counter to our strong conception of citizenship. Most developed countries have property taxes, but none has a deliberately regressive structure. The Commission therefore strongly recommends that council tax is reformed to make it progressive, or at least less regressive. There are two key requirements to any reform package.

The first is to increase the number of bands, particularly at the top and bottom of the scale. This will help to ensure that those with different taxable capacities pay different rates of tax.

- We would recommend that band A is split at least into two, possibly three, thereby differentiating between those living in homes worth less than £20,000 or £30,000 and those in the range to £40,000.

- Likewise we would recommend the splitting of band G, which has a much larger range (from £160,000 to £320,000) between its lower and upper thresholds than any other band.
- In addition band H (£320,000) needs to be split into at least two, and probably more, bands to differentiate between homes worth £320,000 and those worth considerably more. (£320,000 no longer represents a luxurious home in London and the south east.)

The second structural change required is to increase the difference between the tax paid in the bottom and top bands (sometimes known as the 'multiplier'). At present the rate of tax in the top band is three times that in the lowest, giving a multiplier of 3:1. If council tax were made completely progressive, based on real market values of domestic property, this ratio should be around 30:1.[32] We do not recommend this as an immediate reform, since it would involve politically unpalatable increases in council tax (from 18% to over 250%) for those in bands E to H. But it is worth bearing in mind to appreciate just how far from progressive the current system is, and how much the present system effectively benefits the better off.

The reform we recommend initially would increase the ratio of council tax in the top to the bottom band from 3:1 to 7:1. Bands A, G and H would each be split, creating 11 bands in all (see Table 9.2). If this reform were carried out on a revenue-neutral basis—that is, giving the same total yield of council tax—the impact on council tax bills would be as shown in Figure 9.3, based on work done by the New Policy Institute.[33] (The calculation assumes a uniform rate of tax across all authorities.) As the table shows, households in bands A and B would gain significantly. Those in band A1 would pay around £150 a year less in tax, those in band B around £75 less. Those in band G1 would face an increase in their annual tax bill of around £230 and those in band H2 an increase of around £760.

Table 9.2: A reformed system of Council Tax bands				
band	lower threshold	upper threshold	current multiplier (overall 3:1 ratio)	new multipliers (overall 7:1 ratio)
A1		£30,000	6/9	4/9
A2	£30,000	£40,000	6/9	5/9
B	£40,000	£52,000	7/9	6/9
C	£52,000	£68,000	8/9	8/9
D	£68,000	£88,000	1	1
E	£88,000	£120,000	11/9	12/9
F	£120,000	£160,000	13/9	15/9
G1	£160,000	£225,000	15/9	18/9
G2	£225,000	£320,000	15/9	20/9
H1	£320,000	£500,000	18/9	24/9
H2	£500,000		18/9	28/9

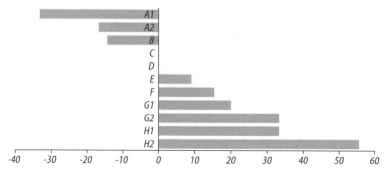

Figure 9.3: The distributional effects of a reformed Council Tax

Percentage change in Council Tax

To obtain full revenue neutrality a 0.5% rise in CT overall is required, equivalent to 7 pence a week for a Band D property. This has not been included in the above calculations.

[Source: New Policy Institute]

It should be noted that those on full Council Tax Benefit will not gain in full from the reform, since they do not pay the full rate of council tax. But it will help improve the incentives to work, since net earnings after tax for those in bands A to C will be higher. The Treasury will of course gain from the reduction in the need to pay Council Tax Benefit as rates of tax fall.

We also believe that the discount on second homes should be abolished, perhaps with some short-term relief for those temporarily in possession of two homes in the process of sale of one of them.

In addition to these reforms we would recommend that valuations are carried out more frequently, perhaps every five years. (Between valuations it might be possible to index values to local house price indices.) This would help to rectify the inequities, between both individuals and local authorities, which arise from relative changes in house prices. It would also act as an economic stabiliser. In the upswing of a business cycle house prices and consumption generally grow faster than income. If through more frequent valuations higher house prices lead clearly to higher taxes, a dampening effect on property price booms should occur.

One further small reform might be proposed.[34] Following common practice in North America, elderly people should be offered the option to defer their council tax bills. The accumulated debt, with interest, could then be settled upon the sale of the dwelling or the death of the surviving resident spouse. Financial markets would allow local authorities to convert these claims into cash. This reform would particularly help elderly people living in valuable houses who do not have the cashflow to meet their tax bill. As well as easing distress, it would reduce the political resistance to making the system more progressive which lay behind the original desire to reform domestic rates in the 1980s.

£

Taxation at the European level

It may seem strange to leap straight from the reform of council tax to a discussion of taxation at an international scale. The particular taxes at issue at these levels are indeed different. But from the point of view of citizenship the essential questions are the same. How is the state accountable to its citizens for the taxes that it raises? Who decides how much tax is raised and therefore how much can be spent?

'Harmonisation' and national sovereignty

In recent years some politicians and commentators have raised fears about the loss of national sovereignty over taxation, arguing that there is an inexorable trend towards the 'harmonisation' of taxes, certainly within the European Union and possibly more widely. There are in fact two different kinds of arguments generally going on here which it is as well to separate out.[35]

The first concerns the phenomenon of 'globalisation'. As we saw in Chapter 6, there is a widespread view that tax rates and overall revenues in all developed countries are now on an inevitable downward trend, because only countries with low taxes will attract mobile capital and labour (though in fact in some cases lower tax rates may actually lead to higher revenue, if firms respond by increasing output). This will in practice undermine national sovereignty over taxation, it is claimed, since countries will find themselves with little effective choice. As we pointed out in Chapter 6, however, tax rates in general, though not insignificant, are not the main determinants of the location decisions of businesses and top executives. Some countries may gain from reducing some taxes (Ireland appears to be an example). But others may equally regard any economic costs of higher taxation as bearable for the higher spending on public services which they finance. National choice over tax levels, in other words, will remain. Globalisation certainly affects the nature of the choice; but we are very sceptical that the importance of taxation levels in investment decisions will become so overwhelmingly important in the foreseeable future that national sovereignty over taxation would be compromised.

The second kind of argument about the sovereignty of national governments over tax policy concerns developments within the European Union. Again there are two different issues here. One is the financing of the EU itself. The European Commission has mooted the idea of the EU having a tax-raising power of its own.[36] (At present it receives its income in agreed allocations from each member state.) But these proposals have not been accepted by member states, and our own principle of citizenship would not support them. The EU has no elected government (the European Parliament has no executive power): it is an inter-governmental, not a federal, body. So although (since the Maastricht Treaty) there is now a formal concept of European citizenship[37], in the current absence of an elected government there is no case in our view for a power of taxation.

The more important argument here, however, is the involvement of the European Union in national tax policy. The EU does have a legitimate interest in this area, since the forms of taxation levied in member states affect the operation of the single market. More generally it can be argued that the introduction of the European single currency gives the EU a stronger interest in taxation policy as an instrument of general economic management. But it is here that concerns about national sovereignty arise. Critics of these developments argue that European rules on taxation—such as on VAT and the proposed 'withholding tax' on overseas savings—are infringements of the right of member states to determine their own tax system. They claim that further European economic integration will eventually lead to the imposition of common or harmonised taxes at a European Union level, thereby undermining national sovereignty in this field. A report drawn up by the European Commission in May 2000, proposing common criteria which member states should use when contemplating national cuts in taxation, has fuelled this argument.[38]

The issue of national sovereignty in economic policy as a whole is complex. There is no question that membership of the European Union does involve a 'pooling' of formal national sovereignty. But one of the justifications for this is that in a global economy collective sovereignty gives each nation more power to direct its own affairs than it would have acting on its own. So long as member states agree the conditions under which tax policy can be decided at a European Union level (and at present all such decisions need the unanimous agreement of member states), the question of where sovereignty for tax policy should lie must be a matter for judgement on the merits of each proposal rather than one of absolute principle. A European-wide policy may be appropriate in some areas, but not in others.

This makes it particularly important to distinguish between the different kinds of taxes which are the subject of debates about harmonisation. The field in which such moves are furthest advanced is that of indirect taxes on internationally traded goods and services. The EU's rules on VAT are already designed to bring national regimes closer together, or at least to stop them diverging—though in fact they have had less effect than often supposed.[39] The aim is to reduce the distortion of competition (leading to cross-border shopping and smuggling) caused by differential tax rates on products which can be traded easily across national frontiers. Harmonisation in this field is desirable and we would support its further development. This could include excise duties and potentially some environmental taxes, such as on business energy use (we discuss this further in Chapter 13). As we pointed out in Chapter 6, however, such harmonisation does not necessarily have to be downwards. It can in principle mean countries with low rates bringing them up to the level of those with higher rates.

The issue of the taxation of mobile capital is another on which the EU has also sought collective agreement. In the absence of a common system, nationals of one country may be able to evade domestic tax by depositing their savings in another country with a different tax rate or system. For this reason a common approach is again sensible. After considerable arguments over the proposal for a so-called 'withholding tax' on non-resident savings, agreement on a system of information-sharing about such savings (which can then act as the basis for national tax regimes) has now been achieved.

The third field in which there are said to be strong pressures towards harmonisation is corporate taxation.[40] In general business taxes are a subject we have not covered in this report. But it is worth saying that harmonisation in this field does not look at all likely in the short or medium term. There are in fact some grounds for arguing that it would be beneficial, levelling the competitive playing field across the single market. But in present circumstances it would be almost impossible to achieve. The regimes of corporate taxation in the different member states are very different, with taxes levied on different activities and bases and at different rates. So long as these differences remain, it is not at all clear what convergence would actually mean, still less whether it could be achieved. It is important to recognise that harmonisation here would have to apply to all business taxes, not just individual ones (in profits, payroll, energy, or whatever): it is the total tax burden faced by firms which is the important factor for competitiveness, not how this is distributed between different kinds of tax.

The third field of dispute here is more general. The largest claim made by critics of European involvement in tax policy is that attempts by the EU to manage the economy following the introduction of the euro will inevitably require a more interventionist approach to taxation. Member states will be required to follow common taxation policies, with the overall shares of taxation in national income being forced onto a convergent path. As a Commission we do not know how powerful any pressures of this kind might prove to be in the future. But it is not our view that they follow inevitably from membership of the single currency. (On the contrary, there is an argument that economic management in the euro zone will require *greater* decentralisation of taxation powers to member states and regions than currently, rather than more centralisation. With a single interest rate right across the European Union, a more decentralised taxation system might help to smooth out regional imbalances in employment and growth.)

What we would wish to say is that if such pressures do arise they would have a powerful impact on our conception of democratic citizenship. So long as the EU remains an inter-governmental body, and the democratically elected European Parliament does not decide on European public spending we believe that decisions on the overall share of taxation in national income are a matter for elected national governments to decide, not the EU. The share of taxation determines the level of spending, which in turn determines the provision of public services. These are vital political issues which should be decided by the people through their democratically elected governments. At present the Maastricht Treaty limits the level of borrowing of member states, but rightly does not say how high or low the levels of spending and taxation should be. (The same level of borrowing can occur at any level of tax and spending.) Given the current structure of the EU, it is important in our view that the share of taxation remains an issue of national democratic sovereignty. This follows, we believe, from the principles of citizenship and accountable government we have espoused.

Part Three:
The reform of key taxes

10 | Making income tax fairer

The basic structure of income tax

Income tax is the largest single form of tax in the UK tax system, accounting for a quarter of all government revenues. For most individuals it is the most visible of taxes, deducted weekly or monthly on wageslips and / or subject to an annual self-assessment return. For much of the past twenty years it has also been the most politically sensitive tax, with a succession of reductions in the basic rate guaranteeing headlines at budget time. Yet in fact the history of the income tax system over this period is rather more complex than is sometimes appreciated.

> ### Box 10.1: Income Tax
>
> The main kinds of income subject to income tax are earnings from employment and self-employment, some social security benefits, pension payments during retirement, profits from business, income from property, bank and building society interest and dividends on shares. Incomes from certain social security benefits are not liable to income tax. Income tax is also not paid on certain savings products such as National Savings Certificates and Individual Savings Accounts.
>
> Income tax in the UK operates through a system of allowances and bands of income. Each individual has a personal allowance, which is deducted from total income before tax in order to reach **taxable** income. Taxpayers under 65 years old receive a personal allowance of £4,385,

while older people are entitled to higher personal allowances subject to a taper above an income limit of £17,000.

Taxable income is subject to different tax rates depending upon the 'tax band' that income falls within, as given in the table (2000-01 figures).

Allowance or tax band	Gross income per year (individual with personal allowance only)[1]	Taxable income per year	Rate of tax (%)
personal allowance (aged under 65)[2]	£0-£4,385	£0	
lower rate band	£4,385-£5,905	£0-£1,520	10%
basic rate band	£5,905-£32,785	£1,520-£28,400	22%
higher rate band	over £32,785	over £28,400	40%

1 Tax relief on private pension contributions increases the effective allowances and therefore shifts the thresholds for each band upwards.

2 Personal allowances for people aged over 65: individuals aged 65-74: £5,790; aged 75 and over: £6,050; married couples aged 65-74: £5,185: aged 75 and over: £5,255.

The income tax system now includes a number of tax credits which reduce income tax liability. These include the Working Families Tax Credit (introduced in October 1999) and the Children's Tax Credit (to be introduced in April 2001). The latter is in part a replacement (though restricted only to taxpayers with children) for the Married Couple's Allowance and Additional Personal Allowance which were abolished (for those aged under 65) in 2000. These tax credits are described in Box 10.3.

Most income tax on earned income is deducted at source by employers under the Pay As You Earn (PAYE) scheme. The UK system is 'cumulative': when calculating tax due each week or month, the employer considers the income not simply for the period in question but for the whole of the tax year to date. This cumulative system allows relatively few tax returns to be issued, since for those with relatively simple affairs no end-of-year adjustment to the amount of tax already paid is necessary. Under the system of self-assessment introduced in 1996-97, around a third of income taxpayers, mainly people with higher incomes and multiple income sources, are required to complete tax returns.

Over 26 million individuals pay income tax in the UK; its yield in 2000-01 was projected to be £95.9 billion (net of tax credits), or 25.5% of total revenues.

[Source: Andrew Dilnot et al, A Survey of the UK Income Tax System, Briefing Note No 9, Institute for Fiscal Studies, 2000]

The income tax story, 1979-2000

Looking at the period since 1979, a number of major kinds of changes have been made to, or have affected, the income tax system. We shall deal with two important ones—the taxation of savings, and the introduction of tax credits—in a separate section below. Here we deal with the ways in which the basic system of rates, allowances and thresholds has altered over the last twenty years.

The first two changes have run in parallel, though far more attention has been paid to one than the other. In 1979, before Margaret Thatcher won her first election, Britain had an income tax system characterised by a number of tax bands and rates—reaching 83% on earned income and 98% on investment income. At the same time, however, several allowances and reliefs enabled particular kinds of expenditures to be deducted from income before calculation of the tax due. Thus a very progressive tax schedule was in practice applied to a relatively narrow tax base. (The tax 'base' is the range of income on which tax is paid.)

The Conservatives' tax reforms dramatically changed this picture. The top rate of tax was slashed twice—to 60% in 1979, and then to 40% in 1988. Meanwhile the basic rate was steadily reduced, from 33% to 23% by the time of the 1997 election. The first of the Conservatives' income tax cuts, in 1979, was financed by an increase in VAT from 8% to 15%. (This was a significant shift from direct to indirect taxation, to which we shall return.) But thereafter part of the reductions in tax rates was financed by an expansion of the earned income tax base. The value of the various tax allowances was gradually reduced, with some (such as life insurance tax relief) abolished altogether. This process has been continued under the Labour government, with the final abolition of both mortgage interest relief and the married couple's and additional personal allowances, and the lowering again of the basic rate of tax, to 22%. In addition the Labour government has introduced a lower rate band at 10%, for the first £1500 (now £1520) of taxable income. (A lower rate at 20% was first introduced by the Conservatives in 1992, for a wider band of income.) In comparison with 1979, therefore, the tax system for earned income now applies much lower rates to a considerably wider tax base.

At the same time, however, a third and much more subtle change has been occurring, one barely noticed in political debate. This is that the starting thresholds for the basic and higher tax rates have been falling in relation to earnings. (The threshold is the level of taxable income beyond which the particular tax rate is paid.) In most Budgets, the Chancellor raises the thresholds for both the basic and the higher rate by the level of inflation: indeed, he or she is statutorily obliged to do so unless Parliament intervene. But prices in general do not rise as fast as earnings, so the number of people who fall into each tax band tends to rise over time, and the yield from the tax therefore increases almost imperceptibly.

This effect (known as 'fiscal drag') has been particularly noticeable for the higher rate of tax—not least because its threshold was actually frozen in cash terms in four out of the first five budgets of the 1990s. Since 1979 the higher rate threshold has therefore not kept pace even with price inflation, let alone earnings. Over the same period there has been a very significant rise in the number of people earning high incomes. The combined result has been a substantial growth in the number of taxpayers falling into the higher rate bracket: from under 700,000 in 1979 (less than 3% of income taxpayers: these included individuals paying at 40% or higher), to 2.3 million, or 9%, now.[1] (By contrast, the personal allowance, which governs the point at which income tax begins to be paid, has been rising faster than inflation.)

The fourth change, strictly speaking, does not involve income tax at all. This is to the structure of National Insurance contributions. As we have already noted, National Insurance (NI) is not, properly understood, a tax: it is a social insurance system through which contributions made out of earnings generate entitlements to benefits of various kinds—notably the basic state pension and benefits during periods of unemployment, incapacity and maternity. Employers, as well as employees and the self-employed, contribute to it. Yet National Insurance can often look like a form of income tax—it is deducted from employees' wages and salaries by the same PAYE system, and to the individual taxpayer its most immediate effect is to increase the effective tax rates on earnings.

This effect has arguably been reinforced by the changes made to the National Insurance system over recent years. These have brought the structures of income tax and NI contributions much more closely into alignment. From April 2001 NI contributions will start at the same threshold as income tax (the personal allowance), for both the employed and (in terms of earnings-related Class 4 contributions) the self-employed as well as for employers. At the other end of the scale, National Insurance remains subject to an Upper Earnings Limit (UEL) above which contributions are not paid. (The 'tax base' for National Insurance is therefore much narrower than for income tax.) But the UEL has gradually been brought closer and closer to the higher rate tax threshold. Whereas in 1991-92 the gap between them was over £8,000, by April 2001—when the UEL will be £29,900 and the higher rate threshold £32,335[2]—the gap will be under £2,500. This makes for a much smoother progression in the combined rate of income tax and National Insurance. In addition, National Insurance is now charged on various kinds of benefits in kind received by employees from their employers. (The NI system is described in Box A.1 in the Annex, and is discussed further there.)

The effects of the changes

From the point of view of our conception of citizenship, and in the light of the principles set out in Chapter 5, many of these changes made to the income tax system over the last twenty years are to be welcomed. The reduction in the number of rates of tax, the expansion of the tax base, and the alignment in the structures of National Insurance contributions and income tax have all contributed to the greater transparency and clarity of the system. In particular, the abolition of most reliefs and allowances has reduced the gap between the income which people perceive they earn and the concept of 'taxable income'. This has surely helped public understanding of the system.

There have been other advantages too. Many of the former reliefs and allowances for particular kinds of expenditure—mortgages and life insurance, for example—introduced distortions into the market for these products, encouraging these forms of saving above others simply on the grounds of their tax advantages. Since most of them were products bought disproportionately by the better off, they also effectively subsidised the spending of the wealthy—especially since relief was given at the marginal rate of tax, giving those paying at the higher rate more benefit than those on the basic rate. Abolition has been entirely for the good.

The same is true in the Commission's view of the abolition of the married couple's allowance. This has not only broadened the tax base. It has ended the inequitable treatment of marriage and other forms of cohabitation. As we discussed in Chapter 4, we do not believe that marriage status should be relevant to the tax system. The tax system should be neutral between different lifestyles where no social harms are caused. There is a strong case for the tax system to support adults with children, both on grounds of horizontal equity—acknowledging the extra costs faced by parents—and to help reduce child poverty. (We discuss this further below.) But children are raised in many kinds of household, and marriage *per se* is not in our view a relevant consideration.

Marginal and average tax rates

The other advantage of the broadening of the tax base is that it has enabled marginal tax rates to be reduced without an equivalent reduction in total yield. As we argued in Chapter 5, this is in general a valuable principle. It enables average tax rates to be kept up even while marginal rates come down. (The average rate is the proportion of an individual's total income paid in tax; the marginal rate is the proportion of tax paid on an additional pound of income.) Since it is the marginal rate of tax which can have an effect on work incentives, while it is the average rate which determines both total revenues and the progressivity of the system, this is highly desirable.

The reduction in the very high marginal rates of tax which existed before

1979 is clearly welcome. Very high marginal rates can certainly affect incentives for work and enterprise, particularly for those who are internationally mobile and could seek to work or set up businesses elsewhere. Very high rates also encourage tax avoidance and evasion. But the effect of marginal rates under, say, 50% is less easy to gauge. It depends partly on the range of income over which different rates are levied: the higher the income range, the less impact a given rate is likely to have, both because there are fewer people earning high incomes and because each pound has less marginal value. But it also depends on the balance between the mutually contradictory effects (known as the 'substitution' and 'income' effects) which taxation can have on behaviour. On the one hand an increase in the marginal rate of tax reduces the reward from working, which may encourage some people to work less (or put less effort into a business). But for people with a target income, on the other, an increase in marginal rate may make them work harder and longer to achieve it. Thus individuals with the same incomes facing the same marginal rate will often react differently, because their preferences are not the same. (This may be particularly true of men and women with different family responsibilities.)

In these circumstances the economic effects of a given set of marginal tax rates cannot be straightforwardly assessed. The best that can be said is that the tax system should be structured so that marginal rates (combined with indirect tax rates[3]) should not be so high as to deter most people from working as much as they would like. In practice, given the reductions in rates over the last twenty years, concerns over incentives now apply far more to the bottom of the income scale than to the middle or top. For it is people on social security benefits into low-paid employment who suffer the highest effective marginal rates of 'tax' or deduction rates. These occur when benefits are withdrawn and tax and National Insurance contributions start to be paid as income rises. In some circumstances a combined withdrawal or effective tax rate of over 90% can be faced[4]. Unemployment traps, in which people experience almost no financial gain from getting a job, and poverty traps, where people working longer hours or moving to higher-paying jobs find themselves little better off, can both be seen as the worst examples of work disincentives in the current system.

The lengthening of the 'tapers' for many social security benefits and means-tested tax credits (through which benefit is withdrawn gradually as income rises) have reduced the effective marginal tax rates faced by many people. Indeed, the basic rate of tax is a relatively insignificant factor for many people at the bottom end of the income scale in comparison with changes to the rates and tapers of benefits and tax credits.[5] For this reason arguments over work incentives now have very little place in discussions over the basic rate of tax, or vice versa. If there is a concern to assist more people into employment, or to target tax cuts to the lowest income groups, the basic rate is not the issue. We shall return to this—and to parallel discussions over the higher rate—below.

Inequality and the progressivity of income tax

Recognition that successive reductions in the rates of income tax (once the very high rates of the 1970s had been abolished) may not have had much effect on work incentives is important. For the changes in income tax rates that have occurred over the last twenty years have had three definite impacts which from the point of view of citizenship have not been positive at all. Indeed in the Commission's view they have been seriously damaging.

The first, as we argued in Chapter 1, is the political and media obsession with the basic rate. The basic rate of income tax is important, of course: it is the marginal rate which applies to the majority of taxpayers. But the totemic quality it has acquired over the last two decades obscures other crucial features of the tax structure. The amount of tax people actually pay is also determined by the thresholds at which tax rates start (including the personal allowance), the range of income on which it is paid, the reliefs they can claim, and, now, on the interaction of tax rates with tax credits. It also depends on the rates of indirect tax. It would be helpful therefore if the basic rate *per se* became less significant in the way politicians and the media discuss the tax system.

Second, the yield from income tax as a proportion of total tax revenues has declined since 1979: from 29% to under 26% (See Table 3.6). It is not in fact true (as sometimes thought) that this change has been accompanied by a significant shift to indirect taxation: the combined proportion of VAT and other taxes on expenditure has risen by only 1% in the same period (from 28% to 29%). But it is nevertheless the case that, had the proportion of income tax been maintained at its former level, this would have allowed a *reduction* in the proportion of indirect tax. In particular, it could have prevented the very significant increase in the rates of VAT imposed in this period. (As a proportion of total tax revenues VAT receipts doubled between 1979 and 1997, from 8% to 16%.) Since income tax is progressive in structure, while VAT is regressive, this effective shift has been regressive overall. Given our citizenship concerns about the growth of inequality, and the principle of progressivity set out in Chapter 5, the reduction in the proportion of total tax revenues accounted for by income tax is a particularly regrettable effect of the cut in rates made over the last twenty years.

Our third concern amplifies this point. As we noted in Chapter 1, and as Figure 10.1 illustrates, over the last two decades there has been a significant growth in income inequality. Up to the mid-1990s, in fact, inequality in the UK rose faster than in every other industrialised country except New Zealand.[6] (In some countries, inequality fell.) There have been a number of reasons for this. At the top of the income scale, earnings have grown rapidly, with significant numbers of people—over 200,000—now earning salaries in excess of £100,000 a year.[7] At the bottom, both the rate of unemployment and the number of households with no earners has risen. Because benefits have only been raised in line with prices over this period, those dependent on them have fallen further behind average earnings. And as we saw in Chapter 3, the tax system has not managed to slow down this growth of inequality.

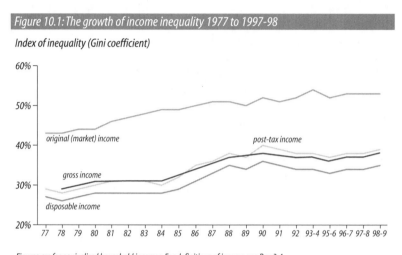

Figure 10.1: The growth of income inequality 1977 to 1997-98

Index of inequality (Gini coefficient)

Figures are for equivalised household incomes. For definitions of income, see Box 3.4

[Source: Tim Harris, 'The effects of taxes and benefits on household incomes 1998-99', Economic Trends, April 2000]

Income tax on its own of course is highly progressive. As Table 10.1 shows, the average rate of tax rises steeply as income rises. Indeed, as we have seen, there is a built-in mechanism to ensure that some of the growth of income inequality is reflected in higher marginal rates: as more people have earned higher incomes, and as the threshold for the higher rate of tax has fallen in relation to earnings, more people have been brought into the higher rate. But this mechanism has had to act against the general reduction in tax rates which has occurred over the last twenty years—including the reduction to 40% of the top rate of tax paid on any level of income.

Table 10.1: Income Tax liabilities for individuals by income range 1999-2000

Range of total income (lower limit)	Average rate of tax
£4,335	1%
£5,000	3%
£7,500	7%
£10,000	11%
£15,000	14%
£20,000	16%
£30,000	19%
£50,000	27%
£100,000	33%

[Source: Inland Revenue Statistics 1999]

Unfortunately, the policy of reducing income tax rates has outweighed the built-in mechanisms. The income tax system is less progressive now than it was twenty years ago. The result, as Figure 10.1 shows, is that disposable incomes (incomes after income tax has been paid) have grown more unequal in this period to exactly the same extent as pre-tax incomes have done. In other words income tax, which is the principal method the tax system has for reducing inequalities, has not over this period achieved this end. When indirect taxes are incorporated into the analysis, the effect is even more startling. As we saw in Chapter 3 and as Table 3.6 showed, post-tax incomes have not only grown more unequal over the last twenty years: the growth of inequality has been *greater* than for pre-tax incomes. The tax system, that is, has not only not reined back the growth of inequality in pre-tax incomes which has occurred over this period; it has managed to worsen it. From the point of view of our strong conception of citizenship, this is the most serious criticism of all the policy changes made over the last twenty years.

These trends, then, constitute the starting point for the Commission's approach to reform of the income tax system. We are concerned that those on the highest incomes, having enjoyed a rapid growth in earnings and, often, investment income over the last two decades, are not now paying a fair share in taxation. We do not suppose that rising inequality can be reversed simply through the tax system. But we do believe that the burden of taxation can be made fairer. Because of its essentially progressive structure, it is the income tax system which will almost certainly be the main vehicle for achieving this objective.

£

Proposed reforms

One reform which would help to make the tax system as a whole more progressive would be a shift in the balance of different kinds of tax: notably, an increase in the proportion of total tax revenues taken through income tax and a reduction in the proportion taken from indirect taxes. But the issues raised by this option concern indirect taxes as well as direct ones: we shall therefore consider it in the next chapter. In this chapter we shall examine how the structure of income tax itself can contribute to a fairer and more inclusive society.

Progressivity and redistribution

The principal way of making the income tax system fairer is to make it more progressive. There are two obvious approaches to doing this. One is to ask those on higher incomes to pay more in tax; the other is to reduce the tax paid by those on lower incomes. Of course, these two methods could be combined: the revenues raised by increasing the tax on the affluent could be spent on reducing the tax paid by the less well off. The 'gradient of progressivity' would be made steeper.

But another approach might be aimed at those in the middle of the income distribution. There are grounds to change the *shape* of the tax schedule. At present the tax schedule includes a rather dramatic leap from a marginal rate of 22% to one of 40% at around £33,000 gross annual income.[8] In terms of the overall range of incomes (from zero to, say, £200,000 plus), this leap to the highest rate of tax takes place quite low down. In fact, when National Insurance contributions are included, the marginal rate structure takes on an even stranger shape. With the Upper Earnings Limit for NI currently standing at £27,820 per year, there is actually a drop in the combined marginal rate of income tax and NI from 32% (22% income tax + 10% NI) back to 22% until the higher rate of income tax kicks in at £32,785. (This is shown in Figure 10.7.) One way of making the income tax system fairer would therefore be aimed at 'smoothing' the shape of the marginal (and average) rate structure. This could be done either by increasing the number of tax bands or changing the thresholds at which they begin and end.

Each of these three ways of increasing the fairness of the income tax system would rebalance the shares of taxation, towards those on the highest incomes and away from those further down. But none of them can benefit the people right at the bottom. This is because the poorest individuals—indeed a third of all adults in the UK (around 14 million people)—do not have high enough incomes to pay income tax at all. So no changes to the rates or thresholds of income tax can help to raise their living standards. If we consider the main measure of inequality to be a relationship between the incomes of those at the top of the income distribution and those at the bottom, adjustments to the income tax system alone cannot address it. For this reason the income tax system on its own is not as useful a vehicle for redistribution of this kind as is sometimes believed.

We cannot in fact consider how to raise the incomes of those at the bottom unless we include public spending in our analysis. As we argued in Chapter 5, the progressivity of the overall system of tax and spending matters just as much as, if not more than, that of the tax system alone. Therefore a fourth method of increasing progressivity also needs to be considered. This is to increase public spending in ways which will benefit low-income individuals and households. Such spending might take the form of direct financial transfers—social security benefits, pensions or tax credits. Or it could be on other kinds of measures which help to raise the incomes of poorer individuals and households indirectly—employment schemes such as the New Deal, lifelong learning and training programmes, support for childcare, and so on. If such spending is financed in part by raising the tax share contributed by the afflu- ent, a relatively direct redistribution from the top to the bottom of the income distribution will be achieved.

It is worth commenting briefly on this concept of 'redistribution'. It can often sound as if this is a static process taking place at a single point in time, in which money is somehow expropriated from rich people and handed over to poorer ones. But this is not actually what happens at all. As we saw in Chapter 3, the combined system of taxation and public expendi- ture is *already* redistributive: inevitably and considerably so, since the better off pay much more in tax than those on low incomes and receive fewer direct benefits. So when we speak of 'redistribution' what is actually meant is a change in the existing pattern of taxation and spending, in which a somewhat larger proportion of the incomes of the better off is taxed every year and a rather higher proportion of spending is directed at (or a smaller amount of tax is taken from) the less well off. This does not necessarily mean, it should be noted, that the richer groups are made (privately) worse off: they will be worse off than they would have been in the absence of the change, but higher gross incomes may still leave them with more money overall.

Redistribution, it should be noted, can also occur 'horizontally', to partic- ular groups in the population. As we saw in Chapter 3, the Labour government has achieved a considerable redistribution of this kind towards adults with children, both in recognition of the extra costs all parents face in bringing up children and as part of its strategy to reduce child poverty. Further measures, notably the Children's Tax Credit from 2001 and the Integrated Child Credit from 2003, are planned. But again, various forms of public spending (such as Child Benefit) will be as important in achieving this goal as the tax system alone.

With these different possible objectives in mind, and conscious (in line with the principles we set out in Chapter 5) of the need to ensure that the system provides continuing incentives to work and enterprise, the Commission considered various possible ways of making the structure of income tax more progressive. We first examined mechanisms which would involve no change in total revenue (that is, which would be 'fiscally neutral'); we then relaxed this assumption to consider approaches which would involve additional spending as well. Four options are examined below:

- Reform of the personal allowance
- A new top rate of income tax
- Raising the National Insurance Upper Earnings Limit
- A new middle rate of income tax

The personal allowance

Our first proposal concerns the personal allowance. This is an allowance of income that can be received tax-free by every taxpayer. For a person under 65 (there are additional 'age allowances' for people aged 65-74 and over 75) the allowance is £4,385pa in 2000-01.

This may seem straightforward. But in fact the personal allowance works in a rather strange way. Since the allowance is deducted from gross income, it effectively reduces the amount of money on which an individual pays his or her top rate of tax. Its value to the taxpayer therefore depends on his or her highest tax rate. For most people, who pay at the basic rate of 22%, it is worth £964.70 (£4385 x 22%). But its value to a top rate taxpayer is £1754.00 (£4385 x 40%), or nearly twice as much. For the 3 million people whose top rate of tax is 10%, on the other hand, it is worth only £438.50.

This disparity in the value of the personal allowance is inequitable. It also contributes to the opacity of the income tax system. When a Chancellor raises the personal allowance in the Budget, it appears to be of equal value to all taxpayers, when in fact it benefits the better off much more than those on low incomes.

For both these reasons the Commission proposes that the present personal allowance should be replaced by a Flat-rate Personal Allowance (FPA) worth exactly the same amount to every taxpayer (with sufficient tax liability to be able to claim it in full). We would propose that this should initially be set at around the value of the present allowance to a basic rate taxpayer (£964.70): for simplicity, this might be £1,000. The easiest way of understanding how this would work is to think of the income tax schedule as having, not an initial personal allowance, but a flat-rate *refund*. Tax would be calculated on all income earned (minus pension contributions) and then each taxpayer would effectively be given back £1,000 off their tax bill. Those whose bill did not come to £1,000 would simply pay no tax at all (they would not receive the difference). In this way the allowance would be worth exactly the same in cash terms to every taxpayer, up to a maximum of their tax liability—which of course would mean that as a percentage of income it would be worth much more to those on low than to those on high incomes.[9]

In the absence of any other changes, the Flat-rate Personal Allowance would change the tax schedule, as given in Table 10.2.

Table 10.2: The flat-rate personal allowance: income tax thresholds		
Threshold (gross income, excluding pension contributions)		
Tax rate	Current system	With a flat-rate personal allowance
10%	£4,385	£0
22%	£5,905 (= £4,385 + £1,520)	£1,520
40%	£32,785 (= £4,385 + £28,400)	£28,400

In practice, no one with an income below £4,385 per year would be liable to income tax, as their FPA would cancel out their liabilities. The 10% band would thus effectively disappear,[10] while the 40% band would be entered at significantly lower income, significantly raising marginal rates of tax for many people. Raising the current tax liability of people near the higher rate threshold is not the purpose of this reform, however. We would therefore propose that if an FPA were introduced, the higher rate threshold should be simultaneously raised, sufficiently to ensure that no-one was made worse off by the change at the time. For an FPA of £1,000, this would involve raising the higher rate to £32,600. The cost of introducing such a reform would then be £758m.[11] Since higher rate taxpayers would all be compensated, and 22% taxpayers would be more or less unaffected (they would gain the small difference between the £964.70 current allowance and the £1,000 FPA), this money would effectively be 'spent' on all current 10% taxpayers (those earnings under £6,000 pa), who would enjoy a small benefit.

In this way the introduction of a Flat-rate Personal Allowance would have a small progressive impact among taxpayers. (It would not, of course, affect non-taxpayers at all.) But this would not be its principal purpose. The aim would be to create a new, more progressive *structure* of income tax. After an FPA were introduced, any rise in the personal tax threshold would benefit lower income groups by the same amount (in cash terms) as higher income groups, and by more in relative terms, instead of (as now) benefiting the better off by more. Imagine, for example, that inflation is 5% and the personal allowance is raised in the Budget (through indexation) by this amount. Under the present system the personal allowance would rise from £4,385 to £4,605. This would be worth £22 a year to a 10% taxpayer, £48 to a 22% taxpayer and £88 to a 40% taxpayer. But under a flat-rate allowance a 5% increase would be worth £50 to everyone. This is patently fairer. And at the same time the tax system would be made more transparent: not only because the value of the personal allowance would be more easily understood, but because the tax schedule could be expressed in simple gross terms rather than through the more difficult concept of 'taxable income'.

The top rate of income tax

The top rate of income tax in the UK is 40%. As Table 10.6 shows, this is low by international standards. The top rate is entered at around £33-£36,000 of gross annual income (depending on pensions contributions).

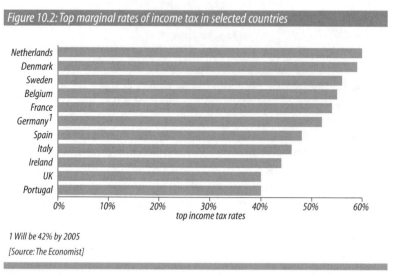

Figure 10.2: Top marginal rates of income tax in selected countries

1 Will be 42% by 2005
[Source: The Economist]

In the Commission's view this structure is not appropriate, for two reasons. First, it is inequitable that those earning around £35,000 of gross annual income pay the same marginal rate as those earning £100,000 and £1 million. With the growth in higher earnings over recent years, £35,000 is in relative terms no longer an extremely high salary (though it is still in the top 10% of the income distribution).[12] As we noted above, whereas in 1979 fewer than 700,000 people (under 3% of income taxpayers) paid the higher rate of income tax of 40% or above, the figure now is 2.3 million, or 9%. The progression of income tax rates would be smoother if there were more than one rate applying above average earnings.

Second, and more simply, we believe that the very affluent should contribute more to the common good through the tax system. This is partly in order to address rising inequality, on the citizenship grounds we have previously discussed. But it is also partly because we believe that the very well off are not presently charged a level of tax which reflects their ability to pay.

This is partly because of the remarkable growth of incomes among very high earners. Between 1996-97 and 1997-98, the number of individuals earning more than £100,000 a year rose from 153,000 to 186,000, an increase of 21% in a year. Their combined gross earnings rose from £26.7bn to

£40.4bn, an increase of 51%. But the level of their combined deductions and reliefs rose from £1.93bn to £3.91bn, an increase of 102%. Hence the average tax rate for individuals earning over £100,000 fell from 35% to 33%.[13] This does not seem to us to be an appropriate state of affairs. In a society where there are great needs, both for improved public services and to eliminate poverty, we believe those groups in society who have benefited most from rapidly growing incomes and wealth should pay more in tax than they do at present.

We therefore believe that a new top rate of tax should be levied on higher incomes. This rate should be somewhere in the range 45-50%. If the lower figure were chosen, the threshold should be lower; a rate of 50% would require a somewhat higher starting point. We do not believe that the top rate should be any higher than 50%. This has both a certain symbolism (that no more than half of any tranche of earnings should be taken in tax) and a clear relationship to other countries' top rates.

There is no similarly obvious logic to the level of income above which the new top rate should apply. The lower the income level the more significant the possible effects on work incentives. We would argue that the threshold should be at least £75,000 pa of taxable income, depending on the rate chosen. (Note that a taxable income of £75,000 equates to a gross income of at least £80,000.)

Our own preference on balance is for a rate of 50% above a threshold of £100,000pa in taxable income. This would affect just 200,000 people.[14] Such a threshold would clearly establish the new tax rate as designed to apply only to very high-earning individuals. Note that £100,000 of taxable income is a minimum of £105,000 of gross income, and for most people earning at this level almost certainly (when pension contributions are added in) nearer £120,000. It is very difficult to argue, we believe, that a 50% marginal tax rate at this level would stifle enterprise or lead to international migration at any significant rate. As Figure 10.2 shows, such a rate at such a threshold would by no means be high in comparison with other countries.

We note too that many members of the discussion groups in our public attitudes research argued that those on the highest incomes should face a higher rate of income tax, and it was above an income level of around £100,000 pa that it was generally felt this should apply.[15]

The principal motivation for proposing a higher top rate is to ensure a more progressive income tax system. But there would be little point in it if the additional revenues gained were small. In fact they are not. The Inland Revenue calculates that a 50% top rate on taxable incomes of over £100,000 would yield £2.9 billion in 2000-01, with an expectation that this would rise by around £200m annually over the next few years as more people enter this income bracket.[16]

Use of the revenues

In these circumstances the question arises as to what should be done with this money. Clearly one option would simply be to add it to the Treasury's general funds, to be spent on public services of various kinds. The most overtly redistributive method would be to spend it on measures which would raise the incomes of, and provide other opportunities for, those beneath the thresholds of the income tax system. However we believe it would be more appropriate if the additional revenues were used to rebalance the burden of the tax system itself. This would ensure that the purpose of the new rate—to achieve a fairer share of the tax burden—was clear and publicly understood. By keeping the reform revenue-neutral it would also ensure that the overall share of taxation in national income was not raised.

In line with the discussion above, this would suggest two broad ways in which the revenues could be used. First, they could reduce the tax paid by low-income taxpayers. There are a number of methods by which this could be done, but the simplest would be to raise the personal allowance. £2.9 billion would enable the personal allowance (on the current system) to be raised by just over £500, to £4,895.[17] This would take around 800,000 people out of income tax altogether, with significant impacts on household incomes for those with low earnings. It would have the added advantage of reducing the administrative costs of the tax system.[18]

The second option would be to use the revenues, or some of them, to 'smooth' the progression of income tax rates. As we have already observed, the fact that over the last two decades the 40% threshold has not risen in line with earnings has brought many people into the higher rate tax bracket who would not have been in it—on equivalent earnings—a few years ago. In this sense the point at which marginal rates jump from 22% to 40% has been brought lower and lower down the income distribution. There is therefore a case for raising the threshold somewhat to bring it more into line with its former position.

This would clearly not benefit those on the lowest incomes: the primary beneficiaries would be people currently just above the current 40% threshold whose marginal rate would fall to 22% if it were raised. (It would also benefit everyone else in the top rate bracket, who would pay 40% tax on a smaller proportion of their income.) But tax reforms—as with reforms in other fields—need not only be aimed at benefiting the poorest groups. As we argued in Chapter 5, one of our aims in this report is to strengthen the general legitimacy of the tax system. The increasing number of people paying the higher rate as its threshold comes down relative to earnings is sometimes seen as inequitable. It seems to us that raising the threshold—on condition that this is financed by a new top rate of income tax—that is, that the money to do this comes from those *above* this level, not those below—is not an unreasonable proposition.

According to calculations done for the Commission by the Inland Revenue, raising the threshold by £1,600 to £30,000pa of taxable income (around £35,000 gross) would take 420,000 people out of the higher rate tax bracket. It would cost around £1 billion. But this would still leave around £1.9 billion for measures benefiting those towards the lower end of the income distribution. For example, such a reform might be combined with an increase in the personal allowance of £250 to £4,635, thereby removing nearly half a million people (480,000) from income tax altogether. The combined effect of these measures (the new top rate of income tax, a higher 40% threshold and a higher tax allowance) would then benefit 27.8 million people, with only 200,000—the new higher rate taxpayers—losing out.[19] (It should be noted that all income taxpayers earning up to £100,000 taxable income per year would benefit from this, so in terms of incentives many more entrepreneurs and others would gain than would lose.)

These two proposals are of course only illustrative. Our aim here is not to recommend a single 'package' from among the possible permutations. The important point is political. It lies in the signal that such a combination of reforms would send. This is that the very affluent in our society should make a larger contribution to society through the tax system. But the aim in taxing them more is not punitive (or a product of any so-called 'politics of envy'). It is designed to create a fairer, more progressive structure of income tax. Such a message, we believe, would help improve the general legitimacy of the tax system, reducing the sense that people have of its unfairness, and hence increasing their 'connection' with it.[20]

The National Insurance Upper Earnings Limit

We noted above that when National Insurance contributions were included in to the schedule of marginal income tax rates, a rather strange picture emerged. Because the Upper Earnings Limit (UEL) for NI is reached at a lower point than the 40% threshold, the combined marginal rate of income tax and NI actually falls (from 32% to 22%) at an annual income level of £27,820 before rising again to 40% at around £33,000. This is shown in Figure 10.3. In terms of progressivity this 'kink' between the UEL and the higher rate threshold is anomalous.

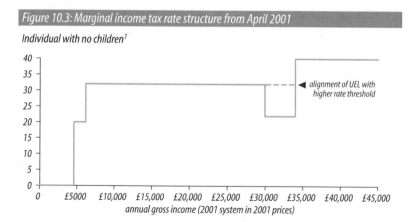

Figure 10.3: Marginal income tax rate structure from April 2001

Individual with no children[1]

◄ *alignment of UEL with higher rate threshold*

annual gross income (2001 system in 2001 prices)

1 A slightly different marginal rate structure applies to individuals with children resulting from the introduction of the Children's Tax Credit. For a childless person under 65 years, includes all pre-announced measures; employee class 1 NICs only.

Some commentators have suggested that the Upper Earnings Limit be abolished altogether. This would create (in the present tax system) a marginal tax rate of 50% on all earnings from the present higher rate threshold upwards. The claim is that the base for National Insurance should be the same as for income tax: at present higher earnings are effectively exempted from making contributions, reducing the progressivity of the system as a whole. But this would mean imposing a combined marginal 'tax' rate of 50% relatively low down the income distribution. The argument also fails to recognise that NI contributions are not a general tax. They create entitlements to specific benefits (the basic state pension, contributory job seeker's allowance, maternity allowance and so on) which are paid at a single rate to everyone who qualifies irrespective of the value of contributions made. The Upper Earnings Limit therefore has a purpose: it limits the contributions which higher earners are expected to make in return for flat-rate benefits. If the UEL were abolished, the revenues generated would not currently be available for general Treasury use: they would have to go into the National Insurance Fund. As such they would require other reforms of the NI system. Abolition of the UEL could not therefore be considered simply as a tax reform. (The National Insurance system is discussed in more detail in the Annex.)

Rather than abolish the UEL, we would therefore propose that its level should be aligned with the threshold for the higher rate of income tax. This would effectively continue the process of closing the gap between the two which has been implemented over the last decade. Alignment would raise £600m in extra contributions. In order to ensure that no-one under the higher rate threshold lost out from this, we would suggest that these funds be used to cut the principal rates of National Insurance on a revenue-neutral basis.

Modelling by the Institute for Fiscal Studies shows that this could be done by reducing the main NI rates by just 0.21%. (The contracted-in rate would fall from 10% to 9.79%; the contracted-out rate from 8.4% to 8.19%; and the Class 4 rate from 6% to 5.79%). This would leave average household incomes marginally higher in all but the top decile, ie for the richest tenth of the population, whose average net loss would be £1.20 per week.[21] This would we believe be a worthwhile structural reform.

A middle rate of income tax?

We noted above that the current schedule of marginal income tax rates involved a significant leap from 22% to 40% at the higher tax threshold. One way of 'smoothing' the progression of rates would therefore be to introduce an extra tax band somewhere between 22% and 40%. There were, after all, two bands at 25% and 33% (reduced to 30% in 1979) before the former was abolished in 1980. Creating a band at, say, 30% would enable the basic rate to be reduced—which would benefit all those on lower incomes beneath the new rate threshold.

To see how this might work we modelled a new structure of income tax rates at 10%, 20%, 30% and 40%. The threshold for the 30% rate was chosen as the level which would finance a cut in the basic rate to 20% (ie the package was fiscally neutral). This turned out to be £16,500 per year. So the structure in terms of taxable income was as set out in Table 10.3.

Table 10.3: A middle rate of income tax: thresholds		
Rate	Starting threshold	
	taxable income	gross income*
10%	£0	£4,385
20%	£1,520	£5,905
30%	£16,500	£20,885
40%	£28,400	£32,785

excluding age allowances and pension contributions

Looking at this schedule it is important to remember the difference between marginal and average rates. A 30% rate of income tax on incomes above £20,885 (including the personal allowance) looks very high—until it is realised that only 20% has been paid on all income (from the 20% threshold of £5,905, including the personal allowance) up to this point. Indeed, one of the main advantages of an extra band of this kind would be to focus attention away from marginal rates and on to average rates, thereby aiding public

understanding of the system. In fact the distributional effects of this structure
would be extremely favourable, as shown in Figure 10.4. All deciles of household income except the richest one see an average increase in post-tax
income, with significant gains, in terms of pounds per week, going to those
in the bottom half of the distribution. Only in the top three deciles are more
than 10% of households made worse off.[22]

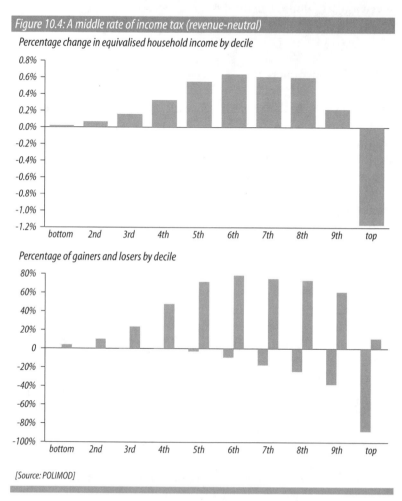

Figure 10.4: A middle rate of income tax (revenue-neutral)

Percentage change in equivalised household income by decile

Percentage of gainers and losers by decile

[Source: POLIMOD]

The Commission sees several advantages in a structure with an additional
rate band of this kind. The first is the distributional effect, as just observed.
Second, such a structure would make the tax system more flexible, enabling
different rates to be adjusted to raise different amounts of money, with more
targeted distributional impacts. In particular, it would enable significant
revenues to be raised on people in the upper half of the income distribution
alone, unlike the present single basic rate which hits more or less everyone.

(We return to this below.) A system of multiple rates takes attention away from the single basic rate, which would help create a more mature political debate.

However we can also see strong arguments against. An extra band would make the tax system more complex, particularly for those completing self-assessment forms and for the calculation of taxation on savings interest. One of the advantages of the current wide basic rate tax band is that most individuals with more than one source of PAYE earnings, and/or savings outside tax-exempt ISAs, do not have to adjust their tax through self-assessment. It is deducted at source at the correct (basic) rate. With an extra band starting at £16,500 per year, many would have to do so, since some would fall into the new marginal rate while others would not. This would add to compliance and administrative costs.

These grounds of complexity persuade us that as a revenue-neutral reform on its own the introduction of a middle rate band would not be worth the cost. (Though if, as seems likely, more people end up completing tax returns over the coming years the force of this objection will decline). But we also considered the option of a middle rate band as a structural reform in circumstances where the government was seeking support for a rise in tax revenue to pay for additional long-term spending.

Raising more revenue

With the current structure of income tax there is only one simple way for the government to gain significant extra revenue for higher spending, should it seek to do so. This is a rise in the basic rate. A rise in the higher rate would of course be possible: but since each 1p rise raises only £720 million, a significant increase in spending, say, £4 billion, would require a rise in the higher rate of 5.5%: that is, to at least 45%. This would substantially change the nature of the higher rate and might well have significant incentive effects on work and enterprise in the economy as a whole. By contrast, if £4 billion were to be raised from the basic rate, the rise would need to be only 1.5%, to 23.5%. The reason for this difference is simple. Only 2.3 million people pay the higher rate, whereas over 23 million pay the basic rate. So a small rise in the latter raises a lot of money in comparison with the former.

In general the Commission's view is that, if a government were seeking significantly more tax revenues for public spending, a rise in the basic rate is the most transparent, equitable and probably politically acceptable way in which this could be done (assuming a new top rate of 45-50% had already been created). (We leave aside the possibility of special or windfall business taxes, such as the mobile phone licence auction or windfall tax on privatised utilities.) However we are also conscious that the distributional effects of a basic rate rise are not ideal. Such a rise affects all taxpayers with incomes above £5,905 per year, including many in the lower half of the income distribution. Since in general we would prefer that lower-income households were not taxed more highly than they are at present, it would be fairer if a way of raising the same amount of money could be found which concentrated the increase in the top half of the income distribution.

A middle rate band could achieve this.[23] It has the specific advantage in these circumstances of being able to protect from a tax increase all those with incomes less than a given threshold. Thus, for example, it would be possible to protect all those under £20,885 gross income (£16,500 taxable income), as in the proposal above. Since this is not far from the level of average earnings, such a proposal would effectively ensure that only those in the top half of the earnings distribution paid more in tax.

The Commission compared this proposal with a simple rise in the basic rate to raise the same amount of money—an additional £4 billion for public spending. A rate of just over 29% was required to start at a threshold of £16,500 annual taxable income.[24] The results are shown in Figure 10.5.

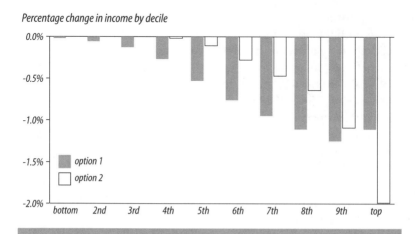

Figure 10.5: Raising £4 billion

Rate structure

Current	Option 1: Basic rate increase	Option 2: New middle rate
10% up to 1520	10% up to 1,520	10% up to 1,520
22% up to 28400	23.54% up to 28,400	22% up to 16,500
		29.4% up to 28,400
40% above that	40% above that	40% above that

Percentage change in income by decile

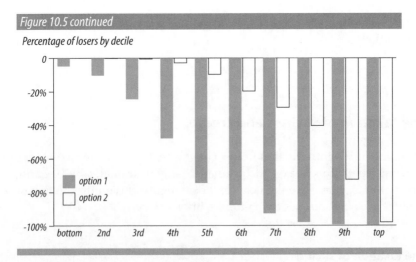

Figure 10.5 continued

Percentage of losers by decile

Figure 10.5 shows that the distributional advantages of raising this sum of money through an additional middle rate tax band are considerable. Whereas average post-tax incomes in every decile are reduced by the basic rate increase, with the new middle rate there are no losses until the fourth decile and the average loss does not reach 1% of weekly income until the ninth decile, ie the richest 20% of the household population. Overall only 27% of households lose out from the introduction of the new middle rate, compared with 74% from the increase in basic rate.

Politically, we can see the difficulties that a middle rate of 29% might cause: the public would have to understand the difference between marginal and average rates. An increase in the basic rate to 23.5% is much simpler to comprehend and may look superficially smaller. But we do not believe that it would be impossible to make it clear to the public how an extra band would affect their income—and if this were done, the preponderance of 'winners' over 'losers', coupled with the intrinsic fairness of protecting the worse off, might make this option more politically acceptable than an across-the-board basic rate increase. If it were decided to introduce the new rate with a lower threshold, so as to protect only those on genuinely low incomes (gross annual incomes of £15,000 and below, say), the required middle rate would be that much lower, and therefore possibly even more politically acceptable.

Certainly, this illustrative example suggests to the Commission that a new middle rate should be seriously considered in the event that a government sought a sustained increase in public spending paid for through higher income tax, or if changes in tax administration made an increase in the number of bands administratively less costly. (A short-term or cyclical increase in tax would not justify a change in the tax structure.) The disadvantages of an additional rate, which we have noted, would remain; but they might well be worth paying for the greater progressivity that such a rate could achieve.[25]

£

The taxation of savings and credits

We noted in the introduction to this chapter that there were two other areas in which the income tax structure had changed dramatically over the last twenty years. These are the taxation of savings and the introduction of 'tax credits'. We shall discuss each of these briefly in turn.

The taxation of savings

Contrary to widespread public misperception (see Chapter 2), savings in the UK are not taxed. What is taxed is the income from savings: the interest earned on bank and building society accounts, unit trusts, stocks and shares and other kinds of investments. Or rather, *some* of the interest is taxed. For the major change which has been made in this field over the past two decades has been to take much of the country's savings out of tax altogether. Before 1983 investment income was not only included for tax assessment, it was subject to a further 15% tax surcharge. Since then both Conservative and Labour Chancellors have sought to make moderate levels of income from saving tax-free.

This has been done through the creation of tax-exempt savings and investment vehicles, initially PEPs (Personal Equity Plans) and TESSAs (Tax-Exempt Special Savings Accounts), now ISAs (Individual Savings Accounts). These have simplified the tax system for many people, doing away with the need to declare interest payments, dividends or capital gains. But the consequence has been a narrowing of the tax base. By putting money into a PEP, TESSA or ISA, as into a pension, an individual reduces the income on which tax is charged. The benefits, inevitably, have largely accrued to the relatively well-off, who save much more than those on low incomes. For a given level of revenue, therefore, the overall effect has been regressive.

On the other hand, these reforms have rationalised the tax treatment of the main kinds of savings, as Table 10.4 shows. Now pensions, owner-occupied housing (since the abolition of mortgage interest relief) and ISAs are all taxed in more or less the same way. Capital put into ISAs and owner-occupied housing comes out of post-tax income, but the returns are tax-free. (The returns on housing are the imputed rent that would otherwise have had to be paid, plus the capital gain on sale.) Meanwhile contributions to personal and occupational pensions are made out of pre-tax income, but when the pension is taken (apart from a 25% lump sum) the payments are taxed. Although the point of taxation is different, these are more or less equivalent zero tax rates. Only non-ISA interest-bearing bank and building society accounts, along with stocks and shares and life insurance, are taxed both at the point of contribution and return—though in the latter capital gains are only taxed above an annual allowance (£7,200 in 2000-01). Of course, the amounts that can be saved in the various tax-exempt vehicles are different: the ISA limit is £7,000 per year, whereas up to 15% of earnings can be saved in a pension without limit, and there are no limits at all on housing.

Table 10.4: The tax treatment of saving				
Asset	Contributions	Returns		Withdrawals
		Interest or dividends	Capital gains	
Interest-bearing accounts	Taxed	Taxed	--	Exempt
Shares	Taxed	Taxed	Taxed[1]	Exempt
Life assurance	Taxed	Taxed	Taxed	Exempt
Owner-occupied housing	Taxed	Exempt	Exempt	Exempt
ISAs	Taxed	Exempt[2]	Exempt	Exempt
Private pensions	Exempt	Exempt	Exempt	Taxed[3]

1 above an annual allowance
2 plus 10% dividend tax credit
3 except for a 25% tax-free lump sum

[Source: Lucy Chennells et al, The IFS Green Budget, Institute for Fiscal Studies, 2000]

In theory there are sound arguments for reversing these reforms: broadening the base of taxation to include all savings income would allow lower rates overall and a more progressive structure. But we believe there are even stronger reasons not to change the now well-established tax treatment of savings. As we argued in Chapter 5, there are good economic and social grounds for encouraging both short- and long-term savings through tax incentives. The propensity to save has fallen over recent decades: if people are to have greater financial security, both during their working lives and in old age, they need to be given encouragement to save. If pension contributions and ISA returns were taxed, the relative attraction of owner-occupied housing as a form of saving would increase, fuelling house price inflation. (As well as this result being politically unattractive, it would be very difficult to assess the value of the inputed income from housing in the absence of reliable market rents.)

In general therefore we believe the present arrangement for taxing savings to be broadly appropriate, apart from the one remaining anomaly in the system, which is the tax-free pension lump sum. This effectively makes the tax rate on the return to pensions saving not simply zero but negative. Some tax advantages to saving in a pension over (say) an ISA are probably desirable. But higher rate taxpayers already get pension contributions relieved from tax at 40%, although with lower retirement income they will probably pay tax on their pension at 22% (or whatever the basic rate will be when they retire). In addition, employers' contributions to a private pension are not subject to National Insurance, so can be larger than would be the case if the money were directly invested by the employee. In these circumstances we are unconvinced that the tax-free nature of the lump sum is necessary to encourage people to take out pensions, or is an otherwise appropriate use of public funds. Given that there is already considerable debate at present about the rules for the use of private pension funds on maturity, we would propose that the tax-free lump sum be included in a review of these.

Tax credits

The final major change in the tax system implemented by the present Labour Government is the introduction and increasing use of 'targeted' tax credits. The introduction of tax credits is clearly an important development in the combined systems of taxation and social security. The Government regards them as one of its most important innovations. Box 10.2 lists those already introduced and announced and others planned.

A 'tax credit' is a deduction from income tax due. 'Targeted' tax credits are means-tested or withdrawn as income rises. There are essentially two kinds. The Working Families Tax Credit (which replaced the old Family Credit social security benefit) and the Disabled Person's Tax Credit (which replaced the old Disability Working Allowance), are 'in-work credits', aimed at raising the incomes of those in relatively low-paid employment. The important feature of this first type of tax credits is that they use the income tax system for their delivery, but not for their assessment.26 Entitlement is worked out on the basis of family income, as it would be if they were means-tested benefits (although this is now done by a unit in the Inland Revenue, rather than by the Benefits Agency). The credits are then 'delivered' to most of those entitled through deductions from income tax on the payslip, with employers taking on some of the burden of their administration. A second important feature of these kinds of credits is that recipients whose tax liability is less than their tax credit entitlement receive a positive payment in their pay packet—a sort of 'negative income tax'. Lone parent employees must have the tax credit paid in the paypacket by their employer. But couples can elect to have a direct cash payment instead, to the partner who is not the main wage-earner; so for them the credit is neither delivered nor assessed by the

Box 10.2: Tax credits

The following have been introduced, announced or proposed by the Government. Figures for 2000-01.

Working Families Tax Credit *(WFTC)*

An in-work benefit or credit for families with children. Announced in the 1998 Budget, it replaced Family Credit (FC) in October 1999. It is conditional on at least one adult working for a minimum of 16 hours per week. The basic credit for each family is £53.15 per week, plus additions for children depending on age (£25.60 for a child under 16 and £26.35 for a child aged 16-18) and £11.25 for working more than 30 hours or more per week. The credit is reduced by 55p for every £1 of family income, after income tax and National Insurance, above £91.45 per week.

Childcare Tax Credit

An addition to the WFTC that covers 70% of the cost of registered childcare used by WFTC recipients. Once entitlement to the basic WFTC has been exhausted, the childcare tax credit is reduced by 55p for every additional £1 of income.

Children's Tax Credit *(CTC)*

Announced in the 1999 Budget and to be introduced in April 2001 as a replacement for the married couple's allowance. One credit will be available to each family with children. It will reduce the tax liability of the family by a maximum of £520 a year. For higher-rate taxpayers, £1 of the credit will be withdrawn for every £15 of income taxed at the higher rate. This new credit will be payable to all families with one or more children aged under 16 living with them.

Disabled Person's Tax Credit *(DPTC)*

A credit based on the WFTC paid to disabled people who work at least 16 hour a week. Unlike the WFTC, it is not conditional on having children. In 2000-01 the maximum value of the credit is £53.15 (as in WFTC there is a full-time addition of £11.25 for those working 30+ hours) and the credit is reduced by 55p for every pound of net family income (after tax and NI) above £91.45.

Integrated Child Credit *(ICC)*

Proposed by the government in November 1999 for introduction in 2003. Involves integrating the support for children given under Income Support, Job Seekers' Allowance, Working Families Tax Credit and Children's Tax Credit into a single benefit.

Employment Tax Credit *(ETC)*

Proposed by the Government in November 1999 for introduction in 2003. Involves extending the work-related credit in WFTC to individuals and couples without children.

Pension Credit

Proposed by the Government in November 2000 for introduction in 2003. Expected to be a credit for pensioners with modest amounts of income above the Minimum Income Guarantee. Not clear whether it would be either assessed or delivered through the tax system, at least in the longer term.

[Source: Adapted and updated from Lucy Chennells et al, The IFS Green Budget: January 2000, Institute for Fiscal Studies, 2000.]

tax system. (Family Credit was automatically paid to the main carer in this way, as a cash benefit.)

The Children's Tax Credit to be introduced in April 2001 is of the second kind. Effectively replacing the Married Couple's Allowance and Additional Personal Allowance, it will be both assessed and delivered through the income tax system, and available to one taxpayer per family. It will not be available to people with incomes below the tax threshold, so will not be able to be received as a positive sum. It will also be withdrawn on a taper for higher rate taxpayers.

Using the tax system for delivery

The government's aims in introducing these targeted tax credits have been clearly laid out.[27] The increased generosity, and shallower tapers, of in-work tax credits are intended to help attack the unemployment and poverty traps. But these changes could have been made under their predecessor social security benefits too. As a Commission on taxation, we did not see it as part of our remit to comment on those aspects of in-work tax credits which are shared with benefits, such as the impact on work incentives or wage levels.

The government, however, is clear that it wants to see targeted tax credits, and it wants the public to see them, as part of the tax system. Indeed, it describes the income tax system as now having a series of rates, from minus 200 per cent (when the Working Families Tax Credit is a net payment) to plus 40 per cent.[28] In this context there are clearly questions which arise about the use of the tax system for the delivery and assessment of these credits. It is important to distinguish between the separate issues that arise here.

The government argues that the use of the tax mechanism and paypacket will help to reduce the stigma of receiving in-work social security benefits for recipients, and will make it more visible that work pays; this could therefore increase take-up of financial help and have positive labour market effects. In addition, although this is more implicit than explicit, the fact that WFTC has been accounted as a tax expenditure (and therefore treated as revenue foregone), rather than public expenditure, can be seen as offering the potential to increase its generosity, given the perceived constraints on social security spending. More fundamentally, it is argued that the identification of tax credits with paid employment and taxation, rather than worklessness and benefits, will also increase the flexibility for governments to increase such payments in future.

Clearly, if take-up of financial help increases, if paid employment is seen as more worthwhile, and if governments have greater flexibility to increase transfer payments, this is to be welcomed. (The Commission certainly welcomes the increased generosity of these credits over their predecessor benefits.) However, set against these potential advantages of linking in-work support to tax and pay, and delivering it through the tax system, are some disadvantages.

First, although in theory there is choice for couples over whether to get WFTC through the paypacket to the main earner or as a cash payment to the main carer, there is some doubt whether the main carer will in practice get the payment in the cases where it matters most. Mothers are in general less likely to have control over the spending of the tax credit, which will not be separately labelled as a payment for children.[29] Payment via the employer also raises issues in itself. Employers are made more aware of their employee's financial/family circumstances, and in any dispute with their employer the employee loses access not just to their earnings but also temporarily to the supplement. The administrative workload on employers is also increased.

Second, we do not believe that in the long run the use of accounting conventions is a sustainable way of winning public support for welfare policy. Justifiable public expenditure should be counted and argued for as such. And this is linked too to the third issue, which arises from our concern for a shared citizenship. By separating support for 'hardworking families'— via its link with pay and tax—from the support available for those not in the labour market, we fear there may be a risk of undermining public acceptance of the latter.

Given these advantages and disadvantages we await an assessment of the impact and operation of the Working Families Tax Credit with interest. It may be advisable to delay the extension of the delivery of income supplements through the tax system, using employers, until such an evaluation is available.[30]

Using the tax system for assessment

Using the tax system for assessment as well as delivery of 'targeted' assistance is a more radical step. Over the last few decades, there have been various attempts to construct models of an integrated system of tax and benefits.[31] On some occasions, the current Government has described its development of tax credits as moving towards this goal. As a Commission on taxation, it was not our remit to examine the social security system, and we have therefore not investigated the potential advantages and disadvantages of such integration.

However, there is one issue which falls squarely within our areas of concern and which has already arisen in particular in connection with the Children's Tax Credit—and will do so with the forthcoming Integrated Child Credit, if it also uses income tax assessment to withdraw entitlement as taxable income rises. This is the implications of 'targeted' tax credits for independent taxation.[32]

These implications, whilst differing for each tax credit, arise because these are family supplements which are intended to be related to family income— either by means-testing or by withdrawal of the supplement as income rises higher up the scale, or both. But they will be operated within an income tax system which is based on individuals having a tax liability relating only to their own income. (If the credits were not related to income, no income assessment would be required, and no issues about independent taxation would arise.) The Children's Tax Credit will have to be claimed by the partner who pays higher rate tax, if either of them does, so that it can be withdrawn as income rises. It is not yet clear how the Integrated Child Credit will work; but if it is to be part of a seamless income-related system, it is likely that the tax assessments of couples will need to be linked, thus breaching the principle of independence.[33]

As we argued in Chapter 5, the principle of individual independence—which includes autonomy, as well as privacy—is an important part of the tax system. But we also pointed out in that chapter that principles conflict. There is clearly a tension in this field: between the independence of individuals in tax matters and the aim of redistributing towards lower-income households. In general we believe that assessment of family income through the tax system should only be done when the advantages clearly outweigh the disadvantages of breaching the principle of independence.[34]

11 | Taxes on spending

Indirect taxes are taxes levied on the purchase of goods and services. The UK has two broad kinds of indirect taxation: value added tax (VAT) and various excise duties. These are listed in Box 11.1. Although indirect taxes are paid to Customs and Excise by firms rather than consumers, they are generally reflected in the price of products, so ultimately it is consumers on whom they largely fall.

Box 11.1: Indirect taxes

Value Added Tax (VAT) is calculated as the difference between the sum of a firm's purchases and the sum of its sales. In practice firms pay over to Customs and Excise the difference between the amount of VAT they pay and the amount they receive. The standard rate of VAT, levied on most goods and services, is 17.5%, with a small number of products exempted or zero-rated and some charged at 5%.

Excise duties are individual taxes levied on a number of products. Excise duties on beer, wine, spirits, tobacco and petrol/diesel are flat-rate taxes levied per pint, per litre, per packet, etc. Tobacco products are also subject to an **ad valorem** tax of 22% on the total retail price, which includes the flat-rate duty and VAT.

Excise duties 2000-01 (April 2000 prices)			
Good	Duty (pence)	Duty as a percentage of price (%)	Total tax as a percentage of price (%)
Packet of 20 cigarettes:			
specific duty	181		
ad valorem	87	70.7	88.2
(22% of retail price)			
Pint of beer	26	14.4	29.3
Wine (75cl bottle)	116	35.5	50.4
Spirits (70cl bottle)	548	44.6	59.5
Petrol (litre)	51	70.3	85.2
Unleaded petrol (litre)	49	74.8	89.7
Diesel (litre)	49	73.6	88.5

Insurance premium tax applies to most general insurance where the risk insured is located in the UK (eg motor, household, medical, income replacement and travel insurance). It is designed to act as a proxy for VAT, which is not levied directly on financial services such as insurance because of difficulties in implementation. The tax is levied at a standard rate of 5% of the gross premium, though if a policy is sold as an add-on to another product (eg travel insurance when buying a holiday) a higher rate of 17.5% is payable. Long-term insurance, such as life insurance, is exempt. The tax is forecast to raise around £1.6 billion in 2000-01.

Air passenger duty is levied on air travel from UK airports at £10 for flights to UK and European Union destinations and £20 elsewhere. From April 2001, air passenger duty on economy flights within the EU will be halved from £10 to £5, and flights from the Scottish Highlands and Islands will be removed from duty. First and club class duty will remain at £10 for destinations in the EU and will rise from £20 to £40 to other destinations. Air passenger duty is estimated to raise £1 billion in 2000-01.

Betting and gaming duties. General betting duty is a duty levied at 6.75% on the total money staked on off-course bets made with a bookmaker or the Horserace Totalisator Board (the Tote). Pool betting is liable to pool betting duty at the current rate of 17.5%. **Gaming duty** is based on the 'gross gaming yield' for each establishment where dutiable gaming takes place. This consists of the total value of the stakes, minus players' winnings, on games in which the house is the banker, and participation charges, or 'table money', exclusive of VAT, on games in which the bank is shared by players. Gaming duty is levied at marginal rates of between 2.5% and 40% according to the amount of gross gaming yield. Duties on betting and gaming are expected to raise around £1.4 billion in 2000-01.

[Sources: HM Customs and Excise, Annual Report 1998-99, 1999; Andrew Dilnot et al, A Survey of the UK Tax System, Institute for Fiscal Studies, 2000]

In this chapter we shall examine, first, some general arguments about the relative balance between direct and indirect taxes, and then more specific issues relating to VAT and the so-called 'sin' taxes on alcohol, tobacco and gambling. We shall deal with petrol duty and other taxes with environmental aims and impacts in Chapter 13.

£

The balance of direct and indirect taxation

Politically, at least until recently, indirect taxes were widely regarded as much easier to raise than direct taxes. Under the Conservative governments of 1979-1997, VAT was raised, first from 8% and 12% to 15% and then a second time to 17.5%, while over the last two decades excise duties on petrol, tobacco and wine (but not other forms of alcohol) have been raised by more than the rate of inflation. New indirect taxes, such as on insurance premiums and air travel, have also been introduced.

The politics of indirect taxation

There is a theoretical reason why one might prefer indirect to direct taxes. Indirect taxes can in some sense be described as 'voluntary', since they are paid only if and when purchases are made. Unlike taxes on income or savings, which are levied automatically, the amount of indirect tax a person pays is—in principle at least—under his or her own control. If one never bought anything, one wouldn't pay any of these taxes. This is an argument often heard on the libertarian right, but it will strike most people as a bit too abstract to be worth much. Avoiding tax by restricting one's consumption isn't a strategy many will wish to adopt.

It is also sometimes argued that indirect taxes are preferable to direct taxes because they don't have comparable disincentive effects on work. But this is incorrect. The financial appeal of work depends on the goods and services which can be bought with the income earned. If the price of these is higher as a result of higher indirect taxes, the effect of lower income taxes will be cancelled out.

The attraction of indirect taxation to politicians has in fact been intensely pragmatic. Indirect taxes are generally less visible to the individual taxpayer than direct taxes. People can see how much they pay in income tax on their monthly or weekly payslip and (if they have one) their annual tax return. But indirect taxes are paid through the price of goods, and the amount is rarely made clear. Few shops price their goods exclusive of VAT and then add the tax; unlike many countries, UK law does not require till receipts to show the tax separately. Where excise duties are concerned, the variation in rates means that most consumers have no idea how much of the price of the good—a bottle of wine, say, or a packet of cigarettes—is actually tax. (The answer in fact is that, at the present time, around 50% of the price of a standard bottle of table wine is tax; and fully 79% of a packet of cigarettes.[1]) When indirect taxes are raised, there is a flurry of media attention at the time of the Budget, but thereafter the impact generally disappears from view. Since consumers are so used to prices rising for reasons other than tax, the initial tax increase after the Budget may itself not be fully noticed.

In general over the past twenty years this relative invisibility has made indirect taxes attractive for Chancellors seeking to raise extra revenue. In the last couple of years, with political attention focused on so-called 'stealth' taxes, this situation has changed somewhat. After the protests of the summer and autumn of 2000, few people are now unaware of the levels of petrol duty. But it remains true that it is almost impossible for most people to tell how much they pay in indirect tax. This point was made frequently in the discussion groups held as part of the Commission's research into public attitudes.[2] The situation can perhaps be characterised as one in which most people are aware that they pay high rates of indirect taxes but few know, in relation to their own income, exactly how high or how much.

From the Commission's point of views, what was most striking about this was that people *know* that they do not know. This contributes to the strong sense of 'disconnection' which people now feel about the tax system. As we saw in Chapter 2, the accusation of 'stealth' has made a considerable public impression. Many people now appear to feel that indirect taxes are almost a 'ruse' allowing governments to take money in an underhand, invisible way. They resent this; indeed, a number of members of the discussion groups argued that, however unpopular income tax rises might be, at least with direct taxes one knew what one was paying. With indirect taxes it was virtually invisible.

The feeling that the continued growth of indirect taxation is somehow 'underhand' can only be detrimental to the wider legitimacy of taxation. For the Commission this in itself would be a reason to seek to slow down the increases in indirect tax rates which have occurred over the last twenty years. But there is another, equally powerful. This is that indirect taxes are essentially regressive in their effect.

Since the same rate of tax is paid by all consumers, taxes on spending bear more heavily on those who are poor than on the better off. The £17.50 in VAT paid on £100 worth of expenditure by a person earning, say, £10,000 a year represents a much higher proportion of income than the same £17.50 for a person on £100,000. This effect is exacerbated for those goods which form a higher proportion of household expenditure for people on low incomes than those with high incomes. Taxation of such items is particularly regressive.

(Note that the converse is the case for goods which are bought only by the rich. A tax on caviar, for example, would be progressive.)

Shifting the balance

Over the last twenty years, as we saw in Chapter 3, the proportion of income tax in total tax revenues has fallen by 3%, from 29% to 26%. Although the proportion of indirect taxes has risen by only a small amount, from 28% to 29%, this includes a doubling of the proportion of VAT (from 8% to 16%). We argued in the last chapter that this partial shift from direct to indirect taxes was regressive overall, since if direct taxation had not fallen, indirect taxation would not have had to rise at all.

One option which could be explored for making the tax system more progressive, therefore, would be to reduce indirect taxation and shift the burden instead back onto direct taxes, notably income tax. In theory any of the indirect taxes could be chosen for reduction. In practice, however, the scope is rather limited. The only indirect taxes which raise serious sums of money (enough to cut the basic rate of income tax by 1p, for example) are VAT and the excise duties on alcohol, tobacco, petrol and vehicle licences. Apart from VAT, all of these have purposes beyond simple revenue-raising: they are all at least partly incentive-based taxes designed to discourage social harms. As we shall see later in this chapter and in Chapter 13, reducing any of them (with the exception of vehicle excise duty—though we have other, environmentally-linked proposals for this) would cause serious ill effects on behaviour, with wider social costs.

The only serious candidate for a reduction in indirect tax, financed by a rise in income tax, is therefore VAT. But here there are other problems. For under EU rules on VAT harmonisation, the furthest that the UK's 17.5% rate of VAT can be cut is to 15%. (Lower rates are allowed for products with current VAT rates less than this.) Would such a reduction have a significant enough effect to make it worthwhile?

We modelled this option. A VAT rate of 15% (on the same goods and services as now) would cost around £4 billion. It would therefore require an increase in the basic rate of income tax to 23.5%.[3] As Figure 11.1 shows, the distributional effect of such a change would be favourable. Over 85% of the households in each of the bottom four deciles would gain, and 59% of all households. (Many of those in the bottom deciles, of course, have incomes too low to pay income tax at all.)

The problem, however, is that the gains are not very significant in cash terms—an average of around £1.50 per week for households in the second an third bottom decile. And this assumes that firms cut prices by the full 2.5%. In practice it is quite likely that prices will not fall uniformly by this amount—it would be relatively easy for both suppliers and retailers in many markets which are not completely competitive to 'lose' a small price cut of this kind in other price changes. If this happened the gains would become relatively invisible, while the costs—the higher rate of income tax—would be only too visible. For these reasons we do not believe that such a change would be politically attractive or sensible.

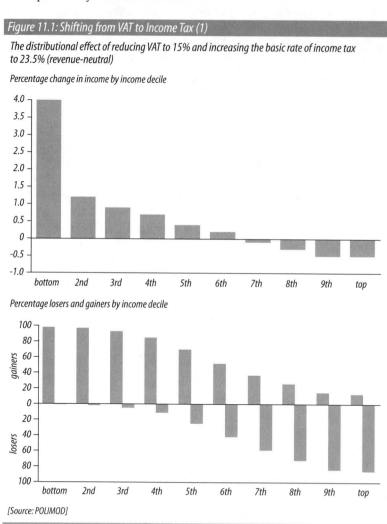

Figure 11.1: Shifting from VAT to Income Tax (1)

The distributional effect of reducing VAT to 15% and increasing the basic rate of income tax to 23.5% (revenue-neutral)

Percentage change in income by income decile

Percentage losers and gainers by income decile

[Source: POLIMOD]

But what if VAT were cut further than this? Although not currently allowed under EU rules, we see no reason to rule it out altogether as a policy option: it is at least worthwhile knowing what effect it would have. So we modelled a cut in VAT to 12.5%. This would require an increase in the basic rate of income tax to 25%.[4]

The results are shown in Figure 11.2. The basic impact is the same as for the 15% VAT rate, but on a larger scale. Again 86% of households in the bottom four deciles gain from the measure, and 60% of all households. But now the gains are rather more significant: £2.80 per week on average in the third bottom decile, £3.25 in the second lowest and fully £5.50 in the lowest. In the top two deciles the loss is limited to 1% of income, or £5-£7.50 per week.

Figure 11.2: Shifting from VAT to Income Tax (2)

The distributional effect of reducing VAT to 12.5% and increasing the basic rate of income tax to 25% (revenue neutral)

Percentage change in income by income decile

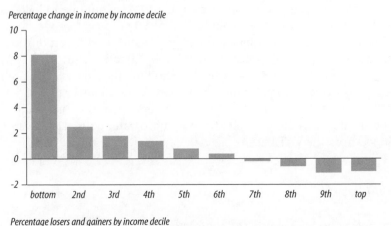

Percentage losers and gainers by income decile

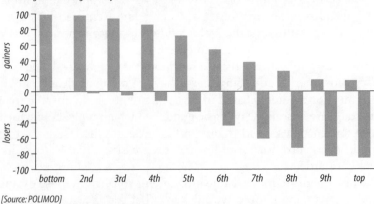

[Source: POLIMOD]

These results, which are revenue-neutral, seem to us to be very attractive. In principle we would therefore approve such a reform. This cannot be recommended as a viable option under present EU rules, and (as we explained in Chapter 9), we accept the rationale for VAT harmonisation. Given that the UK's VAT rate is already among the lowest of all EU countries, it seems very unlikely that these rules will be changed. But in principle they are not immutable. Indeed it may be that they are too restrictive of individual countries' freedom to choose their tax rates and should be reviewed to see whether a progressive change of this kind, reducing VAT to around 12.5%, should be made possible.

£

Value Added Tax

The aim of a possible reduction in the rate of VAT would be to increase the progressivity of the tax system. But VAT is in fact not as regressive as it might be. This is because it is not levied on all goods and services produced in the economy. A number of products have a 'zero rate', with certain others exempted. (The difference is concerned with how the VAT is calculated and collected by firms.[5]) A small number of goods attract a lower rate of 5%. (See Box 11.2.) Overall around 56% of all consumer expenditure is taxable at the standard rate, with 3% taxable at the reduced rate. Fully 41% is therefore excluded from the VAT base.[6]

The VAT base

There are various grounds for these reduced rates and exemptions from VAT. Financial services, insurance and rents are exempted because of the difficulty of separating out the 'value added' in these products. Businesses with low turnover are exempted to ease the burden of administration. We cannot find any reason for the exemption of large ships—since very few ordinary consumers tend to buy these, they are not in any case a final product. But most of the items listed in Box 11.2 are given favourable treatment because they are in some way 'basic goods' which all households, including those on low incomes, need to buy to live a decent life. They are therefore the goods whose taxation would be most regressive—that is, most likely to hit the poor hardest.

Of course there are major value judgements implicit in these exemptions and reductions. Few people would deny that food, water, domestic fuel and children's clothes are essential goods (though adult clothes are surely essential too). Public transport too comes plausibly into the same category: most people on very low incomes do not have access to a car, and public transport is therefore for them a basic good. But international passenger transport hardly counts as a basic good. And is there really any justification for including postal services in this list? After all, 98% of homes in the UK

Box 11.2: Items subject to lower rates of VAT	
	Estimated cost of foregoing 17.5% taxation 1999-2000 (£ million)
Zero rating	
Food	£7,800
Construction of new dwellings*	£2,750
International passenger transport	£1,800
Domestic passenger transport	£1,750
Books, newspapers and magazines	£1,300
Children's clothing	£1,100
Water and sewerage services	£950
Drugs and medicines on prescription	£650
Ships and aircraft above a certain size	£350
Vehicles and other supplies to people with disabilities	£200
Supplies to charities*	£150
5% rate	
Domestic fuel and power	£1,800
Energy saving materials and equipment	n/a
Women's sanitary products	£35**
Residential building conversion (from 2001)	n/a
Exempted	
Rent on domestic dwellings*	£2,650
Rent on commercial properties*	£1,650
Betting, gaming and lottery	£900
Private education	£900
Health services*	£550
Postal service	£400
Burial and cremation	£100
Finance and insurance*	£100
Businesses with low turnover	£100
Total	**£27,950**

* Figures for these categories are tentative, subject to a wide margin of error.
** Figure for 2001-02

[Source: HM Customs and Excise, Annual Report 1998-1999, 1999]

now have a telephone[7]—another method of communication—and telephone charges are subject to VAT. By far the bulk of expenditure on postal services is commercial, not domestic—and courier services are taxed.

And what of books and newspapers? Here lies a more subtle value judgement. Books and newspapers are what economists call 'merit goods'—products which are regarded (or at least, were regarded in 1973 when these categories were established) as intrinsically good for the people. Books and newspapers are exempt from VAT for the same general reason that museums and art galleries have free entrance (or used to have): they are believed to be 'improving' for the public and should as such not be financially discouraged. Other forms of entertainment and information media, such as cinema tickets, sales of TVs and radios, digital TV subscriptions and Internet usage, are by contrast 'vatable', for the same reason that free entrance doesn't apply to swimming pools: these are not (it is assumed) so good for you. At the same time the list of exemptions produces other oddities. Pornographic magazines are exempt from VAT, since they fall into the same general category as, say, Bibles. Many people who take small-sized clothes have realised that they can buy large children's sizes much more cheaply than small adult ones. Private education services are exempted only if provided by not-for-profit organisations (such as public schools); no such condition is required of private health services.

A uniform rate of VAT?

Unsurprisingly, these anomalies have led many commentators to call for the categories of goods subjected to different rates of VAT to be rationalised. Indeed, some have argued that exemptions and lower rates should be abolished altogether, with a single rate of VAT applied to all goods and services.[8] There are three main grounds for arguing this.

First, differential rates of VAT have an essentially 'distortionary' effect on consumption behaviour. People buy more food, books and stamps than they would otherwise, and fewer products of other kinds. To an orthodox economist, this generates a 'welfare loss': people get less satisfaction out of their consumption choices than they would if prices were not distorted in this way. At a more philosophical level, differential tax rates appear simply unfair: they penalise someone who prefers cinema-going to reading books on no other grounds than their wholly legitimate and private likes and dislikes. (This is an example of 'horizontal inequity': for the same level of expenditure the film-goer pays more tax than the book-lover.)

Second, if the purpose of zero-rating is to benefit those on low incomes, it is not a very efficient way of going about this. Though zero-rating means that poor households pay less on the designated goods, so do the rich, who could afford to pay the tax. Indeed, the rich actually benefit more from zero-rating than the poor do: though the proportion of total spending on the basic goods is higher among low-income households, it nevertheless rises in absolute terms with income. If the intention is to tax people on low incomes less, it would be more efficient if this were done directly rather than indirectly—by taxing their incomes rather than their expenditures less. Raising social security benefit levels would be another way of focusing assistance on low income households.

The third argument for extending the coverage of VAT to all goods and services is that to do so would allow the rate levied to be lower for the same level of revenue. In fact, if VAT were to be applied at a single rate to all goods and services, including those currently exempt, a rate of just under 10% is estimated to be sufficient to yield the same level of revenue as at present.[9] This would be a very significant reduction, with a marked effect on relative consumer prices (some would rise, others fall.) It would have a number of benefits, illustrating the more general case for broad-based taxes with low rates. In the first place, low rates would seem likely to be intrinsically more acceptable to the public. They are almost certainly more flexible: it would appear to be politically easier to raise a rate from, say, 10% to 11% than from an already high 17.5% to 18.5%. And perhaps most importantly, low rates are much less likely to result in tax evasion. At 17.5% firms and customers have a strong incentive to evade paying VAT, and with cash sales this is relatively easy. At a lower rate the benefits of evasion are less: the risk-benefit calculus is weaker, and the moral duty not to evade may appear stronger in comparison.

So there would appear to be good reasons to propose a uniform rate of VAT. What is the case against?

The simple answer, of course, is that it is illegal under European Union rules. In practice, unless such rules can be changed, the option is therefore not practically available. But the stronger argument against a uniform VAT rate is one of principle. It would be regressive. Although the higher tax on currently exempt goods would be counterbalanced by the lower tax on goods currently charged at 17.5%, the combined effect would hit poorer households in general more heavily than richer ones, since a higher proportion of their income is made up of currently exempt goods. In fact our modelling shows that, though there would be gainers and losers from such a change at each point in the income distribution, on average households in each of the bottom 60% would be made worse off. Between 10% and 20% of households would face tax rises of at least £5 per week.[10] (See Figure 11.3).

Figure 11.3: A uniform rate of VAT (revenue neutral)

The distributional effects of a flat-rate VAT at 9.76%

Percentage change in income by income decile

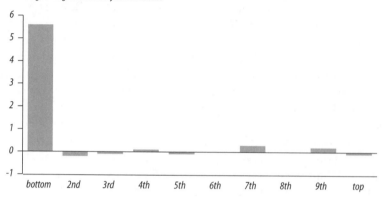

Percentage losers and gainers by income decile

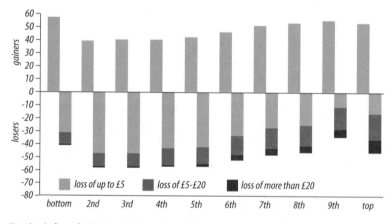

Note that the figures for the bottom decile may be unreliable.

[Source: POLIMOD]

Compensation

But this is not the end of the story. Advocates of a single rate of VAT are well aware of its regressive effects. They argue not for a fiscally neutral rate, but for one which generates some additional revenue which can then be spent on compensating those poorer households that are made worse off by the change.[11]

The Commission modelled such a proposal. An illustrative single rate of 11% was used. This would generate additional revenue to the Exchequer of around £5 billion. This was then spent compensating low income households by raising the rates of all means-tested benefits, notably Income Support and Working Families Tax Credit. An increase in benefit rates of around 11% made the whole package fiscally neutral. For a single person on Income

Support this would amount to around £5 per week.[12]

The results are instructive (see Figure 11.4). On average, households in the bottom half of the income distribution gain. The richest 50% of the population, by contrast, lose out, on average, with the richest losing the most. So it would appear that this proposal does what its advocates seek: namely to reduce distortion and lower VAT rates while overall not hurting—and even benefiting—people on low incomes.

Unfortunately, the real story is not that simple, as the bottom half of Figure 11.4 shows. First, these average gains and losses disguise a much more complicated picture. Although a majority of the poorest 50% of households gain from the measure, over a third do not. And some of the losses are very large. Between 8% and 18% of households in the bottom five deciles lose more than £5 a week, with 1-3% losing as much as £20. At these income levels these are significant amounts.

Figure 11.4: A uniform rate of VAT with compensation for low income households

The distributional effects of a flat-rate of VAT at 11% with all means-tested benefits raised by 10.83% (revenue-neutral)

Percentage change in income by income decile

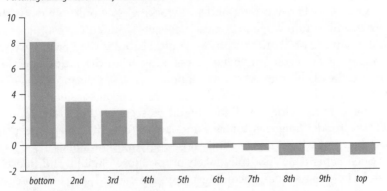

Percentage losers and gainers by income decile

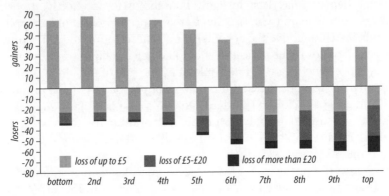

[Source: POLIMOD]

The reason for this is that people's consumption patterns very widely. Some people buy a lot of currently exempt goods, others fewer. The former group will inevitably lose more than the latter. It is impossible to devise compensation which affects everybody equally, since compensation can only be targeted by household characteristics or income levels, not expenditure patterns. Any compensation package, however generous, will over-compensate some groups while under-compensating others. As the Conservative Government found with the poll tax, correcting this would require an ever more complex and expensive—and ultimately unsuccessful—system of payments.

In fact what is striking is that the proportions of households losing £5 or more under the simple uniform rate proposal (Figure 11.3) and the proposal including compensation (Figure 11.4) are hardly different. As the uniform rate rises the impacts become more regressive, so greater compensation is needed to counter them. In other words, raising the money to pay for compensation wipes out much of the benefit that compensation brings.

But there is a second problem with the package which is also important. Raising benefit rates by over 10% could have a major influence on the labour market. For some people it could make for a significant change in the balance of incentive between working and not working. It would almost certainly require the minimum wage to be raised. It is very difficult to estimate exactly what the impacts on work incentives would be, but if they were very significant many of the economic benefits resulting from the reduced distortion and reduced evasion might be outweighed.

At the same time an increase in dependence on means-tested benefits without an increase in living standards should be seen as undesirable in its own right. (The model suggests that the number of benefit units dependent on Income Support would rise by 10%, those on working families Tax Credit by 24%.) Such benefits are not fully taken up by those eligible, and households which do not claim them (including many pensioners) will therefore not be compensated. They will simply pay more. At the same time, raising prices and increasing benefits may lead in many households to an effective transfer of resources from women (who usually do the principal household shopping) to men (who usually receive the benefits), the so-called 'purse to wallet' problem. (Compensation for higher prices, it should be noted, will to some extent occur anyway, since benefits are uprated at least by the rate of inflation.)

For all these reasons the Commission is not persuaded by the proposal for a uniform rate of VAT. The standard economic case is not as strong as many economists assume. Not only would the distributional effects be extremely painful to many people on low incomes—even after compensation—but the wider economic impacts might also be seriously adverse.

In essence the problem here is the UK's high levels of inequality. If one were designing a tax system in an ideal world, a uniform rate of VAT would make sense. But introducing this in a society where there is deep poverty and high unemployment is simply too damaging for too many people.

But even if the fully-fledged proposal is rejected, there might still be a case for rationalising the categories of goods currently exempt from VAT. There are clearly anomalies in the list of goods which are exempt or zero-rated and comparable goods which are not. But we have little desire to raise indirect taxes in general further and we are conscious of how politically unattractive the idea of levying VAT on (say) postage, books or newspapers would be. The lobbies against are powerful, the revenue gain small and the effect regressive. In respect of some other currently zero-rated and exempt goods the argument is more compelling. We would propose that the possible rationalisation of the list of zero-rated and exempt goods might be a suitable subject for review, perhaps by the Royal Commission on Taxation whose establishment we recommended in Chapter 7.

£

'Sin' taxes

Excise duties are levied on a number of products, some of which (those with environmental aims and effects) are discussed in detail in Chapter 13. Here our focus is on the so-called 'sin' taxes—duties on tobacco, alcohol and gambling. These bring in sizeable revenues—£5.7 billion in the case of tobacco, £6 billion for alcohol and £1.5bn for gambling.[13] But they have recently been the subject of increased questioning as a result of the rise of smuggling and cross-border shopping.

It is widely thought that Chancellors almost always raise excise duties on tobacco and alcohol. But in fact over the last twenty years only cigarettes and wine have seen real increases in taxation. The tax on cigarettes was 70% of the retail price in 1979, compared with 79% in 1999; on wine the average rate has risen from 47% to 51% in the same period. Tax rates on beer and especially spirits have fallen: from 34% to 30% and from 77% to 61% respectively.[14]

The justification for taxing 'sin'

'Sin' taxes are misnamed. The argument for taxing the consumption of alcohol, tobacco and gambling services is not that these are intrinsically immoral activities. It is that they cause social harm. As we argued in Chapters 4 and 5, the Commission believes that the discouragement of social harm is an important purpose of the tax system. It is for this reason that taxation of these activities is justified.

The harm is two-fold. First, each of these forms of consumption is addictive. As such each tends to reduce the autonomy of the individuals affected. Since individual autonomy is a fundamental requirement of citizenship and a free society, its diminution through addiction should be regarded as socially highly undesirable. Second, all these forms of consumption have social costs. Some of these are direct costs to other people: excessive alcohol consumption, for example, is a factor in many cases of domestic and street violence, and contributes to many deaths and injuries on the roads.[15] The families of compulsive gamblers and alcoholics are almost always deeply affected by their addiction. Other costs are financial: notably the costs to the NHS of treating lung cancer, other tobacco-caused respiratory problems and alcohol-related diseases. Smoking in particular is the single greatest cause of premature death and preventable illness in Britain, killing 120,000 people a year. An estimated £1.7 billion pa is spent by the NHS treating smoking-related illness and disease. For these reasons, reducing smoking is a key health objective of government.[16]

But if the taxation of these activities is justified in principle, there remains a question mark over the rates of taxation currently levied. It is sometimes argued that such taxes can be justified only up to the point at which the revenues received equal the costs of the NHS treatment they generate. At this point, it is said, tobacco and alcohol consumers are paying the social costs they cause. But this argument is invalid. First, as we have already argued, the social costs are not measured simply by the cost of treatment. Second, the aim of the tax is not simply to pay for the social costs. It is to discourage the activity which causes them. It is to bring down consumption, particularly in the care of tobacco, that high and possibly even rising levels of taxation are justified.

There is an important counter-argument, however. This is that these taxes are regressive—for some of them, doubly so, in fact. They are regressive in the straightforward sense that all indirect taxes have a larger proportionate impact on the poor than on the rich. But tobacco and beer duties are also regressive because these forms of consumption are proportionately highest among people on lower incomes. A large proportion of the revenues from all these taxes is collected from relatively poor people.

The Commission is concerned about these regressive effects, particularly given the evidence that for many people on low incomes, especially women, cigarettes can provide a valuable 'treat' and relief from stress.[17] But ultimately we believe that the social harm caused by consumption of these goods is a more important consideration. The reduction of such consumption would improve the health of many people on low incomes. Indeed, it can be argued that if sin taxes are effective in reducing consumption, the benefits to individuals from this are *progressive*—benefiting people on low incomes proportionately more than those on high incomes. (The financial gains from not smoking are worth more to those on low incomes than to those on high incomes.) We welcome the Government's proposal that aids to help people give up smoking, such as nicotine patches, should be free to those on low incomes through the NHS.[18]

Smuggling and cross-border shopping

A second argument is now commonly used against these excise duties. This is that rates are now too high in comparison with rates levied abroad.

In the case of tobacco and alcohol taxes, there is a serious concern that the high rates of duty imposed in the UK are encouraging the growth of both illegal smuggling and legitimate cross-border shopping. Both these activities affect employment in the UK tobacco and drink industries and in retailing. Smuggling moreover leads to increased levels of criminality, both among members of the public purchasing cigarettes and alcohol on the black market and in the organised crime operations now heavily involved in these trades. Widespread use of the black market encourages disrespect for the law and for taxes. It is also likely to lead to increased consumption, as black market prices are considerably lower than those on duty-paid goods. For this reason, it is now sometimes argued that excise duties on tobacco and alcohol should be reduced.[19]

It is certainly true that UK duties on both tobacco and alcohol are higher than in most other European countries. Duty on beer, for example, is six and a half times higher in the UK than in France, and duty on cigarettes over twice as high.[20] There is also no question that smuggling and cross-border shopping are serious concerns. The Government estimates that almost one in five cigarettes smoked in the UK is now smuggled, and without further action this could rise to one in three within a few years. Smuggling costs the Treasury an estimated £2.5 billion pa in lost revenue, with a further £85 million lost from legitimate cross-border shopping.[21] For alcohol the loss from cross-border shopping is estimated at £290 million pa, and from cross-Channel smuggling £215 million.[22]

However these facts do not automatically imply that the tax rates either on cigarettes or on alcohol should be reduced. Clearly there are different concerns here. One is simply tax revenue. If tax rates are cut, the consumption of duty-paid products will increase, but the revenue obtained per unit will decline. Whether or not total tax receipts will rise or fall then depends on the elasticity of demand for the good. Estimates by the Institute for Fiscal Studies suggest in fact that cuts in duty on tobacco, beer and wine would all lead to reduced revenues. On spirits the current tax rate appears to be close to the rate that maximises revenue, meaning that either a cut or an increase in duty would lead to a fall in tax receipts.[23]

It is generally agreed that reducing duty would cut the 'white van trade' in small-scale cross-Channel smuggling. But it is by no means clear that it would significantly affect larger-scale cigarette smuggling. A very substantial proportion of smuggled cigarettes comes from countries where duty is negligible. Bringing UK tobacco duty rates closer to those of other EU countries would have little effect on these products. As the Government has pointed out, other EU member states, such as Spain and Italy, which have relatively low tobacco duties, also suffer from serious smuggling problems.[24]

For these reasons the Government argues that cutting duty is not the appropriate method to reduce smuggling. Instead it is strengthening a range of 'physical' controls, including scanners at freight ports, greater numbers of Customs officers, fiscal marks on duty-paid packets and increased punishment for those caught with smuggled goods.[25] Broadly speaking we agree with this strategy. Any reduction in duty would lead to an increase in consumption both of alcohol and cigarettes, which would increase the social harms they cause. But the effectiveness of the anti-smuggling strategies will clearly need to be kept under review.

Electronic commerce: a threat to taxes?

A similar problem of high comparative duties has arisen in respect of UK betting taxes. But here the 'cross-border' shopping is occurring by telephone and on the internet. Over the last year there has been an increasing move towards 'tax free' betting in these ways via offshore locations such as Gibraltar and Ireland, where a deduction of 3% is made in comparison with the 9% combined duty in the UK. So far general betting duty revenue has not declined, but Customs and Excise estimate that if all telephone betting moved offshore the revenue loss would be £50 million.[26]

The Government has made two responses. In an effort to restrict offshore betting it has banned advertising for these services. And it has proposed reforms to the structure of betting duty to enable UK bookmakers to compete more successfully. These would either require bookmakers to account for duty based on the location of the person placing the bet; or would base the duty on the gross profits of the bookmaking business. We are doubtful about the effectiveness of the advertising ban. The options set out for reform of betting duty however look sensible in principle and practice.

The deeper issues raised by the development of internet betting concern the taxation of electronic commerce more generally. As we observed in Chapter 1, a number of commentators have argued that the rapid growth in internet-based transactions threatens national tax revenues, as companies and their sales disappear into 'cyberspace' where the tax authorities may not be able to find or identify them.[27] There are two principal issues here.

The first is the loss of visibility. As more and more goods and services are purchased electronically, it is claimed, it will be much harder for the tax authorities to trace the transactions and to levy the appropriate sales taxes on them. But we need to be careful here. No transaction is itself visible to the taxman: there is no essential difference in ordering a book, say, or an article of clothing, over the phone or by post, or indeed in person. The transaction is identified for tax purposes through the records of the selling firm, not via the medium of the order. The internet is certainly increasing international purchasing; but again the physical good must still enter the country however it is ordered, and the tax will be levied, as normal, at the border customs.

The threat to sales taxes (VAT and excise duties) from e-commerce, therefore, is more specific. The products which can more easily escape notice are those which actually have no material existence at all, but which are digitally transferred directly from seller to consumer. Software, music, videos, publications, financial and other services: an increasing volume of goods is now being purchased this way. But again two caveats must be entered. The number of products which can be sold in digital form is still not very large: no-one has yet invented the electronic hamburger or digitally-transmitted car (or indeed, computer). And even for those products which can be sold digitally, again the chief source of information to the tax authority is the selling firm's sales records. It is true that the internet is breeding many new small firms, some of which need little physical space in which to locate, and which may therefore seek to evade the tax authorities. But this is a familiar problem which the internet does not qualitatively change. Indeed, since e-commerce is generally conducted by credit card, the possibility of evasion from the use of cash is actually reduced in comparison with the situation in many small service firms now.

It is now recognised that one of the key issues in the development of electronic commerce is the need for 'trust' between sellers and buyers. When the company from whom one is buying is not visible, the product is not testable before purchase, and payment is by credit card, customers naturally wish to be confident that they are dealing with a legitimate and reputable supplier. But this then assists the tax authorities. To win their customers' trust, web-based companies and operations are increasingly finding that they must publish their address and other details which prove their existence and reliability. But the tax authorities can then use these to trace the company and its transaction records.

The much more serious problem for taxation caused by the internet—one which is causing rather more concern among tax authorities—is identifying which country or region should have jurisdiction.[28] A piece of software might be sold by a company in California to a consumer in the UK via a server in the Bahamas. Where should it be taxed? And how can a simple tax regime be applied? This problem is exacerbated by the ease with which firms doing business over the internet can now locate in low tax countries: this is one of the major reasons for the growth of investment in tax havens. As electronic commerce increases, the possibility for avoidance through relocation becomes greater.

These are serious problems, and as the volume of electronic commerce grows (as a percentage of total sales it is still at present very small) they will become more so. But we are not convinced that they constitutes a crisis for the taxation system as a whole. The key requirements are, first, effective enforcement, so that tax evasion is sought and punished; and second, international cooperation, so that a clear jurisdiction for every transaction can be identified by agreement. The OECD has already begun this process, and the general conclusions it draws from its work on this subject are relatively reassuring.[29] Many of the claims about the risks to tax revenues from electronic commerce would appear to be exaggerated. The internet does increase the possibilities for evasion, and will almost certainly encourage further relocation to offshore operations, but the scale of the threat appears at the moment to be relatively limited. So long as international cooperation is maintained, neither indirect taxes on the electronic sale of goods and services, nor business taxes on the enterprises themselves, look likely to suffer serious losses of revenue over the next few years.

12 | Taxing wealth:
the reform of inheritance tax

The taxation of wealth

In Chapter 10 have argued that those on the highest incomes in society should make a larger contribution to social goods through taxation. From a citizenship perspective the growth of income inequality is a serious concern. But there is another aspect of inequality which—though it tends to receive much less public attention—is equally important. This is the distribution of wealth.

> **Box 12.1: Wealth**
>
> *An individual's wealth consists of the accumulated total of her savings and capital. It includes financial savings and investments; owner-occupied housing and other property of various kinds; and pension rights. Some forms of wealth, such as stocks and shares, earn their holders income; others simply have a capital value which may or may not appreciate over time (such as a house or an antique). Most forms of wealth are 'marketable'—that is, they can be sold; rights to occupational and personal pensions are the notable exception.*

The distribution of wealth in the UK is extremely unequal—more unequal, in fact, than the distribution of income. And the trend has been increasing in recent years. The Inland Revenue estimates that the wealthiest 10% of the population own 52% of the country's total marketable wealth—an increase from 49% in 1982. Meanwhile the top half of the population own 93% of all marketable wealth, up from 91% in 1982.[1] At the other end of the scale, the proportion of households with no wealth at all is also rising: an estimated 10% of the population today have no savings or capital to fall back on, compared with just 5% twenty years ago.[2]

Moreover this trend is set to continue. The increasing use of share options as a way of paying executive salaries in the private sector, coupled with the growth of more general equity-sharing schemes, will boost personal wealth further. But only a small proportion of the population will share in the rewards. Those missing out will include not just the low paid and the unemployed, but also workers in the public and voluntary sectors where there is no equity to hold. Rising house prices, particularly in the south east of England, are further widening the gap between owner-occupiers and those whose housing is rented. Meanwhile an increasing number of second generation homeowners are now inheriting the houses of their parents, creating a kind of 'wealth windfall'.

Does this matter? Some degree of wealth inequality is inevitable in any market economy. Indeed, the opportunity to accumulate wealth is as valid an incentive to economic performance, for both entrepreneurs and employees, as higher pay. But the gross inequality in wealth distribution exhibited in the UK is a concern because of the effect it has on equality of opportunity.

Wealth conveys considerable advantages. Those with wealth can borrow more than those without, enabling them to enjoy a higher level of consumption. Wealth provides financial security, the comfort of knowing that unemployment or other misfortunes need not bring immediate poverty. It is difficult to set up a business without some starting capital. It is almost impossible to get on the housing ladder without an initial deposit. Parental wealth is linked with children's educational attainment. For all these reasons lack of capital entrenches the disadvantage of those on low incomes, and the advantages of the well off. If opportunity is to be extended more widely, it is important that wealth is distributed likewise. One source of wealth to which these arguments apply especially strongly is inheritance, which consolidates inequality across generations.

This is clearly all relevant to the tax system. It suggests the idea that wealth as well as income should be taxed. If wealth confers advantages in the same way as income—and indeed may in some cases simply be income in another form—it should not be treated differently by the tax system. And it suggests a particular focus on the taxation of inheritance.

Of course, taxation alone cannot generate an ideal distribution of wealth. While it can seek a larger contribution to public revenues from the wealthy, and can even encourage them to distribute their wealth more widely, it cannot enforce a redistribution to the wealth-less. After discussing wealth and inheritance taxation, therefore, we shall also consider a possible scheme which could do just this.

A wealth tax?

Wealth is currently taxed in the UK only through Inheritance Tax (IHT). Though sometimes thought of as a tax on wealth, Capital Gains Tax (CGT) is actually a tax on the *return* on capital, not the capital itself (like income tax on investment income). CGT is described briefly in Box 10.2. Inheritance tax is levied on the estates of the deceased (see Box 12.3).

Box 12.2: Capital Gains Tax

Capital gains tax (CGT) is levied on gains arising from the disposal of assets by individuals and trustees. The first £7,200 of an individual's capital gain is exempt from tax (the threshold for trusts is 50% lower).

The present Government has introduced a number of reforms to the structure of CGT. There are now different rates for business and non-business assets; and the effective tax rate is determined by the length of time the asset has been held. A taper operates so that the percentage of the gain chargeable to tax is reduced the longer the asset is held. The aim is to encourage assets to be held for longer, this being believed to support business investment.

No of complete years for which asset held	Non-business assets		Business assets	
	Percentage of gain chargeable	Equivalent rate for higher rate taxpayer	Percentage of gain chargeable	Equivalent rate for higher rate taxpayer
0	100	40	100	40
1	100	40	87.5	35
2	100	40	75	30
3	95	38	50	20
4	90	36	25	10
5	85	34	25	10
6	80	32	25	10
7	75	30	25	10
8	70	28	25	10
9	65	26	25	10
10 or more	60	24	25	10

Primary residences are exempt from CGT. In addition relief from CGT is available for certain types of investment in business and venture capital assets through the Enterprise Investment Scheme. Revenues from CGT in 1999-2000 are estimated as £3.4 billion.

Neither of these instruments therefore taxes the wealth available to the individual taxpayer. CGT is a levy on specific increases in wealth, but only when these are realised. IHT taxes wealth, but only on death. For many years, therefore, the idea of a wealth tax has been advocated in some quarters.[3] Such a tax would be levied each year—or perhaps every three or five years to reduce the burden of compliance—on the assets held by each individual above a lower threshold. All assets, including property, financial assets, businesses and valuable items, would be included, valued at their market price. If the aim were to ensure that only the genuinely wealthy were liable for the tax, the lower threshold could be quite high—say £250,000. Very low rates of tax (1% to 3%, say) would then yield significant sums.

In theory a wealth or capital assets tax of this kind would enable both capital gains and inheritance tax to be abolished, since gains would be captured in the annual valuation of wealth and estates would already have been taxed each year. In practice, however, CGT is an important instrument to prevent avoidance. It discourages wealthier individuals from converting a large part of their incomes into capital gain in order to reduce their income tax liability. The abolition of CGT would therefore not be desirable.

In any case a wealth tax would have three serious disadvantages. First, it would have relatively high administrative and compliance costs. The requirement to value all assets every year, or even every few years, would place quite a burden on taxpayers, and there would be ample opportunity for disputes with the tax authorities over the valuations. Second, the tax would be likely to lead to considerable evasion. The wealthy tend to be well advised by tax accountants and there would be plenty of ways of hiding assets, not least through the use of offshore tax havens and private bank accounts. The mobility of capital today makes flight abroad a serious likelihood. Third, the tax would make no distinction between assets that yield an income and those that do not. Asset-holders whose wealth was largely in non-income-generating forms might well find it quite difficult to pay the tax, leading to enforced sales of property. In some cases this might not be desirable.

For all these reasons we do not believe that a wealth tax is an appropriate or feasible instrument today. Rather, we believe that the same objective, to tax the advantages that accrue from wealth, can be achieved through a reform of inheritance tax. It is to this, therefore, that we now turn.

Inheritance tax

Inheritance tax in its current form was introduced by the then Chancellor Nigel Lawson in 1986. 'Inheritance tax' is something of a misnomer, in fact, since it is levied not on people who inherit, but on the estates of the deceased. In fact it bears virtually no relation to the amount that any individual inherits, either from the estate in question or over a lifetime. It should therefore really be called an estates duty (as indeed existed before 1975).

Box 12.3: Inheritance tax

Inheritance tax is levied at a flat rate of 40% on estates above a threshold value of £234,000 (2000-01). Estates handed over to a surviving spouse are generally exempt, along with lega-cies to charities and political parties. There are also a number of reliefs for agricultural property, family and private businesses, and works of art and other significant treasures of national importance.

To restrict avoidance, gifts made seven years or less before death are subject to inheritance tax, on a sliding scale:

Number of years before death that a gift is made	Tax rate
0-3 years	100%
3-4	80%
4-5	60%
5-6	40%
6-7	20%
over 7	0%

Exemptions are allowed, however, for gifts of up to £3,000 a year to one person and up to £250 a year for any number of people; while there is a specific exemption of up to £5,000 (depend-ing on who the recipients are) for wedding gifts. Lifetime gifts made outside the seven-year period do not come within the tax at all.

Inheritance tax is projected to yield around £2.3 billion in 2000-01.

Perhaps, the most remarkable feature of inheritance tax today is how few people pay it. The main reason is that it is only levied above a threshold of £234,000. The vast majority of people leave less than this when they die (though rising house values have brought more into it over recent years). But it is also because, for the very rich, the tax has become largely voluntary. By passing on one's wealth during one's lifetime—so long as this is done more than seven years before death—legacies can be made completely tax-free. At the same time, a series of reliefs and exemptions, such as for agricultural land, forestry and private businesses, along with the availability of tax-limit-ing devices such as trusts, provide ample means of avoidance for those with good advisers. The result is that only about 3% of estates end up paying inheritance tax.[4] These are mainly the affluent but not very rich: those whose houses bring them above the threshold but who do not have sufficient savings to feel confident about giving them away before they die.

Since we do not know how much wealth is given away during lifetimes (outside the seven year rule, no-one has to declare it), it is impossible to say for certain how much wealth is bequeathed each year, and therefore exactly what the effective rate of tax is. But there are some figures available. In 1996-97 the net value of the estates of people who died during the year was just over £25 billion. Of this, £12 billion was in estates bigger than the (then) inheritance tax threshold of £200,000. £3 billion was left to surviving spouses, and was therefore tax exempt, while other exemptions and reliefs reduced the chargeable figure to just £7.3 billion. Tax paid was £1.45 billion, which represents a yield of just 6% on the net value of the estates.[5]

Objections to the current inheritance tax

There are a number of objections to the current structure of inheritance tax. The first is the basic principle. Exempting most inheritance and gifts from taxation runs against the principle of equality of opportunity. Indeed there is something rather odd about a tax system which taxes income earned from hard work and talent relatively heavily (through income tax) while leaving unearned income largely exempt. If anything, the reverse should be the case.

The second objection is to the formal incidence of the tax. An estates tax bears no relation to the ability to pay of those who inherit. All taxes levied on death are really taxes on legatees, since it is they, rather than the deceased, who are deprived of assets they would otherwise have had. (As Winston Churchill said, an estates duty pretends 'to tax the dead instead of the living.'[6]) Levying the tax on the estate means that no account can be taken of the circumstances of the person who inherits. The same tax is borne whether an inheritor receives one-tenth of the estate or all of it; whether he or she has received many other legacies or none; whether he or she is related to the legator or not; and whether he or she is wealthy or poor. UK inheritance tax therefore bears little relation to most people's notions of equity.

It is for this reason that most developed countries have abandoned estates taxes levied on the deceased and replaced them by more strictly named inheritance taxes levied on legatees. Many of them then use this to have different tax rules for different kinds of recipient: a number, for example, charge less tax to the spouse or children of a donor than to a brother or sister, and more to those not in the immediate family.[7]

The third objection is to the exemption of lifetime gifts. This creates an obvious loophole which encourages the wealthy (who can afford to give away their wealth before death) to avoid paying tax. To the recipient, gifts are no less a contribution to unearned income than legacies; the tax system should therefore treat them in exactly the same way.

The seven year rule in the UK inheritance tax goes some way towards closing the loophole, but not very far. And it introduces a rather morbid feature. As one tax expert has put it, the rule 'represents a state-created lottery... in which a donor is obliged to engage in a gamble with the state on the length of his life. If he survives the statutory period he wins; if not, the state wins and the family loses. Yet the earlier a man dies, the greater his family's need is likely to be'.[8]

Again, virtually all other developed countries have recognised the problem of gifts and have gift taxes as a result. In some (such as Germany and

Sweden) the gift tax is completely integrated with inheritance tax; in others it is applied separately.[9] The UK used to have a gifts tax too: it was called Capital Transfer Tax, and was abolished in favour of inheritance tax in 1986.

£

A capital receipts tax

There are thus strong grounds for reform of the current system of inheritance tax. There are a number of ways in which the present inheritance tax could be reformed to address its current defects. One would be simply be to scale back some of the reliefs it offers for agricultural and business property, through which much IHT avoidance is conducted. Another would be to introduce a more progressive sliding scale of rates, coupled with a lower starting threshold. A third option would be to shift the tax to a donee rather than a donor basis: ie levied on the recipient of the legacy rather than the person making it.

In the Commission's view, however, a more thoroughgoing reform is possible, which combines all of these and some other features. We would propose the introduction of a Capital Receipts Tax. This would tax not just inheritances but all receipts of capital or 'accessions', whether legacy or gift. The model for such a tax is the Capital Acquisitions Tax levied in Ireland. This tax, incorporating inheritance, gift, discretionary trust and probate taxes, was introduced in 1976 and reformed in 1982, and appears to have worked well.[10] Its operation provides a model which reform in the United Kingdom could follow.

A Capital Receipts Tax (CRT) would differ from the current inheritance tax (IHT) in four main ways.

- It would be levied not just on legacies but on gifts, received at any time and from any source. This would include gifts of money, artefacts (such as cars and jewellery) and property. There would be a lower value (de minimis) limit below which gifts were not liable and did not have to be declared. Tax would be charged on the market value of the gift.
- It would be levied on donees (those receiving) rather than donors (those giving). In this way it would be a genuine inheritance tax rather than an estates tax.
- It would apply a cumulative principle to accessions. That is, the tax would be charged not on individual legacies and gifts but on the cumulative total of all accessions received in the donee's lifetime. In this way it would take account of all the recipient's accessions, whenever received and from whatever source.

● It would have a lower exemption threshold than IHT, and a progressive rate structure. Small accessions would not be taxed at all; as the cumulative total increased the tax rate would rise.

Advantages

At this stage of the argument our main purpose is to set out the principle and basic structure of a capital receipts tax rather than its detailed design. Before discussing the possible rates of tax and other features, therefore, it is as well to consider the arguments in its favour, and those against.

A capital receipts tax of the kind proposed would have three major advantages over the current inheritance tax system. First, and most importantly, a capital receipts tax would encourage the wider distribution of wealth. By levying the tax on the donee rather than the donor, an incentive is provided to distribute estates among larger groups of beneficiaries. To give an example, imagine that we introduced the tax with a lower threshold of £50,000 (ie no tax is paid on the first £50,000), and a starting rate of 20%. Now let us imagine an estate worth £200,000. If the estate is left to only one person, he or she will be liable to tax of £30,000 (20% of £150,000). If it is split equally between two people, they will each pay tax of £10,000 (20% of £50,000.) If it is split between four donees, none of them will pay any tax, since each will receive £50,000.

This effect is reinforced both by the cumulative principle and the progressive rate structure. A donor who wants her wealth not to be taxed will have an incentive to give to a donee who has not received previous capital receipts rather than to someone who has. And the smaller each receipt given from the same initial estate, the lower the rate of tax which will be charged. In these ways a capital receipts tax would tend to encourage the dispersal of estates and thereby the more equal distribution of wealth. It is, after all, not large estates which perpetuate inequality, but large inheritances, and it is therefore these which we should wish to reduce. Put another way: whereas current IHT only reduces inequality by giving private assets to the state, a capital receipts tax would have the additional effect of encouraging the 'private' redistribution of wealth.

Second, a capital receipts tax would reduce avoidance, closing the loophole by which lifetime gifts are largely exempt from tax, and ending the lottery of the seven year rule. The cumulative principle would ensure that tax could not be avoided simply by splitting gifts to the same donee.

Third, a capital receipts tax would increase horizontal equity. Under IHT people who choose not to make gifts, who are insufficiently secure to do so, whose wealth is in a form which makes giving away part of it difficult, or who are simply unlucky in calculating their date of death, have a greater liability to tax than others with the same size of estate. The inequity is suffered, of course, by the inheritors, not those who have made the choice to give or not. Under CRT the tax liability would be the same. A CRT would treat a person whose accessions came from one source or in one 'go' the same as someone receiving the same value of gifts from many sources or at different times.

Disadvantages

If a capital receipts tax has these advantages over the current inheritance tax, what arguments might be used against the reform?

One is the claim, sometimes made, that any increase in inheritance tax would reduce saving and provide disincentives to enterprise. In fact there is very little evidence of this. Most lifetime saving is not undertaken for the purpose of bequest, but simply for security and later consumption. The majority of people only begin to think seriously about the size of their legacies when they reach a certain age, at which time most of their saving has been completed, and their saving habits have become ingrained. And insofar as the rates of tax do affect some people's incentives, it is not clear how. As with an income tax, two contrary effects can work simultaneously. On the one hand an individual trying to build a target capital sum to bequeath will be required to work and save harder to reach it; on the other, the person weighing effort or sacrifice against reward may be discouraged into working and saving less. Which of these will be the stronger will depend on the individual.

In fact if anything the economic argument works in the opposite direction. Whereas the effect on potential donors is not clear, the incentive for donees is all one way. Since a tax reduces unearned wealth, it can only increase the incentives to work and save for the recipients. One might even go so far as to say that a higher inheritance tax is a positively pro-enterprise measure: it encourages those who might otherwise rest on the laurels of inheritance to go out and work for their wealth.

The second potential disadvantage of a capital receipts tax is that it would have higher administrative and compliance costs than the current IHT. By levying the tax on donees rather than donors (of whom there are inevitably fewer), by requiring all recipients of gifts above the exempt level to declare them to the tax authorities, and by requiring a lifetime record of gifts received, a CRT would inescapably increase the administrative requirements on both authorities and taxpayers.

We do not believe, however, that this would be excessive. The computerisation of tax collection and the introduction of self-assessment have already provided the basic structure into which a capital receipts tax would fit. The additional requirement to record gifts and to maintain records over time would not add greatly to the existing burden, though there would be extra costs arising from the need to value some gifts. Some of these costs are already incurred, of course, under the present seven year rule for gifts (with the additional problem that donees have to be traced). The Irish capital acquisitions tax has operated at about the same level of cost per unit of revenue as that of income tax on the self-employed.[11] We believe that additional costs on this scale are acceptable in return for the benefits—and the likely increased revenue—which the tax would bring.

The third possible disadvantage is the problem of evasion. As an estates duty, calculated at the time of probate, the present inheritance tax is easy to collect and difficult to evade. (Evasion, of course, is not the same as avoidance.) By requiring recipients of legacies and gifts to declare them, a capital receipts tax would appear to make evasion much easier.

With respect to legacies, there is a relatively simple way of preventing evasion. This is to prohibit the distribution of legacies by the executors of an estate until the tax liability of the legatees has been calculated. The tax could then either be paid by the legatee before receiving the legacy in full or by the executors, with the legatee receiving the sum net of tax. With respect to gifts, preventing evasion would be rather harder. For gifts of land and property, the existing requirement to have title deeds officially stamped (which in themselves attract stamp duty) provides a mechanism for automatic notification to the tax authorities. For other kinds of gifts, there would have to be a reliance on self-declaration. But this could be buttressed by giving the Inland Revenue the power to require donors as well as donees to declare their gifts. This would create an additional means of tracing transfers. Some evasion is still likely; but with high enough penalties and well-publicised enforcement it should be possible to keep this to a minimum.

£

The design of a capital receipts tax

Rates

At what rates should the tax be levied? This is obviously a matter of judgement. It depends partly on how much revenue it is hoped to raise from the new tax. In fact it is difficult to predict the yield from a reformed tax, both because we do not know the present value of gifts and because the tax may lead to a different distribution of legacies (it is indeed hoped that it will). The indicative tax rates proposed below are therefore based on a judgement about what seems—and will be seen by the public—to be fair. The principle of a capital receipts tax is our main concern; the rates are the legitimate subject of further debate.[12]

We would propose the following:

- A lower limit of £2,000 for gifts received from any single donor in any one year. Gifts valued below this sum would not have to be declared. To catch 'gift-splitting', several gifts from one donor would be counted as a single gift. This sum is high enough, we believe, to keep most ordinary gifts (for birthdays, weddings, etc) outside the tax, while not so high as to allow excessive avoidance by a variety or succession of annual donations.[13] It is the figure used in Ireland.

- A threshold for the tax of £80,000. This would apply on a cumulative lifetime basis. All gifts and legacies above £2,000 in a year would have to be recorded. So long as the cumulative total remained below £50,000, no tax would be paid. Tax would begin to be paid above this sum.

- Including the threshold, a progressive rate structure could be designed as follows:

Up to £80,000	nil	(on the first £80,000)
Next £80,000	20%	(on the amount from £80,000 to £160,000)
Next £80,000	30%	(on the amount from £160,000 to £240,000)
The remainder	40%	(on the amount above £240,000)

How would the tax charges produced by these kind of rates compare with the tax paid under the present IHT? The answer depends of course on how many people an estate is bequeathed to. The larger the number of legatees, the less tax is paid. For example, on an estate of £210,000, which would be exempt from tax under the present IHT, the overall tax rate of the proposed CRT works out at 15% (£31,000) if the estate is left to one person, but only 5% (£5,000 each) if it is left (equally) to two, and nothing at all if it is left to three people.

For larger inheritances, in line with the principle of progressivity, the tax rates rise. But in many cases the tax paid will be less than under the present system. For example, if an estate of £600,00 is left equally to three people, the total tax charged to them under the proposed CRT would be £84,000 or 14%, compared with £146,000 (24%) under the present IHT. So it is by no means the case that a CRT inevitably means higher tax. As we have argued, the advantage of a capital receipts tax is that the tax rate falls the more widely the wealth is distributed. Box 12.4 shows some worked examples.

Box 12.4: A Capital Receipts Tax—worked examples

Estate A

Estate A is worth £210,000 (after allowable expenses, such as funeral etc). Under the present IHT, this is under the threshold of £234,000, so no tax would be payable. Under the proposed CRT:

Left to 1 person (£)		Split between 2 people	
Legacy	210,000	Legacy (each)	105,000
Threshold	80,000	Threshold	80,000
Taxable sum	130,000	Taxable sum	25,000
20% on 1st £80,000	16,000	20% on 1st £80,000	5,000
30% on remainder	15,000	Tax paid each	5,000
Total tax paid	**31,000**	**Total tax paid**	**10,000**
Overall tax rate	15%	Overall tax rate	5%

Estate B

Estate B is worth £600,000 (after allowable expenses, such as funeral etc). Under the present IHT, with the threshold at £234,000, the tax paid would be 40% of £366,000 = £146,400. This is an effective tax rate of 24%. Under the proposed CGT:

Left to 1 person (£)		Split between 2 people		Split between 3 people	
Legacy	600,000	Legacy (each)	300,000	Legacy (each)	200,000
Threshold	80,000	Threshold	80,000	Threshold	80,000
Taxable sum	520,000	Taxable sum	220,000	Taxable sum	120,000
20% on 1st £80,000	16,000	20% on 1st £80,000	16,000	20% on 1st £80,000	16,000
30% on 2nd £80,000	24,000	30% on 2nd £80,000	24,000	30% on remainder	12,000
40% on remainder	144,000	40% on remainder	24,000	Tax paid each	28,000
		Tax paid each	64,000		
Total tax paid	**184,000**	**Total tax paid**	**128,000**	**Total tax paid**	**84,000**
Overall tax rate	31%	Overall tax rate	21%	Overall tax rate	14%

Estate C

Estate C is worth £1.5m (after allowable expenses, such as funeral etc). Under the present IHT, with the threshold at £234,000, the tax paid would be 40% of £1,266,000=£506,400. This is an effective tax rate (of the whole estate) of 34%. Under the proposed CRT:

Left to 1 person (£)		Split between 2 people		Split between 3 people	
Legacy	1,500,000	Legacy (each)	750,000	Legacy (each)	500,000
Threshold	80,000	Threshold	80,000	Threshold	80,000
Taxable sum	1,420,000	Taxable sum	670,000	Taxable sum	420,000
20% on 1st £80,000	16,000	20% on 1st £80,000	16,000	20% on 1st £80,000	16,000
30% on 2nd £80,000	24,000	30% on 2nd £80,000	24,000	30% on 2nd £80,000	24,000
40% on remainder	504,000	40% on remainder	204,000	40% on remainder	104,000
		Tax paid each	244,000	Tax paid each	144,000
Total tax paid	**544,000**	**Total tax paid**	**488,000**	**Total tax paid**	**432,000**
Overall tax rate	36%	Overall tax rate	33%	Overall tax rate	29%

Reliefs and exemptions for recipients

The basic structure of the capital receipts tax is straightforward. But many countries modify their equivalent taxes in various ways, as the UK indeed does with the present inheritance tax. There are broadly two kinds of modifications commonly made: reliefs based on the status of the recipient; and reliefs based on the nature of the gift or legacy.

Most countries, including the UK at present, exempt gifts and inheritances between spouses. As recognised by divorce law, assets formally owned by one member of a married couple are generally regarded as belonging to them both. Technically (under the principle of independent taxation) this should entail taxation of 50% of a transfer between spouses, since only half already belongs to the donee; but it is simpler and more comprehensible if all such receipts are exempt. (This accords with the idea that a couple's wealth is held in common rather than 'half each'.) Exemption will often be particularly important in order not to create hardship for a surviving spouse. We therefore recommend this.

Many countries provide relief for gifts and legacies to family members as well as spouses. In Ireland, for example, there are different thresholds for children, for brothers, sisters, nephews and nieces, and for others. This reflects the common feeling that gifts and legacies to family members are 'expected', whereas to non-family members they are simply 'windfalls'. But it is difficult to justify this on principle. If the purpose of the tax is to spread wealth and opportunity more widely, no additional incentive is warranted to keep it within the family—most people will wish to do this anyway. Ability to pay, after all, is unconnected to family relationship.

There is however a problem which emerges here. One way to avoid paying a capital receipts tax is through the practice of 'generation skipping.' Since most people have more grandchildren than children, there will be a lower tax bill if an individual leaves her wealth to her grandchildren rather than her children. If each generation does this, the total amount of wealth left in the family will be the same, but less tax will have been paid. It is for this reason that many countries (Ireland among them) provide relief for children but not grandchildren. Acknowledging this potential loophole, we would recommend a small relief for children.[14]

In common with other countries, we would also exempt gifts and legacies to charities and for other public purposes. Donations of these kinds should be encouraged by the tax system.

Reliefs and exemptions for certain kinds of assets and gifts

Various reliefs may also be given according to the nature of the assets involved. In the first place it is important to have a provision under which tax liabilities can be paid in installments. Many people receiving a non-financial asset (such as a house or piece of jewellery) may wish to hold onto it rather than sell it, but may then find difficulty in paying the tax. Allowing them to spread the payments over a period (the Irish tax allows five years, for example) will ease this problem.

For works of art and other items of national historical, artistic or scientific importance, there is obviously an even stronger case for preventing the break-up or sale of the asset. We would recommend, in line with the present provisions of inheritance tax and the Irish CAT, that such items should be exempt from the tax, but only so long as various conditions relating to public access to them are met. The exemption would last only so long as the item was not sold; if and when it were, the full tax would apply.

The present inheritance tax grants reliefs to two kinds of assets: private and family businesses, and agricultural and forestry land. The rationale is again the desire to avoid the break-up and sale of these assets after they have been transferred. But in practice these provisions largely encourage avoidance. Many wealthy individuals are advised to hold their assets in these forms simply to escape the tax.

With respect to agricultural land, the need to avoid the fragmentation of estates justifies some relief. But to prevent avoidance it is then important that such land cannot simply be sold after transfer. We would recommend a provision similar to that for items of national importance, with the relief lasting only so long as the land remains in ownership. It would be payable on sale.[15] There would be a strong case for limiting such relief to estates under a certain size. The inheritance of large estates is an important means of perpetuating wealth and should not be encouraged through additional incentives. Special provisions to allow the spreading of tax payments over a number of years would assist.

For private and family businesses, the rationale for relief is weaker. The traditional argument used is that taxing an inherited business risks its liquidation, since the inheritor won't otherwise have the money to pay the tax. But there is no reason to treat the inheritor of a business any differently from someone who buys it. The value of a business is related to its future profits. Anyone buying a business judges that its future profits will exceed the purchase price. But if this is the case, these profits will also give the inheritor of a business—who has no purchase price to pay—the income to pay a capital receipts tax. So long as payments can be spread over a number of years, there is no reason to exempt the business from the tax. Indeed, the evidence suggests that relief on current inheritances may positively impede business development. Family members are not always best able to give a business the management and entrepreneurial drive it may need. Sale of the business to new non-family owners may indeed be precisely the stimulus which the firm's long-term survival requires.[16] For these reasons we do not recommend any relief for business assets. A capital receipts tax without such relief would, we believe, work in favour of enterprise and economic efficiency rather than against.

Certain kinds of gifts would be exempt. These would include payments for the accommodation and maintenance of members of a donor's family. A young person living at home could not reasonably be expected to have her notional rent counted as a taxable gift from her parents. Similarly, reasonable maintenance payments for students from their parents should be exempt. We would add exclusions for parental payments for weddings, which do not constitute wealth.

In Ireland school fees and payments for higher education are also excluded. In the UK context, however, this raises an interesting question. Private education in the UK is one of the principal ways in which the advantages of wealth are perpetuated across the generations; it also creates problems for state schools whose intake is unbalanced as a result.[17] One way of recognising the privilege conferred by private education might well be to treat school fees as a gift to the child which would be included in his or her lifetime capital receipts total. Such a provision would clearly need to be considered in the context of other measures relating to private education; we therefore propose it as an option for further debate.

In addition to the need to define gifts precisely, a number of other issues would need resolving in the design of a capital receipts tax. These include the treatment of UK nationals abroad and foreign nationals resident in the UK (the issue of 'domicile'), and the question of trusts. Trusts can be legitimate means of holding assets on behalf of young people or others who are not able to manage it themselves; but they can also be a technique for tax avoidance. There is no simple method of taxing trusts fairly; the method used in Ireland, an annual charge on the value of the trust, would appear to be a useful approach.[18] A capital receipts tax would increase the incentive for those with considerable wealth to place it in a trust to avoid tax, and it is important that such avoidance is minimised.

The transitional period

The final issue which arises in the design of a capital receipts tax concerns the transition from the present inheritance tax system. The simplest way to introduce a CRT would be for everyone to start off with a cumulative total of nil, ignoring all previous legacies and gifts. But if inheritance tax were abolished at the same time, this would considerably reduce the income to the Exchequer while leaving many estates contributing much less than their taxable capacity.

We would therefore propose a seven-year transitional period. All recipients of accessions would have to take account of any capital receipts (over the minimum limit) received in the previous seven years in calculating their tax liability. Gifts made in this period, of course, already have to be remembered by the donor under the seven year rule, so this should not increase administrative complexity. Pre-tax receipts would only be taken into account in determining the rate of tax; they would not be taxed themselves. An exception, however, would be in the case of a person dying after the introduction of the CRT who had made a gift beforehand and within seven years of her death. In this case the gift should be charged to CRT, though for fairness' sake (so as not to diverge from the tax expected when the gift was made) the same taper as used under the seven year rule should be applied.

Since the introduction of a capital receipts tax would lead many people to consider changing their wills, and this could only be done with full knowledge of all its rates and provisions, there would have to be a reasonable period between the passage of the Act and its implementation. The gifts provisions of the tax, however, would need to be applied immediately, or even backdated to the announcement of the legislation. Any gap between the announcement and implementation would encourage the better off to bring their gifts and legacies forward to avoid later taxation.

£

Conclusion

Earmarking a capital receipts tax

Because the extent of gifts and legacies made is not known, the revenues from a capital receipts tax of the kind we have proposed cannot be calculated. However in principle, once the revenues could be estimated, and on the assumption that overall public spending did not need to rise, the introduction of a capital receipts tax would clearly enable other taxes to be reduced.

However there is another option which might also be considered. In line with our general argument that a tax system based on citizenship should aim to promote a fairer society, the primary purpose of the capital receipts tax would be to encourage the wider distribution of wealth. But as we argued earlier, this can only be partially achieved through a tax on its own. Much more could be achieved if the revenues from the tax were also used towards the same end. It is not the principal aim of this report to propose how tax revenues should be used, but in this context—and given our general espousal of earmarked taxes—it is worth mentioning a possible scheme which would have the direct effect of wealth redistribution that we desire.

The proposal is that all young people should receive a capital grant from the state at the age of 18. Such a grant, of perhaps £10,000, would give every young adult an initial wealth 'dowry'. To ensure that the money was not frittered away, but used as an investment in the individual's future, the money would have to be used for approved purposes. This might include education or training; the deposit on a home; or capital to start a new business. The scheme could offer young people advice on how to spend or invest the funds. Proposals for grants of this kind have been made in both the UK and the United States in recent years, attracting considerable attention.[19] For they offer a way of overcoming the huge inequality of opportunity between those young people who inherit wealth from their parents and those who start out with nothing.

The additional feature of such a grant scheme which makes it relevant here is that it could be financed out of the proposed capital receipts tax. Earmarking the tax for this purpose would have a strong rationale, since it would mean that the tax would have a dual effect on the redistribution of wealth—from both its tax and spending elements. Indeed, if people knew that the taxation of their own inheritances was being used specifically to finance opportunity for those with no capital at all, this might considerably increase the public acceptability of the reform. A universal grant would be taxed back from the already or future wealthy: it would be included within the individual's cumulative total under the accessions tax.

As we have already noted, it is difficult to estimate the revenues which the reforms we have proposed would yield. But on 1995 Inland Revenue figures for estates alone, it seems reasonable to suppose that the value of legacies and lifetime gifts made annually now is around £30 billion.[20] There are around 650,000 eighteen year-olds in Britain; so it would cost £6.5 billion to give them £10,000 each. If we assume an allowance of, say, £4 billion for transfers between spouses, this sum would be raised by a capital receipts tax with an overall yield of 25%. If as part of the measure payments to students for higher education were reduced, so that they had to be paid for out of the capital grant (thereby equalising the amounts given by the state to those going to university and those not), the yield required would be less, around 17%. Revenues of this order seem plausible from the rates of taxed proposed. Either the rates of tax or the level of grant provided could of course be adjusted to make sure that the income and expenditure matched.

The proposal for a capital receipts tax does not depend on earmarking it in this way; but it is an additional possibility perhaps worth consideration.

The politics of inheritance

How feasible, politically, is the reform we propose? In principle, for any government committed to widening economic and social opportunity, the measure seems attractive. But it cannot be denied that many people in the UK do have strong objections to the taxation of inheritance. We found this very strongly in the research into public attitudes that the Commission itself undertook for this report. As we saw in Chapter 2, large majorities of the public appear to oppose the principle of taxing inheritance altogether, seeing it as a form of 'double taxation' on income already taxed. We acknowledge that our proposal is unlikely—in the short term at least—to be popular.

This is of course one of the reasons why the present system is so weak. For many older people, the desire to pass on wealth to their children has been a powerful motivation for working hard and saving during their lives. Some have indeed scrimped on their own consumption in order to build up savings for just this purpose. Among such people, suggesting that gifts to offspring should be taxed is unlikely to go down well. By the same token—and in the effective absence of a tax—many of the recipients of parental legacies have come to feel that they have an unconstrained 'right' to them.

These feelings have been given political expression at various times by Conservative politicians, for whom the right to pass on one's hard-earned wealth represents a fundamental freedom and an important incentive for effort. Declaring that he wanted to see wealth 'cascade down the generations,' John Major as Prime Minister indeed sought to abolish inheritance tax altogether.[21]

There is no doubting the feelings behind such arguments; but one should not underestimate either the power of the meritocratic principle. Most people will surely accept that, if income from hard-earned work is taxed, so should be windfall gains unrelated to effort.

In fact it may be that the feeling of an untrammelled 'right' to inheritance is declining as an older generation is replaced by a younger one. Rising living standards, and in particular the growth in home ownership, means that many of those inheriting today already have some wealth of their own. With longer life expectancy, many people's parents die when they (the children) are in their 40s and 50s. They already have homes of their own, pension entitlements, and possibly some savings. Inheriting another home—possibly two, from the parents of both members of a couple—may not then seem quite so much a right or a necessity as it would have done thirty years ago. A tax of less than 20% on the windfall—for this is all that it would be in most cases—may come to seem acceptable.

Few people, after all, are likely to pay very much tax under the rates we propose. Anyone not inheriting a house is unlikely to exceed the £50,000 threshold at all. A cumulative inheritance of £160,000 is required before the tax rate reaches even 10%.

It would be stretching optimism to assert that reforming inheritance tax so that more people paid it would be popular; few new taxes are that. But we believe that public support could be won for a tax which was so clearly more equitable than the one it replaced, and which contributed in this way to fairer patterns of opportunity in society at large.

13 | From goods to bads: environmental taxes

In Chapter 5, drawing on our citizenship principles, we argued that a primary objective of the tax system should be to discourage social harm. All taxes affect behaviour; it is then sensible for behaviours which cause generally-acknowledged damage to society to be subject to disincentives through the tax system. We have already discussed one dimension of this, that of 'sin taxes'. But perhaps the largest field of social harm to which taxes can be applied is environmental degradation.

Few people now doubt that various forms of environmental damage and risk represent some of the most serious challenges facing modern societies. They take many different forms, from climate change caused by rising carbon dioxide emissions to loss of wildlife; from the risks to health from traffic pollution and industrial emissions to the destruction of countryside; from the disposal of wastes to the depletion of fish stocks. This is not the place to rehearse all the different environmental concerns which now animate governments and their publics throughout the world. But as a Commission we acknowledge that these impacts pose a formidable challenge to public policy.

Over recent years taxation has come to be seen as an important tool in tackling environmental damage. As Table 13.1 shows, most OECD countries, including the UK, have introduced environmental taxes of one kind or another. Following the principles we have set out earlier, the Commission regards this as an appropriate and important extension of taxation policy.

Table 13.1: Environmental taxes in European countries

	Austria	Belgium	Denmark	Finland	France	Germany	Ireland	Italy	Netherlands	Norway	Spain	Sweden	UK
Transport taxation													
carbon/energy tax			•	•				•	•	•		•	
sulphur tax		•	•	•				•	•			•	
annual vehicle tax	•	•	•	•	•	•	•	•	•	•	•	•	•
commuting		•	•		•	•			•	•		•	•
company cars	•	•	•	•				•	•			•	•
aircraft noise charge		•	•	•		•	•	•	•	•	•	•	•
Other energy products													
excise tax	•	•	•	•	•	•	•	•	•	•	•	•	•
carbon/energy tax		•	•		•			•	•	•		•	•
sulphur tax		•	•	•				•	•			•	•
NOx Charge			•							•		•	
Agricultural inputs													
pesticides		•	•	•				•		•		•	
fertilisers		•	•					•				•	
Other goods–ECO taxes													
batteries	TBS	•	•							•		•	
plastic carrier bags			•										
disposable containers	DRS	•	•	•				•	DRS				
tyres								•					
CFCs and/or halons	DRS	•	•			TBS		•					•
others	•	•	•	•	•	•	•	•	•	•	•	•	•
Waste													
user charge	•	•	•	•	•	•		•	•	•	•	•	•
waste tax		•	•	•	•	•	•	•	•	•	•	•	•
hazardous waste tax/charge		•	•	•		•			•	•			•
others			•						•				
Water													
user charges	•	•	•	•	•	•	•	•	•	•	•	•	•
water tax		•	•	•	•	•	•	•	•		•		•
water effluent tax/charge		•	•	•	•	•		•	•		•	•	•
others									•				

DRS: deposit refund scheme; TBS: take back scheme

[Source: Stefan Speck and Paul Ekins, Database of Environmental Taxes and Charges, Forum for the Future, July 2000]

In most fields the policy context for environmental taxation is already well established. The UK is either bound by international agreements (such as the Kyoto Protocol on climate change), or is subject to European Union directives (such as on most forms of air and water pollution); or there is a national policy framework in place (such as in transport). Taxation policy will then be one of the instruments through which environmental goals and targets can be achieved. As a Commission we have not been concerned with this wider policy context. In this chapter and the next (which examines the taxation of land), we shall therefore explore only the specific issues concerning tax policy which arise in this field.

£

The case for environmental taxation

The general argument for taxing environmental damage is straightforward. Most forms of environmental damage are 'externalities' of economic activity. That is, they are the costs of production and consumption processes which fall not on the firms and consumers who generate them, but on third parties. The existence of externalities means that the prices faced by firms and consumers in a free market don't reflect all the costs of their decisions. (For example, firms don't have to pay for the pollution they cause; consumers don't have to pay for the disposal of the waste they produce.) Taxing externalities ensures that the price of environmentally damaging activities reflects more of their costs, including their environmental costs. It makes the polluter, rather than the victim of pollution, pay.[1]

Within this general rationale there are two different kinds of argument for levying taxes on activities or products which cause environmental damage. One of these is an argument about how to reduce specific kinds of environmental impact. The other is an argument about the taxation system and how it should be designed.

The environmental argument

The 'environmental' argument is concerned with the most effective and efficient ways of reducing specific forms of harmful environmental impact. There are several kinds of policy instrument which can help to address environmental problems. Traditionally most environmental policy has used legal regulation: either to specify technology or product standards (such as energy efficiency regulations for buildings), or to set emission limits for pollutants to water and air. Some instruments are 'voluntary', such as the labelling of consumer products (intended to encourage consumers to buy more environmentally benign goods), or negotiated agreements with industry associations to reduce pollution. In some cases public subsidies may be used, such as in environmental management schemes for farmers; in others various forms of public provision (such as waste recycling). Over recent years there has been increasing interest in the use of 'tradable permits' for pollution control, where the total amount of pollution permitted is regulated and then firms are allowed to trade the licences between themselves.[2]

Taxation constitutes another possible instrument. An environmental tax charges firms and/or consumers for the damage they cause. Some environmental taxes can be directly applied to the damage: on the volume of waste going to landfill, for example, or on polluting emissions to rivers. But this can often be difficult where the sources of the damage are many and diffuse—as with cars, for example. Here therefore the tax is applied to the initial resource use (petrol) rather than to the damaging emission itself. In either case, by increasing the price of the environmentally damaging activity or product, taxation has the general effect of giving consumers and producers an incentive to cause less damage.[3]

For the environmental argument, the question is then whether, for any particular problem, a tax is the most effective or efficient way of changing behaviour. There are a number of advantages of taxes over other instruments in principle. In particular, a tax is likely to be a more efficient method than a legal regulation. Unlike a legal regulation, which forces all firms to behave in exactly the same way, a tax allows them to choose their own response to the measure according to the costs of doing so. Firms which find it expensive to reduce the damaging activity will prefer to pay the tax, while those for whom reducing the pollution is cheap will cut their damage further. This means that the goal is reached at the lowest total cost; that is, in the most efficient way. The uniform behaviour change of a legal regulation will generally have higher costs.

A further advantage of taxes is that they encourage firms (or consumers) continually to reduce their environmental impacts. Since every additional reduction will reduce the tax bill, there is always an incentive to cut further. Uniform standards by contrast provide no incentive to reduce damage beyond the standard set. This is a very important advantage, since one of the main motors of environmental improvement is innovation: improvements in technology and organisation which increase efficiency. Innovation almost always requires investment. This is likely to be encouraged where there are clear and ongoing financial benefits.[4]

These arguments have helped to persuade policy-makers over recent years that taxes can often be good methods of reducing environmental damage. Nevertheless, any particular environmental tax proposal needs to be compared with other ways of reaching the intended environmental goal to assess its value. Every environmental problem is different; the best mix of instruments (and generally more than one kind of instrument can contribute) will need to be determined separately in each case. This is a question for environmental rather than tax policy.

The taxation system argument: shifting from goods to bads

There is a second kind of argument for environmental taxation, however, which is primarily about taxation rather than the environment. This concerns the efficiency of the tax system as a whole.

All taxes 'distort' economic behaviour, in the sense that by changing the relative prices of different activities or products they make behaviour different from what it otherwise would be. Since most taxes—such as income tax, VAT, capital gains tax, corporation tax—are levied on positive economic activities, they distort behaviour in a generally undesirable way. They reduce the levels of work effort, savings, output, employment and investment. Environmental taxes, by contrast, generate positive behavioural change. Since environmental damage is an externality of economic activity, taxation can be seen as a way of *correcting* existing market distortions.

For any given level of tax revenue, therefore, there is an *a priori* case for saying that the higher the proportion of environmental taxes the more efficient will be the economy as a whole. There will be a lower level of environmental damage and a higher level of economic output and welfare.

In recent years this argument has led to the proposal that environmental taxes should be used not simply to address environmental problems, but to raise revenue. If the use of such taxes allows other taxes (on income or employment, for example) to be reduced within a constant overall total, the result will be a general gain in welfare. This is often described as switching the burden of taxation from 'goods' to 'bads'. In a number of European countries, effecting such a switch has become a specific goal of taxation policy.[5] In the UK it is one of the aims set out in a 'Statement of Intent' on environmental taxation published by the Treasury under the new government in July 1997.[6]

Attention has focused in particular on the possibility of using environmental taxes to reduce taxes on labour, in order to stimulate employment growth. Most countries levy labour taxes on employers—in the UK, employers' National Insurance contributions. These are often seen as a 'tax on jobs': if they were reduced, it is argued, labour would become cheaper and employment would rise. If this can be funded by raising environmental taxes, there will be a general shift in the economy away from sectors which make heavy use of resources and energy towards those which employ more people. The capital intensity of the economy will decline and its labour intensity will rise. Employment will be higher.[7]

The claim that a shift from labour to environmental taxes will increase employment levels as well as improving the environment is sometimes described as the 'double dividend'. A number of economic studies which have modelled 'ecological tax reforms' of this kind appear to show that employment does indeed rise.[8] If this is true, it is obviously an attractive policy prospect. However by no means all economists accept it. The argument centres principally on what happens to wages when labour taxes are reduced. Some economists argue that in the medium term wages will rise to compensate, so wiping out any employment benefit from reducing non-wage costs. Others claim that wages are 'sticky', particularly at the bottom of the income range where unemployment keeps wages low. Unsurprisingly, economic models which treat wage behaviour differently produce different results.[9] Overall the existence of a double dividend remains disputed. Nevertheless, so long as an employment gain, however small, remains a possibility—and there is no evidence that employment will *fall* as a result of a shift in the tax burden—there is likely to be continuing interest from policymakers in this proposal.

Whether or not employment is increased, a shift in the tax burden should increase overall welfare. However this must be set against possible adverse impacts. Since they are environmental taxes are frequently regressive in their impact. There are a few forms of environmental damage which are caused almost entirely by the affluent, such as air travel, whose taxation may be generally progressive. But most forms of environmental taxation—on energy, manufactured goods, foods, waste and so on—will affect all consumers. (Many environmental taxes fall on firms in one form or another, but they are then passed on to consumers in price increases.) As we have already seen, taxes which raise general consumer prices hurt those on low incomes disproportionately more than the better off.

Shifting the tax burden will also change the sectoral distribution of economic activity in undesirable ways. In general it can be expected to penalise manufacturing sectors which have heavy environmental impacts and to benefit less materially intensive service sectors. Even if the overall employment effect is positive, this is likely in the UK to result in adverse impacts on employment in particular regions already suffering above-average unemployment. It may also affect export revenues, depending on how the shift in the tax burden affects different sectors. Some resource-intensive sectors such as paper and steel manufacturing are important exporters, but there are also many exporting sectors—such as financial and information technology services—which would benefit from reduced taxes on labour. Economic modelling suggests that the overall effect on national competitiveness of a shift from labour to energy and transport taxation is likely to be small, though it depends partly on whether similar taxes are levied in competitor countries.[10]

There is another important international dimension to environmental taxation. If the introduction of environmental taxes in the UK led to a substitution of domestically-produced products by imports from countries without equivalent environmental controls, overall environmental damage might not in fact be reduced. There would be little point in the UK reducing its domestic carbon emissions only in order to consume goods produced abroad with the same or greater impact on climate change. In theory it would be possible to ensure that goods produced abroad were subject to taxes on entry to the country, but this would almost certainly fall foul of international trade rules. It would in any case be almost impossible to calculate an appropriate rate of tax adjustment for taxes on inputs to the production process such an energy.[11]

For all these reasons the general desirability of shifting the burden of taxation from economic 'goods' to environmental 'bads' must be tempered in practice by distributional considerations. In the long term a less resource-intensive economy is a very important aim of economic policy, and the Commission believes that taxation policy can make an important contribution to this. We therefore support the long-term goal of shifting the burden of tax. But this will inevitably have to occur sufficiently slowly to allow the structural changes in the economy to occur without unacceptable economic and social damage in the transition. In particular there will almost certainly in the medium term have to be some level of international agreement on the larger environmental taxes, notably on energy, to avoid damage to national competitiveness. As we suggested in Chapter 9, this is an important area for the development of European Union taxation policy.

Recycling and earmarking: using the revenues

In practice one of the key issues in the design of environmental taxes concerns not the tax itself, but the use of the revenues. The two kinds of argument for such taxes have different implications here.

The taxation system argument suggests that the revenues from environmental taxes should be 'recycled' back to the economy through reductions in other taxes. Where the revenues from an environmental tax are large, the impact on the economic sectors concerned will be significant. By recycling the revenues back to those affected—so long as it is on the basis of some criterion other than environmental damage—the overall burden of taxation can be held constant, while the incentives facing economic agents are changed. Thus with each of the three major new environmental taxes introduced or announced in recent years, on landfill disposal, business energy use and aggregates extraction, the bulk of the revenues are being recycled back to the business sector through reductions in employers' National Insurance contributions. This has kept the overall burden of business taxation more or less constant, but shifted its basis (a little) from labour to environmental damage.

There is a competing claim, however, on use of the receipts from environmental taxes. The environmental argument will often suggest that the revenues should be earmarked for environmental spending. Many environmental taxes on their own may not be particularly effective at changing behaviour. Some environmentally damaging activities are 'inelastic' in relation to price—that is, they don't decline by much when the price rises. This is likely to be true, for example, of the Government's tax on aggregates quarrying to be introduced in 2002, and of a tax on pesticides, also under consideration. It would be partially true of a tax on domestic energy consumption. It is also often said of petrol taxation—though in fact the evidence shows that fuel consumption is more responsive to price, particularly in the longer term, than generally appreciated. (We discuss both the latter two taxes further below.)

In these circumstances, there is a good case for using the revenues from the tax to help raise the elasticity of response. By making substitutes for the damaging activity cheaper or by reducing the cost of environment-improving investment, for example, it becomes easier for firms or consumers to reduce the environmental damage they cause. This will make the tax more effective in tackling the problem. Thus, for example, firms subjected to taxes on pollution can be given subsidies or tax breaks for investment in pollution control technology. Households facing a domestic energy tax could be given grants for insulation. Charging motorists to enter congested urban areas is much more likely to reduce car use if there are adequate public transport alternatives available. The revenue from the former can then help to provide the latter. This is of course exactly the principle that the Government has adopted in giving local authorities the power to levy such charges.

As well as using the revenues directly to assist those affected, revenues from environmental taxes might be used on public spending on associated environmental improvements. Examples might be using landfill levy income to pay for recycling services or using a pesticides tax to pay for research into organic and less intensive agriculture.

There is also likely to be another call on the revenues from some environmental taxes. This is to compensate those on whom the tax would have particularly damaging effects. When petrol taxation is raised, for example, it may be appropriate to return some of the revenue to motorists hardest hit by the rise in price. A domestic energy tax might similarly require compensation for those on low incomes. (We discuss these further below.)

As we saw from our own research into public attitudes, earmarking the revenues from environmental taxes in any of these ways is likely to make them more publicly acceptable. Most people now accept that environmental damage needs to be curtailed. In comparison with other taxes, therefore, environmental taxes start from a position of relative advantage in winning public support. But at the same time our research revealed a considerable level of cynicism that environmental taxes really are designed for environmental purposes. There is suspicion that the environmental claim is just a ruse and that in fact such taxes are just another way of raising more money for the Treasury. As we suggested in Chapter 8, earmarking the revenues for environmental spending seems likely to help counter this perception, 'connecting' people better to the purpose of the tax.

Nevertheless, it has to be accepted that the revenues from a tax cannot be spent more than once. There is therefore an inevitable tension between the different options of recycling and earmarking. The environmental impact of the tax will generally be improved through earmarking. But the economic impact will be minimised—and the 'tax shift' argument more clearly manifested—through recycling. In practice, it seems inevitable that, where a new tax has a large revenue yield, governments will have to do some of both. This is indeed what has happened with the landfill tax, climate change levy and aggregates tax. While most of the revenues have been recycled into reduced National Insurance contributions, a small proportion has been earmarked for spending on environmental improvement in the same field. We see no issue of principle which can decide the relative proportions: this must be a matter of judgement in each case. For smaller, more specific taxes with lower yields, we would generally recommend (in line with the principles we discussed in Chapter 8) that all the revenues should be earmarked for associated environmental spending.

One further issue needs to be raised in this context. There is a specific question in the UK about the method chosen for revenue recycling. It has generally been assumed that the best form of recycling is a reduction in employers' National Insurance contributions (NICs). But quite separate from their impact on business costs, reductions in NICs have implications for the principles and financing of the National Insurance system. As we have already argued, National Insurance contributions are not properly a tax: they fund a special system of contributory benefits. Employers' contributions are an important part of this system. Any significant further shift in the burden of taxation which involves reductions in NICs should therefore be undertaken with full consideration of the implications for the National Insurance system.

Environmental tax options

In terms of scale of impact and revenue potential, the key fields for environmental taxation are:

- Energy consumption (non-transport)
- Transport
- Solid waste disposal

All of these areas not only involve serious environmental impacts, but also arise from pervasive and inescapable economic activities. This means that

Box 13.1: Environmental taxes in the UK

- **Landfill tax** Introduced in 1996, the landfill tax is levied on the disposal of waste to land-fill at two rates: £2 per tonne for inactive waste, which does not decay or contaminate land, and a standard rate of £12 per tonne (2000-01) for all other waste. On introduction most of the revenues were recycled into cuts in employers' National Insurance contributions, with a proportion earmarked for environmental spending through an environmental trust. The standard rate will increase by £1 per tonne each year till April 2004, when the government's waste strategy will be subject to further review. The landfill tax was forecast to raise £0.4 billion in 2000-01.

- **VAT on domestic energy consumption** This was introduced by the Conservative government in 1994 at 8%, and reduced by the Labour Government in 1997 to 5%.

- **Climate change levy** A tax on business energy consumption to come into effect on 1 April 2001. See Box 13.2. The levy is forecast to raise around £1 billion in 2001-02. The revenues will mostly be recycled into cuts in employers' National Insurance contributions, with some earmarked for spending on measures to promote low carbon and energy efficiency investment and research and development.

- **Aggregates tax** To come into effect in April 2002, a tax on the quarrying of virgin sand, gravel and crushed rock. These will be charged at £1.60 per tonne. On introduction the revenues will mostly be recycled into cuts in employers' National insurance contributions, with some earmarked for a Sustainability Fund.

- **Fuel duties** Petrol duty is an excise duty levied (in 2000-01) at 51p per litre. There are lower duty rates (differentials) for unleaded petrol and diesel (49p per litre) and for various less polluting fuels, such as low sulphur diesel and liquid petroleum gas (LPG). These are designed to encourage consumers to switch fuels and thereby to contribute less to pollution. The Conservative Government introduced an escalator on road fuel duty of 3% pa in 1993 (later 5%); this was raised by the Labour Government in 1997 to 6% before being abandoned in 2000. Fuel duties were forecast to raise £23.3 billion in 2000-01.

- **Vehicle Exercise Duty** An annual tax on vehicle ownership. The Labour Government has introduced a graded system by which vehicles (both cars and lorries) with larger and less fuel-efficient engines pay higher duty than smaller, more efficient cars. VED is forecast to raise £4.9 billion in 2000-01.

- **Company car taxes** Various reforms have been to the company car taxation regime (to be implemented by 2002) to abolish incentives to drive more miles and to increase incentives to purchase low-emission cars. The Government has also introduced various employer and employee tax regime changes to encourage the use of public transport, cycling and car sharing.

- **Road congestion and workplace carparking charges** Under the Transport Act 2000 (and the Greater London Act 1998) local authorities have been given the power to to introduce urban road congestion charges, with the requirement that the revenues are hypothecated to transport spending for at least ten years. Local authorities have also been given the power to introduce workplace car parking charges, again with the requirement that the revenues are hypothecated to transport spending.

they offer major potential sources of revenue which are unlikely to decline significantly as they affect environmental behaviour. Whereas with some taxes the response of firms or consumers may be to change economic activity so significantly as to reduce the yield from the tax to very little, in each of these cases the pervasive nature of the economic activity concerned makes this very unlikely. There is almost no form of production or consumption which does not use energy and transport and produce solid waste.

There are a number of other fields where there is the possibility of levying taxes on various less pervasive but nevertheless important forms of environmental damage. In these cases the revenues are likely to be lower, though not insignificant (and they could eventually disappear altogether if the tax is effective). There will often therefore be a strong argument for earmarking the revenues for associated environmental improvement. Possible taxes include:

- Charges on polluting discharges to water and air (non-transport)
- Resource extraction taxes (eg aggregates, water, peat)
- Product taxes (eg pesticides, nitrate fertilisers, disposable products, non-rechargeable batteries)
- Taxes on land development (eg site value taxation, countryside housebuilding levy)

In the last few years most of these forms of taxation have come under consideration by UK governments, both Conservative and Labour, and a number have been introduced. Box 13.1 lists the major environmental taxes and associated tax measures now in place in the UK.

In the following sections we discuss the two most controversial areas of environmental taxation, energy and transport, and then refer briefly to some other tax options. We discuss the taxation of land in the next chapter.

£

Energy taxation

Under the terms of the Kyoto Protocol the UK is legally bound to achieve a 12.5% reduction in carbon dioxide and other greenhouse gas emissions on 1990 levels by 2008-12. The Labour Government has a domestic manifesto commitment to a 20% reduction by 2010. It is generally expected that further and more stringent targets will be set beyond this: the Royal Commission on Environmental Pollution has argued that a 60% reduction in UK emissions will be needed by 2050.[12]

Around 90% of primary energy consumed in the UK comes from fossil fuels (gas, petroleum and coal), the burning of which generates carbon dioxide. Of this around a third (34%) is used for transport. The remainder is used for heating, light and power in the household sector (30%), manufacturing industry (22%) and commercial and public services (14%). As a result partly of increased use of gas (instead of coal) for electricity generation, partly of efficiency measures and partly of structural changes in the economy (notably the continuing decline of manufacturing industry), UK carbon dioxide emissions have been falling since 1990. However, without further policy measures being taken they are now predicted to rise again as economic growth occurs in the period up to 2020.[13] It is in this context that energy taxation has been placed on the agenda in the last few years.

Business energy taxation: the climate change levy

In response to its obligations under the Kyoto Protocol the Government is introducing in April 2001 a wholly new tax on the consumption of energy by businesses. The Climate Change Levy will tax the use of electricity, gas and coal in the industrial, commercial, agricultural and public sectors. The levy is expected to raise £1 billion in 2000-01. Most of the revenues are being returned to business through a cut in employers' National Insurance contributions of 0.3%. In addition £150 million of the revenues has been earmarked for schemes to promote energy efficiency and the take-up of renewable energy.

Box 13.2: Climate Change Levy

The climate change levy applies to sales of electricity, coal, natural gas and liquid petroleum gas (LPG) to the business and public sectors. Mineral oil has been exempted because it is already taxed. The effective tax rate in 2000-01 will be 0.43p per kilowatt hour for electricity, 0.15p for coal, 0.15p for natural gas and 0.07p for LPG. Electricity generated from renewable sources of energy such as wind, biomass, hydro and solar are exempted from the tax, along with some 'combined heat and power' plants (which use waste heat for electricity). To protect energy-intensive sectors from undue competition effects the Government has agreed that companies in such sectors which sign 'negotiated agreements' to meet energy efficiency targets will be entitled to 80% discounts on the levy.

The levy is expected to raise £1 billion in 2000-01. Of this most will be used to cut employers' National Insurance contributions by 0.3%. £50 million is to go into an energy efficiency fund which will provide energy efficiency advice and grants for businesses, particularly small and medium-sized ones, and support the research, development and deployment of renewable, low-carbon and energy-saving technologies. A further £100 million in the first year will fund a new system of capital allowances for energy-saving investments. Firms making such investments will be able to deduct 100% of the cost from their corporation or income tax bill.

The Commission welcomes the introduction of the levy. It is expected to reduce carbon dioxide emissions from the business sector by at least five million tonnes a year by 2010, which represents around a quarter of the Government's remaining target (given reductions already achieved) of reducing carbon emissions by 20% from their 1990 level.[14] The levy is therefore a serious contribution to meeting the UK's climate change commitments. We believe it would have been more effective had it been designed as a 'carbon tax' which differentiated more closely between the carbon content of different fuels. But this would have required the tax to be levied 'upstream' at the point of energy production, rather than 'downstream' at the point of sale, which in turn would have meant it became a tax on domestic as well as commercial energy use. The carbon tax proposal therefore ran foul of the Government's commitment not to tax domestic energy further. (We discuss this further below.)

In taxation policy terms the climate change levy is most significant for its use of the revenues. First, 15% of the estimated first year yield has been earmarked to assist energy efficiency measures by business and to support renewable energy technologies. This is therefore an explicit example of using the revenues from an environmental tax to increase the elasticity of response to it. While the evidence shows that many firms can make energy savings which cut their overall costs, there are severe constraints of management time, information and capital which prevent these being implemented, particularly in the small and medium-sized enterprise sector. The energy efficiency advice and grants should help to overcome these barriers, while additional support for renewable, low-carbon and energy-saving technologies will reduce the cost and risk of their development. The 100% investment allowances are also welcome, though it should be noted that these merely defer (rather then reduce) tax liability. They are therefore not properly a form of public expenditure: the funds are recouped by the Treasury over time. There is a strong case for further earmarking of these revenues beyond the first year.

The remainder of the receipts from the levy are being used to reduce labour costs through a cut in the rate of employers' National Insurance contributions. This represents the largest single attempt yet in the UK tax system to shift the burden of taxation from 'goods' to 'bads'. While the overall taxation of business remains more or less constant, the incentives for employment and energy use are changed in a desirable direction—in favour of the former and against the latter.

The climate change levy has attracted considerable opposition from the business sector. But we believe that much of this is unwarranted. Energy costs are a small proportion of total costs for most firms—under 4%. The evidence suggests that most firms can save sufficient energy to ensure that their overall bills are not increased—while the reduction in National Insurance contributions will further reduce their costs.[15] In only a few sectors does energy constitute a major proportion of total costs. In these sectors the Government has made a major concession, allowing firms an 80% discount on the tax if they sign a 'negotiated agreement' to improve energy efficiency. The detail of these agreements is not yet clear, but they are in principle far from ideal. It is almost impossible for the government to know how easily and at what cost firms can reduce their energy consumption. The agreements are therefore likely to be rather inefficient mechanisms which will allow firms considerable leeway in comparison with the tax. There are some legitimate concerns about the effect of the levy on competitiveness in certain sectors, but in the economy as a whole economic modelling suggests only a small impact.[16] Given the UK's legal obligations to reduce carbon emissions, and the importance of the business sector in achieving these, the tax is we believe a necessary component of the national climate change strategy.

In principle, the argument for shifting the burden of taxation from goods to bads—and the need for continuing cuts in carbon dioxide emissions beyond those currently agreed—would suggest that the climate change levy might be increased over time, with corresponding reductions in employers' NICs or other taxes. However, we would wish to see how the levy works, both in cutting emissions and in terms of its sectoral and overall economic impacts, before any further proposals are made. In the meantime, efforts to encourage a convergence of business energy taxation across the European Union—and to encourage other countries, including the USA, to follow suit—should be pursued.

A domestic energy tax?

The Government's climate change strategy recognises that all sectors need to cut their emissions of carbon dioxide, and tax increases have been introduced for business and transport. But this leaves something of an anomaly. The domestic sector contributes 30% of all the UK's carbon dioxide emissions, and in absolute terms no reductions are projected in the period to 2010.[17] But this sector has been exempted from higher prices. Indeed, the opening up of the energy market and tightly regulated retail tariffs have given consumers significant cuts in energy prices over recent years. Domestic electricity and gas prices have fallen by 35-40% in real terms since 1990.[18] These price cuts have been welcome for consumers, particularly those on lower incomes, but they have been very unhelpful for the attempt to reduce carbon emissions from the domestic sector. Falling prices send exactly the wrong signal to households, encouraging wastefulness and making energy efficiency measures (such as insulation) less cost-effective.

The reason that domestic energy has not been subject to the additional environmental taxation imposed on business and transport is that on its own such a tax would be extremely regressive. Poorer households (and those where the members of the household spend a considerable amount of time at home, such as pensioners and parents with young children) spend a much larger proportion of their budget on fuel—about 9% for the bottom 20% of households, compared with under 3% for the top 20%.[19] Many poorer households live in homes with inadequate heating systems and poor insulation. This leaves many of them spending relatively large proportions of their income on energy while still living in cold and damp homes. On government estimates, around 4.3m households suffer from 'fuel poverty' because of the energy inefficiency of their home, with others putting the figure higher.[20] (A fuel-poor household is defined as one which needs to spend in excess of 10% of its income on fuel to maintain adequate heating.) Up to 50,000 people, mainly pensioners, die from cold-related diseases each year.[21] In these circumstances (and if nothing else were done) raising domestic energy prices would not simply be regressive in terms of the comparative effects on rich and poor. It could have terrible absolute effects on some of the most vulnerable people in society.

Politically, this idea has therefore become more or less taboo since the attempt by the then Conservative Government to levy VAT on domestic energy in 1993. Opposed by the Labour Party and a huge campaign in the media by the poverty lobby, which emphasised in particular the effect on poorer pensioners, the Government was defeated in Parliament on its plan to levy the tax at 17.5%. VAT was introduced, but only at 8%. On coming to office in 1997, Labour immediately cut this to 5%, the lowest possible rate under EU rules. This tax cut remains one of the Government's proudest boasts.

There are therefore formidable obstacles, both of policy and politics, to the introduction of a tax on domestic energy. Yet in principle such a tax remains a rational option. For it is not just those on low incomes who are shielded from higher prices by its absence. It is also all other households, including large numbers of people who could certainly afford to pay more for domestic fuel, particularly given the huge cut in prices they have enjoyed over the last decade. Indeed for most people a rise in prices is an important signal to encourage the greater take-up of energy efficiency measures, which remains the environmental goal. (Regulatory measures can also help, particularly higher energy efficiency standards for houses and domestic appliances.) In fact, domestic insulation and more efficient heating and lighting systems can pay for themselves over time in lower energy bills.[22] So a domestic energy tax should not, in fact, raise overall costs for those households which respond to it in the way society wants—namely by improving the efficiency of their energy consumption, and thereby reducing their polluting emissions.

The question remains, however, how to protect poorer households from the effects of such a tax. One way to do this would be to compensate them with financial payments—to raise the levels of social security benefits and the state pension (or the pensioners' winter fuel allowance) so as to cancel out the extra costs which the tax impose. But this has two disadvantages. First, it is a very blunt instrument. Social security payments are made at the same rate to all households that meet certain financial and other conditions. But people's energy consumption varies considerably, depending on the size of their home, the type of energy consumed, the level of insulation and their individual needs. So a compensation package set, say, at the average level of extra cost imposed by a tax would inevitably fail fully to compensate some people (those with above-average energy bills) while over-compensating others (those with below-average bills). Either the compensation package would still leave some poor households worse off, or, if this were avoided by increasing the rate of compensation, it would become very expensive, with much of the extra cost providing net benefit increases to households with low fuel consumption.

The second problem with compensation payments is that they don't deal with the real problem, which is the energy inefficiency of the homes of those on low incomes. Indeed, this inefficiency means that much of the extra money will in effect be wasted, going not to heat the home, but out of the window (literally so in the case of draughts). The aim of policy should not really be to increase the income of such households, but to improve their *capital*: to raise the energy efficiency of their housing.

The task of improving the nation's housing stock is a large one. The Government's Home Energy Efficiency Scheme, which provides heating and insulation improvements for low-income households, has a budget of £365 million over three years.[23] (In addition local authority housing improvement programmes include some energy efficiency spending.) But independent estimates suggest that to improve the energy efficiency of the worst 2.5 million homes a total spending programme of £1.25 billion per annum is needed over at least five years, at a rate of 500,000 homes a year.[24]

Over the lifetime of such an investment programme there are good grounds for believing that at least some of its cost would be recouped in reductions in health, housing maintenance and other public expenditures. (It would also create considerable numbers of jobs.[25]) There is clearly a problem of funding it. But then this provides another rationale for a domestic energy tax. Such a programme could be financed from its revenues. Indeed, if the receipts from a domestic tax were earmarked for the purpose of ending fuel poverty, this would almost certainly make it more publicly and politically acceptable.

A problem would remain, however, with this proposal: that of timelag. If even a large-scale programme of housing investment would take at least five years to reach 2.5 million households in fuel poverty, any tax levied in the meantime would hit at least some of the 'fuel poor' very hard. Once improved the tax would be affordable—indeed, energy bills for such households would almost certainly fall. But until then 'unimproved' households paying the tax would still be worse off.

The goal for policy-makers is therefore to finance the investment in energy-efficient housing while protecting those on low incomes. Our recommendations are two-fold. First, no action should be taken on taxation for two years before the current domestic energy programme is completed in 2002. This will provide a baseline of improved housing stock, and allow realistic projections to be made on further investment needs. We would also expect the number of people living in fuel poverty to have been reduced through other government measures, such as higher pensions.

Second, after 2002 we would propose that a domestic energy tax should be announced, but with implementation delayed for a further three years. This period should be used to provide additional funding for housing investment targeted at low-income households. Such investment could then be financed by borrowing against the future income stream of the tax. In this way the tax revenues could be earmarked for 'advance' spending. At the same time the delay in implementation of the tax would give better-off households a three-year period in which to ensure that the energy efficiency of their own homes was improved. Rather than leave this to the individual householder, it would be most effective if the energy distribution companies were encouraged (or required by regulation) to provide energy efficiency improvement schemes to their customers. Such schemes could be payable over a period through customers' bills, which would in any case be expected to fall.

The aim of these two recommendations is to eliminate fuel poverty before a domestic energy tax was introduced. The Government is committed to eliminating it by 2010: the aim of earmarking the tax revenues in advance would be to increase overall spending beyond the Government's plans and therefore to speed up this process. However, even if this were done the introduction of the tax would still be regressive, with a larger impact on low-income households than on richer ones. We would therefore consider further measures to mitigate its impact on poorer households. This might either be through targeted compensation or through the design of the tax itself.[26]

We would suggest that a domestic energy tax should be levied through a new excise duty rather than VAT. Although VAT would be administratively simpler, an excise duty would allow wider freedom in the setting of rates. It would also help consumers identify its environmental purpose. (Given the present Government's commitments on VAT, it would also be politically easier.) Moreover it would allow the tax to be integrated with the climate change levy in the future to create the more rational option of an 'upstream' carbon tax. We concur with the Royal Commission on Environmental Pollution that in the longer term this is the most desirable option on both environmental and administrative grounds.[27]

Including our proposal for borrowing against future receipts, we believe that the full revenues of a domestic energy tax should be earmarked for domestic energy efficiency programmes, aimed at the poorest households first, for at least the first ten years.

We have modelled the impact of a domestic energy tax at 5%, in addition to the existing 5% VAT. Such a tax would yield revenues of £730m pa. In terms of income the losses would be more or less equivalent in every decile of the household income distribution. No households would lose more than £1 a week.[28] Of course, this modelling is done on present patterns of energy consumption. Our proposal is that such a tax should not be introduced until considerable investment in energy efficiency has been made, so we would expect the impact in reality to be rather smaller.

The introduction of a domestic energy tax should also be accompanied by other measures designed to increase the energy efficiency of homes. These might include compulsory energy ratings for all homes when sold, new standards for domestic appliances, and so on. Taxation alone cannot achieve environmental improvement; it must be one policy measure among several working in the same direction.

£

Transport taxation

Of all indirect taxes, let alone environmental taxes, it is the taxation of motoring which has become the most controversial. When the price of petrol suddenly rose dramatically over a period of a few months in the spring and summer of 2000, the actual cause was a rise in the underlying price of crude oil. But public attention focused on the percentage of the price made up of taxation. As the fuel protesters who took to the streets and blockades and their supporters in the media pointed out, fully three-quarters of the price of a litre of petrol in the UK is tax. This is made up both of excise duty (levied in terms of pence per litre) and VAT (levied as 17.5% of the post-tax price). This percentage has not only been steadily rising over the last twenty years (under both Tory and Labour governments); it is also the highest rate of any country in Europe. (It was the Conservative Government which first introduced the automatic 'escalator' which raised petrol tax every year: initially by 3%, then 5%. The incoming Labour Government initially increased the escalator to 6%, then scrapped it altogether in its Budget in 2000.)

Petrol is not the only component of motoring which is taxed. Vehicle ownership itself is taxed through vehicle excise duty (the tax disc). Charges for car parking operate in many urban areas. And now the Government is giving local authorities two new taxing powers: first, the power to charge motorists for entering urban areas at congested times (congestion charging) and, second, the power to charge employers for the workplace carparking spaces they provide for their employees.

The basic case for taxing motorised transport is straightforward. It has very high social costs. Emissions of carbon dioxide from transport (34% of the total) are rising faster than in any other sector. Petrol- and diesel-driven vehicles are the principal source of local air pollution, emitting a variety of toxic pollutants including carbon dioxide, hydrocarbons and particulates, which cause and exacerbate respiratory disease. Traffic accidents kill over 3,000 people each year, and seriously injure another 300,000. Road congestion and vehicle noise reduce the quality of life for people living in affected streets and areas, while congestion-caused delays to commercial journeys and the delivery of goods cost the economy an estimated £19 billion every year. The total social costs of transport in the UK have been calculated at £44-51 billion annually, considerably more than transport use is taxed.[29]

In defending high petrol duty the Government has tended to use the argument that it raises money for schools and hospitals. This is undoubtedly true: the yield was fully £23 billion in 2000-01. But it is not sufficient justification on its own, for there are other ways in which this money could be raised. It is the external cost of transport which justify this particular form of taxation. But then we need to answer two questions. How far do transport taxes actually have any environmental effect? Do they help reduce vehicle use and thereby cut pollution? The second concerns their social impact. Are transport taxes unacceptably regressive?

Petrol prices and fuel consumption

One of the arguments which is frequently made against the high level of petrol duty in the UK is that it has had no effect on motorists' behaviour. Petrol prices have doubled over the last ten years, but the number of kilometres travelled by car has continued to rise. So it is obvious (it is said) that high petrol prices have not 'worked' as an environmental measure: people have not been deterred from using their cars.

This argument, however, is fundamentally misleading. It ignores the 'counterfactual': what would have happened if petrol prices had *not* risen by so much over this period? Would car use have been even higher? There is now in fact considerable evidence on this question—evidence too rarely invoked in public debate. Car driving *is* inelastic in relation to price: that is, if the price goes up, fuel consumption does not go down by the same percentage. But it is not as inelastic as some people have claimed. For every 10% that petrol prices rise, the evidence suggests that fuel consumption falls by around 3% in the short run (within a few months), but around 6-8% over a longer period (up to around five years).[30]

How is it then that car driving and fuel consumption have continued to rise even as petrol prices have risen (by much more than 10%)? The answer is that *incomes* have risen. Motoring is not just responsive to price. As with all forms of consumption, it is also affected by income. In fact it is more responsive to income than price. For every 10% increase in average real incomes, fuel consumption and traffic increase by more than 10%. Thus, while higher petrol prices have worked to reduce car use, higher incomes have done the reverse—and with greater effect. In fact, given an average increase in real incomes of around 2.5%, petrol prices would have to rise by more than 4% above inflation every year simply to hold fuel consumption constant.[31] To reduce consumption, even higher price rises would be needed. If petrol prices were *cut*, meanwhile, fuel consumption would increase by even more than it has done in recent years.

The effects of petrol prices on traffic levels tend to be less than their effects on the amount of fuel consumed. A price increase of 10% would reduce vehicle mileage by only about 3% in the long run. So to hold traffic levels constant (assuming no other measures were taken) the price would have to rise in real terms by about 10% a year.[32] This is because over time the fuel efficiency of cars rises, saving on fuel but allowing higher mileage per litre. Indeed, this impact on fuel efficiency is an often unrecognised effect of higher fuel prices. As prices rise, consumers regard fuel efficiency as a more important feature of the cars they buy, so manufacturers have a greater incentive to make technological improvements. The last decade has seen steady advances both in the fuel efficiency of petrol-driven cars, and in the development of new fuel technologies (electric 'hybrid' vehicles, liquid petroleum gas (LPG), compressed natural gas (CNG) and hydrogen fuel cells). Since in the medium to longer term it is the development of these alternative fuels and vehicle designs (such as the much lighter and more efficient aluminium 'hypercar'[33]) which are the best hope of significantly reducing the polluting impacts of vehicles, this effect of rising prices on technological innovation is very important.

There is another factor at work here too. Although fuel prices have risen over the last twenty years, the cost of motoring *as a whole* has not. For the purchase price of cars in real terms (ie allowing for inflation) has fallen dramatically. When the growth of earnings is taken into account, we find that it is much cheaper to run a car now than it was two decades ago.[34] Meanwhile the alternatives to cars have been getting more expensive. Average bus and rail fares have risen by 30% in this period.[35] Since car use is also affected by the price of possible substitutes, this again helps to explain the growth of car use even in the face of rising fuel prices.

It is therefore essentially wrong to say that fuel consumption has not been affected by rising petrol taxation. Perhaps more importantly, it can be said with some certainty that reducing petrol duty would cause car use to rise. If governments and political parties are serious about meeting the legally-binding international commitments to reducing carbon dioxide emissions into which the UK has entered, it would seem extremely difficult to avoid the conclusion that high petrol prices continue to be needed. Of course, the higher price need not be made up of taxation. If the underlying oil price rises, as occurred in 2000, it may be that additional taxation is not required. It is after all the total price, not the tax component of it, to which behaviour responds. But the environmental case for using the tax system to maintain high prices—rising at least as fast as inflation, and possibly (given the effect of rising incomes) faster—is a very strong one.

The need for other measures

There are two riders that need to be added to this argument, however. Both concern other dimensions of transport policy, for fuel price increases are not the only mechanism available to help reduce vehicle use. The first is that the elasticity of response to petrol prices is not an independent and fixed factor. On the contrary, people use their cars less when acceptable and competitively-priced alternatives are available. For inter-city journeys this means in particular reducing rail fares and improving services. In local areas it requires lower bus fares and improving the reliability and comfort of bus travel, making walking and cycling safer and in some cities introducing new tram and light rail systems. Carsharing schemes, designing 'safe routes to school' for children, land use planning policies and a variety of other mechanisms are already being introduced by many local authorities to help reduce car use.[36]

At central government level one option which might be considered is to allow employers to give tax-free vouchers for public transport to their employees to encourage non-car commuting, as happens in some US states.[37] At the same time measures can be taken to make alternative fuels cheaper and more readily available. This might include an increase in the availability of grants for car and truck owners to convert their vehicles to LPG or CNG. Additional support could be given to the longer-term introduction of low-pollution hydrogen fuel cell and electric hybrid vehicles. There are many possible measures, both short- and long-term, of these kinds. The point is that spending on them is an important part of making higher fuel prices properly effective.

The second caveat is that higher fuel duties do not have the same impact on all the different environmental impacts of motor transport. They are most effective in reducing carbon dioxide emissions, which correlate reasonably precisely with fuel consumption. But the emissions which cause local air pollution are not proportionate in this way. They vary according to local conditions, being more damaging in urban areas, where traffic is higher and air quality is already worse. Congestion similarly varies by time of day and location. So fuel duty has only a rather blunt effect on these problems.

This is why the Government has also proposed the use by local authorities of road congestion and office carparking charges. Congestion charges can be adjusted to the particular conditions in different places, with highest charges at peak hours and peak rates of pollution, and lower or zero charges at other times. Road congestion charging has worked well in certain cities around the world (such as Singapore) and new 'smartcard' technology should make it administratively relatively simple.[38] In principle we support the use of such schemes. The Government has stipulated that the revenues from them must be earmarked for transport spending for at least ten years. Given the importance (as we have just described) of positive measures to promote alternatives to car use, and with the conditions we set out in Chapter 8, we believe that this is appropriate and will help to win public support.

If there is a concern about such charges it is in fact that many local authorities may be reluctant to introduce them (and associated office car parking charges) for reasons of competition rather than environmental impact. There is an understandable fear that if some towns and cities introduce charges while other, neighbouring, ones do not, retail business and new employers will be attracted away to the latter. For this reason local authorities should be strongly encouraged to cooperate with one another. If this does not happen the Government may need to threaten the transfer of local powers to the regional level. In respect of office car parking, there may be a case for making this a national tax if local schemes are slow to take off.

Is car taxation regressive?

The final issue that needs to be addressed in this field is the social impact of high taxes on motoring. There is an understandable concern that car taxation is regressive.

In fact the distributional impact of car taxation depends on who is being considered. Across the population as a whole, taxing motoring is not regressive, for the simple reason that the poorest households do not have cars. In terms of household living standards, petrol duty increases fall hardest upon households in the middle of the income distribution. The richest households experience on average a rather smaller percentage drop in their living standards, while on average those in the bottom 20% experience little change. However, for those households which do have cars, taxation is indeed regressive. As a proportion of the household budget, low-income households with cars will often spend double the amount spent by those on high income. Increases in fuel duty therefore have the largest impact on living standards in the poorest car-owning households, falling as incomes rise.[39] This picture is complicated by geographical factors. Lack of public transport and longer distances to amenities give people living in rural areas fewer alternatives to the car than those in towns and cities, so at any level of income the impact of fuel duty on rural dwellers is larger. Low-income car-owning households in rural areas are particularly badly hit. Conversely, people living in London, who have the most accessible alternatives to car use (and the lowest levels of car ownership at any level of income) are least hurt. Across the country the impact tends to vary in proportion to population density.[40]

One further point can be made. Given that most low-income households are dependent on non-car modes of transport (public transport, walking and cycling), investing money in these modes has a generally progressive impact. (It also benefits, incidentally, many children and second-driver adults—often women—in households which do have cars.) If the revenues from car taxation are used for this purpose, any regressive effects of the tax need to be offset against the progressive impact of the spending.

An integrated policy

In the light of these arguments the Commission's conclusion is that overall the heavy taxation of motoring is justified on environmental grounds. But we recognise that high petrol taxation is not popular, and is genuinely painful for many people, particularly those on low incomes. We therefore believe that measures should be taken to lessen its impact, especially when crude oil prices also rise. There are two primary ways in which this should be done.

The first is through vehicle excise duty (VED). One important reform has already been made to VED in recent years. The Labour Government has introduced a graded scale of charges according to engine size, so that smaller cars (which are generally more fuel-efficient) pay less than larger ones.[41] In so far as low-income households tend to have smaller cars, this introduces some measure of progressivity. But for any individual size of car VED operates as a flat-rate tax, rather like a standing charge. It is therefore regressive overall, adding considerably to the cost of owning a car for low-income households. At the same time the tax has very little impact on the environmental impact of driving. Once paid for, it does not vary at all with mileage, fuel consumption or pollution.

Our recommendation, therefore, is that higher petrol tax revenues—caused either by higher duties or increases in the underlying price of oil—should be compensated for by reductions in vehicle excise duty. By shifting the burden of tax from ownership onto use, this would be both environmentally more sensible (ensuring that the rate of tax paid was more closely proportional to use) and socially more progressive, since low income households drive less than richer ones. A simple £50 cut in VED for cars up to 1800cc would cost around £800 million a year.[42] Such a reform would leave VED rates in three bands: £50 for cars up to 1200cc, £105 up to 1800cc and the present £155 for cars over 1800cc.

It is worth comparing the effect on motorists of a cut in VED of this kind compared with, say, a 3p cut in fuel duty. For a fairly recent make of 1800c car doing 10,000 miles a year (which is around the average mileage), a 3p cut in petrol duty would save around £36.50.[43] A £50 VED cut would therefore represent a larger annual saving—without tending to increase fuel consumption. (There might be a marginal effect on consumption if lower VED enabled some low-income households to buy a car where before they could not, particularly if this tended to increase the stock of older and cheaper cars. But the equity effects of this, it should be noted, would be positive.) Clearly, those driving larger cars and doing more than around 15,000 miles a year would do better in purely financial terms with a 3p petrol duty cut. But people in this category are almost all on high incomes.

It would be possible in fact to increase the gradient between the top and bottom rates of VED even further, reducing the licence on small cars to an administrative sum, say £20, and increasing it for the least fuel-efficient vehicles. This could be done on a revenue-neutral basis.

One option sometimes proposed is for VED to be specially reduced on cars registered in rural areas. But we would not recommend this. (The proposal to cut VED on all cars will of course benefit rural motorists.) Although poorer rural dwellers are hardest hit by higher fuel prices, the average income of households in rural areas is higher than in most urban areas, so any general cut for rural motorists would disproportionately benefit higher-income households. In the medium term it would encourage more people to move to the countryside, which in environmental terms would not be desirable because of the additional kilometres which would then end up being driven. In any case, we have grave doubts that a scheme of this kind could be properly enforced. Many urban dwellers would surely find ways of registering their vehicles at rural addresses. We can see a justification for compensating low-income rural dwellers for the high cost of petrol. But this should be part of a more general compensation for the higher costs and lower amenities available in rural areas. (Those without cars in rural areas are even more disadvantaged than car users.) The obvious way of doing this would be through special reductions in council tax rates for lower income bands in rural areas.

The second way in which the impact of higher fuel taxes can be reduced is by using the revenues for additional spending on public transport and other non-car transport schemes. We have already argued the importance of alternative modes of transport in enabling people to use cars less. But earmarking the revenues from motoring taxes for such spending would have the added political advantage of making the connection visible.

One of the repeated complaints of the public—frequently repeated in the discussion groups held as part of our own research into public attitudes—is that higher petrol duty revenues over recent years seem to have gone into the 'black hole' of the Treasury rather than into improving the roads or public transport. In these circumstances it is perhaps surprising that the Government has not attempted to link the revenues it receives from fuel duty and its spending on transport more closely. In his 1999 Pre-Budget Report the Chancellor announced that any future increases in fuel duty would be earmarked for transport spending; but then in the subsequent Budget he did not raise the duty. A few months later, however, as part of the 2000 Comprehensive Spending Review, spending on transport was dramatically increased: not just through a capital expenditure programme of £65 billion over ten years but an average rise in current spending of nearly £6 billion a year.[44] Yet when the petrol tax protests erupted soon after—accompanied in the media by the familiar complaint that no transport benefit was seen from the revenues—the Government did little to point to the fact that higher spending on roads and public transport was exactly what was now planned.

Making this connection would, we believe, help persuade the public of the value of higher petrol duties. Clearly, not all of the revenues from petrol duty can be earmarked for transport spending. As we argued in Chapter 8, where there is an independent environmental justification for the level of tax, as we have shown there is in this case, earmarking 100% of the revenues is not necessary. But we do believe that earmarking *increases* in revenue above a baseline would help to 'connect' the public better to the purpose of the tax. The Government could usefully show how the higher revenues received since May 1997 match—and in that sense 'pay for'—its higher transport spending over the three years from 2001-04, and could guarantee again that any further increases will lead to higher spending over and above current plans. These could include the increases in revenue received from VAT and mineral oil duties resulting from higher crude oil prices as well as increases in petrol tax. As we argued in Chapter 8, when clear expenditure and taxation plans have been set out and revenues then exceed expectations, it is incumbent on the Government to explain what will be done with them. In this case earmarking the revenues for transport alternatives is likely to make a particularly useful contribution to the wider project of connecting people to their taxes.

£

Conclusion

Other environmental taxes

There are several other possible environmental taxes. We have not investigated these in detail: they depend on arguments about specific areas of environmental policy which were beyond the scope of the Commission's work. However, from a preliminary examination there would appear to be strong arguments in favour of the following:

- Bringing incineration within the landfill levy. This would acknowledge its pollution impacts and would further encourage reuse and recycling of wastes.
- A general environmental product tax which could be levied at different rates on particular products with adverse impacts for which substitutes are available. This would help to build consumer awareness of environmental damage, particularly if revenues were earmarked (as in several European countries) on associated environmental programmes. Pesticides, artificial fertilisers, peat and non-rechargeable batteries are among possible candidates; each needs careful assessment.
- A European-wide tax on aviation fuel. This is the one form of energy which is at present untaxed. Aviation has considerable environmental impacts, including carbon dioxide emissions, and is growing rapidly. A national tax would clearly be unworkable, but a European-wide tax is regarded as feasible. If legal barriers prove insuperable, a carbon emissions trading scheme for aircraft operators would be an alternative.[45]

The politics of environmental taxes

In general, therefore, the Commission supports the use of environmental taxes where they can contribute both to the reduction of environmental damage and to the wider goal of shifting the tax burden from goods to bads. But we are also acutely conscious of the considerable political obstacles which stand in the way of further development in this field. The 'losers' from environmental taxes—those whose costs are increased—are almost always more vocal than the 'winners' whose overall tax burden falls. The losses are often concentrated among a small number of large industries with high environmental impacts, whereas the gains may accrue much more widely (and many gainers may not realise it until the tax takes effect, since most of the advance publicity concerns the tax to be increased rather than the tax to be reduced). Lobbying against environmental taxes—whether directly by industry or in the media—can then put tremendous pressure on governments to back down, as has been seen with both the climate change levy and petrol taxation.

In these circumstances governments need to ensure that the grounds for levying environmental taxes are made very clear. The key point that needs to be emphasised is what would happen in the absence of the tax. In few areas is the alternative the *status quo*. It is some other form of environmental instrument to tackle the damage instead of the tax. But this is very likely—particularly if it takes the form of a standards-based regulation—to result in higher overall costs and little incentive for innovation. As most businesses will ultimately recognise, a tax is almost always a preferable option. Perhaps most importantly, governments need to remind firms and consumers that a tax does not have to increase their costs. Indeed, the point of it is that it should not: it should result in more efficient production and consumption. The aim of an environmental tax is to change behaviour to reduce environmental impact. Where this is done by changing the methods of consumption or production—through innovation—overall costs can actually be reduced. This is the ultimate objective, and it needs to be emphasised in the face of complaints that higher taxes simply raise costs.

The nature of the alternative is also relevant in terms of tax revenues. Those who seek a reduction in petrol duty, for example, needs to be reminded not just of the environmental impact of even greater traffic congestion and air pollution, but the shortfall in tax revenues which would result. A permanent cut in petrol taxation would require some other tax to be raised. Few of the alternative options are very popular.

Over recent years there has been a considerable increase in the number and extent of environmental tax measures levied in most industrialised countries, including the UK. Both the environmental and the taxation system arguments suggest that this trend should continue. But there needs to be considerable public education about both arguments if this is to be politically feasible. We note that in several European countries governments have established 'Green Tax Commissions' to examine the case for further environmental taxes in an impartial framework. The Environmental Audit Committee of the House of Commons has made a similar call here.[46] We concur: this would make a valuable subject for examination by the Royal Commission on Taxation we have ourselves proposed (see Chapter 7).

14 | Taxing land

The aims of land taxation

The taxation of land is a subject that has fascinated economists and others for two centuries. It has come back to public attention in recent years and in terms of the Commission's objectives offers some important—and potentially radical—opportunities for reform.

The taxation of land value has a unique feature. Unlike virtually all other taxes, it does not in principle have an adverse effect on economic activity. This is because land is fixed in supply. If the cost of holding land rises through a tax, the supply of land does not fall (as, for example, a tax on goods tends to reduce their supply). Since land rental levels are determined by the market, the landowner cannot generally pass the tax on to the user of the land. So the tax has no effect on rents, and no effect on the prices charged by firms or others using the land. It simply reduces the land's value. In this way the entire burden of a tax on land falls on the landowner, reducing his or her wealth. As the great classical economist David Ricardo pointed out nearly 200 years ago—and as many others, from John Stuart Mill to Milton Friedman, have subsequently observed—land value taxation is therefore largely 'non-distortionary': it does not reduce the economic output that takes place on it at all.[1]

The fact that a tax on land falls entirely on the landowner has long been seen as another argument in its favour. For the value of land does not derive primarily from the landowner's own efforts. Land itself (that is, not including the buildings on it) acquires value essentially from two sources. These are its natural attributes (location, topography, soil quality and so on) and its proximity to economic activity and infrastructure (housing, industry, roads, sewerage etc). But neither of these sources of value is of the landowner's making. Indeed, the more the local community develops economically and socially, the more it invests in communal benefits such as roads, housing or whatever, the higher the value of the land. In this way the landowner's wealth, and the income he or she receives from rents, can be regarded as largely unearned: they are the product of the community's activity, not the landowner's. Taxing the land can therefore be justified simply as a way of recouping the wealth the community has generated, which the landowner would otherwise effectively expropriate.

These arguments were most famously expressed by the American Henry George, whose book *Poverty and Progress*, published in 1878, was the world's first best-seller about economics. (HG Wells and George Bernard Shaw, among others, both credited George with converting them to socialism—though George himself was not a socialist.) George argued for the taxation of economic rents at 100%—effectively, for the nationalisation of land wealth. George and his followers proposed that land taxation could actually replace all other taxes, financing the entire public spending budget without recourse to taxes on income or labour. Since the latter inevitably reduced economic activity, whereas a land tax was non-distortionary, George argued that such a shift in the burden of taxation would increase production, employment and wealth.[2]

The radical and impractical nature of the Georgists' 'single tax' proposal has led to its general dismissal in political debate over the last century. But there is no need to see land taxation, in the Georgist fashion, as somehow a panacea for all economic ills. Indeed today the taxation of land is much more sensibly viewed as a form of environmental taxation, with the same advantages as other such taxes. It encourages the efficient use of a scarce resource, penalises activity with external or social costs, and generates revenue which can be used to offset other, less efficient taxes. Seen in this light, there is every reason why land taxation should take its place among the range of taxes available to the modern state.

As with other environmental taxes, there is a further argument which should encourage a debate about land taxation now. Because land is fixed, and cannot be concealed, its taxation is extremely difficult to evade. As we observed in Chapter 1, a number of commentators now argue that the increasing mobility of capital and people, and the development of e-commerce (which makes the territorial location of economic activity harder to determine), are already beginning to undermine certain elements of the tax base. Although as a Commission we have doubts about this thesis, it is certainly possible that taxing fixed assets such as land may come to seem particularly attractive, generating a certainty of revenue where the taxation of income or sales may not.

The current taxation of land

Land in the UK is currently taxed in a number of ways, from income tax to council tax—see Box 14.1. All these taxes have an impact on the market for land, and therefore on wider economic and housing activity. (Since property is an important part of most pension fund portfolios, they also have a more general economic impact.) Considerable revenues are raised from them, including over £30 billion from the uniform business rate, council tax and stamp duty. But their structure nevertheless gives rise to two different kinds of problem.

Box 14.1: Taxes on land

*Income from land—both private and commercial rents—is taxed, like other earnings, through **income** and **corporation** taxes. If land is bought and sold as part of a trading activity, the profits are also counted as earnings and subjected to corporation or income tax. Otherwise the sale of land is subject to **capital gains tax** (CGT), though the sale of primary residences is exempt. The value of land itself is taxed through **inheritance tax**, as part of the estate of a deceased person. (See Boxes 12.2 and 12.3 in Chapter 12.)*

*   **Stamp duty** is charged on the documents conveying the sale of land and buildings. Stamp duty is effectively a form of taxation of land value. It is charged at progressive rates as a proportion of the selling price: 0% for sales under £60,000; 1% from £60,000 to £250,000; 2.5% from £250,000 to £500,000 and 4% above £500,000. The higher rates have been raised in successive Budgets by the present Government. Around £7.2 billion was raised from all forms of stamp duty in 1999-2000.*

*   **VAT** is charged on normal commercial activities associated with selling, leasing, renting or hiring out of land and buildings, for the construction and refurbishment of commercial properties and for the refurbishment of domestic buildings. The construction of new dwellings is zero-rated, along with the conversion of commercial buildings to housing use. From April 2001 it is proposed that the refurbishment and conversion of domestic buildings should attract a reduced rate of 5%.*

*   **Uniform Business Rate** (UBR), sometimes known as the National Non-Domestic Rate (NDDR), is levied on buildings in commercial use. It is calculated by multiplying the rateable value of the property by a national uniform poundage. The rateable value is an official estimate of the annual market rent for the property. The tax bill is therefore the same for properties of the same value wherever in the UK they are located. Empty properties are not liable to UBR. Business properties are revalued every five years, most recently in 2000. UBR is collected by local authorities and redistributed to them by central government but (since 1990) set nationally. It raised £15.6 billion in 1999-2000.*

*   **Council Tax** is levied on domestic properties by local authorities. It is an annual charge based on the market value (assessed in 1991) of the property, with properties divided into value bands for the purpose of the tax. Council Tax raised around £12.8 billion in 1999-2000. (See Box 9.1 in Chapter 9 for more detail.)*

*   Liability for Council Tax and the Uniform Business Rate lies with the occupiers of land, not the landowners, and the taxes reflect the value of the whole property, including the buildings. They therefore fall on the incomes of the occupiers, not on the wealth of the landowners.*

First, there is a set of very specific land-related environmental problems which has emerged over the last few years. These essentially concern the imbalance in the location of development (both commercial and residential) in rural and urban areas. While their causes are complex, and certainly not simply a product of the regimes of land taxation, there are a number of tax reforms which might assist their solution. Second, there is the more general and continuing failure of the present tax system properly to capture economic rent, and in particular to tax the increase in land value caused by community development. The problem here is not that land is not taxed, but that it is taxed in the wrong way, and as a result has an unnecessarily adverse impact on both the economy and the environment.

We shall consider the environmental issues first, and then turn to the more general problem of capturing land value. A number of relatively straightforward reforms will be proposed to deal with the former issues; and a more radical option explored for the latter.

Land taxation for environmental goals

Demand for housing and other development in the United Kingdom is very uneven. There is enormous demand for housing in the south east of England and in certain parts of other regions, particularly on so-called 'greenfield' or previously undeveloped sites in rural and semi-rural areas. At the same time many urban areas, particularly in the north of England, are suffering from dereliction and decline, with low demand for any kind of development, many sites lying vacant and buildings empty, and very low land and house prices. In certain inner city areas there is literally no demand at all: houses cannot be given away. Many of these areas have entered what sometimes seems like an inexorable downward spiral, with little new investment, high unemployment and population emigration. Even in relatively prosperous areas, many town centres have experienced decline, suffering from the relocation of much commercial, retail and leisure development to out-of-town or edge-of-town sites.[3]

This situation is a product of many forces, and geographical disparities are inevitable in any market economy. But there are good reasons from a citizenship perspective for regarding it as undesirable. In the first place, it has made and continues to make a major contribution to the growth of inequality. We have already noted in Chapter 12 how rising house prices, particularly in London and the South East, have increased the wealth of some groups who generally already have high incomes. At the same time, urban dereliction and falling house prices contribute to unemployment and social exclusion, as many inner city areas and urban housing estates attest.

The over-development of the countryside and the decline of urban areas do not just affect those who live there. Since it is the use of land which defines the wider environment in which all of us are located, land in a strong sense belongs to the whole community. People care about what happens to the countryside, and to town centres, because they are in some way 'ours', even though much of them may be privately owned. (This is indeed why the planning system gives rights over development, through the requirement for planning permission, to the community at large rather than to the landowner.) A concern for citizenship is likely to attach particular weight to the vitality of town and city centres. It is in the shared spaces of the urban environment—the streets, squares, riversides and parks—that citizens meet one another and appreciate the bonds of interdependence. The call for an 'urban renaissance' reflects the need not simply to rebuild the physical environment, but to strengthen the public realm.

The trends of development in both countryside and urban areas are the products of market forces, of many thousands of individual decisions about where to live, to locate businesses and so on; but their wider social impacts make them the subject of concern to society at large.

None of this means that there should be no development in the countryside. Much of the pressure to prevent rural development acts primarily to raise house prices, which has extremely adverse distributional effects, particularly on younger people living in areas who find themselves unable to live there. Often the priority must be increasing the amount of social housing. There are legitimate disagreements about how much housing is needed in the countryside; but few now dispute that not all the demand can be accommodated. The Government's target is that 60% (rather than the present 51%) of all new housing development should be built on 'brownfield' (already developed) land rather than greenfield sites.

The question is how to achieve this. The primary instrument is the planning system. But the planning system is an essentially negative instrument; it can prevent development in one place but it cannot force the development into another. Indeed it cannot even properly encourage it. This is why in recent years there has been increasing interest in the use of economic instruments—taxes of various kinds—to do this.[4]

There are essentially two separate, though related, problems here. One is that the present system of land taxation actually contributes to the decline of urban areas. The other is that it does not sufficiently deter 'greenfield' development. Can the system be changed to tackle these problems?

£

Proposals for land taxation

Varying business rates

The principal impact of the tax system on urban land comes through the operation of Uniform Business Rates (UBR). As a uniform tax imposed at the same rate in all parts of the country, UBR provides little help in areas which need to encourage development. Indeed, it tends to do the opposite. On the one hand, in areas of low demand, business rates raise effective rental levels and thereby discourage commercial activity. As industrial activity has declined, rates have tended to rise on commercial and retail properties to compensate. In many town centres, rates are now higher than rents, and can cause particular difficulties for small shops and firms already struggling to compete with out-of-town competitors.[5]

At the same time, in urban areas where there is high demand, business rates do little to encourage landowners to bring forward brownfield sites for development. Since UBR is a charge on occupiers, not landowners, it is not levied on vacant land, and is charged at only 50% on empty properties. Where land values are rising, it often pays landowners to hold on to vacant land and empty property in the hope of being able to secure a higher price or higher rents in the future. While some vacant landholding is necessary to allow property owners to assemble viable parcels of land for development, in others it is simply speculation, and an impediment to brownfield building. There are around 45,000 hectares of vacant and derelict land in England, of which 11,000 is suitable for housing. While not all of this is in areas of high demand, sufficient of it is to represent a serious concern. Meanwhile more than 1.3 million residential and commercial buildings are empty.[6]

These problems could clearly be overcome if business rates were not uniform, but could be adjusted in different areas. A radical way of doing this would be to restore control of the rates to local authorities, and then allow them to charge what they wished. There are indeed strong advocates of this idea, not least (and not surprisingly) the local authorities themselves.[7] But we have already argued against this, in Chapter 9, preferring a power for local authorities to vary business rates if they choose to do so. If that recommendation were adopted no further measures on business rates might be needed to support urban regeneration. If it were not, we would propose a more targeted variation of business rates in different areas. This, we believe, would be highly desirable. In areas of real urban degeneration business rates could be relieved altogether (for time-limited periods), to encourage development. In areas of high demand, vacant land and empty property could be charged full or nearly full business rates to discourage speculation, with a short period of grace allowed for the transition between occupiers.

The variation of business rates would require the designation of different areas, both of low and high demand. The Urban Task Force has already proposed the creation of Urban Priority Areas where regeneration policy (including rate relief and other tax incentives) could be focused. Experience in the United States suggests that this can be very effective (in conjunction with other policies) in stimulating urban regeneration.[8] Our additional recommendation is that areas of high demand also be designated, where the levying of business rates on vacant land (and the raising of rates on empty property) could—according to local conditions—be imposed.[9]

Moreover, we would argue for the use of 'Town Improvement Zones' where local authorities would have the power to vary business rates within certain limits. This could involve a reduction of rates for small shops and enterprises in town centres as a means of assisting their regeneration. It could also allow local authorities, in partnership with local businesses, to levy a special additional rate, with the funds earmarked for improvement in local services which would benefit those businesses—in environmental improvement, traffic management, crime prevention and so on. The Government broadly accepted this approach in its local government White Paper *In Touch with the People*.[10]

VAT on building conversions

Until recently, one of the most glaring anomalies in this general field was the full rate of VAT charged on the conversion and refurbishment of existing housing, while new housing construction was zero-rated. Given the urgent need to upgrade the housing stock, to convert existing buildings into flats and to bring derelict housing back into use, this constituted a highly perverse system of incentives. However, in the November 2000 Pre-Budget Report the Chancellor proposed that conversion and refurbishment of domestic buildings should be charged VAT at the reduced rate of 5%.[11] This is a sensible proposal which we support. It is estimated to cost around £1 billion, although the Joseph Rowntree Foundation, taking into account an expected increase in activity and reduced evasion, suggests the cost is more likely to be around £400 million, and could be even less.[12]

The taxation of greenfield development

These measures, we believe, would help encourage development in urban areas. But they would cost money (in tax revenues foregone); and they would do nothing to discourage development on greenfield sites. For this reason there has been increasing interest in the last few years in the idea of a 'greenfield tax', levied on development on previously undeveloped land.[13]

In the last chapter we noted that environmental taxes can have two purposes. They can provide incentives to less environmentally damaging behaviour; and they can raise revenue which can be used to reduce other taxes or for earmarked environmental spending. As an incentive measure a greenfield levy would be a very blunt instrument. The environmental impact of greenfield development varies in different areas: in some, development on greenfield land may even be quite desirable. (Even the Government, after all, is willing to see 40% of all housing development on such land.) To prevent really significant amounts of greenfield development the rate of the levy would have to be very high; but in that case the tax would also choke off much development elsewhere that was perfectly acceptable.

For this reason the Commission believes that a greenfield tax should be seen primarily as a revenue raising measure. Its purpose would be to raise money which would then be earmarked for urban regeneration. Part would compensate for the reductions in urban taxes proposed above. Part would go to fund other activities aimed at recycling urban land, such as environmental improvements, the remediation of contaminated land, housing refurbishment and so on. (The report of the Urban Task Force offers no shortage of spending options.)

There are two different ways in which greenfield development might be taxed. One is an *ad valorem* tax on the market value of land developed in designated greenfield areas. The other—rather more simply—is to impose of VAT on sales of new houses in such areas.

A new greenfield levy would have the advantage of being a flexible tax clearly labelled with an environmental purpose. At a tax rate of around 5-10% of land value, it is unlikely that the imposition of such a levy would have much impact on market demand. It would probably prevent some marginal development from occurring, but its main effect would be to raise revenue. On the assumption that 40% of development (rather than the present 51%) occurs on greenfield sites, and this is uniform across every region, it is estimated that a tax of 10% would raise around £1.2 billion a year, with lower rates generating proportionately less.[14]

Who would bear such a tax? Although paid by developers, the greenfield levy would in practice primarily fall on landowners, since it would act as a land tax and reduce the value of land. Perhaps most importantly, there is likely to be little or no effect on house prices. The price of houses is determined by the second-hand market (which accounts for 90% of all house sales), so the extra cost of building a new home on greenfield land would not increase its market price.[15] A greenfield levy of this kind, however, would pose some formidable problems of valuation. Where land is newly acquired its value is known. But for land previously acquired the tax would require the land to be valued, adding additional administrative costs and potential dispute into the scheme. Borne entirely by landowners there is a strong risk that it would effectively turn into another 'betterment' tax of the kind which has been introduced several times in the past—and each time abandoned as unworkable. (We discuss this further below.)

We therefore favour the alternative option of imposing VAT on new properties sold in designated greenfield areas.[16] This would have the great advantage of not requiring the design of a new tax (though if it were limited to greenfield development it would require many of the same issues of definition). It would therefore be easy to introduce and cheap to administer. There would be no thorny issues of land valuation: the sale price of the property would be the basis of the VAT charge. As an existing tax it might be more difficult to identify its primary purpose as to raise earmarked funds for urban regeneration, but this should not pose insuperable problems of political presentation. It might even be called a 'land recycling levy'. Most European countries charge VAT on new homes.

Since the main function of such a tax is to raise funds, it should be recognised that the planning system is still the principal mechanism to prevent undesirable greenfield development. The tax is not a substitute for strong and carefully applied planning policy. Indeed, it will be important that the tax does not become a perverse incentive to grant greenfield permissions in pursuit of revenue. VAT has the added advantage here of being a national tax and not one levied on a local or regional basis.

Capturing development value

The measures so far outlined are primarily designed to improve the environmental impacts of development. Their purpose is not to address the basic problem we noted at the beginning of the chapter, namely the increase in the value of land which is enjoyed by landowners but which arises from actions taken by or in the local community. As we have already observed, the value of land is determined to a considerable extent by what happens around it. Even more importantly, it is regulated by the planning permission which is granted on it by the local authority. These factors give rise to 'development' or 'betterment' value.

Under planning law, landowners cannot do whatever they want on land they own: they have to have permission from the democratically elected local government. (In this sense, development rights in the UK are effectively publicly owned.) If a plot of agricultural land is given planning permission for housing, its value rises enormously. The rise in value is effectively created by the community through its local authority, but it is enjoyed entirely by the landowner. The scale of such development or betterment value can be simply illustrated. The typical value of agricultural land in the south east of England is around £7,100 per hectare, while land for residential development (subtracting the value accounted for by the provision of utilities) has an average value of £1,116,000 per hectare, or 157 times as much.[17] This represents a very large windfall for those landowners fortunate enough to share in it.

Enhancement of this kind does not need to wait for planning permission: the mere expectation or hope of it is sufficient. Whenever a bypass is built, the value of the agricultural land alongside it rises hugely, since everyone expects new retail, warehousing and leisure developments to be sited there. (They are usually right.) Many kinds of development will increase the value of land nearby even where no new planning permission is needed. A new housing estate may make local retail sites more valuable; new community or retail facilities will increase local house prices; a new road will raise the value of industrial land. In all these cases, landowners benefit from activities paid for by others in the community. As Ricardo, George and others have argued, the community should properly get at least some of this back.[18]

The capture of development value has not just been a Georgist concern. The present Government is in fact (so far) the only postwar Labour administration not to enact legislation with this aim. In 1947 (in the Town and Country Planning Act), 1967 (in the Land Commission Act) and 1976 (in the Development Land Tax Act), successive Labour Governments tried to tax a share of development value. Each time, the measure was resisted by landowners and repealed by the Conservative Government which followed. The problem in each case was straightforward. Attempting to tax betterment at the point at which development occurred, the measures simply had the effect of discouraging developments from coming forward. Landowners, confident that the legislation would be repealed by an incoming Government, held onto their land, producing an artificial scarcity of development sites.[19]

In fact it was the Conservatives who introduced the only successful form of land value taxation the UK has seen, with their Development Gains Tax of 1973 (actually enacted by the succeeding Labour Government in 1974). Levied at the point of sale of land, this was effectively an enhanced capital gains tax (CGT). Indeed it was subsequently merged with CGT, and as such the specific (higher rate) taxation of betterment value disappeared.[20] Today capital gains tax, with its various 'offsets', 'roll-overs' and other exemptions, and with the reduced rates introduced by the present Government on assets held for more than three years, captures only a small part of development value. It only applies, of course, when land is sold.

It is not quite true, however, to say that betterment value is not captured at all in the UK tax system. Two mechanisms do function in this way. The first is stamp duty, which is charged on all purchases of land, now at a rate of 4% for land worth more than £500,000. The effect of stamp duty is simply to lower land values, so it acts like a land value tax. Again, however, it only applies when land is sold.

The second mechanism is a kind of 'informal' taxation process within the planning system. This is what is generally known as 'planning gain'. It is the mechanism by which local planning authorities require developers to provide, or fund, local infrastructure or other community benefits as a condition of planning permission. Technically called 'planning obligations', their ostensible purpose is to require developers to finance the infrastructure improvements that their developments require, such as new or upgraded roads and drainage. But these 'requirements' can be very generously interpreted—they can include a new local school, health clinic or community centre, restored or improved green spaces and so on. In practice planning obligations have often strayed outside their statutory definition and have become a means of funding a wide variety of local facilities unrelated to the development itself. They are a particularly important method of financing the construction of affordable or social housing.[21]

Insofar as planning obligations go beyond the mere financing of the infrastructure required by the development, they do in practice represent an indirect form of taxation to capture betterment value. The developer has to pay more than the simple development cost; the public authority is relieved of infrastructure spending. But this is a very *ad hoc* system, applied at vastly differing 'rates' in different areas at different times, and therefore scarcely qualifies for the name of development value taxation. It is moreover regressive in effect, since the largest gains are extracted in the richest areas where developers have the largest profits from which it can be taken. For these reasons a number of proposals have been put forward recently for its replacement by a more straightforward and predictable procedure. These include the payment by the developer of pre-determined 'impact fees' (as used in the United States), and the use of standardised environmental and social impact assessments to determine planning obligations (as used in New Zealand).[22] Since both of these would formalise the strict payment for infrastructure—though widely defined—rather than for betterment, we do not intend to discuss them here.

How can development value be better captured? Two options have already been mentioned. Capital gains tax could be reformed and increased for land sales; and/or stamp duty increased. However, neither of these particularly recommends itself. Applicable only when land is sold, they address only a part of the problem; and their remoteness from the development process itself renders them rather blunt in affecting wider change. But in any case, if our previous recommendation is accepted, they are not necessary. For the greenfield levy would act as a tax on development value. Levied as a percentage of development costs, which in turn reflect the increase in land values accrued from planning permission, its effect, as we have seen, would be to reduce land wealth. Since the levy would be charged on the whole of the land value, not just the unearned increment, a 10% greenfield tax would in effect represent something more than a 10% tax on development value—and it would apply not just when land was sold, but when it was developed.

On the other hand, the greenfield levy wouldn't capture development value in non-greenfield areas; and it wouldn't capture it on land which was not being newly developed. For these reasons there is still a case for considering other mechanisms—and in particular for examining the possibility of taxing land wealth directly.

Land value taxation

As we have already observed, the vast bulk of land taxation in the UK is levied through business rates and council tax. Yet because these are charged to the occupier of property rather than to the landowner, they do not have the effect of true land taxation: they fall on the occupier (reducing his or her income) rather than on the wealth of the landowner. As we noted, this means that landowners can leave land empty or derelict and are not charged for it. Perhaps even more important, because rates are based on the current use of the land, they do not encourage its most efficient use. In many towns and cities which desperately need to find land for housing there are, for example, car parks, used car plots and other extensive uses of land whose rates do not reflect the cost to society of such inefficient use.

There is a way of levying rates, however, which would provide an incentive to more efficient use of land and which would also help to capture development value. This is 'land value taxation', and it is used in a number of cities in the United States (notably in Pennsylvania, where it has been extensively introduced over the last three decades), Australia, New Zealand, Hong Kong, South Africa, Japan and South Africa.[23] Land value taxation differs from the present UK system of business rates in three main respects.

First, it is levied on the landowner, not the occupier. This means that it does not have the adverse impact on economic development that business rates have, but causes instead a reduction in land values. Assuming a market rent is already being charged, the landowner cannot in principle pass the tax on to the occupier.

Second, it is levied not on the current market value of the property on the land, but on the *unimproved* value of the land alone. That is, the valuation method disregards any buildings or other improvements on the land. It reflects simply the advantages of situation, quality, proximity to facilities and infrastructure and so on, along with the expected planning permission which might be granted. In this sense the tax falls only on those aspects of the land which are not of the landowner's making—the 'unearned increment' created by the actions of the wider community.

Third, it requires the identification of potential planning permissions for all parcels of land, and then the valuation of the land, not on its actual use, but on the assumption of its 'best' or most economically productive use within that permission. This means that the tax provides an incentive for the most efficient use of land, since any use but the most efficient is charged at a higher effective rate. The tax would be levied on all land, including vacant land.

There is a particular way in which land value taxation can be introduced into an existing rating system which has worked successfully in Pennsylvania and elsewhere and has recently attracted interest in the UK.[24] This is what is known as the 'split-rate' or 'two-tier' property tax system. Business rates are divided into two tiers: on the land and on the buildings. An 'Owner's Land Tax' is charged to the landowner as a percentage of the value of the unimproved land, as described above. An Occupier's Rate is then charged to the occupier on the basis of the market or rental value of the buildings, as at present. In this way the land value taxation element can be introduced gradually over a period. The split at first can be very small, with the largest part remaining the Occupier's Rate. But gradually over time the proportion of the total rate charged to the landowner can be increased by varying the percentage rate applied to the land value. As this occurs, the incentive to construct new buildings and to improve existing ones grows, while the incentive to hold under-used land and to speculate declines. Experience in Pennsylvania suggests that a gradual shifting of the burden of the total tax—around 10% each year for ten years—within a revenue-neutral framework gives an appropriate time for landowners and firms, and the land market, to adjust.[25]

Introduction of a split-rate system of this kind was discussed by the Urban Task Force report, but regarded as a future development rather than a present recommendation. In principle it has attractions, but there are two significant objections in the British context.

The first is valuation. At present land is valued (by the Valuation Office) every five years for business rates. An annually adjusted land tax requires an annual valuation of land. On the other hand, the valuation process would be much simpler than for the present rating system, which, since it is based on the rental value of property, requires every building to be examined. Since the basis of valuation for a land value tax is only the land itself, which does not vary between neighbouring buildings, a cheaper 'mass valuation' technique could be used: block by block in urban areas, rather than building by building. If the initial land valuation were conducted as part of the ordinary five-yearly valuation for business rates, subsequent re-valuations would no doubt be easier. The difference in cost between the two systems is not clear however. A biennial rather than annual valuation process could in principle be used.

The second and more serious conceptual concern lies in the planning system. Land value taxation requires every land site to have an outline planning permission. It is this planning permission which to a considerable extent determines the value of the land, as we have seen.

In the United States and other countries where land value taxation has been introduced, a zonally-based planning system is used. This allocates land in a development plan into different zones, with the planning permission in each zone being fixed and known. There is therefore no question of what the planning permission is for any parcel of land: it is given by its zoning.

The UK planning system, however, operates on a different principle. Planning permission is discretionary and depends on the nature of the development proposal which is brought forward. Local planning authorities produce development plans which set out the criteria and principles of planning permission, but they do not lay down what may or may not be done on an individual land site. Planning permission is ultimately decided on a case-by-case basis by the local councillors on the planning committee (with appeals being taken to the Secretary of State).

This would make the introduction of land value taxation in the UK very problematic. Every land site in a district would require an 'advance' or 'likely' planning permission, which would then determine the tax levied. This would make taxation rates subject effectively to the discretion of planning officers or councillors. While no doubt broad bands for valuation could be used to minimise the number of disputes, such a system nevertheless seems likely to create considerable conflict between landowners and planning authorities. It would be possible for taxes to be refunded if the actual planning permission granted on a site subsequently differed from the advance permission, but this could only occur where a new development was proposed.

A further problem might arise from the pressure which the new valuation method placed on landowners to develop their land to its fullest economic potential. Since the land value is based on its 'best' (most profitable) potential use under the advance planning permission, any land use which generated a lower return than this would face a high cost. This is indeed part of the aim of the tax: to encourage the most efficient use of land. But 'efficiency' need not simply be equated with 'most profitable'. There may well be many land uses—for example, small corner shops, or simply open spaces—which provide valuable amenities to the local community but which are not economically the most profitable. It would be essential that all considerations of this kind were taken into account in the granting of planning permissions if the diversity and colour of local communities were not to be extinguished by a monolithic valuing system.

With the introduction of much more detailed development plans over recent years the UK planning system has become in some senses less discretionary. We now have a so-called 'plan-led' system, which is intended to give landowners and the community at large more certainty over likely planning permissions. In principle this should make it easier to issue advance planning permissions for all land sites. Nevertheless, we are not convinced that such a form of taxation would be compatible with the UK planning system, a system which has many advantages and which we would wish to retain. Given the administrative cost of introducing a new tax system, and the incentives to develop vacant and derelict land which our proposals on the variation of business rates provide, we cannot recommend its introduction.

We do however accept that land value taxation is in principle a better way of levying business land taxes than the present system of business rates. We therefore suggest that further research is done in this field, including a pilot scheme in one or two local authority areas. A pilot scheme would allow both the cost and difficulty of valuation and the compatibility of the tax with the planning system to be investigated.

**Part Four:
Conclusion**

Chapter 15:
Paying for progress

During the period that the Commission on Taxation and Citizenship has met, from October 1998 to October 2000, the subject of taxation has returned to the top of the political agenda. As the Government has come to acknowledge the role that taxes have had to play in funding its programme of higher public spending and lower government debt, the phrase 'tax and spend' has even undergone a mild rehabilitation. It can now, at least, be invoked without automatic pejorative associations.

This is welcome. Taxing and spending is what all governments, of all colours, inevitably do. The recognition in politicians' rhetoric that taxes can be good—that they fund spending on public services which improve the quality of people's lives—is an important advance on the terms of debate of most of the last two decades.

But it is not enough. Indeed in the Commission's view it would be deeply unfortunate if the restoration of the idea of 'taxing and spending' simply returned public debate to the language of the past. For society has changed; and as the research into public attitudes conducted for this report has shown, the public have changed too. In terms of taxing and spending, they can no longer be taken be granted. The deep sense of alienation that people feel from the taxes they pay—what we have called 'disconnection'—puts all government on a knife-edge. Taxes *should* be regarded as legitimate; as we have argued strongly in this report this is essential if support for public

spending is to be properly underpinned. But at present it has to be acknowledged that taxes are widely experienced as a deadweight, a cost which
people bear for sometimes barely perceptible gain. No government wishing
to maintain taxation at present levels, let alone increase it, can be wholly
comfortable in these conditions.

There are two principal kinds of remedy. The first of these was beyond the
remit of this report; but it is without doubt the most important. This is to
improve the quality of public services. It is the perceived decline in public
services—particularly in comparison with an improved private sector—
which most concerned those who took part in our research; more than the
level of taxes *per se*. There is in our view little question that addressing this is
the most vital task for government today. Many reforms are now being put in
place; no-one should underestimate how difficult they will be, or the time
significant improvement will take to achieve. But achieving it is vital. 'Tax and
spend' will no longer do. It must be, always, 'tax, spend and improve'. We
doubt that public support for the first will survive failure to sustain the last.

But we also do not believe that the improvement in services will be
enough on its own, particularly if its pace is inevitably slow. In the
Commission's view the public also need to be 'connected' more directly and
visibly to the taxes they pay and to the public services which these finance.
For as our research showed it is not just a dislike of poor public services
which fuels 'tax resistance'. It is the feeling of not knowing where one's taxes
are going, what they are being used for, even how much tax one is paying.
People feel in the dark about this whole subject, confused and aware of their
own ignorance. It is no wonder then that they suspect governments waste
the monies they receive; but it is also little surprise if people feel they pay too
much.

Attempting to tackle this sense of 'disconnection' has therefore been a
central theme of this report. The proposal for earmarking certain taxes,
including (despite some reservations) a new fully hypothecated tax for the
National Health Service; our suggestions for improving the information
made available to the public on taxation and spending, including the
Citizen's Leaflet sent to every household; our recommendation for the independent auditing of government performance by a new Office for Public
Accountability; the suggestion that new mechanisms be used to involve the
public in taxing and spending choices—all these measures, we believe, will
help to enhance the public's sense of 'connectedness'. It is to the same end—
tying taxation firmly to the democratic process—that we have also proposed
the granting of proper tax-raising powers to the devolved institutions in
Wales and Northern Ireland (to match those in Scotland), and to local
government.

We are conscious that many of these recommendations tie the hands of
government. Earmarked taxes are less flexible than ones paid simply into the

Treasury pool. Independent auditing of government requires a more rigid system of objectives and targets and performance measures. Our proposal for a more publicly visible Office for Public Accountability and a standing Royal Commission on Taxation to investigate the impacts of new and existing taxes might even be seen as trying to take the politics out of tax altogether. Would it not be better, we could be asked, if governments could be trusted simply to govern according to their own lights, with maximum flexibility; if their accountability to the public was achieved simply, as of old, through the ballot box?

Well it might; but unfortunately we do not believe that such a view of government and its relationship to the public can be sustained in current conditions. As we found in our public attitudes research, government (of all parties) is too tarnished in the public mind: it would be difficult, indeed, to overstate just how cynical many members of the public have become about the competence and honesty of the politicians who govern them. In these circumstances we believe it is essential that the relationships of accountability and involvement between government and public are enhanced; and that the transparency of the government process is increased, even if this comes at the cost of some flexibility. Nothing we have proposed will take decisions about taxation and spending away from those democratically elected to make them. But such decisions must be seen to be accountable; and debates about them must be conducted with an informed public. It is politicians who need to take the lead in this, presenting information about taxes, spending and public service performance to the public openly and honestly. Our recommendations are designed to help this process.

We acknowledge that there is a wider debate to be held here about the nature of democratic governance in modern society. The renewal of the 'civic contract' between citizens and their government of which we have spoken will require more than the changes in taxes, scrutiny and information which have been our main concern in this report. We hope our proposals will contribute to such a debate.

We note, too, the reward potentially available here for those who seek it. Despite all their misgivings about the taxes they pay and the governments they pay them to, the public have not rejected the idea that they might pay more. If they can genuinely see that more money would help to improve the quality of public services, we found significant majorities prepared to pay their share. As we have observed in this report, the United Kingdom is not a highly taxed country by European standards; it is certainly, as the Prime Minister has argued, an 'under-invested' one.

This should, however, be a fair share. A second theme we have pursued in this report is the distribution of the burden of tax and public spending. We have noted how the rapid growth in incomes at the top of the scale over the last twenty years, accompanied by falling relative incomes at the bottom, have left Britain a less inclusive, more divided society, with high levels of poverty. As we have argued, the system of tax and public spending already and inevitably undertakes an important measure of 'redistribution'. But policy changes over the last two decades have not kept pace with—indeed in some cases have exacerbated—the growing inequality of market incomes. We believe that those earning the highest amounts in society cannot now be said to be paying a fair share towards the public purse. The reforms we have proposed to income tax, the introduction of a new inheritance tax and the changes suggested to the structure of council tax are all designed to make the tax system fairer.

Our proposals do imply, we are happy to acknowledge, that the system of tax and public spending should become more 'redistributive'. Indeed, the Labour Government's first four budgets, as we have shown, have already helped to do this. We believe that this should be debated openly. What some have called 'redistribution by stealth' is not in our view a sustainable strategy. Building a decent society, in which everyone feels they have a stake, in which genuine equality of opportunity and security are available to all, cannot be done invisibly. It must be argued for, promoted, defended. The vision of economic and social progress we have suggested, and the methods by which it will be paid for, need to be properly understood through public debate.

The same applies, too, to our argument that the tax system should be used to discourage social harm, particularly in relation to environmental damage, the third major theme of this report. As has been made abundantly clear recently in relation to petrol taxation, this goal too must be defended explicitly if its implications are to be publicly supported. There can be no 'hidden' environmental taxes either.

All these themes spring from what we have called the 'strong' conception of citizenship. We believe it is important that this should be properly articulated. Decisions about taxation and public spending are not simply questions of day-to-day political conflict. As we have argued in this report, they spring from fundamental beliefs about the relationship between individual citizens and their government; and of the relationship between citizens themselves within society. A fair system of taxation and spending which provides high quality public services for all can no longer be assumed; it must be argued afresh from fundamental values and principles about what constitutes progress in today's world.

For in the end political choices over taxation and public spending are choices about the kind of society we wish to be. At the start of the 21st century the UK has different directions open to it. They need to be faced head on.

Annex:
National Insurance

National Insurance (NI) is not, strictly speaking, a tax: it is a system of social insurance. But it often looks like a tax: employees' contributions are deducted from payslips like income tax, employers' contributions function rather like a payroll tax, and the rates and thresholds of both can be changed by Chancellors in Budgets like those of taxes. Perhaps more importantly for the Commission, the interesting feature about National Insurance is that it is earmarked. The National Insurance contributions paid by employees, employers and self-employed people go into a separate National Insurance Fund, not into the central Treasury pool. The social security benefits paid out under the National Insurance system come from this Fund, not from general revenues.

It was not the Commission's remit to investigate the contributory principle, or the National Insurance system as a whole, since this would have involved examining the entire system of social security benefits. However, the earmarked nature of NI was inevitably of interest. In principle, according to the arguments we set out elsewhere in this report (see especially Chapter 8), earmarking should make people feel more 'connected' to the National Insurance system than to the tax system proper. The recent furore over the 75 pence increase in the basic state pension may suggest some basis for this assumption. Yet much discussion of NI in the media suggests that it is in decline, if not in crisis. Why should this be?

The design and purpose of National Insurance

In its details, the National Insurance system is very complex, but its general features are straightforward enough. Paying contributions earns employees and self-employed people entitlement to social security benefits which are paid out of the National Insurance Fund. These benefits are designed primarily for income replacement in periods when the claimant is not expected to be able to get earnings from work—principally unemployment, sickness, incapacity, maternity and retirement—along with the death of a spouse. (The range of benefits for which self-employed people qualify is narrower than for employees.) The benefits paid do not usually depend on the income or wealth of the recipient: the 'contributory principle' means that in most circumstances all those who have paid their contributions, however poor or wealthy, are entitled to the benefits. Although the emphasis of the UK scheme has always been on minimum subsistence levels (rather than the maintenance of living standards, as in continental social insurance systems), several benefits used to have an 'earnings-related' element. Now, however, with the exception of the remaining earnings-related element in the pensions system, virtually all are flat-rate—paid at the same level for everyone, without reference to the earnings they are replacing. (The National Insurance system is explained further in the box below.)

The National Insurance system is what we have described as a 'flexible' form of earmarking: as well as employers and employees, the Treasury can also contribute from general revenues. Its annual payment fluctuates according to the needs of the Fund. When contributions from employers, employees and the self-employed are insufficient to pay out the required benefits (for example, in periods of very high unemployment), the Treasury contribution is increased; when receipts exceed benefits, and the working balance recommended by the Government Actuary, it is reduced to zero. (The Treasury is not, however, reimbursed in these instances: the Fund accumulates a surplus for later use; the flexibility therefore operates in only one direction.)

The National Insurance system is intended to fulfil several purposes. For the individual, as explained above, it aims to be an insurance scheme, covering against loss of earnings due to circumstances such as unemployment, incapacity or maternity. It is also a form of life-cycle saving, taking money from people when they are young and working and giving it back to them in retirement. For society, it is a means of preventing poverty (through insurance), and also a redistributive mechanism. Because contributions are earnings-related, but benefits are flat-rate, and because not all income groups suffer unemployment (or indeed sickness or incapacity) equally, the system tends to take more from the better off and give out more to the less well off.

The intention, however, is that this should be done in such a way as to 'bind in' the middle classes to the social security system.

Box A.1: National Insurance

The National Insurance Fund receives income from employees, employers, self-employed people and, when required, the Treasury (general taxation). It pays out benefits to replace income in a variety of contingencies: mainly old age (the basic state pension, and in future the state second pension), and others such as unemployment, incapacity, maternity and the death of a spouse. The NI Fund does not contain the accumulated entitlements of every contributor. Payments each year are financed by contributions in the same year (sometimes known as 'pay-as-you-go').

Unlike income tax, National Insurance contributions (NICs) are not charged on investment income, state or private pensions, or social security benefits; they are calculated fully and finally in relation to a particular pay period, rather than being cumulative; and they are paid on a tranche of income, rather than on total income less allowance(s), like income tax. Employees pay contributions only on a slice of their earnings: between a 'primary threshold' (£76 per week in 2000-01) and an upper earnings limit (UEL, currently £535 per week). The standard rate is 10%. (The UEL puts a ceiling on the level of earnings used to calculate earnings-related benefits.) Employers now start to pay National Insurance contributions (NICs) once an employee's earnings reach the 'secondary threshold', which is linked to the personal tax threshold. The standard rate is 12.2%, and there is now no ceiling. People who are contracted out of the state earnings related pension scheme, and their employers, pay lower contributions. Self-employed people pay a flat-rate contribution (currently £2 per week), plus a percentage of profits between certain limits; the upper profits limit is the annual equivalent of the weekly upper earnings limit. They have rights to fewer benefits.

Both employees and self-employed people with lower earnings are exempted from paying contributions, but in consequence usually build up no entitlements to National Insurance benefits. However, there are exceptions. Employees are now deemed to have paid contributions on earnings between the former 'lower earnings limit' and the new 'primary threshold'—in effect, they are zero-rated on this slice of earnings. A variety of groups are 'credited' with contributions (treated as though they had paid them), including people on various social security benefits in or out of work; credits can be used to help qualify for benefits, although usually some actual contributions must also have been paid. 'Home responsibilities protection' also protects the right of people looking after children to the basic state pension.

The National Insurance system now finances some 47 per cent of all social security spending, with more than eighty per cent of this total going to pay retirement pensions. It was recognised from the start that some people not in regular employment would not be able to build up sufficient contributions, so a separate system of means-tested benefits was also established, of which Income Support is now the principal component. However, the numbers dependent on means-tested benefits have increased far beyond those envisaged in the 1940s, partly because no solution was found to the problem of paying variable housing costs from largely flat-rate, subsistence level benefits.

In addition to NI benefits, there are various other kinds. Some benefits are now administered and/or paid for by employers (such as statutory sick pay and maternity pay.) 'Categorical' benefits, of which child benefit is an example, are neither contributory nor means-tested; they are paid either to meet additional costs or to replace income, and can be claimed by anyone, regardless of means, whose status qualifies them (in the case of child benefit, by being responsible for a child). A fourth type of benefit has now been introduced by the current Government: tax credits, usually paid through the tax system and varied according to the income of the recipient and their partner.

The Government Actuary reports annually on the National Insurance Fund, forecasts future developments and makes recommendations about the level of National Insurance contributions and Treasury grant required. In 1999-2000, contributions from employees and self-employed people were estimated as over £22 billion, and contributions from employers over £28 billion. These funds were able to pay out all NI benefits and maintain a working balance in the Fund without a Treasury grant. The Treasury grant was reduced from 1981 onwards, and abolished after 1988-89, but reintroduced in reduced form from 1993 onwards to maintain flexibility. In practice, from 1998-99 onwards, however, no Treasury grant has been paid, as contributions have been sufficient. Indeed, the surplus in the Fund was calculated at £5.9 billion in 1999-2000.

[Source: Social Security Committee, Session 1999-2000, Fifth Report, HC 56-1, The Contributory Principle, Vols. I and II, June 2000; and Department of Social Security, Facts and Figures 2000, 2000]

The earmarked nature of the National Insurance system has kept it separate from the tax system proper, with employees' contributions identified in their own right on their payslips, and employers' contributions effectively acting as a payroll tax. Public attitude surveys suggest that the earmarked nature of the system gives people a greater sense of 'connectedness' to their NI contributions than to their taxes in general. While many people have only a very general idea of which benefits the NI system funds, they are aware that their contributions generate entitlements, and the contributory principle *as a principle* retains substantial support.[1] Perhaps for this reason, governments have generally felt more able to raise National Insurance contributions than income tax. Remarkably, considering the similarity of the effect on people's incomes, the Conservative governments of 1979-97 were able to raise National Insurance contributions five times without apparent public reaction, even as they were simultaneously cutting income tax.[2] Benefits were not increased in parallel; indeed, various cuts were made, to both entitlements and value.

Recent trends

In recent years, however, there have been indications that the basis for the sense of 'connectedness' built into the National Insurance system is being eroded. The National Insurance Fund remains formally 'hypothecated'. But in some ways NI is coming to look less like a separate social insurance system, under which people's expectations of clearly-defined entitlements would have to be honoured by governments, and more like just another part of the general tax system without such guaranteed outcomes. A number of trends have contributed to this. Some of them are the result of social and economic changes with which all developed countries have been grappling: an ageing population, higher unemployment and greater participation of women in the labour market. But others are the result of deliberate government policy. They have combined to put the system's purposes under increasing strain.

First, and perhaps most important, has been the decline in the relative value of National Insurance benefits. After 1980, the Conservative Government ended the mechanism under which long-term benefits, including the state retirement pension, were uprated each year on the basis of the increase in average earnings or prices, whichever was higher (in practice, earnings). Instead increases were tied to prices, which tend to rise more slowly. The value of these benefits has therefore not kept pace with the general rise in living standards. This must have become particularly obvious to those on middle and higher incomes, with the abolition of most of the earnings-related elements of benefits further exacerbating this effect.

Beveridge himself had seen the NI system as providing a flat-rate floor of income, which people could build on. But the result of recent developments is that NI now provides in relation to current expectations an ever more minimal insurance scheme for large numbers of people contributing to it. Many people on average earnings and above already qualify for private insurance coverage via their employers (especially occupational pensions and permanent health insurance); others pay personal insurance premiums to private schemes, if they can do so. Most such people are now relying on their occupational and/or personal pensions to give them a reasonable living standard in old age, since the state pension is expected to make only a very small contribution to retirement income in the longer-term future. Similarly, the benefit levels the state now pays without a means test for unemployment, sickness and incapacity entail a significant fall in income for anyone even on average earnings; hence the increasing use of private and employer-provided insurance—and even more, simple savings—to cover some of these eventualities. Although NI benefits can add to these, since they are not means-tested, they are contributing a smaller proportion of people's anticipated replacement income. Many people, however, cannot obtain private insurance (for example, to cover the risk of unemployment); for others, the premiums are unaffordable, or the exclusions mean they do not qualify. For those who do not qualify for private insurance on the basis of their employment, therefore, the decline of NI benefits is of greater significance.

The downward trend in the value of most NI benefits relative to earnings has continued under the present Government. In the longer term, the Government wants to raise the proportion of pensioners' income coming from private schemes and reduce the proportion coming from the state. In the shorter term, its strategy has been to increase the level of payments to pensioners, but not by restoring the earnings link for the basic retirement pension. It has argued that many people are now retiring on occupational pensions which provide a reasonable income. The priority therefore, it argues, is to direct money not to all pensioners through the NI system, but to those in poverty. Extra money has been 'targeted' on poorer pensioners through the means-tested 'Minimum Income Guarantee' outside the National Insurance system. This Minimum Income Guarantee (or Income Support under another name) is being uprated in line with earnings. Some benefits have been paid universally, such as the winter fuel allowance and the free TV licence for older pensioners. But these have also not been part of the NI system: they are *ad hoc* extras.

This development reflects the second trend, which is the declining value of the National Insurance system as a mechanism for poverty prevention and redistribution. National Insurance is also less than comprehensive in its coverage of the population. The post-war contributory system was established when the economy was expected to stay in full employment, most jobs were full-time, and it was thought that most male breadwinners would be supporting non-earning wives. Today, with the increased prevalence of part-time working, high levels of long-term unemployment, many more lone parents, and other social changes, the same structure leaves large numbers of people outside the system (though, conversely, many more women have begun to qualify for NI benefits in their own right). Although some excluded groups, such as unemployed people and those caring for elderly or disabled relatives, are 'credited' with contributions when they are not earning, these usually have to be matched by some employment-based record to gain entitlement to benefit. Many part-time workers, most of them women, earn too little to participate in the NI system at all.

As a result of these and other developments, therefore, the non-contributory element of the social security system—funded by general taxation, and based on means-tested and categorical benefits—has grown proportionately much larger. The ability of the benefits system as a whole to fulfil the goal of poverty prevention has been weakened, since categorical benefits are often paid at too meagre a level for realistic income replacement, and means-tested benefits are only available when people are already in poverty.

Third, the contributory principle itself has become more blurred, and the NI system has been further eroded. Both Conservative and Labour governments have tightened the conditions of eligibility for various benefits, a process which tends to undermine people's sense of entitlement.

Unemployment Benefit, for example, used to be paid for a year, and be distinguished sharply from means-tested Income Support. By reducing the period to six months, making the two benefits much more similar in structure and rules, and even calling them by the same name (Jobseeker's Allowance), the Conservative Government made it difficult to tell the difference between them. Now the Labour Government, in its Incapacity Benefit reforms, has introduced another form of means-testing (technically abatement, or offsetting) into the NI system, requiring occupational pensions above a certain level to be taken into account in determining the amount of Incapacity Benefit paid. The number of people entitled to Incapacity Benefit has also been reduced—though for some other benefits the Government has widened eligibility, and some groups have been given new entitlements to contributory benefits.[3] The current Government argues that its attitude towards the National Insurance system is pragmatic—that it builds up or cuts back NI benefits, and/or changes conditions of entitlement, where appropriate for its broader welfare reform goals. But on balance the contributory system has continued its decline over the last few years.

Fourth, there have also been changes on the financing side. The Conservatives raised NI contributions while cutting some entitlements. The structure of NI contributions, for both employees and employers, is now increasingly being aligned with that of income tax. (It is thereby, of course, also becoming less regressive). There is still an Upper Earnings Limit for employees; it had been declining in relation to earnings, but is now being raised in real terms in two successive years. The Contributions Agency, which collects contributions, has been merged with the Inland Revenue. And government ministers increasingly refer to National Insurance contributions as a tax.

'Disconnection'

Combined, these developments threaten increasingly to undermine the sense of National Insurance as a separate and distinctive part of the fiscal and welfare systems, under which contributions paid guarantee meaningful entitlements. Public opinion surveys show a widespread expectation that benefits will gradually come to be restricted to fewer people, and that their value in relation to earnings will continue to decline, eventually (if the trend continues) to more or less nothing. As the divergence between earnings-related contributions and non-earnings-related benefits grows larger, public faith in the system appears to be diminishing: while it is approved in principle, current trends leave little confidence in its worth. In the public opinion research undertaken for the Commission, NI contributions did not usually seem to spring quickly to mind when taxes were discussed, and they were seen to be building up personal entitlements in a way that other taxes generally did not. But both this and other research shows that more people are now starting to see NI contributions as in practice just another form of tax.[4]

The National Insurance system therefore provides an example of the 'disconnectedness' which we have argued afflicts the tax system as a whole. However, the NI system was designed specifically to achieve such a sense of connection. Whereas with the general tax system people have perhaps never felt that they knew precisely what they were paying for, National Insurance was meant to create just such an understanding. But now a part of the system which earmarked identifiable benefits for its citizens is widely perceived as no longer doing so—or at least not as it promised to do. And at the same time (although this may not be widely known), there is a surplus in the NI Fund, now amounting to some £5.9 billion, according to the Social Security Select Committee.[5]

As with the tax system proper, this may become a vicious circle. One option for welfare reform has for some time been to strengthen the NI system, asking people to pay higher contributions for better benefits (or at least benefits which do not decline in relation to general living standards). The real level of the Upper Earnings Limit is already being increased. But if the public believes that since governments have reneged on their commitments in the past they can do so again in the future, governments are unlikely to feel confident in asking people to pay higher contributions. So one of the ways in which 'reconnection' might occur can get ruled out—because governments believe that the public do not feel sufficiently connected. This is parallel to the dilemma progressive governments face over taxation and public services in general.

Any social security system of course needs to change in relation to new economic and social circumstances, and all developed countries have faced problems in adapting to new conditions.[6] Many people may disagree with the recent changes in the NI system; but it is not unreasonable that such a system should look different now from how it looked twenty or more years ago. But in the UK, these changes have been happening without explicit public debate, let alone the negotiations with 'stakeholders' common in continental Europe[7]—or even a proper acknowledgement by government that they amount overall to a decline in the NI system. The various ways in which National Insurance has changed—under both Conservative and Labour governments—have occurred incrementally and cumulatively, without an explicit decision on their combined effect, and without, by and large, a specific moment of public recognition. It is hardly surprising in these circumstances that people feel disconnected and cynical. It is not just that the system is not working in the way they had expected, but that this has happened without anyone ever explaining what is going on, or engaging in sustained public discussions about the purposes and problems of the NI system. The public are likely to feel not just let down (because the policy has changed), but also deceived.

It has been argued by some commentators that governments will continue using the separate term 'National Insurance'—because this is a more publicly acceptable way of raising money than income tax—but that the system itself is otherwise effectively dying.[8] If the public comes to believe this too, cynicism about governments and their honesty in matters of taxation is likely to increase. If governments can change the nature of the contract established in an earmarked tax without explicitly engaging in a debate with the public, the sense of 'disconnectedness' which people feel about the tax and spending system as a whole may well grow deeper.

Reform and debate

From the citizenship perspective which aims to 'connect' people better to their taxes, the current condition of the NI system is therefore profoundly unsatisfactory. But what should be done?

We need to distinguish between specific reforms to the NI system which may be possible, and the more general approach which government takes to the issue. We are primarily concerned here with the latter: the need to address the growing gap between public expectations of the NI system and its reality. In short, we believe there must now be a proper public debate about the future of National Insurance. Its gradual, incremental, undeclared decline needs to be ended, and all major political parties told to face the electorate squarely with an honest account of the issues at stake. From the point of view of citizenship and connectedness, it is important that decisions are made in public, after full debate—and with a clear explanation of what they mean for the public's contributions and the benefits they can expect in return.

It was not within the remit of the Commission to study alternative policy approaches to NI in detail, since the financing of social security benefits is inseparable from the nature of the benefits themselves, and this is a subject ranging far beyond the tax system. But there are three general routes which governments could take.

The first is to maintain the present policy direction, but with a much more explicit statement of what this will involve. It would acknowledge that, without earnings linkage, National Insurance benefits will decline in value relative to general living standards over time, and explain what this trend would mean in practice. Since NI benefits are not means-tested they would not be completely worthless to those on higher incomes, but they would make up a small and declining proportion of income. At the same time, the government would use any additional resources differently, including targeting them on priority groups—and would make clear, again, that this is what it was doing. In the case of pensioners, for example, as described above, the Government's strategy is to set a higher 'Minimum Income Guarantee' (means-tested benefit) level, and to pledge to increase this in line with earnings; to abolish the state earnings related pension scheme and replace it with the state second pension; and to introduce a 'pension credit' enabling pensioners with small savings or incomes just about the Minimum Income Guarantee level to receive a benefit.

It seems to us that if such a policy approach is to retain the name 'National Insurance', it must at least involve no further erosion of the contributory principle, and no extension of means-tested benefits. The NI system would need to be redefined as a way of funding a minimal basic pension (and other income replacement benefits) for everyone, while most of the welfare system was organised through non-NI-based benefits, private insurance and savings. Over time, this would almost certainly involve engineering a decline in the size of the National Insurance Fund—to be achieved by cutting employees' and/or employers' contributions. Such a policy would also be likely to have implications for taxation, savings and private insurance payments.

The second option would be a rejuvenation of the National Insurance system, essentially by re-establishing the 'contract' embodied in its earmarking. Several different (and separate) kinds of reform might be made.[9] One set of reforms would seek to make the contract between the government and the citizen more transparent. The government is already proposing to give NI contributors a card setting out their contributions record and the pension to which this entitles them. As a symbol of 'reconnection' this is an important initiative, and it might be extended to other NI benefits as well. Another option would be for the Fund itself to be administered not directly by government but by independent organisations (perhaps mutual societies owned by contributors). This might help to reduce the public anxiety that governments can always renege on long-term contracts made by their predecessors. It might also enable a more sensible public debate to occur if and when the NI system needs to be revised in the context of new social and economic circumstances. Such a revision could occur as a negotiation between the organisations responsible for administering the Fund, the contributors, employers and the government, rather than simply by government fiat.

Finally, and more radically, the benefits provided could be re-examined. One option could be to extend coverage to new contingencies, such as parental or educational leave and long-term care. Another might be for the earnings-related element of benefits to be restored, perhaps in return for additional contributions made voluntarily by those who wished to. Both these reforms would help to ensure that those on average incomes and above continued to regard the system as of value to them. Additional contributions might even be organised as a separate 'funded' system, invested and managed by the private sector. And benefit upratings might themselves be tied again to increases in earnings, to ensure that beneficiaries kept up with the general rise in living standards.

Any extension of benefits, of course, would be expensive, requiring higher NI contributions in the longer term. Some of the extra revenue might be obtained by extending the contributions base, for example by raising or abolishing the Upper Earnings Limit on employee contributions and the profits limit for self-employed people, or by including investment income etc. But the implications for contribution rates would also have to be squarely faced. The system would provide more; but it would also cost more. If administration and ownership of the Fund were at arm's length from government, and entitlements were on record, the public might feel the system sufficiently protected from possible future changes in government policy to make this worthwhile. The strengthened earmarking of the system, it could be argued, would help ensure its integrity. While the transition to a system along the lines of the continental European model is almost certainly impossible in the British context, National Insurance might in these ways be made to feel less like a tax and more like a true social insurance scheme.

The third possible direction would seek to overcome the problem of declining public confidence in the NI system by abandoning earmarking altogether. The rationale here would be that an earmarked system which has lost, or is losing, its legitimacy is worse than no earmarking at all: it poses a higher risk to public trust in the wider tax system. National Insurance, on this view, cannot any longer serve its multiple purposes well, even if reformed, and is bound to increase the sense of disillusionment if it continues to try.

So on this model National Insurance would be abolished, and payments would be integrated into the tax system. Contributions for employees and self-employed people would be merged into income tax, while employers' contributions became a payroll tax, or were even (in due course) converted into the economically more efficient corporation tax. Social security benefits would be financed, like other public expenditure, out of general Treasury revenue. It would need to be decided who was then eligible for the various benefits: with the contributory principle gone, new criteria would need to be established. In terms of financing, this proposal would increase the progressivity of the system, since income tax has no Upper Earnings Limit, and includes investment income. But its cost would depend on the structure of benefits decided upon. And its effect on the distribution of incomes overall would also depend on the new structure of benefits, and on any behavioural changes resulting from this policy move.

As a Commission on taxation, not benefits, it is not our role to choose between these options. The issues are extremely complex, relating at least as much to the structure of social security benefits as to the methods of financing. But we do believe that a broad choice between them will need to be made in the near future. The current sense that the National Insurance system is drifting slowly but inevitably into decline is neither healthy nor sustainable. It is important that the purpose of taxes is clear, and their functioning understood by the people asked to pay them.

We therefore believe that there needs to be a full public debate on the principles and future of the National Insurance system. This is a crucial area of public policy for citizenship—both because of the vital importance of social security for the prevention of poverty and the building of social cohesion, and because of the implications for the sense of 'connectedness' which we have outlined. An open public debate would enable these issues to be properly articulated.

Appendix 1:
Members of the Commission

Chair: Lord Plant of Highfield
Professor of European Political Thought at the University of Southampton

Professor Raymond Plant is a political theorist who has written extensively on political philosophy and public policy, with a particular focus on citizenship and social welfare. He was appointed to the Chair of Politics at Southampton University in 1978. He became Master of St Catherine's College, Oxford, in 1993. He returned to a research professorship at Southampton in January 2000. His books include *Political Philosophy and Social Welfare*; *Philosophy, Politics and Citizenship*; *Conservative Capitalism in Britain and the United States* and *Modern Political Thought*. He chaired the Labour Party's Commission on Electoral Systems, whose report (the Plant Report) is widely regarded as a major contribution to the literature on voting and elections. He is a regular contributor to the press and was for three years a columnist for *The Times*. He was made a Labour Peer in 1992.

Fran Bennett
Independent social policy analyst and policy adviser on UK poverty for Oxfam

Fran Bennett was Director of the Child Poverty Action Group from 1987 to 1993, having been Deputy Director from 1983 to 1987. She was social security adviser to the Joseph Rowntree Foundation Inquiry into Income and Wealth which reported in 1995. She has also written and advised extensively on social policy issues for a number of organisations, including the Commission on Social Justice and the National Association of Citizens Advice Bureaux. She acted as a consultant to Oxfam GB in the development of its anti-poverty programme in the UK and is now a policy adviser for Oxfam on UK/EU poverty issues. She is also the editor of the Social Policy Digest in the *Journal of Social Policy*.

Jonathan Charkham
Company director and former adviser to the Governor of the Bank of England

Trained as a barrister, Jonathan Charkham was for ten years Managing Director of Morris Charkham Ltd before entering the Civil Service in 1969, where he became Under-Secretary and Director of the Public Appointments Unit. He joined the Bank of England in 1981 and served from 1985 to 1993 as Chief Adviser, then Adviser to the Governor, covering relations with heads of major British companies. On secondment from the Bank, he founded and directed PRO NED (Promotion of Non-Executive Directors). He is presently a non-executive director of The Great Universal Stores plc and Leopold Joseph plc and on the London Advisory Committee of the Industrial Bank of Japan. He was a member of the Cadbury Committee and has written widely on corporate governance. He is a Visiting Professor at the City University Business School.

Ruth Evans
Former Director of the National Consumer Council

Ruth Evans was director of the National Consumer Council from 1992 to 1998. Her previous career was largely in the voluntary sector. From 1981 to 1986 she was Co-ordinator of the Maternity Alliance. In 1986 she was appointed Deputy Director, and later Acting Director, of MIND, the National Association of Mental Health. After a period as General Secretary of War on Want, she worked as a management consultant with the Department of Health. In 1999-2000 she chaired an Inquiry into paediatric cardiac services at the Royal Brompton and Harefield Hospital Trust. She is a lay member of the General Medical Council; a member of the Human Genetics Commission; a Trustee of the Money Advice Trust; and non-executive director of the Financial Ombudsman Service and of Liverpool Victoria Friendly Society.

Roger Jowell
Director of the National Centre for Social Research

Roger Jowell was the co-founder of SCPR, now the National Centre for Social Research and Britain's largest social research institute, and has directed it since it was set up in 1969. He is also a Visiting Professor of Social Research at the LSE, the Director of the British Social Attitudes survey series and the Co-director of the Economic and Social Research Council's Centre for Research into Elections and Social Trends (CREST). He is a fellow of the Royal Statistical

Society and an Academician of the Academy for the Social Sciences. He chairs the Association for Research Centres in the Social Sciences. His main research interests are in measuring and interpreting value change in society and its relationship to demographic factors, political attitudes and voting behaviour, subjects on which he has written and lectured extensively in Britain and abroad.

Julian Le Grand
Richard Titmuss Professor of Social Policy at the London School of Economics

Julian Le Grand is an economist who has written extensively on social policy and philosophy, with a particular specialism in health policy. He is a Senior Associate of the King's Fund and an Honorary Fellow of the Faculty of Public Health Medicine. He has acted as an adviser to the World Bank, the European Commission, the World Health Organisation and the Departments of Health and Social Security on welfare reform, health policy and social exclusion. He is currently a Commissioner on the Commission for Health Improvement; previously he served on the boards of two health authorities and was the vice-chair of an NHS acute trust. He writes regularly for the press and appears frequently on radio and television. He is a founding Academician of the Academy for the Social Sciences.

Peter Lehmann
Chairman of the Energy Saving Trust and former Commercial Director and member of the Board of Centrica

Peter Lehmann is the Chairman of the Energy Saving Trust, an organisation set up by the Government and the energy companies to promote energy efficiency. He is an independent adviser to the Water Regulator. He is Chair of the Standards Committee of the Benefits Agency (BA), which monitors the standards of decision-making in the BA and makes recommendations for improvement. He is also currently working as an adviser to several continental gas and electricity companies. He is a member of the Board of Race for Opportunity and a Trustee of Project Full Employment. He was, until the end of 1998, the Commercial Director and a member of the Board of Centrica, the company demerged from British Gas. He was responsible there for strategy and was involved in Centrica's major commercial divisions and in political and regulatory relationships. Previously he worked for British Gas for 25 years in a wide range of positions.

Professor Elizabeth Meehan
Jean Monnet Professor of European Social Policy and Professor of Politics, School of Politics, the Queen's University of Belfast.

Professor Meehan has researched and written extensively in the areas of citizenship, gender, social exclusion and European politics. Her books include *Equality, Politics and Gender* and *Citizenship and the European Community*. She is Life Vice-President of the Political Studies Association of the UK and board member of the Research Council for the Humanities and Social Sciences in the Republic of Ireland. She was a Commissioner of the Northern Ireland Fair Employment Commission until it was superseded by the Equality Commission, a director of Democratic Dialogue (Northern Ireland) and a trustee of the Scarman Trust. She is a founding Academician of the Academy for the Social Sciences.

Jim McAuslan
Deputy General Secretary of the Public and Commercial Services Union

Jim McAuslan worked in the Inland Revenue during the 1970s and 1980s before being appointed the Inland Revenue Staff Federation's first full-time Education, Training and Campaigns Officer. He is now Deputy General Secretary in the newly-amalgamated civil service union, PCS, and heads the Headquarters Bargaining Unit responsible for 81,000 members in the Inland Revenue, Customs & Excise and the Valuation Office. He serves on the European Public Service Union Taxation Committee and is Chair of Unions 21.

Sir Nick Monck
Former Permanent Secretary at the Department of Employment and Second Permanent Secretary (Public Expenditure) of the Treasury

Nick Monck joined the Treasury in 1969, following posts at the National Economic Development Office and as senior economist at the Ministry of Agriculture in Tanzania. In 1976-77 he was principal private secretary to Denis Healey. During his period at the Treasury he worked on energy, employment, social security, science and industrial policy, privatisation, financial institutions, inflation and monetary policy. Since retiring from the civil service in 1995, he has worked as a consultant on public finance and expenditure in Eastern Europe, Latin America and Africa. He is a former Chairman of the British Dyslexia Association and former Deputy Chairman of IMRO. He is a non-executive director of Standard Life.

Stephen Nickell
Professor of Economics at the Centre for Economic Performance, London School of Economics

Stephen Nickell is the author of numerous books and papers in the areas of corporate performance, investment, wage determination, unemployment and labour market institutions. Formerly Professor of Economics at the University of Oxford and Director of the Research Programme in Corporate Performance at the Centre for Economic Performance at the LSE, he is now a member of the Monetary Policy Committee of the Bank of England.He is a Fellow of the British Academy.

Brian Pomeroy
Former Senior Partner of Deloitte Consulting

Brian Pomeroy was formerly Senior Partner of Deloitte Consulting. He trained as an economist and an accountant and played a leading role in developing public-private partnerships and utilities regulation in the UK and overseas. He continues to act as a consultant in this field, as well as holding a number of public and non-executive appointments. He is Chairman of Centrepoint, the charity for homeless young people.

Holly Sutherland
Director of the Microsimulation Unit in the Department of Applied Economics at the University of Cambridge

Holly Sutherland is an expert in tax-benefit modelling who has written extensively on taxation and welfare policy and poverty. She currently co-ordinates the 15-country EUROMOD project to build a European-wide model for the examination of the distributional effects of social and fiscal policies, and she has recently co-authored *The Arithmetic of Tax and Social Security Reform: a User's Guide to Microsimulation Methods and Analysis* and edited *Microsimulation Modelling for Policy Analysis: Challenges and Innovations*. In 1988-1990 she was Secretary/Researcher to the Fabian Society Taxation Review Committee.

The following were original members of the Commission whose changes of position required them to resign during the Commission's period of enquiry and who are therefore not signatories to its final report:

Paul Johnson (member of the Commission to September 2000)
Former Head of Economics of the Financial Services Authority and previously Deputy Director of the Institute for Fiscal Studies

Paul Johnson was Deputy Director of the Institute for Fiscal Studies when the Commission was established, and later became Head of Economics of Financial Regulation at the Financial Services Authority. He has also worked as an adviser in the Cabinet Office. His work has focused on pensions, social security and taxation. He was a member of the Pension Provision Group, established by the Secretary of State for Social Security, and is author of numerous articles and books on taxation, social security and pensions.

Wendy Thomson (member of the Commission to June 1999)
Former Chief Executive of the London Borough of Newham

Wendy Thomson was Chief Executive of the national charity Turning Point and Assistant Chief Executive of Islington Council before joining Newham Council in 1996. At Newham she took a leading role in tackling poverty and in urban regeneration and was a member of the Government's Urban Task

Force. She has written widely on social policy, local government and public sector management.

Secretary to the Commission: Michael Jacobs
General Secretary of the Fabian Society

An economist, Michael Jacobs was formerly a Research Fellow in the Department of Geography at the London School of Economics and an ESRC Research Fellow in the Centre for the Study of Environmental Change at Lancaster University. Prior to becoming an academic he was a Director, then Managing Director, of CAG Consultants, where he worked on community-based urban regeneration and environmental policy, principally with central and local government. He has written widely in environmental economic and politics: his books include *The Green Economy*, *The Politics of the Real World* and *Greening the Millennium? The New Politics of the Environment*.

Appendix 2:
The Commission's terms of reference

Basing its deliberations upon the concept of citizenship, and with the objective of helping to renew trust in public institutions and promoting social cohesion, the Commission will:

- Consider the aims and principles of a taxation system appropriate to the UK at the beginning of the 21st century.
- Examine the current structure and operation of the UK tax system, and recent changes to these, in the light of these principles and aims.
- Analyse the possibilities, advantages and disadvantages of reform to the tax system in the following areas, and any others regarded as appropriate by the Commissioners:
  - The tax base—the activities on which taxation is levied.
  - The tax incidence—the people or organisations on whom tax is levied.
  - The level of government (local, regional, national, European and international) at which taxes are levied.
  - The hypothecation (earmarking) of taxes, and other mechanisms to relate taxation to public expenditure.
  - The political process by which taxes are set.
  - The mechanisms of tax collection.
- Examine the relationship between the tax system and other objectives of government, including: macroeconomic management; microeconomic efficiency; social justice; environmental protection; gender equality; and the provision of public services.

Appendix 3:
Written and oral evidence

The following submitted written evidence to the Commission:

- The Adam Smith Institute
- J B Bracewell-Milnes
- The British Property Federation
- British Retail Consortium
- The Chartered Institute of Taxation
- Christian Action Research and Education
- John Collins
- Council for the Protection for Rural England
- Don Draper
- Alan Hall
- Colin Harbury
- The Henry George Foundation
- Noel Hodson
- The Industry-wide Group on Stamp Duty
- The Institute of Economic Affairs
- Low Incomes Tax Reform Group of the Chartered Institute of Taxation
- David Oliver (N W Brown and Co)
- Public and Commercial Services Union
- The Royal Institute of Chartered Surveyors

- The Royal Society for the Protection of Birds
- Professor Cedric Sanford
- TaxAid
- Trades Union Congress

The following individual experts met the Commissioners and discussed various issues with them:

- Tony Atkinson
- John Chown
- Owen Connellan
- Graeme Cottam
- Evan Davies
- Andrew Dilnot
- John Hills
- Nathaniel Lichfield
- David Oliver
- Tony Travers

The following very kindly read parts of the text:

- Bob Evans
- Chris Hewett
- David Maddison
- Kitty Ussher
- Tony Vickers

The Commission is very grateful to all of the above for their contributions to its work.

Appendix 4:
Public attitudes research methodology

Discussion (focus) groups

This was a small-scale qualitative research project. Eight groups were convened, involving 59 people in all, in Banbury, Sheffield, Birmingham (Sutton Coldfield) and Outer London (Barnet). All the groups were mixed men and women. The group members were selected at random by the following criteria:

- *Group 1* High income older (income £30,000 plus; aged over 40)
- *Group 2* High income, younger (income (£30,000 plus; aged 18-39)
- *Group 3* Middle income, older (income £15,000-£30,000; aged over 40)
- *Group 4* Middle income, younger (income £15,000-£30,000; aged 18-39)
- *Group 5* Low income, older (income up to £15,000; aged over 40)
- *Group 6* Low income, younger (income up to £15,000; aged 18-39
- *Group 7* Middle or high income, Conservative views (income over £15,000, Conservative closest to views)
- *Group 8* Middle or high income, Labour views (income over £15,000, Labour closest to views)

Each group met once for around an hour and a half. They were led by an experienced moderator using a topic guide of questions, issues and information on issues concerning taxation. A small payment of £20 was made to respondents. The groups were held in June 2000.

Opinion surveys

Ten questions were placed on the Office of National Statistics monthly Omnibus opinion survey between 19 June and 7 July 2000. 1,717 adults aged 16 and over took part. Weighting was used to correct for unequal probability of selection caused by interviewing only one adult per household.

One question was put on an ICM Omnibus survey between 25 and 27 August 2000. 1006 adults took part.

Appendix 5:
The POLIMOD model

In several places this report cites modelling conducted for the Commission using POLIMOD, the tax-benefit microsimulation model constructed and maintained by the Microsimulation Unit in the Department of Applied Economics at the University of Cambridge.

POLIMOD uses representative household survey micro-data from the Family Expenditure Survey to calculate tax liabilities and social security benefit entitlements before and after policy reforms.[1] It demonstrates the distributional effects of policy changes in the context of their revenue cost.

'Models do not give answers, they give insights.'[2] The modelled scenarios using POLIMOD in this report should be treated as illustrations, not forecasts. All model results based on survey data are subject to sampling error and some types of results are sensitive to particular assumptions. Here the main issues to bear in mind when interpreting the results used in this report are briefly described.[3]

Throughout the baseline policy, incomes and prices are as in 2000-01, with some changes that have been announced in detail for 2001-02 also assumed to be in place.

Some tax changes have an identifiable impact on individuals—income tax being the prime example. Other taxes, such as indirect taxes, only make sense to consider at the level of the spending unit, or household. To aid comparisons and to allow the modelling of combinations of direct and indirect taxes, the household is used as the unit of analysis throughout. While convenient, it is recognised that this choice implicitly assumes equal sharing of income and resources within the household to an extent that may not always take place in reality.

In exploring the impact of tax changes on the income distribution households are ranked according to their disposable incomes (after direct tax and benefits) which are 'equivalised' to take account of differences in household size and composition (using the McClements scale). When considering indirect tax changes households are ranked by disposable income less indirect taxes. (Thus the decile groups used in Chapters 11 and 13 are slightly different from those used in Chapter 10.) Some results are presented in terms of the number or proportions of 'gainers' and 'losers'. These are defined to be households better or worse off by at least 10 pence per week.

Income tax changes

It is known that people with very high incomes are under-represented in the underlying survey data. For this reason in Chapter 10 the modelling of tax changes affecting high incomes does not use POLIMOD, but instead relies on the Inland Revenue's model based on a sample of income tax returns.

Indirect tax changes

Estimates from POLIMOD do not in general incorporate the effect of any changes in behaviour that may come about following a shift in policy. In Chapters 11 and 13, where changes in indirect taxes are modelled, we make the assumption that the change is borne in full by consumer prices and that consumers do not change the quantity of goods that they purchase following a price change.

Other changes

Most of our modelling relates to tax changes. However, in Chapter 11 the effects of using the means-tested benefit and credit systems to compensate low-income households following the introduction of a uniform rate of VAT are explored. These results are clearly sensitive to the assumptions that are made about the rate of take-up of these benefits and credits, since there is evidence to show that take-up of means-tested benefits is much less than complete.[4] It is assumed in this chapter and throughout that take-up behaviour corresponds to the take-up proportions estimated by the Department of Social Security for the main means-tested benefits. For example it is assumed that some 20% of lone parents do not receive the Working Families Tax Credit to which they are entitled (on the basis of estimates for Family Credit, its predecessor), and that 15% of people of working age do not receive the Income Support to which they are entitled. It is assumed that take-up behaviour is not affected by changes in the size of benefit entitlements.

Notes

Introduction

1   Alan Hedges and Catherine Bromley, *Public Attitudes Towards Taxation*, Fabian Society, 2000.

Chapter 1

1   OECD, *Revenue Statistics 1999*, 1999. (This is analysed further in Chapter 3).
2   See Alan Hedges and Catherine Bromley, *Public Attitudes Towards Taxation*, Fabian Society, 2000. The results are summarised and discussed in Chapter 2.
3   HM Treasury, *Budget 2000*, HC 346, Stationery Office, 2000 (and see Chapter 3).
4   See Philip Gould, *The Unfinished Revolution*, Little, Brown and Co, 1998.
5   HM Treasury, *Budget 2000*, *op cit* (and see Chapter 3).
6   Zoe Smith, *The Petrol Tax Debate*, Briefing Note 8, Institute for Fiscal Studies, July 2000; HM Treasury, *Budget 2000*, *op cit.*.
7   Typical was a rather absurd exchange in the House of Commons in December 1999, when a series of Tory questions to Treasury Minister Andrew Smith asking whether the share of tax in national income had risen in the past two years was met with a series of replies to the effect that it was due to fall in the next two. See *Hansard*, 16 December 1999, pp385-88.
8   On 14 March 2000. The full briefing was published in *The Guardian* on 15 March.
9   Our own Commission indeed experienced this. A pamphlet published by the Fabian Society in December 1999 drawing on some of the Commission's work (*Citizens and Taxes* by Selina Chen, Fabian Society 1999), noted in half a sentence the Red Book table showing that the tax share in national income had risen slightly. The pamphlet was actually about how citizens could be better 'connected' to their taxes; but it was this 'admission' that became the

subject of headlines in the *Daily Mail* and *The Times*. ('Fabian Society agrees that tax burden is up', *The Times*, 29 December 1999; 'Yes, tax burden is rising says Blair's own think-tank', *Daily Mail*, 20 December 1999.)

10   Certain newspapers regularly provides examples of this schizophrenia, calling for tax cuts in one editorial and higher spending on favourite causes such as nurses' pay in another.

11   Michael Portillo, 'How we can offer increases in public spending while reducing taxes', *The Times*, 30 October 2000.

12   John Hills and Orsolya Lelkes, 'Social security, selective universalism and patchwork redistribution', in Roger Jowell *et al* (eds), *British Social Attitudes: The 16th Report*, Ashgate 1999.

13   Roger Jowell and Catherine Bromley, 'Tax, public opinion and voting', unpublished paper prepared for the Commission on Taxation and Citizenship, National Centre for Social Research, 1998, based on Gallup polls of voting intention 1992-97.

14   MORI, monthly polling results, cited in Jowell and Bromley, 'Tax, public opinion and voting', *op cit*.

15   Giles Radice and Stephen Pollard, *Southern Discomfort*, Fabian Society, 1992; Radice and Pollard, *More Southern Discomfort*, Fabian Society, 1993; Radice and Pollard, *Any Southern Comfort?*, Fabian Society, 1994.

16   Gould, *Unfinished Revolution*, *op cit*.

17   Hedges and Bromley, *Public Attitudes Towards Taxation*, *op cit*.

18   Howard Glennerster and John Mills (eds), *The State of Welfare*, 2nd edn, Oxford University Press, 1998.

19   Those saying they trusted British governments (of any party) to place the needs of the nation above the interests of their own political party 'just about always' or 'most of the time' fell from 39% in 1974 to 22% in 1996. Just 9% of people trust politicians to 'tell the truth in a tight corner'. A quarter of people 'strongly agree' that MPs quickly lose touch with the the the public. See John Curtice and Roger Jowell, 'Trust in the political system', in Jowell *et al* (eds), *British Social Attitudes: The 14th Report*, Ashgate, 1997, pp89-109.

20   Michael Johnston and Roger Jowell, 'Social capital and the social fabric', in Jowell *et al* (eds), *British Social Attitudes: the 16th Report*, Ashgate, 1999.

21   The exact figures are 48% in 1973 and 35% in 1996. Those saying the system 'could be improved quite a lot' or 'a great deal' rose from 49% in 1973 to 63% in 1996. Curtice and Jowell, 'Trust in the political system', *op cit*. Confidence in the political system and participation among young people are even lower. See Helen Wilkinson and Geoff Mulgan, *Freedom's Children*, Demos, 1995.

22   Curtice and Jowell found that support for different forms of constitutional reform was highest amongst those with least trust in the system. 'Trust in the political system', *op cit*.

23   Robert Harris, 'The effects of taxes and benefits on household income, 1998-99', *Economic Trends*, No 557, April 2000.

24   John Hills, *Income & Wealth: The Latest Evidence*, Joseph Rowntree Foundation, March 1998.

25   Department of Social Security, *Opportunity for All: Tackling Poverty and Social Exclusion*, First Annual Report 1999, Cm 445, Stationery Office, 1999; and *Opportunity for All One Year On: Making a Difference*, Second Annual Report 2000, Cm 4865, Stationery Office, 2000; Department of Social Security, *Households Below Average Income 1998-99*, 2000.

26   Sir Donald Acheson *et al*, *Report of the Independent Inquiry into Inequalities in Health*, Stationery Office, November 1998

27   Market or original incomes are incomes before taxes have been taken or benefits paid. In 1978 the share of market incomes of the top 20% of the household population was 14 times that of the bottom 20%; by 1998-99 it was 17 times. (Harris, 'The effects of taxes', *op cit*)

28   Hills and Lelkes, 'Social security', *op cit*.

29   *Ibid*.

30   See Department of Social Security, *Opportunity for All One Year On*, *op cit*.

31   See for example OECD, *Growth, Equity and Distribution*, OECD Economic Outlook 60, 1996.

32   See for example Diane Coyle, 'What price the welfare state in a brave new economy world?', *The Independent*, 4 April 2000; 'Caught in a global trap: Treasury tax options are narrowing', leading article, *The Guardian*, 25 February 2000.

33   See for example Vito Tanzi, *Globalisation and the Future of Social Protection*, IMF Working Paper 00/12, International Monetary Fund, 2000.

34   See for example Charles Leadbeater, 'Goodbye, Inland Revenue', *New Statesman*, 3 July 1998.

Chapter 2

1   Alan Hedges and Catherine Bromley, *Public Attitudes Towards Taxation*, Fabian Society, 2000.

2   See for example John Hills and Orsolya Lelkes, 'Social security, selective universalism and patchwork redistribution', in Roger Jowell *et al*, (eds), *British Social Attitudes: The 16th Report*, Ashgate, 1999.

Chapter 3

1   This figure for the share of spending in 1999-00 uses the Government's treatment of tax credits, counting them as 'tax expenditures' (ie as subtractions from tax revenues) rather than public spending. If they are counted as public spending, spending in 1999-2000 would be 38.0% rather than 37.7%.

2   *Financial Times*, 19 July 2000.

3   HM Treasury, *Comprehensive Spending Review*, Cm 4011, Stationery Office, 1998.

4   Department of Social Security, *Annual Report 1999-2000*, Stationery Office, 2000.

5   HM Treasury, *Budget 2000*, HC 346, Stationery Office, 2000.

6   HM Treasury, *Spending Review 2000*, Cm 4807, Stationery Office, 2000.

7   See OECD, *Revenue Statistics 1965-98*, 1999.

8   The indirect tax figures include the estimated incidence on households of intermediate taxes paid by businesses such as employers' National Insurance contributions, business rates and duties on fuel and vehicles used by business. These figures allocate nearly 67% of total tax and NICs to households and about 55% of general government expenditure. Taxes and expenditure which cannot reasonably be allocated to households, for example corporation tax and spending on defence and law and order are excluded.

9   Andrew Dilnot *et al*, *A Survey of the UK Tax System*, Briefing Note No 9, Institute for Fiscal Studies, 2000.

10 Michael Myck, *Fiscal Reforms Since May 1997*, Briefing Note No 14, Institute for Fiscal Studies, 2000. The analysis covers 53% of all tax and benefit changes; those such as changes in corporate taxation, employer NICs and the climate change levy, which only indirectly affect household incomes, are not included. It allows for the full implementation of announced measures due to be introduced in April 2001. It does not include the impact of the national minimum wage or of lower unemployment arising from macroeconomic management or the New Deal programmes; nor of any changes in behaviour (such as increased participation in the labour force) resulting from the reforms.

11 Holly Sutherland and David Piachaud, *How Effective are the Government's Attempts to Reduce Child Poverty?*, Centre for the Analysis of Social Exclusion, LSE, CASEPaper 38, 2000.

Chapter 4

1   William Hague, 'The Moral Case for Low Taxation', speech made to Politeia, 14 March 2000, Conservative Central Office.

2   See for example Robert Nozick, *Anarchy, State and Utopia*, Blackwell, 1974.

3   FA von Hayek, *Law, Legislation and Liberty*, 3 vols, Routledge and Kegan Paul, 1976; F A von Hayek, *The Constitution of Liberty*, Routledge, 1960. Milton Friedman and Rose D Friedman, *Free to Choose: A Personal Statement*, Secker and Warburg, 1980. See also K. Hoover and R. Plant, *Conservative Capitalism in Britain and the United States*, Routledge, 1989.

4   Gabriel Stein, *Tax Freedom Day 1999*, Adam Smith Institute, 1999; Maurice Saatchi and Peter Warburton, *The War of Independence: A Declaration*, Centre for Policy Studies, 1999.

5   Keith Joseph and Jonathan Sumption, *Equality*, J Murray, 1974.

6   Neo-liberals commonly underestimate the cost of protecting negative rights. In a free market society the risk

is that social disorder would increase these costs very considerably. The present case of Russia is instructive in this regard: the chronic crisis of a state unable either to collect its taxes or to enforce the rule of law. See Stephen Holmes and Cass Sunstein, *The Cost of Rights: Why Liberty Depends on Taxes*, W W Norton, 1999 and Stephen Holmes, 'What Russia teaches us now', *American Prospect*, Vol 33, July/August 1997.

7   This argument is due to Charles Taylor, 'What's wrong with negative liberty?', *Philosophical Papers*, Clarendon Press, 1985.

8   See Amartya Sen, *Development and Freedom*, Oxford University Press, 1999.

9   This point has been made very precisely by the philosopher Anthony de Jasay, who is otherwise sympathetic to a very limited government approach:

> There is a not too far fetched sense in which the production of any public good at public expense is *ipso facto* redistributive, if only because there is no unique, 'right' way of apportioning the total cost to be borne amongst members of the public according to the benefit derived by each from a given public good. Some can always be said to get a bargain, a subsidy, at the expense of others. Thus the distinction between the production of public goods and explicit redistribution is a matter of arbitrary convention.

> *[Anthony de Jasay, The State, Blackwell, 1985, p106]*

10   Hague, 'The Moral Case', *op cit*.

11   Hayek, *The Constitution of Liberty*, *op cit*.

12   OECD, *Health Data 1999*, 1999.

13   Hague, 'The Moral Case', *op cit*.

14   This term is borrowed from Alan Gewirth, *Reason and Morality*, Chicago University Press, 1979.

15   It should not be thought, incidentally, that this implies that 'contribution' is in some way measured only through employment and payment of income tax. Every citizen pays taxes, whether through VAT, excise duties or council tax.

16   *Encouraging Citizenship*, Report of the Commission on Citizenship, HMSO, 1990.

17   Joel Slemrod, *Why People Pay Taxes: Tax Compliance and Enforcement*, Ann Arbor, University of Michigan Press, 1992.

18   There may even in some instances (such as hospital accommodation) be a case for allowing various kinds of optional charges into some services to meet the demand for higher standards amongst those who can pay. This may be preferable to their opting out altogether, though it raises significant issues of equity of its own.

19   See Robert Puttnam, *Making Democracy Work*, Princeton University Press, 1993; Francis Fukuyama, *Trust: The Social Virtues and the Creation of Prosperity*, Hamish Hamilton, 1995.

20   See for example OECD, *Environmental Taxes in OECD Countries*, 1995.

Chapter 5

1   See for example Institute of Chartered Accountants Tax Faculty, *Towards a Better Tax System*, ICA, 2000; Jacob Braestrup, *A Guide to the Simplification of the British Tax System*, Adam Smith Institute, 2000; Taxaid, submission to the Commission on Taxation and Citizenship, July 1999; 'Brown urged to simplify "complex" system', *Financial Times*, 10 April 2000; Simon London, 'Will tax become a burning issue?', *Financial Times*, 9 September 2000.

2   See especially Institute of Chartered Accountants, *Towards a Better Tax System*, *op cit*.

3   'Tax experts question 558-page Finance Bill; call for Royal Commission into taxation', news release, Chartered Institute of Taxation, 11 May 2000.

4   These are known as the 'income' and 'substitution' effects. For a discussion see J A Kay and M A King, *The British Tax System*, 5th edn, Oxford University Press, 1990.

5   This is based on what is known as the 'Laffer curve'. See Kay and King, *The British Tax System*, *op cit*.

6   House of Commons *Hansard*, Written Answers, 18 May 2000, Cols 261-262W.

7   HM Treasury, *Supporting Children Through the Tax and Benefits System*, The Modernisation of Britain's Tax and Benefits System No 5, 1999; Paul Gregg *et al*, *Entering Work and the British Tax and Benefit System*, Institute for Fiscal Studies, 1999.

8   See for example William Hague, 'The moral case for low taxation', speech to Politeia, 14 March 2000, Conservative Central Office.

9   'Vertical equity' refers to equity between people or households on different incomes (achieved in a progressive system).

10   Institute of Chartered Accountants, *Towards a Better Tax System, op cit.*

11   See for example 'Survey: gimme shelter', *The Economist*, 29 January 2000.

12   As we pointed out in Chapter 3, the Government presently has two rules for borrowing (the 'golden rule' and the 'sustainable investment' rule) which set its acceptable limits. The principle of sufficiency obviously depends on the desired level of public expenditure. As we argue in the next chapter, the level of taxation and public expenditure need to be determined together: the point at issue here is that once the overall levels of taxation and spending have been determined, the system needs to generate the required revenues.

Chapter 6

1   HM Treasury, *Budget 2000*, HC 346, Stationery Office, 2000; HM Treasury, *Spending Review 2000*, Cm 4807, Stationery Office, 2000. Taxation here includes National Insurance contributions. All years given are year-ends; ie 1999 is 1998-99 and so on.

2   OECD, *Revenue Statistics 1999*, 1999.

3   See for example Michael Portillo, 'A weight around Britain's neck', *Financial Times*, 16 March 2000; Institute of Directors, 'Why the UK needs lower taxes', Economic Comment, July 1997.

4   Cited in Charles Leadbeater, 'Goodbye, Inland Revenue', *New Statesman*, 3 July 1998.

5   See for example D Swank, 'Funding the welfare state: globalisation and the taxation of business in advanced market economies', *Political Studies*, Vol 46, No 4, 1998; J R Hines, 'Tax policy and the activities of multinational corporations', *Working Paper 5589*, National Bureau of Economic Research, 1996.

6   Stephen Bond *et al, Corporate Tax Harmonisation in Europe: A Guide to the Debate*, Institute for Fiscal Studies, 2000.

7   The OECD calculates that total direct investment from the richest seven countries into Caribbean and South Pacific tax havens grew more than fivefold between 1985 and 1994, to over $200 billion. By 1994 26% of the assets and 31% of the net profits of American multinationals (though only 4.3% of their workers) were located in tax havens. Survey 'Gimme Shelter', *The Economist*, 29 January 2000; James Hines and Eric Rice, 'Fiscal paradise: foreign tax havens and American business', *Quarterly Journal of Economics*, 1994.

8   *The Economist*, 5 August 2000; PriceWaterhouseCoopers, *Individual Taxes 1999-2000: Worldwide Summaries*, Wiley, 1999.

9   OECD, *Harmful Tax Competition: An Emerging Global Issue*, 1998; OECD, *Progress in Identifying and Eliminating Harmful Tax Practices*, 2000; European Commission, *Towards Tax Coordination in the European Union*, COM (97) 495, 1997.

10   See for example Henry Anron and William Gale (eds), *Economic Effects of Fundamental Tax Reform*, Brookings Institute, 1996.

11   Willi Leibfritz *et al, Taxation and Economic Performance*, Economics Department Working Papers No 176, OECD, 1997. Reviewing the literature on this subject the paper concludes that 'the effects [of taxes] on economic performance are ambiguous in some areas and unsettled and controversial in others'.

12   James McCormick, 'Brokering a New Deal' in James McCormick and Carey Oppenheim (eds), *Welfare in Working Order*, IPPR, 1998.

13   Leibrifiz *et al, Taxation and Economic Performance, op cit.*

14   See for example Maurice Saatchi and Peter Warburton, *The War of Independence; A Declaration*, Centre for Policy Studies, 1999; Alan Duncan and Dominic Hobson, *Saturn's Children*, Politico's, 1998. The figure of 30% has been suggested by the Institute of Directors: see 'Why the UK needs lower taxes', Economic Comment, July 1997. The case for lower taxation in principle was made by William Hague in a speech on 14 March 2000 ('The moral case for low taxation', Conservative Central Office). A more sophisticated approach is given in V. Tanzi and L. Schuknecht, *The Growth of Government and the Reform of the State in Industrial Countries*, IMF Working Paper, December 1995.

15   OECD, *Health Data 1999*, 1999; see also 'National Health Care Expenditures and Projected Tables 1997-2007', US Health Care Financing Administration website, November 2000.

16   Tim Harris, 'The effects of taxes and benefits on household income, 1998-99', *Economic Trends*, No 557, April 2000. See also Tania Burchardt and John Hills, *Private Welfare Insurance and Social Security*, Joseph Rowntree Foundation, 1997.

17   House of Commons, *Hansard*, Written Answers, 9 May 2000, Cols 331-332W.

18   John Hills and Orsolya Lelkes, 'Social security, selective universalism and patchwork redistribution', in Roger Jowell *et al* (eds), *British Social Attitudes: The 16th Report*, Ashgate, 1999. When people were asked this question, they were reminded that higher spending might require higher taxes.

19   Carl Emmerson *et al*, *Pressures in UK Healthcare: Challenges for the National Health Service*, Institute for Fiscal Studies and the King's Fund, 2000.

20   See for example Tom Bentley, *Learning Beyond the Classroom*, Routledge, 1998; and Charles Leadbeater, *Living on Thin Air*, Viking, 1999.

21   David Reynolds, 'Commentary', in Gavin Kelly (ed), *Is New Labour Working?*, Fabian Society, 1999.

22   Department for Education and Employment Annual Reports 1995 and 1999; National Committee of Inquiry into Higher Education, *Higher Education in the Learning Society* (the Dearing Report), HMSO, 1997.

23   Lucy Chennells *et al*, *The IFS Green Budget 2000*, Institute for Fiscal Studies, 2000; OECD, *Education Database*, 1999. The figures are for 1997, the last available year for comparison. The EU average for health but not for education is weighted, so that larger countries account for a greater share.

24   Department of Social Security, *Opportunity for All: Tackling Poverty and Social Exclusion*, Cm4445, Stationery Office, 1999.

25   David Gordon *et al*, *Poverty and Social Exclusion in Britain*, Joseph Rowntree Foundation, September 2000.

26   Carl Emmerson and Andrew Leicester, 'A Survey of the UK Benefits System', Briefing Note No 13, Institute for Fiscal Studies, 2000.

27   See OECD, *Employment Outlook*, June 2000; McCormick, 'Brokering a New Deal', *op cit*.

28   HM Treasury, *Spending Review 2000*, *op cit*.

29   OECD *Education Database* and *Health Data*, *op cit*.

30   'Brown's untold riches', *Financial Times*, 25 October 2000. See also HM Treasury, *Pre-Budget Report*, Cm4917, Stationery Office, 2000.

31   A worked example may illustrate this point. Imagine in year 1 you have an income of £20,000, and the share of taxation (which you pay exactly) is 37%. This means that you pay tax of £7,400, and have net disposable income of £12,600. Now imagine that in year 2 your earnings grow by 3%, and at the same time the government raises the tax share to 38%. Your income is now £20,600, and your tax bill is £7,828 (38% of £20,600). This leaves a disposable income of £12,772 (£20,800-£7,828).

Chapter 7

1   See for example John Curtice and Roger Jowell 'Trust in the political system', in Jowell *et al* (eds), *British Social Attitudes: The 14th Report*, Ashgate, 1997.

2   See for example Geoff Mulgan and Robin Murray, *Reconnecting Taxes*, Demos, 1993.

3   Curtice and Jowell, 'Trust in the political system', *op cit*.

4   See for example J Fishkin, *Democracy and Deliberation: New Directions for Democratic Reform*, Yale University Press, 1991; John Stewart, *Further Innovation in Democratic Practice*, School of Public Policy, University of Birmingham, 1996.

5   *Modernising Government*, Cm 4310, Stationery Office, 1999.

5   HM Treasury, *Comprehensive Spending Review*, Cm 4011, Stationery Office, 1998; HM Treasury, *Public Services for the Future: Modernisation, reform, accountability*, Cm 4181, Stationery Office, 1998.

7   HM Treasury, *Spending Review 2000*, Cm 4807, Stationery Office, 2000; HM Treasury, *Public Service Agreement 2001-2004*, Cm 4808, Stationery Office, 2000.

8   *The Government's Annual Report*, Cm 3969, Stationery Office, 1998; *The Government's Annual Report*, Cm 4401, Stationery Office, 1999; *The Government's Annual Report*, Stationery Office, 2000.

9   See for example Michael Power, *The Audit Society*, OUP, 1999.

10 HM Treasury, *Public Service Agreements 2001-2004*, *op cit.*

11 Alan Hedges and Catherine Bromley, *Public Attitudes Towards Taxation*, Fabian Society, 2000.

12 UK National Audit Office, *NAO 2000 Annual Report: Helping the Nation Spend Wisely*, 2000.

13 Audit Commission website (www.audit-commission.gov.uk); National Audit Office website (www.nao.gov.uk).

14 NAO, *NAO 2000 Annual Report*, *op cit.*

15 'Who audits the auditors?', *The Economist*, 10 June 2000.

16 We note that the Commons Liaison Committee, which consists of the Chairs of all the select committees, has recommended that committee members should not be appointed by the whips. (*Shifting the Balance: Select Committees and the Executive*, HC300, March 2000.)

17 HM Treasury, *Budget 2000*, Stationery Office, March 2000 (leaflet).

18 Ideally, each would be individually addressed through the electoral roll, with additional ones delivered unnamed for addresses not entered on the roll. This would allow the leaflets to be enclosed with self-assessment forms without duplication, by deleting self-assessment taxpayers from the list based on the electoral roll. There is an obvious rationale for including the leaflet with self-assessment forms if possible, since this is when people concentrate most closely about their tax. But clearly the cost of a more complicated delivery system such as this would need to be examined.

19 For example, the education total announced as £19.2bn was made up of year-on-year increases of £3bn, £3.5bn and £3.2bn. So by normal conventions it should have been announced that at the end of the third year spending would be £9.7bn higher than the base year figure. To get £19.2bn the Government took the £9.7bn, then added what would be spent in year 1 (£3bn) and in year 2 (£3bn + £3.5bn = £6.5bn).

20 Treasury Select Committee, 4th Report of Session 1998-99, *The 1999 Budget Report*, House of Commons Paper No 325, April 1999. Another recommendation we would make is that in addition to the actual and cyclically adjusted budget balance year by year, which is already shown in the Red Book, the table should also show separately cyclically adjusted revenue and spending as a percentage of GDP. It would moreover be preferable if these tables treated the cost of Working Family Tax Credit as public expenditure, in line with the international statistical standard ESA 95.

21 David Brodie, Taxaid, submission to the Commission on Taxation and Citizenship, July 1999.

22 Saul Levmore, 'Taxes as Ballots', *University of Chicago Law Review*, Vol 65, No 2, 1998.

23 'Tax experts question 558-page Finance Bill; Chartered Institute of Taxation call for Royal Commission', news release, 11 May 2000.

24 Marshall Task Force, *Economic Instruments and the Business Use of Energy*, HM Treasury, 1998.

25 Department of the Environment, Transport and the Regions, *Modern Local Government: In Touch with the People*, Cm 4014, Stationery Office, 1998.

Chapter 8

1   See Carolyn Webber and Aaron Wildavsky, *A History of Taxation and Expenditure in the Western World*, Touchstone, 1986.

2   The powers are granted by the Greater London Authority Act 1999 and the Transport Act 2000. The earmarking must be maintained for at least ten years.

3   See for example Ranjit S Teja and Barry Bracewell-Milnes, *The Case for Earmarked Taxes*, Institute of Economic Affairs, 1991.

4   The classic exposition of this case is J M Buchanan, 'The economics of earmarked taxes,' *Journal of Political Economy*, vol 71, 1963.

5   See for example Geoff Mulgan and Robin Murray, *Reconnecting Taxation*, Demos, 1993.

6   This is an illustration only: the two are no longer connected. Indeed it was because the revenue and the

spending need diverged so far that the hypothecation was abandoned.

7   See for example Andrew Dilnot (ed), *Options for 1994: The Green Budget*, Institute for Fiscal Studies, 1993; or Evan Davies, *Public Spending*, Penguin, 1998.

8   In practice, this problem may not arise. The Government has announced a ten year transport spending plan which includes capital spending allocations for local authorities (Department of Environment, Transport and the Regions, *Transport 2010: The 10 Year Plan*, Stationery Office, 2000). It is therefore committed to a certain level of central funding over ten years, on top of any revenues which local authorities raise from congestion and workplace parking charges. So for the ten years in which earmarking is legally required, it should be possible to say that all the charge revenues are genuinely additional. Since the central government funds will be available, and ring-fenced for transport spending, it will not be in the interests of any local authority to reduce the level of its bid just because it has the new charge revenues coming in. Some councils may still reduce their current spending, but they are unlikely to do so for capital spending—and it is towards the latter that the earmarked charge revenues are mainly expected to go.

9   Department of Culture, Media and Sport website, November 2000 (figure to September 2000).

10 Alan Hedges and Catherine Bromley, *Public Attitudes Towards Taxation*, Fabian Society, 2000; and see Chapter 2.

11 DETR, *Transport 2010, op cit*.

12 In an NOP poll conducted for Greenpeace in September-October 2000, 68% of respondents said they 'would be happier' paying the current rate of fuel duty if some of it was earmarked for spending on 'reducing pollution…by investing in public transport and developing green fuels'. The same proportion said they would prefer 3p of the duty to be earmarked for such spending than to be cut. 'New poll shows public back current fuel tax if revenue is spent on the environment', news release, Greenpeace, 5 October 2000.

13 It is true that some environmental taxes (such as a pesticides tax or greenfield building levy) will not of themselves have much effect in changing behaviour, due to the low level of responsiveness (elasticity) of the affected firms or consumers. In these cases the tax may effectively only be justifiable with the associated earmarking. The incentive effect of petrol duty is for the same reason sometimes disputed. But such taxes are still incentive-based, not merely revenue-raising. They are not without environmental impact: they send important policy and 'cultural' signals about environmental damage, they force polluters to pay for the harm they cause, and they can have quite strong incentive effects at the margin, not least on the possible growth of the damaging activity. Hence they must still be set with regard to their environmental and economic impact, not simply at a rate to raise revenue. This is discussed further in Chapter 13.

14 It is possible that even with broad definitions of spending, a desirable new tax may end up bringing in more revenue than it is rational to spend on a related area. The tax may prove itself an effective incentive, or otherwise relatively efficient, or easy to collect, or have other qualities which make it sensible to maintain it at a rate which can no longer justify an associated spending programme. Then the government may simply have to say that the earmarking has been abandoned, or reduced to 50% of the revenues, or whatever. There is no point in a mechanism designed to increase the legitimacy of taxes ending up impeding their basic effectiveness. But equally, the possibility that at some point in the future this might occur hardly seems a reason to forego an important way of connecting people to their taxes in the present. We trust that if, it were to occur, governments could be honest enough to say what had happened, and to explain what they had done in response. This is, after all, what this exercise is all about.

15 Hedges and Bromley, *Public Attitudes Towards Taxation, op cit;* and see Chapter 2.

16 Department of the Environment, Transport and the Region, *Modern Local Government: In Touch with the People*, Cm 4014, Stationery Office, 1998.

17 'Town votes for 10pc rise in council tax to avoid cut in services', *The Guardian*, 24 February 1999.

18 Similarly, a tax and public service pledge might be used to help increase the public acceptability of a new or reformed tax. In Chapter 12 we propose the introduction of a reformed tax on inheritance. We believe that such a tax is in principle desirable in its own right; and, if required, the revenues from it could be spent on any area of government (or used to cut another tax). But we also suggest a scheme to which the revenues might be earmarked to increase both its incentive effect and its legitimacy. The earmarking here would be loose, in the sense that the tax would not be dependent on the spending programme. If the latter were abolished, the tax would still operate. But the form it should take, we believe, would still be of the 'pledge' kind. It is the defining of the improvement target and its subsequent public auditing which is what reconnects the citizen to the tax—and to the spending it finances.

19   See for example Alan Milburn, 'Reinventing Healthcare: A Modern NHS Tomorrow', speech to the Institute for Public Policy Research, December 1999.

20   The British Social Attitudes survey has asked people since 1983 what they think of the idea of limiting NHS services just to those with low incomes, while everyone else takes our private insurance. The highest level of support for this idea was in fact in 1983 when just 29% supported it, compared with 64% opposed. In 1998 the proportions were 26% in favour and 72% against. Roger Jowell *et al* (eds), *British Social Attitudes: The 16th report*, Ashgate, 1999.

21   Lucy Chennells *et al*, *The IFS Green Budget 2000*, Institute for Fiscal Studies, January 2000. The figures depend on how the 'European average' is calculated, and how fast it is growing. The figure of 8.5% (for the four years to March 2005) is based on a weighted average of European countries, in which larger countries count for more, and assumes that the average spending on health in other European countries (as a proportion of GDP) remains the same from 1994 to 2005. Given that other countries face similar pressures on health spending to the UK, the latter is a very conservative assumption. By the time we have reached the European average, that is, it will no longer be the average.

22   See OECD, *Educational Database*, 2000.

23   HM Treasury, *Spending Review 2000*, Cm 4807, Stationery Office, 2000.

24   Total income tax revenues are projected to rise by £5.8 billion from 1999-00 to 2000-01. If a health tax were 50% of total income tax, its revenues would rise by £2.9 billion. Health spending is due to rise by £4.9 billion. So £2 billion extra would need to be raised by the health tax. A 1p rise in the basic rate of income tax currently raises £2.65 billion. So a 0.75p rise in the basic rate of health tax would raise £2 billion. (*Budget 2000*; Treasury ready reckoner.) The increase could of course be financed in any number of other ways: raising the top rate of the health tax, reducing the thresholds etc.

Chapter 9

1   Catherine Bromley *et al*, *Revisiting Public Perceptions of Local Government: A Decade of Change*, Department of the Environment, Transport and the Regions, 1999.

2   International Foundation for Election Systems (IFES) website, November 2000.

3   By 'sub-national' here we refer to levels below that of the nation state. Scotland and Wales (and England) are nations, but only the United Kingdom as a whole is a nation state. The use of the term 'sub-national' is intended to avoid the obvious scope for linguistic confusion here; we emphasise that the nation below which it refers is the United Kingdom as a whole. We use 'sub-UK-national level' where possible.

4   One illustration of this is the number of statutory instruments brought forward to regulate local government activity. During the 1950s and 1960s, an average of 69 statutory instruments were enacted annually. This increased to an average of 102 per year in the 1970s and 1980s. By 1996 it was 245. Another is the use of specific grants earmarked for particular local services, such as police, community care and under-5s education. By 1998-99 these amounted to nearly 19% of gross revenue spending by English local authorities. Cited in the Select Committee on Environment, Transport and Regional Affairs, Eighth Report, *Local Government Finance*, May 1999.

5   See for example Magnus Linklater, 'Salmond spends a costly penny', *The Times*, 18 March 1999. Strictly speaking the SNP's proposal was to rescind the 1p cut in income tax due to come into force in April 2000.

6   This is not quite true, in fact. Both the Scottish Parliament and the Wales and Northern Ireland Assemblies have an indirect power to raise money for their own public spending through the expedient of withholding revenue support grant to the local authorities in their jurisdiction. However this would not increase total public spending determined by these institutions. It should also be noted that the Scottish Parliament has the power to change the forms of local taxation: it could abolish or reform council tax if it so wished, and could return business rates to local control. For a clear account of the division of powers in the new constitution, see Vernon Bogdanor, *Devolution in the United Kingdom*, Oxford University Press, 1999.

7   The Northern Ireland Assembly has less discretion over the allocation of public spending than the Scottish Parliament or Wales Assembly: more of its central government grant is ring-fenced for particular purposes.

8   The so-called Barnett formula is used to allocate changes in the grants made to Scotland, Wales and Northern Ireland. Based on per capita income there is a case for saying that this is now overly generous to Scotland and Northern Ireland in particular, especially in comparison with the allocations made to some English regions. See Iain McLean, 'A Fiscal Constitution for the UK', in Selina Chen and Tony Wright (eds), *The English Question*, Fabian Society, 2000.

9   A point originally made by the Layfield Committee on Local Government Finance in 1976 and widely accepted since, though never resolved. (Layfield Committee, *Local Government Finance: report of the Committee of Enquiry*, Cmnd 6453, HMSO, 1976.) See also the Select Committee on Environment, Transport and Regional Affairs, *Local Government Finance, op cit.*

10   Local Government Association, *Modernising Local Government: Reforming Local Government Finance*, response to Government consultation papers, LGA, 1998.

11   Bromley *et al*, *Revisiting Public Perceptions of Local Government, op cit.* Similarly, over 60% of respondents thought that business rates were set mainly by local government or equally by local and central government.

12   See Bogdanor, *Devolution in the United Kingdom, op cit.* The Primrose Committee on Irish Finance argued that it was a 'a first principle of sound government that the same authority that has the spending of revenue should also have the burthen, and not infrequently the odium, of raising that revenue. That one should have the unpopular duty of providing the same, and another the privilege of expending them, is a division of labour that leads to disaster.' The 1976 Layfield Committee on Local Government Finance argued that 'whoever is responsible for spending money should also be responsible for raising it, so that the amount of expenditure is subject to democratic control.' (Layfield Committee, *Local Government Finance, op cit*)

13   Local Government Association, *Modernising Local Government, op cit.*

14   The Layfield Committee on Local Government Finance, *op cit*, in 1976; the Hunt Committee of the House of Lords in 1996 (Select Committee on Relations Between Central and Local Government, *Rebuilding Trust*, HL Paper 97, 1996); and the House of Commons Select Committee on Environment, Transport and Regional Affairs, *Local Government Finance, op cit.*

16   House of Lords Select Committee, *Rebuilding Trust, op cit*; and the Select Committee on Environment, Transport and Regional Affairs, *Local Government Finance, op cit.*

16   Department of Environment, Transport and the Regions, *Modernising Local Government Finance: A Green Paper*, 2000.

17   For a useful discussion of these and some other alternatives see for example Guy Hollis *et al*, *Alternatives to the Community Charge*, Joseph Rowntree Foundation, 1990.

18   For a detailed study see Stephen Smith and John Hall, *Local Sales Taxation*, Institute for Fiscal Studies, 1995.

19   Layfield Committee, *op cit*; see also M Ridge and Stephen Smith, *Local Taxation: The Options and the Arguments*, Institute for Fiscal Studies, 1991; A J G Isaac, *Local Income Tax: A Study of the Options*, Joseph Rowntree Foundation, 1992; Liberal Democrat Party, *Financing Federalism*, 1992.

20   A second, more fundamental option would be to move from the present system of cumulative PAYE to a simple PAYE system with year-end adjustment. This would allow employers to levy a single, slightly above-average rate of local income tax for all employees, doing away with the need for multiple tax tables. At the end of the year all income taxpayers would be required to complete a self-assessment form, on which their total tax for the year would be adjusted according to the tax rate levied by their local authority. Those living in areas levying a below-average tax rate would receive a rebate, those in above-average areas would be required to pay the difference. In Chapter 6 we rejected the universal use of self-assessment on the grounds that the gains in the transparency of the tax system were not worth the additional administrative and compliance costs. However if a local income tax were introduced the advantages in terms of reducing employers' costs would be considerable, and such a system might well then be worthwhile. The year-end assessment would certainly ensure that local income tax were visible to taxpayers.

21   CACI, *Paycheck*, 1999.

22   A careful transition mechanism would be needed, in which equalisation grants were adjusted not only for different needs and taxable capacity for council tax but also for different capacities for local income tax. Initially all local authorities would receive the same amount of income from the three new sources (grant, council tax and local income tax) as they received under the former system from two. Over time the central

grant would continue to be adjusted for changes in taxable capacity and need but not for changes in local income tax rates decided by the local authority.

23   Department of Environment, Transport and the Regions, *Modernising Local Government Finance, op cit*.

24   Antony Seeley, 'The Scotland Bill: Tax-Varying Powers', House of Commons Library Research Paper 98/4, January 1998.

25   'Town votes for 10pc rise in council tax', *The Guardian*, 24 February 1999. See also *Local Government Association, Local Referendums and Citizens' Ballots*, discussion paper, April 1999.

26   The Government has expressed its own interest in this idea. See Department of the Environment, Transport and the Regions, *Modern Local Government: In Touch with the People*, Cm 4014, Stationery Office, 1998.

27   For a discussion see Laura Blow, John Hall and Stephen Smith, *Financing Regional Government in Britain*, Institute for Fiscal Studies, 1996.

28   It is of course possible with such an arrangement that one tier of government might choose to reduce income tax at the same time as another raised it. It is part of the democratic process that elected governments at different tiers should sometimes be in conflict. If two tiers of government did cancel each other out by simultaneously raising and reducing income tax, each change would be reflected in changes in spending at those tiers, and would become part of the political debate in each jurisdiction. The combined effect might look odd, but it would reflect real choices at each level.

29   The Government's proposals were set out in its White Paper *Modern Local Government: In Touch with the People*, Cm 4014, July 1998.

30   See John Muellbauer and Gavin Cameron, 'Twelve reasons to reform the council tax and five essential reforms', unpublished paper, April 2000; Peter Kenway and Guy Palmer, *Council Tax: The Case for Reform*, New Policy Institute, 1999.

31   Tom Clark *et al, Does Council Tax Benefit Work?*, Institute for Fiscal Studies, 1999.

32   Department of the Environment, Transport and Regions, 'Exemplifications of changes to council tax', Local Government Finance Review Paper LGA2/CT2, September 1997.

33   The modelling and other tables and figures used here are taken from Kenway and Palmer, *Council Tax: The Case for Reform, op cit*. The gains and losses by band use the average band D council tax for 1997-98 of £688. The calculation of the changes to the band D rate necessary to ensure revenue neutrality derive from a model based on the distribution of dwellings by band in England in March 1998, taken from *Local Government Financial Statistics*, 1998. Revenue neutrality is defined as council tax revenue net of council tax benefit.

34   This proposal is made in Muellbauer and Cameron, 'Twelve reasons to reform the council tax', *op cit*.

35   For a discussion of these issues from contrasting perspectives see for example Tim Congdon, *European Tax Harmonisation and British Taxes*, Politeia, 1999; and Kitty Ussher, *The Spectre of Tax Harmonisation*, Centre for European Reform, 2000.

36   European Commission, *Financing the European Union, Commission Report on the Operation of the Own Resources System*, October 1998.

37   Elizabeth Meehan, *Citizenship and the European Community*, Sage, 1993; Antje Wiener, *'European' Citizenship Practice: Building Institutions of a Non-State*, Westview, 1999.

38   'EU States agree tax cut rules', *Financial Times*, 22 May 2000.

39   C Ussher, *The Spectre of Tax Harmonisation, op cit*.

40   See Stephen Bond *et al, Corporate Tax Harmonisation in Europe: A Guide to the Debate*, Institute for Fiscal Studies, 2000.

Chapter 10

1   Andrew Dilnot *et al, A Survey of the UK Tax System*, Briefing Note No 9, Institute for Fiscal Studies, 2000..

2   This assumes that both the UEL and the higher rate threshold will be unchanged in real terms.

3   It is a common error to assume that only direct tax rates matter to work incentives. If reduced income tax rates are paid for by higher taxes on consumption (such as VAT and excise duties), the real rewards to work may be

unchanged. The individual will have more income, but it will be able to buy fewer goods and services. We will return to this in Chapter 11.

4 House of Commons *Hansard*, Written Answers, 18 May 2000, Cols 261-262W. Marginal deduction rates above 70% are caused through the interaction of various combinations of the Working Families Tax Credit, Housing Benefit and Council Tax Benefit.

5 See Paul Gregg *et al*, *Entering Work and the British Tax and Benefit System*, Institute for Fiscal Studies, 1999.

6 John Hills, *Income and Wealth: The Latest Evidence*, Joseph Rowntree Foundation, 1998.

7 Inland Revenue, direct communication.

8 It is 'around' £33,000 because of the impact of tax relief for pensions. The threshold for the 40% rate is £28,400 pa of taxable income in 2000-01, and the personal allowance is £4,385. This gives a basic gross income threshold of £32,785. But most people at this level of income will be paying into a personal or occupational pension. The actual threshold in terms of gross income will therefore for most people be considerably higher.

9 The flat-rate personal allowance could in technical terms be described as a non-refundable credit: tax would be reduced either by the level of the credit (if the tax bill were more than this), or the tax liability before the credit (if the credit were larger). Another way of looking at it is that if the FPA were set at £964.70, this would be similar to limiting the personal allowance to the basic rate. But it would have one major difference: the FPA would reduce the tax paid by those on the 10% rate of tax (giving them the full £964.70), whereas limiting the current personal allowance to the basic rate would not (10% taxpayers would get only £438.50). The FPA would therefore be more progressive.

10 Under such a system it would probably be sensible for the 10% rate applying in the low rate tax band gradually to be reduced to zero. This would eventually eliminate the lower rate band altogether, raising the rate of the allowance. Eliminating the band altogether in a single year would be expensive, costing £3.6 billion, but a gradual reduction might be possible. See Lucy Chennells *et al*, *The IFS Green Budget 2000*, Institute for Fiscal Studies, 2000. Under a flat-rate personal allowance, the abolition of the 10% rate would require the allowance to rise to £1,180.

11 Modelling for the Commission using POLIMOD.

12 Inland Revenue, *Inland Revenue Statistics 1999*, Stationery Office, 1999.

13 Inland Revenue, *Inland Revenue Statistics 1998 and 1999*, Stationery Office, 1998, 1999.

14 Inland Revenue modelling for the Commission.

15 See Chapter 2, and the full report, Alan Hedges and Catherine Bromley, *Public Attitudes Towards Taxation*, Fabian Society, 2000.

16 House of Commons *Hansard*, Written Answers, 28 July 2000, Col 1012W.

17 Inland Revenue website, Ready Reckoner Table 1.6.

18 Another way of redistributing the revenues to low income taxpayers would be to reduce the lower (10%) rate of tax. Although with this level of revenue it could not be reduced to zero (this would cost around £3.6 billion) this might then become a target in the future: in effect it would mean an even larger personal allowance. Alternatively the scope of the 10% band could be broadened—though this would have a slightly less progressive distributional impact than abolishing it. This is discussed in Chennells *et al*, *The IFS Green Budget 2000*, *op cit*.

19 Calculation by the Institute for Fiscal Studies. Modelling for the Commission by the Inland Revenue Analytical Services Division. These measures are not in fact revenue neutral; they generate a combined yield of £340 million. This would therefore allow the personal allowance to be raised by somewhat more than £250.

20 Introducing a new top rate of income tax would have certain other impacts on the tax system as well. It would almost certainly require the top rate of capital gains tax to be raised to 50%. We would argue however that private pension contribution relief for 50% taxpayers should remain at 40%.

21 Chennells *et al*, *The IFS Green Budget 2000*, *op cit*. It should be noted that the UEL and higher rate threshold can never be completely aligned, since they apply to different bases of income. Pension contributions are subtracted from gross income for income tax but not for National Insurance. However the anomalies caused by this cannot be removed without changing the basis either of NI or of income tax.

22 Modelling for the Commission using POLIMOD.

23 Theoretically another way of doing this would be to raise the personal allowance at the same time as the basic rate. But in fact we found it was not possible to do this and protect incomes below £16,500 while simultaneously raising £4 billion.

24   Modelling for the Commission using POLIMOD.

25   If, as suggested above, the 10% rate were simultaneously abolished, perhaps financed in part from the revenues from a new top rate, the number of bands beneath the top rate would not in fact have to rise.

26   The distinction between using the tax system for delivery alone, or for assessment and delivery, is made by Jane Millar, in 'Benefits for children in the UK', in M Mendelson and K Battle (eds), *Benefits for Children: A Four Country Study*, Joseph Rowntree Foundation and Caledon Institute (forthcoming).

27   HM Treasury, *Supporting Children Through the Tax and Benefit System*, The Modernisation of Britain's Tax and Benefit System No 5, 1999.

28   *Ibid*.

29   The government is planning to address this by effectively abolishing WFTC and splitting its functions into two—helping children and promoting paid work—with one payment to the main carer (Integrated Child Credit) and one via the paypacket (Employment Tax Credit).

30   It would in our view be important, in any such review of the extension of tax credits, that the whole personal tax/benefits system is considered together—including those benefits which are not suitable for conversion to tax credits.

31   See, for example, Andrew Dilnot *et al, The Reform of Social Security*, Oxford University Press, 1984.

32   Similar issues arise in connection with the existing tax credits, such as the WFTC; but since these tax credits are currently only delivered, rather than assessed, through the tax system, the issues involved seem to us to be about the most appropriate unit of assessment for social security benefits—a debate which the Commission has not seen as part of its remit.

33   Chennells *et al*, in *The IFS Green Budget 2000* (*op cit*) includes a discussion of the Integrated Child Credit and its implications for independent taxation. One issue which we do not discuss here is the operation of a cohabitation rule within the new system, to identify those whose incomes should be considered together; this has been a familiar issue within the benefits system but has not been so central within the tax system.

34   There are some compromises which could be made in this particular policy area, such as limiting the range(s) of income over which the payment has to be income-related.

Chapter 11

1   HM Customs and Excise, *Annual Report 1998-1999*, Stationery Office, 1999.

2   Alan Hedges and Catherine Bromley, *Public Attitudes Towards Taxation*, Fabian Society, 2000 (see Chapter 2).

3   Modelling for the Commission using POLIMOD.

4   Modelling for the Commission using POLIMOD.

5   Zero-rated goods have no VAT levied on the final good or on the inputs used in its production. Exempt goods have no VAT levied on the final good sold to the consumer but firms cannot reclaim VAT paid on inputs. Thus exempt goods are in practice liable to a 4-7% rate of VAT, depending on the firm's costs and the nature of suppliers.

6   Andrew Dilnot *et al, A Survey of the UK Tax System*, Institute for Fiscal Studies, 2000.

7   Office of National Statistics, *Social Trends 2000*, Stationery Office, 2000.

8   See for example Evan Davies and John Kay, 'Extending the VAT base: problems and possibilities, *Fiscal Studies*, Vol 6, No 1, 1985.

9   Modelling for the Commission using POLIMOD.

10   Modelling for the Commission using POLIMOD.

11   Davies and Kay, 'Extending the VAT base', *op cit*

12   Modelling for the Commission using POLIMOD.

13   HM Treasury, *Budget 2000*, HC 346, Stationery Office, 2000 (see Chapter 3).

14   Dilnot *et al, A Survey of the UK Tax System, op cit* It is important to be clear what 'raising' one of these duties means. Tobacco and alcohol taxes are levied in absolute terms—so many pence per unit. (There is also an *ad valorem* component to tobacco tax, while gambling taxes are wholly *ad valorem*.) This means that, if left

unchanged, the revenues received fall in real terms over time, as inflation erodes their value. Therefore when a Chancellor raises these duties in a Budget by the rate of inflation, this should not be treated as a tax rise. Although the consumer will no doubt notice the price increase immediately after the Budget, in fact over a period of a year—assuming that the basic price of the product does not change unusually—the price will rise only by the rate of inflation, as would be expected with any product, taxed or not. Only if the duty is raised by more than the rate of inflation can it be said that the tax rate has risen.

15   Department of the Environment, Transport and the Regions, *Combating Drink Driving: Next Steps*. Consultation paper, February 1998 ; Institute of Alcohol Studies, *Alcohol and Crime*, Factsheet, October 2000.

16   Department of Health, *Smoking Kills*, Stationery Office, 1998.

17   Alan Marsh, *Poor Smokers*, Policy Studies Institute, 1994

18   Department of Health, 'Government action in response to Select Committee report on the tobacco industry', press release, 30 October 2000.

19   See for example Tobacco Manufacturers' Association, *The Chancellor's Budget 2000*, February 2000;

20   Lucy Chennells *et al*, *The IFS Green Budget*, Institute for Fiscal Studies, 2000.

21   HM Customs and Excise and HM Treasury, *Tackling Tobacco Smuggling*, March 2000; Chennells *et al*, *The IFS Green Budget, op cit*

22   Chennells *et al*, *The IFS Green Budget, op cit*.

23   *Ibid.*

24   HM Customs and Excise and HM Treasury, *Tackling Tobacco Smuggling, op cit*.

25   *Ibid.*

26   HM Customs and Excise, *Budget 2000*; Press release C&E1, 'Reform of Betting Duty', 21 March 2000.

27   See for example Charles Leadbeater, 'Goodbye, Inland Revenue', *New Statesman*, 3 July 1998; and *Living on Thin Air*, Viking, 1999.

28   OECD, *Electronic Commerce: A Discussion Paper on Taxation Issues*, 1998; OECD Committee on Fiscal Affairs, *Report to Ministers on Implementing the Ottawa Taxation Framework Accords*, June 2000. See also Inland Revenue and HM Customs and Excise, *Electronic Commerce: The UK's Taxation Agenda*, 1999.

29   *Ibid.*

Chapter 12

1   Inland Revenue, *Inland Revenue Statistics 1999*, Stationery Office, 1999 (provisional 1996 figures).

2   James Banks and Sarah Tanner, *Household Saving in the UK*, Institute for Fiscal Studies, 1999.

3   See for example A B Atkinson, *Unequal Shares: Wealth in Britain*, Allen Lane, 1972.

4   Office for National Statistics, *Britain 2000: The Official Handbook*, Stationery Office, 1999.

5   Inland Revenue, *Inland Revenue Statistics 1999, op cit*.

6   Winston Churchill, *Lord Randolph Churchill*, Macmillan, 1960.

7   Ken Messere, *Tax policy in OECD Countries: Choices and Conflicts*, OECD, 1993.

8   Cedric Sandford, 'Towards a Real Inheritance Tax', *Accountancy*, January 1988.

9   Messere, *Tax Policy, op cit*.

10   For a full account of the Irish tax, see J Condon and J Muddiman, *Capital Aquisitions Tax*, 12th Edition, The Institute of Taxation in Ireland, 1999. The proposal for an accessions tax for the UK was comprehensively argued as long ago as 1973 in C T Sandford *et al*, *An Accessions Tax*, Institute for Fiscal Studies, 1973. This has been an invaluable source for the present report.

11   Irish Institute of Taxation website.

12   One possibility would actually be not to have separate rates for the capital receipts tax at all, but simply to include all receipts within an individual's income tax return. In any year in which a gift or legacy was received, its taxable value would be added to the individual's income and the total charged at the relevant rate of income tax. Large receipts could be spread over several years, so as not to create huge liabilities in any one

year. There is some logic and simplicity to this proposal, but it would not create a very progressive rate struc- ture. Effectively there would be only two rates: 22% and 40% (the basic and higher rates of income tax). Depending on the number of years over which a capital receipt could be spread, most significant inheritances would end up being charged at 40%. This would almost certainly require a rather high initial threshold, defeat- ing the point of bringing more inheritances into the tax system. For these reasons—and in line with practice in other countries—we believe that a capital receipts tax should have its own progressive rate structure.

13   It would be possible for a wealthy person to give £2000 to her child every year for 50 years, giving the later an effective exemption of £150,000 rather than £50,000. In theory this could be repeated by any number of other donors, increasing the effectively exempt sum. But this will surely be rare. In choosing the lower limit some balance must inevitably be struck between administrative cost and the risk of avoidance.

14   We would also propose relief for children and grandchildren under the age of 18 whose parents are dead. In these circumstances there are obviously strong grounds for ensuring that such children have adequate finan- cial support; some relief (on a sliding scale) is therefore appropriate.

15   A time limit during which the relief applied has sometimes been suggested; we see no particular rationale for this. There would need to be special provisions to allow the rationalisation of estates by the sale and purchase of particular parcels of land.

16   See for example the classic study by Jonathan Boswell, *The Rise and Decline of Small Firms*, Allen & Unwin, 1972.

17   See for example Andrew Adonis and Stephen Pollard, A Class Act, *The Myth of Britain's Classless Society*, Penguin Books, 1998.

18   See Condon and Muddiman, *Capital Acquisitions Tax, op cit*. The issue of trusts is discussed in detail in C T Sandford *et al, An Accessions Tax, op cit*.

19   See David Nissan and Julian Le Grand, *A Capital Idea: Start-Up Grants for Young People*, Fabian Society, 2000; Bruce Ackerman and Anne Alstott, *The Stakeholding Society*, Yale University Press, 1999.

20   Inland Revenue, *Inland Revenue Statistics 1999, op cit*.

21   John Major, speeches to the Conservative Party Conference, 11 October 1991 and 13 October 1995, Conservative Central Office.

Chapter 13

1   The 'polluter pays' principle is an important part of environmental policy. But contrary to the view sometimes expressed, it is not only environmental taxes which make the polluter pay. Regulatory measures generally have the same effect.

2   For a general discussion of environmental policy instruments, see for example Judith Rees, *Natural Resources: Allocation, Efficiency and Policy*, 2nd edn, Routledge, 1990.

3   In theory, the tax should be set at the level which reflects ('internalises') all the external costs of environmen- tal damage. In practice it is often difficult to calculate these in monetary terms. So taxes are generally set, either at the level it is estimated will achieve a particular target for damage reduction, or to yield a target revenue.

4   For a general discussion of environmental tax policy, see Ernst von Weiszäcker and Jochen Jesinghaus, *Ecological Tax Reform*, Zed Books, 1992; Stephen Tindale and Gerald Holtham, *Green Tax Reform*, Institute for Public Policy Research, 1996; Tim O'Riordan (ed), *Ecotaxation*, Earthscan, 1997.

5   This includes Belgium, Denmark, Finland, France, Germany, Italy, the Netherlands, Sweden and Switzerland.

6   HM Treasury, 'Statement of Intent on Environmental Taxation', July 1997.

7   See for example O'Riordan, *Ecotaxation, op cit*.

8   For a survey see A Bosquet, 'Environmental tax reform: does it work?—a survey of the empirical evidence', *Ecological Economics*, 34, 2000. See also the discussion in O'Riordan, *Ecotaxation, op cit*.

9   Bosquet, 'Environmental tax reform', *op cit*.

10   Paul Ekins and Stefan Speck, *Environmental Policy, Carbon Taxes and Competitiveness*, Forum for the Future, 1998.

11 Paul Ekins and Stefan Speck, 'Proposals of environmental fiscal reforms and the obstacles to their implemen-
    tation', *Journal of Environmental Policy and Planning*, 2000.

12 Royal Commission on Environmental Pollution, *Energy—The Changing Climate*, 22nd Report, Cm 4749, 2000.

13 *Ibid*.

14 HM Treasury, *Budget 2000*, HC346, Stationery Office, 2000.

15 Paul Ekins, *Ecological Tax Reform, Environmental Policy and the Competitiveness of British Industry*, Forum for the
    Future, 1998.

16 *Ibid*.

17 Royal Commission on Environmental Pollution, *Energy—The Changing Climate, op cit*.

18 *Ibid*.

19 Office for National Statistics, *Family Spending 1997-8*, 1998.

20 Department of the Environment, Transport and the Regions, *Fuel Poverty: The New HEES—A Programme for
    Warmer, Healthier Homes*, May 1999.

21 *Ibid*.

22 Royal Commission on Environmental Pollution, *Energy—The Changing Climate, op cit*.

23 Department of the Environment, *Transport and the Regions, Fuel Poverty: The New HEES, op cit*.

24 Campaign for the Warm Homes Bill Strategy, 1999.

25 *Ibid*.

26 One way of doing this might be to charge a lower rate of tax (or no tax at all) to households in the two or
    three lowest council tax bands (A, B and C). Since most (though not all) low income households live in homes
    in lower bands this would target the relief reasonably well. In terms of administration, this proposal has been
    made for water charging and is generally regarded as feasible by the water companies. Most domestic ener-
    gy is similarly delivered straight to households by electricity and gas distribution companies, so data on
    homes is readily available. For the few low-income households living in homes in higher council tax bands
    (mainly elderly people), additional targeted compensation could be given.

27 Royal Commission on Environmental Pollution, *Energy—The Changing Climate, op cit*.

28 Modelling using POLIMOD for the Commission.

29 The congestion figure comes from the Confederation of British Industry; the total external costs from David
    Maddison *et al, Blueprint 5: The True Costs of Road Transport*, Earthscan 1996. The other figures are from the
    Department of the Environment, Transport and the Regions, *A New Deal for Transport: Better for Everyone*, Cm
    3950, Stationery Office, 1998.

30 Stephen Glaister and Dan Graham, *The Effect of Fuel Prices on Motorists*, Automobile Association, 2000.

31 *Ibid*.

32 *Ibid*.

33 See Ernst von Weiszäcker *et al, Factor Four: Doubling Wealth, Halving Resource Use*, Earthscan, 1997.

34 Stephen Glaister, 'Tax disc losers', *The Guardian*, 16 October 2000.

35 *Bulletin of Public Transport Statistics Great Britain 1999*, Stationery Office, 1999.

36 DETR, *A New Deal for Transport, op cit*.

37 Institute for Public Policy Research, *Transport Tax Options for the Pre-Budget Report*, October 2000.

38 DETR, *A New Deal for Transport, op cit*.

39 Laura Blow and Ian Crawford, *The Distributional Effects of Taxes on Private Motoring*, Institute for Fiscal Studies,
    1997; Ian Skinner and Malcolm Skinner, *Transport Taxation and Equity*, Institute for Public Policy Research, 1998.

40 Glaister and Graham, *The Effect of Fuel Prices on Motorists, op cit*; Skinner and Fergusson, *Transport Taxation and
    Equity, op cit*.

41 HM Treasury, *Budget 2000, op cit*.

42 Institute for Public Policy Research, *Transport Tax Options for the Pre-Budget Report, op cit*.

43 *Ibid*.

44 Department of the Environment, Transport and the Regions, *Transport 2010: The Ten Year Plan*, Stationery Office,
    2000.

45   Brendon Sewill, *Airports Policy—A Flawed Approach*, Aviation Environment Federation, 2000; Chris Hewett and Jane Foley, *Plane Trading*, Institute for Public Policy Research, 2000.

46   Environmental Audit Committee, 8th Report, Session 1998-99, *The Budget 1999: The Environmental Implications*, 1999.

Chapter 14

1   David Ricardo, *The Principles of Political Economy and Taxation* (1817), Everyman Library Edition, J M Dent, 1911.

2   Henry George, *Progress and Poverty* (1878), condensed version, Hogarth Press, 1953.

3   Urban Task Force, *Towards an Urban Renaissance*, E & F N Spon, 1999.

4   *Ibid.*

5   Nicholas Falk, 'Resourcing the Revival of Town and City Centres', *Built Environment*, Vol 24, No 1, 1998.

6   Urban Task Force, *Towards an Urban Renaissance*, *op cit*.

7   Local Government Association. *Modernising Local Government: Reforming Local Government Finance*, response to Government consultation papers, LGA, 1998.

8   Urban Task Force, *Towards an Urban Renaissance*, *op cit*.

9   This seems to us a much simpler method of tackling the problem of vacant land than the general imposition of a Vacant Land Tax which was recommended in the KPMG report on economic instruments accompanying the Urban Task Force report. (Urban Task Force, *Fiscal Incentives for Urban Housing: Exploring the Options: A Report for the Task Force* by KPMG, DETR, 1999.) A vacant land tax, apart from being a new measure requiring new legislation, would not discriminate between areas where demand was high and where it was low. As the report concedes, to overcome this it might need to be accompanied by complex variations in the capital gains tax regime, which would then just weaken the effect of the tax. Use of tax varying powers allows the measure to be targeted where it is most needed. (It should be noted that Compulsory Purchase Orders could also be more widely used than they tend to be today to deal with vacant land.)

10   Department of the Environment, Transport and the Regions, *Modern Local Government: In Touch with the People*, Cm 4014, Stationery Office, 1998.

11   There is a further anomaly which needs correcting. On listed buildings, VAT is charged for repairs, but not for alterations. This creates incentives to change rather than maintain historic buildings. In the Pre-Budget Report in November 2000 the Government said this would be investigated.

12   House of Commons *Hansard*, 4 June 1998; Bob Evans and Richard Bate, *A Taxing Question: The Contribution of Economic Instruments to Planning Objectives*, Town and Country Planning Association, 2000.

13   The Government itself raised the possibility in its White Paper *Planning for the Communities of the Future*, Stationery Office, 1998. The Urban Task Force considered the idea but recommended more research be conducted on it. A greenfield tax (in different forms) has been proposed by the Civic Trust (*Housing and Regeneration—How a Greenfield Levy Can Help*, Civic Trust, 1998) and the Town and Country Planning Association (Bob Evans and Richard Bate, *A Taxing Question*, *op cit*.)

14   These calculations have been made by the Royal Institution for Chartered Surveyors, 'The Economic Impact of a Greenfield Tax', unpublished paper, 2000. The proportion of the sale price of a new house which comes from the land value varies between 20% and 50%, depending on the area. This means that the extra added to housebuilding costs by a 10% tax would be at most 5% and in some areas only 1%.

15   *Ibid.*

16   This is proposed by Evans and Bate, *A Taxing Question*, *op cit*.

17   These calculations have been made by RICS, 'The Economic Impact of a Greenfield Tax', *op cit*, using figures from the Valuation Office, *Property Market Report*, October 1999. The differences are somewhat smaller in other parts of the country, where pressure for housing is less. In the north east, for example, the average values are £8,000 per hectare for agricultural land and (subtracting 30% for the value of utility services) £371,000 for residential, a multiple of 46.

18   The converse is of course also the case. Some developments can blight or otherwise reduce the value of local

property. But in these cases, when the blighting is specifically caused by the action of public authorities, they may be required to compensate property owners or to buy their properties from them.

19   V H Blundell, *Essays in Land Economics*, Economic and Social Science Research Association, 1993.

20   *Ibid*.

21   P Healey, M Purdue and F Ennis, *Gains from Planning? Dealing with the Impacts of Development*, Joseph Rowntree Foundation, 1993.

22   On impact fees, see Barry Goodchild and John Henneberry, 'Impact Fees for Planning', Royal Institution of Chartered Suveyors research publications, 1994; Malcolm Grant, 'Impact Fees: Could They Work Here?', unpublished paper, Department of Land Economy, University of Cambridge, 1998, and the Urban Task Force Report, *Towards an Urban Renaissance, op cit*. On environmental and social impact assessment, see Nathaniel Lichfield, Community Impact Evaluation, UCL Press, 1996. In addition the Countryside Agency has proposed the systematisation of planning obligations as 'development obligations': *Planning for Quality of Life in Rural England*, Countryside Agency, 1999.

23   See R V Andelson (ed), *Land Value Taxation Around the World*, Schalkenbach Foundation, 1997.

24   This is taken from Nathaniel Lichfield and Owen Connellan, *Land Value and Community Betterment Taxation in Britain: Proposals for Legislation and Practice*, Lincoln, Institute, 2000.

25   A Hartzok, 'Pennsylvania's Success with Local Property Tax Reform: The Split Rate Tax', *American Jouranl of Economics and Sociology*, Vol 56, No 2, 1997.

Annex

1   Bruce Stafford, *National Insurance and the Contributory Principle*, DSS In-house Report 39, 1998; Fabian Society, *Public Attitudes on the Future of Welfare*, Research Findings, 1998.

2   National insurance rates for employees were raised in each of the Conservative Budgets from 1980 to 1983 (from 6.5% to 9%), and then again in 1993 (to 10%). Reduced rates for lower earners were introduced in 1985.

3   This sense that governments have broken an implicit 'contract of entitlement' may actually be felt most strongly in relation to long-term care, where changes in the qualifying conditions have forced many more elderly people to pay for themselves. Since long-term care was never part of the national insurance system, this cannot be counted as part of the decline of the contributory principle; but the distinction is not clear in many people's minds, and this has probably contributed to the general sense that governments have reneged on their welfare contract.

4   Stafford, *National Insurance and the Contributory Principle, op cit*; Fabian Society, *Public Attitudes on the Future of Welfare, op cit*.

5   Social Security Committee, Fifth Report, Session 1999-2000, HC 56-1, *The Contributory Principle, Volumes I and II*, June 2000.

6   The pay-as-you-go system in the UK has addressed the problem of an ageing population largely by reducing its (state) benefit levels in relation to general living standards. Continental systems have attempted to restrain the growth in expenditure, but in various different ways; they have also focused on making changes to qualifying conditions for benefits and/or agreeing additional contributions or taxes to fund them. (See, for example, Richard Disney, 'The European way of ageing', *Financial Times*, 10 October 2000; Jochen Clasen (ed), *Social Insurance in Europe*, Policy Press, 1997.

7   Peter Taylor-Gooby, 'No time to talk', *The Guardian*, 4 October 2000.

8   See for example Nicholas Timmins, 'The death of universalism', *Financial Times*, 22 November 1999.

9   Several of these were recommended by the report of the Commission on Social Justice (*Social Justice: Strategies for National Renewal*, Institute of Public Policy Research/Vintage, 1994). The recommendation on long-term care was put forward in the report from the Joseph Rowntree Foundation Inquiry, *Meeting the Costs of Continuing Care: Report and Recommendations*, Joseph Rowntree Foundation, 1996. The Social Security Committee, in its recent report (see note 5), also made several suggestions for reform.

Appendix 5

1   Data from the Family Expenditure Survey are Crown Copyright. They have been made available by the Office for National Statistics (ONS) through the Data Archive and are used by permission. Neither the ONS nor the Data Archive bears any responsibility for the analysis or interpretation of the data reported here.

2   Performance and Innovation Unit, *Adding It Up: Improving Analysis and Modelling in Central Government*, Stationery Office, 2000.

3   See G Redmond *et al*, *The Arithmetic of Tax and Social Security Reform: a user's guide to microsimulation methods and analysis*, Cambridge University Press, 2000, for more information.

4   Department of Social Security, 1999, *Income Related Benefits: Estimates of Take-Up in 1996/7 (revised) and 1997/8*, Analytical Services Division.

The Fabian Society—individual membership

Radical thought—searching debate

Join the Fabian Society, the UK's premier left-of-centre think tank

As a member, you will receive:

- *Fabian Review*
  Our quarterly magazine *Fabian Review* combines authoritative political analysis with stimulating comment, interviews with leading political figures, head-to-head debates, book reviews and lively readers' letters.

- *Pamphlets on key political and policy idea*
  Always readable, often provocative, covering diverse subjects and from original perspectives, Fabian pamphlets keep our members ahead of the political agenda.

- *50% off books and in-depth policy reports*
  Our popular paperback books explore major political themes, our policy work generates far-reaching recommendations for government.

- *Advance notification of conferences and events*
  Our conferences are an opportunity for critical examination of new political ideas and the issues facing the Labour Party. As a member you will be the first to know about all major events.

- *Access to over 70 local groups*
  Membership gives you access to an active nationwide network of local groups which hold meetings and discussions and develop local research.

- *FREE membership of the Young Fabians for all those under 31*
  Currently 1,000 strong, the Young Fabians publish their own magazine, Anticipations, and organise meetings and conferences.

Call us on 020 7227 4900 to find out about our latest offers for new members or email join@fabian-society.org.uk. Please put 'info' in the subject line.

Recent publications from the Fabian Society

Public Attitudes Towards Taxation

Alan Hedges and Catherine Bromley

Public Attitudes Towards Taxation is the full report of the research into public attitudes which was undertaken for the Commission on Taxation and Citizenship in 2000. Using the results from both a focus group study and quantitative opinion polling the report examines public understanding of and attitudes towards the tax system as a whole; attitudes towards the rates and overall burden of taxation and its fairness; and views on the quality of public services and the accountability and trustworthiness of government and politicians. It explores the public's willingness to pay higher taxes and the effect on this of proposals to hypothecate or earmark taxes. It examines attitudes towards direct taxes, indirect taxes and inheritance tax. This is an invaluable background document to the report of the Commission on Taxation and Citizenship.

Alan Hedges is an independent researcher specialising in qualitative public attitudes work; Catherine Bromley is Co-director of the British Social Attitudes survey at the National Centre for Social Research.

70 pages ● December 2000 ● £10.00

Environmental Modernisation—The New Labour Agenda

Michael Jacobs

Jacobs presents an original analysis of the politics of New Labour and the environment. Arguing that the environmental movement has been tied too closely to green ideology, Jacobs shows how environmental issues are bound up with current trends in globalisation, individualisation and risk. He offers the Government a distinctive environmental discourse and policy agenda.

'Jacobs has made a trenchant and articulate contribution to what has become a rather turgid debate' Jonathon Porrit. 'Excellent' *New Statesman'*. A devastating analysis' *The Guardian*

50 pages ● October 1999 ● ISBN 07163 0591 7 ● £6.95

Coping with Post-Democracy

Colin Crouch

Colin Crouch argues that we are entering a new phase of politics, which he characterises as 'post-democracy'. After the brief moment of mass democracy in the mid-20th century, he argues political life is once again being dominated by an elite and professionalised oligarchy, as was the case prior to the explosion of mass political movements at the end of the nineteenth century. Whilst there is much is common with this 'pre-democratic' state, the specific characteristic of the emerging phase is the increasingly institutionalised nature of corporate influence.

Crouch does not make a case for resisting these developments; hence 'coping' with post-democracy. Rather he argues that, in this new context, egalitarians have to reassess their relationship with a political system which is no longer well-suited to achieving their ends.

52 pages ● December 2000 ● ISBN 07163 0598 4 ● £6.95

The English Question

Edited by Selina Chen and Tony Wright—Robert Hazell, Mary Hickman, Gordon Marsden, Iain McLean, Austin Mitchell, Gerry Stoker, Tony Wright, Gary Younge

Devolution to the Scottish Parliament and the Welsh Assembly leaves an unresolved question at the heart of the United Kingdom. What is the future of England? This book explores both the nature of, and possible answers to, the 'English Question'. It examines different models of government, including an English Parliament, devolution to English regions, and the idea of 'city regions' with elected mayors. It calls for a new 'fiscal constitution' to govern the geographical distribution of public spending. Revisiting the historical myth of England, the book questions the notion of Englishness both from the left and from minority ethnic perspectives.

With contributions by leading thinkers drawn from the academic and political worlds, this collection provides a rich array of insights into how political relationships, identities and structures in the UK could evolve in the future.

'A lively new collection of essays' Peter Riddell *The Times*
'An important new book' Donald MacIntyre *The Independent*
'Fascinating' Stephen Pollard *The Express*

116 pages ● April 2000 ● ISBN 07163 6002 0 ● £8.95

The Third Way—New Politics for the New Century

Tony Blair

Tony Blair sets out his vision of the Third Way as a modernised social democracy, committed to social justice and the goals of the centre-left but flexible, innovative and forward-looking in the means to achieve them.

'An important pamphlet, an important moment' Will Hutton.

20 pages ● September 1998 ● ISBN 07163 0588 7 ● £4.50

The New European Left

Edited by Gavin Kelly—Donald Sassoon, Thomas Meyer, Jos de Beus, Anne-Marie Lindgren, Laurent Bouvet and Frédéric Michel

With social democratic governments in power throughout most of Europe the left of centre has a historically unique opportunity to shape a more progressive era of European politics.

The New European Left explores the ideas, policy debates and electoral pressures which are determining the governing agenda in four key European countries—Germany, France, Sweden and the Netherlands. An introductory chapter by Donald Sassoon, leading commentator on European politics, draws out lessons for the UK from the experiences of the left of centre across Europe.

'The left now has the opportunity to shape a new European policy agenda. This book is an excellent guide to the latest social democratic thinking in Europe—it is of direct relevance to current debates in Britain.' Professor Andrew Gamble, University of Sheffield

72 pages ● November 1999 ● ISBN 07163 6001 2 ● £9.95

Second Term Thinking series

The Labour Party looks likely to win an historic second term at the next General Election. This provides an unprecedented opportunity to develop a radical policy agenda. The Fabian Society's publication series **Second Term Thinking** is intended to make a significant contribution to the development of innovative policy options across a range of areas. Second Term Thinking aims to stimulate debate both on the key strategic and philosophical directions of the post-election Government and the policies that will manifest them.

Reports have been published on giving start-up grants to eighteen year-olds, compulsory voting and paid parental leave. These will be followed by a report on how the New Deals for the unemployed might be taken forward to respond more effectively to areas of high unemployment and proposals for reform to the private school system, recommending greater collaboration between the state and independent sectors. Topics to be addressed in further publications include transport, health and culture.

Second Term Thinking Reports are £7.50 each or £30 for the series of eight. To order, please contact the Fabian Society on **020 7227 4900** or visit our website at **www.fabian-society.org.uk**.